Engd by J.C. Buttre, New York.

Jeffn Davis

From a recent Photograph taken from Life

LIFE OF JEFFERSON DAVIS,

WITH A

SECRET HISTORY

OF

THE SOUTHERN CONFEDERACY,

GATHERED

"BEHIND THE SCENES IN RICHMOND."

CONTAINING

CURIOUS AND EXTRAORDINARY INFORMATION OF THE PRINCIPAL SOUTHERN CHARACTERS IN THE LATE WAR, IN CONNECTION WITH PRESIDENT DAVIS, AND IN RELATION TO THE VARIOUS INTRIGUES OF HIS ADMINISTRATION.

BY

EDWARD A. POLLARD,

AUTHOR OF "THE LOST CAUSE," ETC., ETC.

Issued by subscription only, and not for sale in the book stores. Residents of any State desiring a copy should address the publishers, and an agent will call upon them.

NATIONAL PUBLISHING COMPANY,
PHILADELPHIA, PA.; CHICAGO, ILL.; ST. LOUIS, MO.;
ATLANTA, GA.

PREFACE.

I HAVE long meditated writing the life of Jefferson Davis, and divulging in this work a mass of curious and extraordinary information which I have possessed, concerning the private and interior history of his Government, in Richmond. It was a most remarkable singularity of the Southern Confederacy, that, though holding out to the world the forms of Republican Government, it was as closely veiled in its operations, as secret and recluse as the most absolute and arrogant despotism. Thus many things happened behind that curtain which Mr. Davis so studiously spread before his Government, of which the world has as yet no knowledge, and of which even people living in Richmond, and in the shadow of that Government, have had only the faintest conception, or, at best, a chequered and imperfect revelation.

The writer may say, without vanity or self-assertion, that he is peculiarly fitted to be the biographer of Jefferson Davis. He was near him during the whole war. He had occasion to study his character assiduously, and to pursue him in his administration with a curious and critical industry; and his opportunities as a journalist, in Richmond, enabled him to learn much of the veiled mysteries and inner scenes of the weak and anomalous government that wrecked the fortunes of the Southern Confederacy. The writer thus obtained much of the secret and unwritten history of the Confederacy, involving Mr. Davis; information which, for obvious causes, he could not give to the newspaper press, and which, since the war, he has not yet published in any of his memoirs, for *peculiar and impressive reasons.*

The fact is, the writer has been, for a long time, persuaded by friends standing between him and the Confederate President, to withhold the work he now contemplates, as it was thought it would give information concerning various conspiracies and vengeful plots in the war, which might be used against Mr. Davis on his expected trial, or might inflame against him a fatal prejudice. For this reason alone, the writer has, for a long time, deferred the publication he has now determined upon; and he may claim that in this he has shown an extreme and punctilious regard for Mr. Davis's safety. But he can no longer defer to this solicitude for Mr. Davis; it has become a mere punctilio, since there is no longer now a reasonable expectation that the Ex-President will ever be brought to trial, or be disturbed in the foreign land, in which he is reported to have descended to the commonplaces of trade and an unnoticed existence. At least, it would be unreasonable that the writer should longer weigh a calculation so tender and remote against a debt severely due to history.

Jefferson Davis should have a truthful and acute biographer, one who would do something more than echo the shallow clamors and interested opinions of the day. Whatever the estimate of his person, he performed a great part in history; and his character, mixed, angular, abounding in surprises, full of caprices and apparent inconsistencies, is precisely that which affords the most interesting and vivid subjects for biography. The writer is conscious of attempting a high and difficult task—an extraordinary work. He comes to it not only with ample literary preparation, but with an unusual animation. He has been accused of personal hostility to Mr. Davis; and is to-day, perhaps, in all his literary capacities, most widely known to the country as censor of the Confederate Chief. He repels the accusation of any prejudice, in the very front of his work; he is able and willing to do exact justice to Mr. Davis; and if he ever attacked him it was through supreme devotion to a great cause, and from a just resentment toward the man who misguided and wrecked it.

Those who suppose that they will find in the work of the writer a declamation against Mr. Davis—a mere amplitude of rhetoric, or an excess of passion—will be disappointed. The writer designs to give *facts*, many of them new, and all of them capable of distinct and impressive evidence. He proposes to address himself to the serious and inevitable historical question :—*Who were responsible for the failure of the Southern Confederacy?*—and on this issue he will insist upon asserting that rule familiar to the world, that those who assume power are responsible for its discharge, according to the exact measure of their assumption, and that responsibility in any great cause is not to be squandered through subordinates. To do this, indeed, would be to scatter and enfeeble all the lessons of history; to render impossible its unity of narrative and to nullify its philosophy. Responsibility must rest somewhere in history; it naturally and inevitably ascends; and in regarding Mr. Davis as the prime cause of the failure of the South in the late war, the author has but simply recognized and submitted to the great law of logic in historical composition :—that, in political affairs, where a certain result is clearly not an accident or misadventure, but must have come from a well defined cause, that cause ultimately and inevitably rests in the head of the government.

As the author has said in another historical work: "Jefferson Davis cannot escape the syllogism that has been applied to every public ruler since the world began. However he may be plastered with 'glittering generalities;' however paltry publications may consult the passions of the hour; however newspapers, made up of dish-water and the paste-pot, may deprecate the vigorous inquiries of history and counsel the suppression of unpleasant facts; however partisans may dress the leaders in garish colors and the brilliant and exaggerated uniform of a class, the question comes at last: How are those failures of the Confederacy, which are accounted errors, and not misfortunes, to be ascribed, if not to the folly of rulers? Mr. Davis was supreme in his administration, and singularly unembarrassed in directing and controlling public affairs. There was no question of disconcerted authority. For the major part of his administration he had a servile Congress, a Cabinet of dummies, and a people devoted to his person." * * * *

In these circumstances, the responsibility of President Davis was well defined, and, taken along with his autocracy, was almost exclusive. But it is not necessary to insist upon this rigidity of construction. The author has simply sought to place Mr. Davis in his true logical position as President of the Southern Confederacy. He has not been content to rest on secondary causes, or disposed to enter the province of hypothesis and over-refinements; and he has done nothing more than apply to Mr. Davis's four years of Presidential life the same rule of responsibility that is familiar in all history, and has been applied to every administration of public affairs in the annals of America.

It is thus that the author, with no disaffection toward Mr. Davis, and with no design to discriminate personally against him, yet feels impelled by the reasonable logic of history to make him, as it were, a head and centre of responsibility in the late war, and to gather around him the causes of the failure of the Southern Confederacy. He risks himself upon the *facts* of his work, not upon its ingenuity. He designs a severe narrative, and he challenges the naked application to it of the common rules of logic. It has already been said that Mr. Davis had determined to reply to this work. If so, he is welcomed to the task, and is challenged to the combat. He shall have facts to oppose; and in such conspicuous, stern, and unrelenting contest, the world will decide who falls, who retreats, or who covers himself with defeat.

Finally, the writer, careless as he is in the just sense of history of the person of Mr. Davis, and disdaining whatever criticisms may grow out of personal feelings, is yet sensible that he has undertaken a great and serious work, and protests that he approaches it in a becoming and collected spirit. He attempts no mean and evanescent commentary on the late war. In betaking himself to a literary task, excelling all his former ones, and in which he is fired by various desires, he proudly ventures to produce a work that will not only interest these present times, but that "will live" permanently and assuredly, if even among the humbler monuments of the historical literature of America.

EDWARD A. POLLARD.

CONTENTS.

INTRODUCTION.

CHAPTER I.

CHAPTER II.

CHAPTER III.

CHAPTER VII.

CHAPTER VIII.

CHAPTER IX.

CHAPTER X.

CHAPTER XI.

CHAPTER XII.

CHAPTER XIII.

CHAPTER XIV.

CHAPTER XV.

CHAPTER XVI.

CHAPTER XVII.

CHAPTER XVIII.

CHAPTER XIX.

CHAPTER XX.

CHAPTER XXI.

CHAPTER XXII.

CHAPTER XXIII.

CHAPTER XXIV.

CHAPTER XXV.

CHAPTER XXVI.

CHAPTER XXIX.

CHAPTER XXX.

CHAPTER XXXI.

INTRODUCTION

A Theory of the Greatness of Men—Two interesting Reflections—A New Rule in the Composition of Biography—Application of it to Jefferson Davis.

THE greatness of men—the titles they hold to the memory of mankind—is generally achieved in a comparatively short period of life. It would be a curious and not invaluable speculation to estimate the average period in which the supreme fame of men, notable in the world's memory, is accomplished. Such fame usually extends over but a small segment of life, although the exceptions to the rule are not a few. We might indeed risk the statement that the average of the historical mission scarcely exceeds a decade. The career in which great names are accomplished generally occurs on the plane of middle life, and is bounded, on the one hand, by the obscurity of earlier years and, on the other, by the natural retirement of old age. This law of greatness is essentially a very general one, largely qualified by exceptions; but it certainly exists, and one cannot have read history attentively, if he has not observed in what comparatively brief and contracted spaces of human life, that fame which entitles men to the memory of the world, has been achieved. Two valuable and interesting reflections occur on this subject.

There are many ambitious men who mourn the shortness of life, and as they advance in years are disposed to despair of time in which to accomplish their hopes of fame. It is a common despondency of eager and sensitive aspirants, reckoning their years against their achievements. But it is a despondency that may be cured and re-animated by observing within what boundaries of years the most numerous examples of historical greatness have occurred, and on what short leases of time great names have been won. It is a sovereign peculiarity of genius to contain always in itself illimitable possibilities of greatness; there is no telling when it may assert itself and blaze forth to the admiration of mankind, and its possibility and confidence of distinction it, alike, releases only with life. But even men of lower faculties than genius need not despair of the narrow chance of historical fame, because of the accumulation of obscure years, as long as they have a margin on the natural feebleness and seclusion of old age. The greatest memories in history are spanned but by a few years; and the brave aspirant for fame, not actually stricken by age, has no reason to mourn that he has not time wherein to achieve his passion for glory.

But we have another reflection on this subject besides its consolation to ambition—a particular reflection, and one applicable to the work before us. It concerns a new rule in the composition of Biography. What is memorable in men's lives in a historical sense, and most valuable to know, generally, as we have already maintained, takes place within a limited number of years; and within this compass are to be found, we are persuaded, the proper limits of Biography. The reader wants to know principally the historical part which the man performed; and what of his life extends on either side of this space is really so marginal and subordinate that the philosophical biographer may dwell but lightly on it. If this rule diminishes the field of a particular class of literature, it is really to improve it, to cultivate its true value under a healthy system of contraction, and to concentrate and raise its interest. We protest against that tedious and jejune Biography, which relates the lives of men in the style of annals, each year having its event; which has no idea of the distribution of incidents; and which follows the subject with equal detail from the cradle to the grave. Something of course must be allowed for tracing the growth of character and bringing up the man to the period in which he is distinguished; the career, indeed, must be exhibited as a whole and in its proper relations; we only insist that in the life of the greatest men, there is a particular and often contracted period wherein its true interest resides, and that all outside of this crowded space may be treated but slightly and subordinately as scarcely different from the commonplaces of any average human life. It is within the experience of almost every reader of Biography how often he has been offended and wearied by minuteness of details, which have nothing to do with the real significance of the hero; by accounts of his childhood and early life no way distinguished from the ordinary experience of human creatures; by a puerile faithfulness to every event from the birth to the death; and by dreary relations of incidents neither memorable, nor suggestive, and not even uncommon. It is against this excess of Biography we protest.

We have proposed a rule to ourselves deduced from general observations; and happily it is singularly and even exactly appropriate to our subject. The interest of the life of Jefferson Davis lies within a remarkably limited space of time. It is bounded by well-defined lines, of more than ordinary clearness and severity, and beyond which it is but little important or memorable in the sense of history. His fame and the true significance of his life are chiefly compassed by the four years of the late war. In this dense historical period he moved as a commanding figure; but he had grown suddenly to the stature of greatness, and already he has sunk into obscure occupations and immeasurable neglect.

Adhering to the rule we have already adopted, we may rapidly go over his life up to the threshold of the war, commencing there the elaborate and justly proportioned narrative of his historical career.

CHAPTER I.

Life of Mr. Davis Anterior to the War—His Early Military Career—Abrupt Resignation of It—Eight Years of Retirement—An Early Insight into Mr. Davis' Character—Passion for Self-Culture—His Student-Life—An Imperfect Intellectual Character as the Result of Solitude—Mr. Davis's First Remarkable Adventure in Public Life—The "Pons Asinorum"—Curious Explanation of a Slander—Mr. Davis and the Mississippi "Repudiation"—His Career in the Mexican War—The "V" Movement at Buena Vista—Return of Mr. Davis to Congress—His Senatorial Career.

JEFFERSON DAVIS was born on the 3d day of June, 1808, in that portion of Kentucky which is now Todd county. His family removed to the then territory of Mississippi, while he was a child of tender years. He commenced his education at the Transylvania University, Kentucky, but left it for the West Point Academy, where he graduated in 1828.

He followed the fortunes of a soldier until 1835. He was a cadet from 1824 to 1828; Second Lieutenant of Infantry from 1828 to 1833; First Lieutenant of Dragoons from 1833 to 1835, serving in various campaigns against the Indians; was Adjutant of Dragoons, and at different times served in the Quartermaster's Department. His military life gave considerable promise of distinction; it had already afforded ample fields to gratify a passion for adventure; there was no likelihood that the command of the young officer of dragoons would rust on the Western frontier, where it had already chastised the Camanches and Pawnees, and where it was often detailed on duties of an important and dangerous character; but to the surprise of his companions in arms,

Lieutenant Davis abruptly quitted the service, resigned his commission, and betook himself to the widely removed occupation of a cotton-planter in Mississippi. A short while afterwards, it was known that he had married the daughter of Colonel Zachary Taylor after a romantic elopement, and that he had founded a quiet home in the neighborhood of Vicksburg, where for a long time he was withdrawn from the notice of his former friends and associates.

For eight years after his resignation from the army, Mr. Davis remained in the close retirement of private life, occupying himself obscurely with domestic and personal cares. He was a successful planter, living in comfort, but apparently averse to the social entertainments of that class, a man known only to his immediate neighbors, recluse, inoffensive and unpopular. Such a period of retirement, taking place within that period of matured manhood, when life is most valuable, and when the character may be said to assert itself, and occupying years of which the ambitious nature is generally jealous and eager to appropriate to particular objects, is remarkable enough, in view of the former career of Mr. Davis, and especially in view of its elevated and impassioned sequel. He was not a man who would have been generally estimated as fond of retirement. He had chosen the profession of arms from ambition, and had confessed to an early passion for public distinction. He had resigned that profession without dishonor and without bitterness. There are no traces of any private disappointment in his life which could have forced him into a seclusion in which for so many years he was apparently so well satisfied. It was not the retirement of a misanthrope, or of one whom fortune had offended, or of yet one whom some secret necessity or pain had driven into solitude. He went willingly and easily into retirement;

and for eight years, the future President of the Southern Confederacy, whose name a great war was to carry to the ends of the earth, lived quietly on a plantation, and gave the best part of his manhood to the most peaceful and most obscure pursuits of life.

But this curious interval in the life of Mr. Davis really affords an insight into his character which has not generally been observed. Stormy and ambitious as was his subsequent career, he frequently confessed to a happiness in this period of retirement which could only have proceeded from one of those rare and refined natures, which, however occupied in the world, or however conspicuously placed by circumstances, yet finds a supreme pleasure and luxury in *self-culture*, in the improvement of the mind, not for special effects, but for the delightful consciousness of its progress in power and knowledge. This disposition of Mr. Davis for intellectual pleasures is remarkable throughout his life, and even in the busiest of his public pursuits he is known to have indulged the solitary habits of self-improvement in reading, meditation and private exercises of the mind. He was a student for life, and so from the necessity of his nature. He had the passion for self-culture which is observed in such men—a passion which even the most ambitious pursuits sometimes do not dull, and the most apparently foreign occupations cannot entirely displace.

His retirement to which we have referred was rather that of the scholar than of the planter. He improved it by studies the most various; he adorned his solitude with books; he undertook a course of reading and of literary cultivation of which he never wearied, and evidences of which strangely appeared in his subsequent memorable career. It was in these years of retirement that he mostly acquired that fund of "general learning," that extensive range of culture, which was remarked of him by those who knew him intimately, when the public knew him only as President of the Southern Confederacy; which was curiously displayed within the walls of the prison where he was afterwards consigned; which supported him in that weariness and solitude; which made books his only pleasures there; and of which the most interesting and affecting evidences have been given to the world in the conversations of the "prison-life" of the fallen and fettered chief, whose "learning," in the language of the physician who attended him in pain, in sorrow, in separation from the world, in partial blindness, and in apparently the last infirmities of nature, was yet "almost marvellous."

Within eight years of close student-life Mr. Davis made himself an accomplished scholar, but scarcely more. Here he acquired the extraordinary literary culture which made him in some respects so admirable; but here too he may have derived much of that imperfect intellectual character, which marks those who have but little practical intercourse with men, and who have not mixed knowledge of the world with the information of the scholar. It is this fine mixture which we recognize especially in the highest types of statesmanship, and which we observe in those happy men who command the successes of the multitude along with the appreciation of the few and intelligent. Whatever may be the natural vigor of the mind, it may be impaired by excessive and solitary exercises; a weak and speculative intellectual character is often the result of studies which abstract us from the world; and in the practical conduct of human affairs, the danger of over-refinement is not less than that of a blunt and barren ignorance. Altogether Mr. Davis's period of studious and elegant retirement was not a fortunate preparation for the distinguished and momentous career on which he was to enter.

In 1843, Mr. Davis emerged suddenly from his seclusion, and with brilliant rapidity and a becoming ease won the honors of public life. He entered the arena of politics in the midst of a great excitement and at a time auspicious for an adventurous candidate for distinction. The State of Mississippi was then unusually agitated by a campaign for Governor, and parties were also being organized for the great Presidential contest of the next year. Mr. Davis was placed as a Presidential elector on the Polk and Dallas ticket; and so rapid had been his progress as a popular speaker and so conspicuous his part in the critical Democratic success of 1844 that the next year he was sent to Congress, and in December, 1845, took his seat in the House of Representatives.

Generally an election to Congress may be taken as the *pons asinorum* in the career of the American politician. It is usually prefaced by easier problems of local advancement, and the ordinary experience of the aspirant for public honors is that of successive steps of office leading up to this considerable elevation. The common routine or order of the political career is the local magistracy, the corporation office, the State Legislature—then Congress. Mr. Davis, however, appears to have mounted to the latter place rapidly, and to have disdained the pains of gradual advancement. That he may have been aided in this quick ascent by accidental circumstances is probably true as we have already suggested; but it is none the less certain that he must have made a remarkable display of ripe and vigorous parts to have won such a success so quickly, on his emerging from a profound retirement, and to have made his first appearance in public life as a member of Congress.

His previous connection with the local politics of Mississippi could only have been of the slightest description. Almost from the commencement of his career, he was on the theatre of national politics. This observation is interesting in view of the accusation which has become familiar in Northern newspapers, that Mr. Davis was an advocate of that odious measure, the repudiation of part of the State debt of Mississippi, represented by the bonds of one of her banks. The libel is contemptibly ignorant in point of narrative; the main fact being that at the time the bonds referred to were refused payment, Mr. Davis was in the retirement we have described, having no connection whatever with politics, and the further fact having lately appeared that at a subsequent period of his life he endeavored to raise voluntary subscriptions to pay off these bonds, and thus redeem the honor of Mississippi.

How such a slander could have been persistently and successfully maintained in the face of these facts—even to the extent that many thousand persons in the North and Europe to this day firmly believe and habitually assert that Jefferson Davis achieved his first bad distinction in life as a disciple of repudiation in Mississippi—is remarkable and even curious. It is so much so that the author may afford in this place the explanation of it which has been given him. It appears that in the late war there was an especial effort of the Northern Government to disparage the credit of the Southern Confederacy in Europe; to break down its financial schemes there, and, in proportion, to advance their own. To this mission was appointed Robert J. Walker, a Mississippian, a personal enemy of Mr. Davis, a man of the doubtful trade of a private "financier," and known to be the tool of any pecuniary enterprise; and the first flagitious enterprise of this individual was to publish in all the money markets of Europe a pamphlet representing the then President of the Southern Confederacy as one of the agents of repudiation in Mississippi. What he asserted he knew to be false; but he attached to it an invention of great plausibility. When Mr. Davis was in the Senate of the United States, his State was aspersed for repudiation; and he answered, offering what of defence or of apology he could for an act to which he had been originally opposed, but the wrong of which he was not willing to admit under the force of censure levelled at his State, or to the extent it implied in a debate of recrimination. In this he did nothing more than his duty as a representative —to offer all he could of justification of an act of his State, even one from which he had originally dissented, but which he was not therefore, willing, to submit to the unmitigated censure of enemies and to the excessive and unmeasured reproaches of the revilers of the South. In such a defence of Mississippi, he performed the just and generous duty of a representative, and made an honorable speech to urge what he could of excuse for a measure which he had never advocated, which he never pretended to justify and which he was yet impatient to see turned to excessive and distorted censure by the enemies of his State. It was this speech from which Mr. Walker obtained the color of repudiation, which he published or rather garbled in the capitals of Europe, and through which Mr. Davis is to this day unjustly known as a party to an infamous measure of his State. It is easy to pile occasions upon a fallen man; malice has done its worst upon the unsuccessful chief of the Southern Confederacy; but surely he has enough of reproach to bear without the added burden of those false recriminations which so readily grow in the season of misfortune. Though his life should be greatly accused by the just biographer, the same should be none the less ready to defend it against false accusations as to expose it to truthful censure. On this principle of distribu tion, thus early avowed and illustrated, the author bases his work and trusts its strength and merit.

Mr. Davis was sitting in the House of Representatives when the war with Mexico was proclaimed. It opened a new road to his ambition, and one which led back to his first passion for arms. He resigned his seat in Congress, to accept the command of the Mississippi Rifles—a regiment of which he was unanimously elected colonel—overtook his men at New Orleans, *en route* for the theatre of the war, and by midsummer of 1846 reinforced General Taylor on the Rio Grande. We have neither the space nor design to admit here the details of his military career in Mexico. He played an important part at Monterey, where he charged, without bayonets, on Fort Leneria; he led his command through the streets to within a square of the Grand Plaza, suffering a storm of musketry and grape; and on the subsequent field of Buena Vista, he performed one of the most dramatic incidents of the war, receiving on a suddenly conceived formation of his lines a charge of cavalry, and with a plunging fire from right and left repelling it, the last desperate effort of the Mexicans to break the American lines at the close of the day.

Of this affair a writer, who witnessed the field, has afforded the following vivid description:—"A brigade of lancers, one thousand strong, were seen approaching at a gallop, in beautiful array, with sounding bugles and fluttering pennons. It was an appalling spectacle, but not a man flinched from his position. The time between our devoted band," (the Mississippi Rifles) "and eternity seemed brief indeed. But conscious that the eye of the army was upon them, that the honor of Mississippi was at stake, and knowing that, if they gave way, or were ridden down, our unprotected batteries in the rear, upon which the fortunes of the day depended, would be captured, each man resolved to die in his place sooner than retreat. Not the Spartan martyrs at Thermoplyæ—not the sacred battalion of Epaminondas—not the Tenth Legion of Julius Cæsar—not the Old Guard of Napoleon—ever evinced more fortitude than these young volunteers in a crisis when death seemed inevitable. They stood like statues, as frigid and motionless as the marble itself. Impressed with this extraordinary firmness, when they had anticipated panic and flight, the lancers advanced more deliberately, as though they saw, for the first time, the dark shadow of the fate that was impending over them. Colonel Davis had thrown his men into the form of a re-entering angle, (familiarly known as his famous V movement,) both flanks resting on ravines, the lancers coming down on the intervening ridge. This exposed them to a covering fire; and the moment they came within rifle range each man singled out his object, and the whole head of the column fell. A more deadly fire never was delivered, and the brilliant array recoiled and retreated, paralyzed and dismayed."

On his return from the Mexican war, Mr. Davis quickly reëntered political life, this time with an ascent to the Senate of the United States. He was elected in 1847 to fill a vacancy; but a few months before the expiration of his senatorial term, he returned to the field of local politics in Mississippi, and was an unsuccessful candidate for Governor in the campaign of 1850. From that contest he passed into the Cabinet of President Pierce, and for four years discharged with uninterrupted satisfaction to the army and to the country the duties of Secretary of War. In 1857, he returned to the

Senate, and his term would have continued there until the 3d of March, 1863, had not the war translated him to that career wherein we shall find the dominant interest of his life

It is not our purpose to examine here the political record of Mr. Davis; it will appear in another and special connection, and as bearing on the one great question of separation and war. We do not purpose to burden the reader with the ordinary legislative history of his Congressional terms; we simply sum here, and very briefly, the external events of his life, before the war, designing hereafter to review, as from its threshold, whatever is significant in them on the question of Disunion.

Yet we must say something generally of his Senatorial career. It was the most important part of his public life preceding the war. For several years he sat in this body, in the company of such men as Clay, Webster, Cass, Douglas, Dickinson, and King; and the distinction he obtained for such a time and in such an association cannot be well omitted from his life—especially as we think it a rightful portion of his fame that should survive the war, and be justly distributed to his posterity. The chief interest of his life resides, as we have already suggested, within the limits of the war; and yet beyond this there is something of achievement and of character that the public should remember.

CHAPTER II.

Mr. Davis in the Senate of the United States—Distinction as an Orator—Definition of the term "Eloquence"—Mr. Davis in the World of Letters—Brilliant Remnant of his Reputation—His Style as a Speaker—His Figure and Manners in the Senate—The art of "Self-continence" in Oratory—Reference to Stephen A. Douglas—His "Specialty"—Anecdotes of his Life—How Jefferson Davis Compared with the "Little Giant"—The Former Scorns "Quarter"—The Kansas Controversy—Mr. Davis's Reply to Douglas—A Burst of Temper—A Noble Speech—The Senatorial Career of Mr. Davis, the Most Honorable Part of his Public Life.

MR. DAVIS'S career in the Senate of the United States was not connected with the origination of any great public measure, and had but little of severely historical distinction. He was a quiet member, illustrating in that august assembly a fine eloquence, a studied and refined manner, and a habit rather scholarly than popular. He never had any force as a partisan; he had no reputation as a statesman; he had none of the original resources of a great genius, a creator; but he had a characteristically senatorial manner, a mind variously and richly stored from cultivated leisure, and an eloquence which was without parallel in his times, and, in fact, ascends to comparison with the best models in history of public and deliberative discourse.

It is curious how words, formed at first to express single and distinct things, are carried to secondary significations; how they are extended by popular use to take in adjacent or similar ideas; how special or even technical terms are made at last to comprehend, in the common parlance, the whole generic idea. This peculiarity of the use or abuse of language is well illustrated in the word "*Eloquence*." As a term of art, eloquence has a very distinct and severe meaning; it denotes a quality that is the rarest of human gifts, and which, however difficult of definition, is as unmistakable in its effects as the mesmerism that by subtile influences enchains its subject, possesses all his sympathies, and makes him for the time obey the will and reflect the very sense of the other. It is, in fact, a moral mesmerism: the conversion of an audience into the *alter ego* of the individual, the irresistible command of a sympathy that identifies itself with the speaker, and binds up the hearts of men in one common feeling and affection. It is no more possible to mistake this mysterious power of eloquence than the Promethean fire. It is properly *sui generis*, distinguished from all other faculties of man, mysterious and defying analysis, and so seldom possessed, that Eloquence, taking it as a term of art, may be said to be the very rarest of that rare gift called genius, and those who may be called orators, in the highest sense of the word, may be counted by the tens in the sum of all ages of the world, and in the entire extent of human history.

But the term has been expanded by general use, until at last those even who pretend to a critical and precise use of language, are accustomed to denote as Eloquence almost any kind of powerful or effective speaking. Thus, this word is now generally used to characterize any discourse that answers its ends, whether it be the conviction of the understanding or the persuasion of the will. The vivacity of the intellect is confounded with the play of the passions; the ardor of conviction is mistaken for the heats of fancy and imagination; the lively harangue is termed the effort of Eloquence; and the mere intellectual animation of the speaker passes for the rage of the orator. It is by these natural processes that the term Eloquence has obtained a very extensive meaning. In the literature of our country, we find it freely used to denote general excellence in speaking, and appropriated as a title to fame by men of the most various gifts and accomplishments. It is equally applied to the massive, judicial discourse of Webster, the lively dialectics of Calhoun, the scholarly elegance of Randolph, the well-dressed, agreeable commonplaces of the over-rated Clay, the skilled debate of Douglas, the fiery appeal and fierce exclamations of the passionate and unequal Yancey. All these are orators in the popular sense of the term; and in this sense we shall not dispute their titles to fame, and their claims on the admiration of their countrymen.

Indeed, it is in this general and popular sense that we accept the term Eloquence, and apply it to the subject of this chapter. It would be too severe an affectation to limit now a word that has grown into so large and general a signification; and, therefore, taking it to mean power and excellence in speech, we shall proceed to designate the merit as an orator of one whose character has been but seldom or slightly discussed in this view.

The events of the past few years have not only made the name of Jefferson Davis familiar to the companies of statesmen and politicians; it has been introduced to the world of letters, and discussed there with an interest scarcely second to that it has inspired in the political circle. His exhibitions of scholarship, the fine literary effects of his style, his sonorous State papers, his skilled narration of the origin and conduct of the war, his powerful and sometimes splendid vindication with the pen of the cause of the Southern Confederacy have made him, no matter whatever else of reputation he may have lost or diminished in the struggle, one of the first literary names in America. It has been said that his very numerous and full state papers would make a very ingenious history of the war. They might be collected in another interest, as a model of style, containing, as they do, some of the best and most vigorous English extant in this corrupt literary period of the country, in which the language of our ancestors suffers so much from the zeal of Yankee reformers. But it is as an orator that we propose to regard Mr. Davis in this chapter,—a view in which it is remarkable he has been scarcely considered by his countrymen, although discussed in so many respects, and surrounded and assailed by almost every weapon of criticism. Here his displays during the war were less frequent than with the pen; they were few and but very imperfectly reported; they were almost lost to fame in the dingy records of the Confederate newspapers; but what of well-preserved record he has left, as an orator, in the Senate of the United States is sufficient, we think, to entitle him to a large measure of admiration, to repair, to some extent, other parts of his reputation, and to leave him with an honorable and not lightly adorned name to survive the misfortunes of his purely political career.

The Senate of the United States is undoubtedly the highest school of eloquence in America. It was in this school, where had reigned the triumvirate of Clay, Webster, and Calhoun, where had been the theatre of the greatest and most dignified contests in American politics, where resided the memories of the country's greatest men, that Mr. Davis formed his style. It was a fit school. Of all the living orators of America, Mr. Davis was best suited to address a small and cultivated assembly. No one abhorred more than he did that vulgar and detestable style of eloquence, which the world is disposed to designate as peculiarly *American*, and of which exaggeration is the prevailing characteristic. His sober and classical speech had nothing in common with that Fourth-of-July oratory which captivates the masses; it rejected all extravagances; it had none of that rhetorical excess which has disfigured so many American statesmen. To those accustomed to the inflated style of the hustings and the extravagances of American oratory, it was indeed refreshing to listen to the polished yet forcible language of the Senator from Mississippi, to mark his apt political words, and to hear the hautboy tones of his rich and manly eloquence.

The qualities of Mr. Davis as an orator were of rare and cultivated type. His person realized all that the popular imagination pictured for an orator. His thin, spare figure, his almost sorrowful cast of countenance, composed, however, in an invariable expression of dignity, gave the idea of a body worn by the action of the mind, an intellect supporting in its prison of flesh the pains of constitutional disease, and triumphing over physical confinement and affliction. His cheek-bones were hollow; the vicinity of his mouth was deeply furrowed with intersecting lines; and the intensity of expression was rendered acute by angular facial outline. "In face and form," said one who frequently saw him in the Senate, "he represents the Norman type with singular fidelity, if my conception of that type be correct." Observing him in a casual group of three of the then most distinguished public men of the South, sitting in abstracted conversation in the Chamber of the Senate, the same writer thus continues his description: "Davis sat erect and composed; Hunter, listening, rested his head on his hand; and Toombs, inclining forward, was speaking vehemently.

Their respective attitudes were no bad illustration of their individuality. Davis impressed the spectator, who observed the easy but authoritative bearing with which he put aside or assented to Toombs's suggestions, with the notion of some slight superiority, some hardly acknowledged leadership; and Hunter's attentiveness and impassibility were characteristic of his nature, for his profundity of intellect wears the guise of stolidity, and his continuous industry that of inertia; while Toombs's quick utterance and restless head bespoke his nervous temperament and activity of mind."

Mr. Davis had a personal figure which was commanding in every attitude. His carriage was erect—there was a soldierly affectation, of which, indeed, the hero of Buena Vista gave evidence through his life, having the singular conceit that his genius was military, and fitter for arms than for the council. He had a precise manner, and an austerity that was at first forbidding; but he had naturally a fondness for society, and often displayed tenderness to those with whom he was intimate. When he spoke, he was always self-possessed. His style as a speaker was very deliberate,—sometimes with majestic slowness pouring out his wealth of language, and anon with low searching tones penetrating the ear even more distinctly than the strained utterances of other speakers. His voice was always clear and firm, without tremor; his elocution excellent. The matter of his speeches was invariably sound and sensible. A scholar, but not in the pedantic sense of the term; a man remarkable for the range of his learning, though making no pretensions to the doubtful reputation of the sciolist, his reading was classical and varied, his fund of illustration large, and his resources of imagery plentiful and always apposite.

But what was most remarkable in Mr. Davis's style of eloquence was a manner which we believe constitutes the highest art of the orator—that of apparent *self-continence* in the expression of passion. It is by this peculiar manner, this appearance of suppressing the struggling emotions of the heart and only half speaking what is felt, that the consummate orator often conveys more of passion to his hearers than when his rage "wreaks itself upon expression," and is lost in the storm and multitude of words. It is a nice art,—a magnetic power; and Mr. Davis, of all the speakers whom the author has ever heard in America, had it to perfection. He seldom stormed, he seldom spoke loudly or impetuously; but he often filled the hearts of his hearers with unspeakable passion, and captured their entire sympathies by that evidently forced moderation of tone and language which leaves to the power of *suggestion* much that expression declines to attempt, and is incapable of conveying.

There was another remarkable trait of Mr. Davis as an orator. His eloquence was haughty and defiant, and his manners singularly imperious. He spoke as one who would not brook contradiction, who delivered his statements of truth as if without regard to anything said to the contrary, and who disdained the challenges of debate. With an eye sometimes kindling like the light that blazed on "Diomed's crest;" with a countenance engraven with passion; with a form erect but elastic, he presented the clear-cut, conspicuous front of a proud and dangerous antagonist. The author recollects him in one of the passages of the debate in the Senate on the famous Kansas bill, when he shone as the impersonation of defiant pride, and threw his haughty challenge in the face of a political enemy. Mr. Douglas, of Illinois, had twitted some of his Democratic friends for what he declared their alleged defection, and had promised certain conditions to them when he was able to dictate their restoration to the party. Mr. Davis rose suddenly to his feet, with erect and dilated figure, and, striking his breast, exclaimed proudly and passionately: "*I scorn your quarter!*"

The Senator from Mississippi and the Little Giant of the West met frequently in debate, and often with passionate encounter. There were scarcely any points of comparison between these two men,—the first, the finest orator in the Senate, and the latter, one of the ablest debaters there. Great as he was in some sense, there was no man of his times more over-rated than Stephen A. Douglas; and an estimate of his character here is interesting in illustration of what we may have occasion to suggest elsewhere in this work,—that loose judgment of the public which mistakes a narrow excellence for greatness, and special accomplishments for unlimited capacities.

Mr. Douglas had his specialty. There was no public man in the country of his high grade who was more exclusively a politician. Politics was the specialty of his life, and embraced all his mind. He had no literary accomplishments; he appears to have profoundly read no other history than that of America; and outside the competitions of political life he was wholly unknown. There is something unpleasant in this intellectual scantiness of his life, this devotion to a single pursuit. But Mr. Douglas was certainly the most consummate of politicians, "the Little Giant" in his small world of ambition. He had that ready and intricate skill which comes from the close and narrow study of a specialty, an acuteness carried to the nicest point of perfection by a division of labor. He was so thoroughly a master of the political history of the country as to constantly defeat men who were intellectually above him, by his superiority in facts; and his great power in debate was his minute and remote illustrations drawn from this special fund of knowledge. He had at his fingers' ends all the Congressional Annals and Globes, National Registers, and political encyclopedias of every sort, from "Cluskey's Text-Book" to the briefest *vadè mecum.* In this intricate field of knowledge he had no rival; his illustrations gathered there were weapons, and they sometimes bore down the most formidable arrays of intellect, and scattered the literary ornaments and flowery language of his cultivated competitors.

Mr. Douglas was a peculiar character in the political literature of America. He may be described as a characteristic product of the broad and free life of the West, and his career wonderfully illustrates the developing influences of American institutions. He plunged into politics from the time he first passed the early struggles of poverty, and was free from the concern of livelihood. There are many anecdotes of the perplexed poverty of his youth. He was born in Vermont, worked when he was fifteen years old as an apprentice to a cabinet-maker, and wandered West in a spirit of adventure, so careless and comical as to make his early life at once amusing and instructive. He describes himself on one occasion of his travels in Illinois as reduced in funds to thirty-seven and a half cents. With this sum in his pockets he entered the town of Winchester, in Illinois, and chancing to come upon an illiterate auctioneer selling goods in the street, he offered to keep his accounts. In three days he made six dollars, advanced his views, and on this capital opened a school. The next step was a strident one, and ended with a nomination to Congress.

He lost the election by five votes. But he was consoled by an appointment to the supreme bench of Illinois, and here he obtained the title of Judge, by which he was familiarly known to the day of his death. In 1847 he was elected to the Senate of the United States, and here he at once became famous in recommending a characteristic policy in the foreign affairs of the country.

It may be claimed for Mr. Douglas that he originated the gushing school of "young America," if he did not, in fact, introduce these words for the first time in the political literature of the country. No experiment on public sentiment could have been more happy and captivating at the particular period in which Mr. Douglas first introduced himself to national attention. It was a time when the Cuban question was at its heat, when our foreign relations were deranged and unsatisfactory, when "Anglophobia" had again become a title of popularity, and when reports of constant searches of American vessels by British cruisers on the Gulf of Mexico, the *mare clausum* of America, were spurring public indignation to the rowels. Mr. Douglas was at once for radical and daring measures. He was ready to take possession of "the gem of the Antilles," to annex Canada, and to send a national war vessel on the track of the British cruisers. The party supporting such measures was aptly named "Young America;" it had no distinctive body or organization, but as a sentiment it was definite and characteristic enough to make Mr. Douglas suddenly and immensely famous, and to procure for him an almost intoxicating draught of popularity. His favorite rhetorical figure was an "ocean-bound republic;" he taught a rapid and inflammatory progress; the literature of the day reeked with caricatures of those who opposed this sudden inflation of American pride and ambition. The "old fogy" was a miserable wretch "sitting over the shirt-tail of progress crying woe, woe!" This grotesque term has since become nearly obsolete in our politics, and the *afflatus* of "Young America" has since passed into the general patriotism of the country; but the popularity made out of the passing transport was Mr. Douglas's first stage in fame, on which ensued a long and important career.

It would be merely to repeat some very familiar history to detail Mr. Douglas's record on that peculiar "territorial question" which preceded the late war, and, in fact, was its most obvious and visible occasion. The vexed question of Slavery in connection with the government of the Territories, was the main topic of his public life, and furnished those theatres of debate on which he was such a central and conspicuous figure. The political record has become trite from repetition; but Mr. Douglas's personal history in the controversy is one of vivid and dramatic interest. He realized the most various experience of public opinion, the utmost shifts of adventure in the changeful and intricate controversy extending from the Compromise Measures of 1850 to the opening of the war in the next decade. At one time, he was almost apotheosized, at another time incontinently damned. It was a striking example of "the fickle vulgar," and of the uncertain tides in the life of a great politician. At one time the City Council of Chicago voted Mr. Douglas in the company of "the Benedict Arnolds and Judas Iscariots of history," and thereafter, expunging the record, received him with the honors of a conqueror. In 1854, when he was bearing the burden of the repeal of the Missouri Compromise, it was said that "he could ride from Boston to Chicago by the light of his blazing effigy in the night, and in sight of his hanging effigy by day." On this occasion the indignation of Chicago, the tumultuous metropolis of the West, was again erect, and the Senator, returning to his home, was received by a city bristling with mobs. He attempted to address a crowd from the balcony of his hotel; but they would not hear him, and they drowned his struggling words with insults, and jeers and taunts and shouts of defiance. It was a remarkable struggle of the persistence of a single, brave, and clear-toned speaker, with the clamor of a hoarse and brutal mob. For four long hours, from eight o'clock in the evening, Mr. Douglas struggled for a hearing, edging in a word wherever he could, expostulating, defying, shaming, entreating, as the moods of the mob appeared to vary. Finally, when the hour of midnight was struck, he took out his watch, looked at it very deliberately, and said: "It is Sunday morning; I have to go to church, and you—may go to h—l!"

In the Kansas controversy, and the involved question of popular sovereignty, Mr. Douglas had abundant opportunities of that passionate controversy which his strong and aggressive nature craved. He was never so great and powerful as when spurred by controversy and baited by his political opponents. He had a supreme self-confidence, and his tones of defiance were clear and ringing. Although not an orator in the highest sense, he had an intellectual vividness that was nearly akin to eloquence, and his intrepidity was like an inspiration. When the "Lecomptonites" sought to "read him out of the Democratic party," and a group of Democratic Senators, among whom Jefferson Davis was conspicuous, were constant in their recriminations, he said, with great disdain, that he would return from Illinois a Senator for six years longer, and would then take occasion of further reply to the enemies confronting him, preferring to save time and unnecessary fatigue by "firing upon them in a bunch." At this remark Mr. Davis grew warm, denouncing it as unexampled insolence; and it was on an occasion in the same speech of Mr. Douglas that he struck his breast in a theatrical manner, and declared that he would never accept "quarter" from the Senator from Illinois.

Mr. Davis had his specialties as well as Mr. Douglas; some of them were, perhaps, even narrower than those of the Senator from Illinois; but whatever was the force of the former, in the Senate of the United States, he certainly had a breadth of literary culture to which the Western man could not pretend. Mr. Douglas had a ready reference in the political history of the country, and was, thus, often able to overthrow his opponent on particular questions of party; but Mr. Davis had an immense fund of historical and literary illustration, and excelled his antagonist in the general effect of his speeches taken as a whole. In the brief and ready colloquy, Douglas had no superior in the Senate; in the orderly and elaborate discourse, Davis stood pre-eminent. Whenever it came to the lengthened debate between the two, the latter was likely to carry off the palm of superiority.

Mr. Douglas was particularly sore in the Kansas controversy under the imputation cast upon him by his removal from the position he had long held of chairman of the Committee on Territories. It was a proclamation of a Democratic majority in the Senate, that his doctrine of "squatter sovereignty" was a heresy, a defamation, in fact, of that high principle of popular sovereignty which Mr. Davis himself had avowed in the Kansas-Nebraska bill, and which breathed the true spirit of American institutions. The first impression of the difference between Mr. Douglas and the Southern Democracy—the former contending that the people in the Territories were from the first date of their settlement competent to decide the question of slavery, and the latter contending that they could do so only when the Territory was prepared to ask admission into the Union, and was in the act of assuming the sovereignty of a State—is that of an unimportant and technical question, a mere affair of circumstance and time. But it was a question that really went to the heart of the sectional controversy. Mr. Douglas's "squatter sovereignty" was in fact, a concession to the Anti-Slavery sentiment of the North; it proposed to decide the question of Slavery in the new States by a hasty and disorganized action, in which the facilities of the North for colonization might easily stock a factitious vote and override the rights of the South; it suggested a plan by which a few "emigrant aid societies" might take a "snap-judgment" on southern institutions, even more effective than a Congressional prohibition; and it furnished to the Abolitionists an instrument practically more certain and expeditious than the blunted and undisguised measures with which they had formerly waged a desultory war upon the institution of Slavery.

It was on this broad issue that Mr. Davis repeatedly encountered the Senator from Illinois, and illustrated more than one triumph of luminous and scholarly eloquence over the ingenious vapor of the demagogue. Mr. Davis was but seldom personal or acrimonious in his speeches; when he designed to wound, he was sarcastic rather than aggressive; but more than once in debate with Douglas, he lost his temper, and rushed at his antagonist with an ungovernable violence. There was a marked animosity between the two Senators; one of the most important contests in the politics of America found them face to face; and the combatants were ready to strip their lances as in a controversy of life and death. On one occasion in 1860, Mr. Douglas spoke uninterruptedly for two days in the Senate, hurling defiance at those who had degraded him from the position of chairman of Committee on Territories. Mr. Davis replied at almost equal length; he went over the whole ground of controversy, and made the most telling and complete speech of his life. He disclaimed personalities but with characteristic ingenuity made his very disclaimer the channel of attack, the conduit of scorn and contempt. "Nothing," he declared, "but the most egregious vanity, something far surpassing even the bursting condition of swollen pride, could have induced the Senator from Illinois to believe that I could not speak of *squatter sovereignty* without meaning him." He scorned the narrow rule of proscription on slight differences in parties; but at the same time he accommodated to this a noble declaration concerning the integrity of political opinions. He spoke of that common subject in American politics, the disgraceful compromises of parties for the spoils of office. He said, "I cannot respect such a doctrine as that which says, 'you may construe the Constitution your way, and I will construe it mine; we will waive the merit of these two constructions, and harmonize together until the courts decide the question between us.' A man is bound to have an opinion upon any political subject upon which he is called to act; it is skulking his responsibility for a citizen to say, 'Let us express no opinion; I will agree that you may have yours, and I will have mine; we will co-operate politically together; we will beat the opposition, divide the spoils, and leave it to the court to decide the question between us.' I do not believe that this is the path of safety; I am sure it is not the way of honor."

It was a noble speech; and is referred to here, for much of the character of Mr. Davis in debate, and for something of his elevated moral tone in public life. Naturally passionate, his temper was usually moderated by a fine and cultivated language; ambitious, he yet disdained the low efforts of the demagogue and courted popularity decorously; successful in politics, a man having many propitious opportunities, he was yet never caught in a corrupt bargain, a fraudulent adventure or any affair which could be counted personally dishonorable, or which might not be pardoned to the common spirit of intrigue in the politics of the country. No shadow ever fell upon his personal honor in the Senate of the United States; and even the malign persecution of him in a "lost cause" has failed to find in this part of his life anything of personal reproach, moral delinquency or intellectual weakness.

The career of Mr. Davis in the Senate is undoubtedly the best and most honorable part of his public life. It was singularly pure, elevated, and well-sustained. In whatever other times and characters he was deficient, he will, at least, be known in future and just history as an orator who adorned the highest councils of his country, and as a scholar who has left in his literary compositions models already studied and applauded in two continents.

CHAPTER III.

The Election of Abraham Lincoln, President, not the Cause of the War—A Peculiar Aristocracy in the South—The Power of this Section in the hands of Politicians rather than Slaveholders—Remarkable Speeches in the Convention of South Carolina—The State Conventions Mere Puppets—The Centre of the Conspiracy at Washington—Jefferson Davis Among the Conspirators—Critical Examination of His Record on the Question of Disunion—Its Inconsistency—His Early Extravagances for the Union—His Conduct in Congress in 1850—Prophetic Warning of Henry Clay—Mr. Davis' Ambition to succeed Calhoun—His Effrontery—Connection with the "Resistance" Party of Mississippi as its Candidate for Governor—His Remarkable Explanation of the Designs of this Party—Inconsistency of this Explanation—Mr. Davis enters the Cabinet of President Pierce as a Union Man—Repudiates the "Resistance" Party—His Responsibility for the Kansas-Nebraska Bill—Union Speech in Mississippi—Mr. Davis Regards the Kansas Settlement as a Triumph for the South—He is Bit by the Ambition for a Presidential Nomination—An Electioneering Tour in New York and Maine—"Slaver" of Fraternal Affection—Insincerity of Mr. Davis's Record on the Question of Disunion—The Cause of the South Disfigured by the Ambition of its Leaders, but not therefore to be Dishonored—A Brief History of Disunion—The South Suffered from a General Apprehenson Rather than a Specific Alarm—The Action of her Politicians, neither a Test of Her Spirit, nor a Measure of the Justice of Her Cause—The Condition of Washington, in December, 1860.

THE election of Abraham Lincoln to the Presidency of the United States might have precipitated the Secessionary movement of the Southern States; but it certainly did not produce it. For many years the thought of Disunion had gathered in the South, and it was at last executed by a small number of politicians—for there is nothing more singular in the history of the war, than the narrow and exclusive control, in the South at least, which managed its initiation, compelled the people to it, and brought upon the country the rage of sectional arms.

We shall have future occasion to see how the war was compelled by a few politicians, and to what extent the people were excluded from the early drama of its inauguration. How these few persons were able to do so much can only be understood from the peculiar constitution of society in the South. In that part of the Union there had long been a singular aristocracy—not that oligarchy of slaveholders generally imputed to it—but an aristocracy that was not constituted by birth, wealth, or manners, but that rested mainly on the titles and dignities of public life. The aristocracy of the South is properly described as an aristocracy of politicians—men who had naturally other coincident claims to superiority, who, perhaps, owned slaves, possessed wealth, or might assert some sort of social merit, but who governed the masses and reposed their superiority mainly on the eminence of public office. Such an aristocracy is naturally narrow, restless, and badly ambitious. It had ruled the South for many years; in that part of the Union there was not only a marked and close monopoly of public office, but even some trace of hereditary descent in it; and the greater politicians of the South were as distinct and imperious a class as men in any single occupation have ever formed.

It was this class in the South that had long indulged the thought of Disunion, and that for years had paved the way to its consummation. Many of them saw in it new careers; the more ardent sought in it opportunities of ambition; and not a few old and spent politicians hoped to gratify in it a mean and slothful greed of office. The war took such men neither by surprise nor by force. They had plotted and desired it; they saw in the accommodations of the contest, new fortunes and emoluments for themselves; and they seized with alacrity the occasion to realize the hopes of years.

The first remarkable step of the South ensuing on the election of Mr. Lincoln, was the Convention of South Carolina, which on the 20th of December, 1861, passed an ordinance of Secession, and declared that the State had resumed her sovereignty. In the debates of this Convention there was a tone of congratulation, rather than the foreboding and deprecation which might have been supposed would have prefaced a great and disastrous civil war. "It is no spasmodic effort that has suddenly come upon us," said one of the members; "it has been gradually culminating for a long series of years." "Most of us," declared another, "have had this matter under consideration for the last twenty years." Others, and among them those who had long led in the Disunion party, could not contain their joy at the consummation of their hopes, and spoke with something of the intoxication of success. Mr. Keitt said:—"We are performing a great act, which involves not only the stirring present, but embraces the whole great future of ages to come. I have been engaged in this movement ever since I entered political life. I am content with what has been done to-day, and content with what will take place to-morrow. We have carried the body of this Union to its last resting place, and now we will drop the flag over its grave." Mr. Rhett said more plainly:—"The secession of South Carolina is not the event of a day. It is not anything produced by Mr. Lincoln's election, or by the non-execution of the fugitive slave law. It has been a matter which has been gathering head for thirty years." The consummation of so much of effort and of desire was proclaimed on the day South Carolina passed an ordinance of secession; and after such speeches as those referred to, it is not surprising that the audience in the hall of the Convention, on the announcement of the vote rending the bonds of the Union, should have risen to their feet and hailed the event with wild and impassioned cheers.

But we shall not linger upon the history of the several State Conventions which successively and respectively severed their States from the Union. The early story of the war does not belong there. Its true seat and theatre were in Washington City. There was the true dramatic centre of the conspiracy, there the real spring of the plot; and the State Conventions passing pretentiously their ordinances of secession, and affecting deliberation where all had already been advised, were really but the puppets at the ends of the wires.

The true history of the war takes us then to Washington—takes us to a small but powerful company of politicians who had assumed there the question of peace or war. Among these brilliant conspirators stood conspicuous Jefferson Davis—alert, magnetic, keen in his ambition, his weak health restored by excitement, quickened with nervous transports, a man having many qualities of leadership, a nature easily inflated with great occasions, but without the true and robust pregnancy of a real greatness. For the present, however, he was the most observed of all the Southern Representatives at the capital, and took with facility and grace the position of their leader.

Mr. Davis' record on the question of Disunion was greatly mixed and contradictory—one of those inconsistent careers which could only have been tolerated in the loose habits of American politics, that care but little for the antecedents of public men, have a very feeble estimate of consistency, and are prone to forget whatever is of record in the past, in the busy and tumultuous excitements of a strained and excessive partyism. Mr. Davis had first entered Congress as a fulsome, young declaimer of that easy and popular theme—the blessings of the Union. He had the sophomorial tumour of "the glorious Union" on the brain. He sought to excel in the competitions of devotion to this idol of the populace, and this commonplace of demagogues. In his first important speech in the House of Representatives, delivered in 1846, he had said:—"From sire to son has descended the love of Union in our hearts, as in our history are mingled the names of Concord and Camden, of Yorktown and Saratoga, of Moultrie and Plattsburg, of Chippewa and Erie, of Bowyer and Guilford, and New Orleans and Bunker Hill. Grouped together, they form a monument to the common glory of our common country; and where is the Southern man who would wish that that monument were less by one of the Northern names that constitute the mass?"

Yet in 1850, he had opposed the "Compromise Measures" in the Senate, and was repeatedly rebuked there for the sentiment of disunion. In a private conversation Henry Clay had spoken to him in terms of mingled expostulation and warning. "Come," said the venerable Senator from Kentucky,—anxious to win another vote for what he regarded as the supreme work of his life, then suspended in a divided Congress,—"join us in these measures of pacification, and they will assure to the country thirty years of peace. By that time I will be under the sod, and *you, my young friend, may then have trouble again.*" But the ardent Senator from Mississippi was intractable. He had already conceived the ambition of taking the mantle of Calhoun in the Senate, and in the zeal of a poor and coarse imitation he was already violently affecting all the ideas of the dead statesman and champion of the South. He would lower none of the demands of the South. He announced its *ultimatum* in a high and menacing tone. With a pretension that little became his relations with the venerable Henry Clay, he thus spoke in the Senate, in 1850:—"That I may be understood upon this question, and that my position may go forth to the country in the same columns that convey the sentiments of the Senator from Kentucky, I here assert that never will I take less than the Missouri Compromise line to the Pacific Ocean, with specific right to hold slaves in the territory below that line; and that before such territories are admitted into the Union as States, slaves may be taken there from any of the United States at the option of the owners."—Certainly, John C. Calhoun could not have spoken more distinctly, more imperiously, or with greater arrogation of the importance of himself in the Senate of the United States.

In 1851, after the passage of the "Compromise Measures" Mr. Davis, as if resolved upon the utmost *role* of "disunionist," and probably spurred by his ambition to take the place of Calhoun, removed his opposition to the measures referred to, to the local politics of Mississippi, and had consented to stand as candidate of the State Rights or "*resistance*" party for the office of Governor of the State. He was rebuked by a defeat. A short time thereafter we shall find him modifying his views, and attempting the popular current of a renewed devotion, a restored allegiance to the Union. But in advance of this mark or indentation of his record, there is a passage of history connected with his party campaign of Governor for Mississippi of remarkable interest, and of a significance which appears not heretofore to have been perceived.

The party in Mississippi referred to, as headed by Mr. Davis, was popularly known as the "resistance" party. It recited a long list of grievances. It named no less than six different causes, for which the people of Mississippi might resort to the most extreme remedies. Yet when Mr. Davis, in the month of May, 1860,—a time when he was displaying himself as a conservative supporter of President Buchanan's administration, and probably attempting the new career of a moderator in public life—was reminded in the Senate of having been formerly involved in a scheme of disunion, he explained his connection with the period of Mississippi politics, referred to:—"The case only requires that I should say that *the party to which I belonged did not then, nor at any previous time, propose to go out of the Union, but to have a Southern convention for consultation as to future contingencies threatened and anticipated.*"—Yet a few months later, the same man who had professed the idea of resistance to usurpations of the Federal authority, only to the extent of challenging them in a convention and bringing them before a tribunal of the States—which was indeed the length and breadth of Calhoun's doctrine of "nullifaction"—was demanding *disunion* for evils not greater than that which the Mississippi resistants had "anticipated," and was ready to rush to the arbitration of the sword!

But we return to the chronological order of Mr. Davis's record. In 1852, impressed by the election of the previous year in Mississippi, he openly repudiated the scheme of disunion, to the extent of supporting the nomination of Franklin Pierce for President, and actually abandoning the party which had nominated the Presidential ticket of Troup and Quitman upon the distinctive platform of State Rights and separation. He was rewarded with a place in President Pierce's Cabinet. Here he played the part of an intense Union or compromise man; and it is a significant incident, showing what views were held of his disposition in Mr. Pierce's Cabinet, that he was sought by the friends of Stephen A. Douglas as an intermediary to obtain the pledge of the President's approval of the Kansas-Nebraska bill—"the

Pandoras' box"—in advance of its introduction into Congress. And he did obtain it, and thus became directly responsible for a measure, which the Democratic party in the South afterwards sought busily to disown, and to ascribe to the ambition of Mr. Douglas.

In 1857 Mr. Davis returned to the Senate of the United States. He marked his way to the capital by a speech delivered at a small town in Mississippi, professing increased devotion to the Union. He spoke with eloquence on this subject, and with something of the profusion of the enthusiast. He would not disguise the profound emotion with which he contemplated the possibility of disunion. The fondest reminiscences of his life were associated with the Union, into whose military service, while yet a boy, he had entered. In his natured manhood he had followed its flag to victory; had seen its graceful folds wave in the peaceful pageant, and again its colors conspicuous amid the triumph of the battle-field; he had seen that flag in the East, brightened by the sun at its rising, and in the West, gilded by its declining rays—and the tearing of one star from its azure field would be to him as the loss of a child to a bereaved parent!

In 1858, after the battle with the Douglas party, and when the South was regarding what it thought a doubtful field, Jefferson Davis was among the first to re-assure those who were disposed to despair of the Union, or were distrustful of the prospects of the South, after a combat so hard-fought, so elaborate, and through which it was so difficult to run the line of victory, and to determine where success rested. He declared in a public letter to the people of his State that the "Kansas Conference bill" was "the triumph of *all* for which we contended."

During the recess of Congress after the settlement of the

Kansas question, Mr. Davis, bit by the ambition of a Presidential nomination, commenced to go through all the wretched affectations of a candidate for this position—those demagogical devices in dinners, serenades, etc., that making of occasions of *national* significance, that traditional coquetting of sections, that deprecation of partisanship, those ingenious equivocations and agreeable platitudes, which have generally been taken among American politicians as an unfailing sign of an aspiration to the White House at Washington. He commenced the unmistakable routine of a candidate for the Presidency.

He travelled North. In October, 1858, he spoke in Faneuil Hall, Boston. A few days later he addressed an immense Democratic meeting in New York. In reply to an invitation to attend the Webster Birthday Festival, held in Boston, he wrote, with withering indignation, of "partisans who avow the purpose of obliterating the landmarks of our fathers," and of men "whose oaths to support the Constitution had been taken with a mental reservation to disregard its spirit." He asked "to be enrolled among those whose mission is by fraternity and good faith to every constitutional obligation, to ensure that, from the Aroostook to San Diego, from Key West to Puget Sound, the grand arch of our political temple shall stand unshaken." He penetrated even to Maine as knight-errant of the Union, and candidate for the White House. He accepted a serenade in Portland "without distinction of party." "The occasion was," said a local journal, "in every respect the expression of generous sentiments, of kindness, hospitality, friendly regard, and the brotherhood of American citizenship." The Senator from Mississippi, the head of the old "Resistance" party, the *quondam* competitor for the mantle of Calhoun, had suddenly become the apostle of "nationalism" and the messenger to the

North of peace and of love, beyond all Southern men of his day. His affection for the North ran actually into slaver. He surpassed the usual pledges of demagogues; he loved the people around him not only as brothers, but he proposed to dedicate his infant son to the Portlanders. It was a singular ceremony of devotion. "If," said the orator, "at some future time when I am mingled with the dust, and the arm of my infant son has been nerved for deeds of manhood, the storm of war should burst upon your city, I feel that, relying upon his inheriting the instincts of his ancestors and mine, I may pledge him in that perilous hour to stand by your side in the defence of your hearth-stones." He hoped that the flag over his head "would forever fly as free as the breeze which unfolds it," and after this invocation, scarcely original, he sat down under it amid tumultuous cheers.

Such was the man who, in December, 1860, appeared in Washington, chief among the Southern Disunionists, angered by disappointed ambition, and eager for a new career—anxious to play the grand game of compensation in his fortunes, as leader of a revolutionary movement.

In the record we have recited there is an insincerity which cannot be overlooked. We are not permitted to doubt that Jefferson Davis, in his leading part in the Secession conspiracy at Washington, was moved by personal ambition, when we consider the antecedents of his public life, his recent, and yet raw disappointment of a Presidential nomination, his nervous and restless nature, and his passion for leadership. But to these remarks the author must attach an explanation to defend himself against misconstruction. The reflections which he has cast upon Mr. Davis and other politicians of the South by no means include the cause for which they acted, and the merits and justice of it are certainly not to be confounded with the unworthiness of some of its partisans. Because the cause of the South was defaced by the personal ambition of politicians, we have no right to conclude that it was neither just nor meritorious.

Indeed, every candid historian must admit that the causes of Southern complaint had accumulated up to the time of President Lincoln, and that the election of this man was to a certain extent, the signal of the aggravated prosecution of the irrepressible conflict, which he himself had declared, between the institutions of the South and the ideas of the North. Disunion was not so much the speculative project of the Southern mind, as it was the growing bitter fruit of Northern injustice. The history of the idea of Disunion is curious and desultory. It had first appeared in the North, and was first announced in Congress in a speech of Mr. Quincy, of Massachusetts, delivered in 1811; it was next developed in the Hartford Convention; it was renewed on the memorable measure of the Missouri Compromise, in 1819; it disappeared for more than a decade from the politics of America; it was violently revived by the Tariff discussions of 1831–2; and it thereafter progressed through a multiplication and perplexity of causes, which it would take too much space here to arrange in detail, and of which it has well been stated, "the acts of oppression could not be stated in precise words or estimated in figures." In truth, any attempt at such detail must essentially be defective, so various had become the forms of hostility to the South which the North displayed. At the time of President Lincoln's election, this hostility of the North had become so pervasive and popular, that it eludes analysis, and renders specifications unnecessary; it could no longer be measured by political acts; it had become habitual through every expression of Northern opinion; it was in its literature, its pulpit, its social offices, its daily conversations; it had grown to such proportions, and was so reaching and subtile in its ramifications, that the intelligent and philosophic historian must observe that the protest of the South was not so much against any particular series of political measures as against the whole current of Northern sentiment, the entire animus of that section on the subject of so-called slavery.

The mind of the South had really come to disdain specifications on this subject. It suffered from a general apprehension rather than a specific alarm; and the election of Abraham Lincoln was a vague addition to this uneasiness rather than a particular cause of complaint. Whether the South might have been reassured at this time by any act of legislative wisdom; whether her grievances admitted of compromise, and whether an adjustment could have been made which would have spared the extremity of the sword, is one of those questions so entirely dependent on speculation, and so untried by facts, that the opinion of mankind is likely to remain long divided on it. The partial action of her politicians on this subject, affords no true test of it. They, we repeat, were concerned at Washington, with their own schemes of personal ambition, rather than with a work of public interest; and yet in referring again to their narrow and selfish control of the affairs of the South, we are forced to reflect, that even under that system of aristocratic rule which badly adorned public life in the South, these men could not have asserted so complete a command of the issue of Disunion, had there not been among the people of the South a wide and deep-seated dissatisfaction to impel them, and to sustain the experiment of a new government. It is always difficult to say what share personal ambition has in causing wars and revolutions; it must always be mixed more or less with general causes;

and, in the case to which we are referring, while making justly prominent the motives which we believe governed those who precipitated war from Washington, we by no means imply that other causes did not co-operate with them, or that the merit of Southern resistance is to be measured by the selfishness of a few men who assumed to represent it.

These men had come to Washington in December, 1860, full of the idea of Disunion, many of them bursting with ambition, and some eager to vent their arrogance in Congress, where they had before suffered anything of reproach or of defeat. The South, and the whole country, were in anxious and dumb expectation, rather than in the condition of positive and pronounced ideas; and it was precisely in this undetermined state of public opinion that a few politicians might assume the largest control of public affairs, and determine by rapid measures the destinies of a nation. Such was the condition in which a Congress, the most memorable in American history, and yet the most trivial in some respects, met; and in which the message of James Buchanan, the weakest and most plausible of Presidents, was given, not only to his country, but to an interested and anxious world.

CHAPTER IV.

Remarkable Effect of the Message of President Buchanan—A Spectacle in the White House—A Singular Pause in the Movement of Secession—Mr. Keitt's Remarks on the Situation—The Southern Leaders Actually Abandon the Scheme of Disunion—It is Resumed on Major Anderson's Occupation of Fort Sumter—A Question of Concealed Importance—How the Question of "the Forts" determined the War—Mr. Floyd's Adroitness—Secret History of the Junta of Fourteen in Washington—A Revolutionary Council in the Shadow of the Capitol—Their Extraordinary Usurpations—Jefferson Davis and "the Committee of Three"—True Date of the Commencement of the War—Why Mr. Davis was Chosen Leader—In the First Programme of the Southern Confederacy, R. M. T. Hunter, of Virginia, Designed for President—How he Lost the Position of Leader—A Fatal motion in the Senate—Comparison of the Claims of Hunter and Davis for the Position of Leader.

THE message of the President, delivered to Congress, in December, 1860, had an effect which has not been duly appreciated in history, and which was scarcely recognized in the newspapers of the day. Mr. Buchanan was timid, secretive, ingenious; one of those time-serving politicians, who had managed to keep constantly in public life, not an ostentatious partisan, but a traditional office-holder, an "old public functionary," one of those men who make extraordinary successes in the political arena without the force of merit and through the sheer ingenuity of the demagogue. He had neither courage nor intellectual decision. "To see him," said a distinguished Virginia politician, who visited him during the impending difficulties of the country, "cowering beneath the full-length portrait of Andrew Jackson on the mantelpiece of the reception-room of the White House, munching a dry cigar, and asking querulously what he could do, or what he should do, was more than human patience could endure, or human pity tolerate." This despicable old man was grotesquely balancing on the question of peace and war. He was apparently resolved to trifle with the time-service of a great occasion, and he was desperately anxious to save the remnant of his administration from the imputation of a civil war.

But perhaps his message was more artful than weak. However low and unworthy the motive which dictated it, nothing could have better answered the purpose of giving a pause to the movement of Secession, of suspending it, and of delaying, if not pacifying the excitement of the country. This result it performed with admirable ingenuity; and his message had thus a certain value in history, a decided appreciable effect, which has never been justly estimated in the accounts of this period. It took the sting from Secession; it neutralized for a time the complaints of the South, and it removed those immediate causes of alarm on which the Southern leaders had calculated to agitate their section and to precipitate its decision. If the country did not avail itself of this season of reflection, it was not Mr. Buchanan's fault. For nearly a month he held the Secession conspiracy at bay, and if the interval was not improved by the sober second thoughts of the people, they have themselves to blame for the loss of an opportunity.

The author was in a company of Southern members of Congress when the information was first obtained, some days in advance of Mr. Buchanan's message, that it disclaimed "coercion," that it contained nothing to interrupt or to exasperate the movement of Secession, that it referred to it without menaces, and had nothing about it but the tone of a weak expostulation. The news had a dampening and curious effect. The question at once occurred whether the South could be put out of the Union without the force of added exasperation; and indeed what reason could be urged for fresh anger or alarm, when the General Government disclaimed the idea of force, and there possibly might be found a provision in the Constitution to save that collision of arms, which the wisest of the Southern leaders knew was necessary to complete their scheme of separation, and to plant its line with a permanent animosity and discord. It was a baffling question. The conspirators had already lost more than half their capital—there was to be no coercion; and when Mr. Keitt, of South Carolina, shook himself, "tetered," and declared, in his characteristic way, from major to minor premise, that the President had "blocked the game," and that they must wait for contingencies, there were none of the company to gainsay him.

The remarkable fact is historically certain that for several weeks after Mr. Buchanan's message, the Southern leaders abandoned or suspended the scheme of disunion, and had resolved simply to keep the question open as a standing menace, and possibly as a means of compelling future terms. They could scarcely do more than maintain an equivocal attitude; they dared not pursue the idea of disunion in the face of the concessions of Mr. Buchanan, or without occasions to refresh the excitement of the South. At the first meeting of Congress, they were confident of an early separation of the South, and almost treated it as an accomplished fact; now these same men in their private conversations, suggested the possibility of a settlement, advised their constituents not to sell, from alarm, property which they happened to own in Washington, and gave out the idea—none the less forcible because it was unwilling—that there might possibly be a peaceful solution of the troubles of the country. Those who lived in Washington in this period of hesitation, will well remember how balanced were the rumors of that time. It was a marked interval in the history of the conspiracy of disunion. Whether, on the hypotheses of certain events, the Secessionists might have been baffled and overruled, is a question we are not permitted to discuss; for in this season of suspense came an event, one apparently slight and accidental, which decided it at once, and, more than any single incident, determined for the country the calamity of war.

This event was the surreptitious capture of Fort Sumter, in Charleston Harbor, by the Federal forces under Major Anderson. It occurred on the 16th of December, 1860. It was on its face a slight event; there is no evidence that there was a deliberate design in it; it had been undertaken, to be sure, in contravention of the equivocal policy of the President, and of his express pledge that the military status on the Southern coast should not be disturbed; it was merely the transfer of a Federal garrison to a more advantageous post; and yet it was an event which was vitally significant in the estimation of the Southern leaders, which interrupted all efforts for peace, and which, finally, more than any thing else, determined the alternative of war.

To understand the great importance of this event, and its extraordinary weight on the impending issue of Secession, it is necessary to make some explanations.

The Southern States were full of arsenals and forts, which commanded their rivers and strategic points. The value of these forts was vital, in a military point of view, and with the army of the United States once transferred to them, the General Government would have been put in a position that might have paralyzed Secession, or secured an almost decisive advantage for the Federal power at the very commencement of the war. A few men in the country saw this. While the general public was but little concerned about the Federal forts in the South, many of which had been neglected for years, some of which were yet without garrisons, and not a few of which were not even known by name to persons of ordinary information, there had been a quiet estimate of their importance by the Southern leaders at Washington from the moment they had first meditated the consequences of Secession. They saw readily enough that if the General Government secured possession of these forts, it could establish communications with the South, which the latter could scarcely cut off without the aid of a great fleet; and that if it was once determined at Washington to reinforce these positions against a chance to take them by surprise, or *coup de main,* the South would have lost an opportunity which it would be impossible to regain and incurred a disadvantage which it would be most difficult to repair.

The question of the forts was one of concealed importance in the minds of the Southern leaders. As long as attention might be diverted from them, the South could still hold within reach the opportunity of possessing them and securing a powerful advantage, and might thus afford to suspend the question of war, and to linger some time at least in the discussion of peace measures. But the signal came at last for action. The alarm which ensued on the movement of Fort Sumter appeared to the public of that day very disproportionate; a huge exaggeration of an event that might be explained on the commonest hypotheses; but those who thought so did not understand its terrible significance to the Southern leaders, and their sudden interpretation of it as a signal that the Government had at last understood the importance of the forts, and might yet throw a chain from the Atlantic to the

Mississippi on the dreaming genius and relaxed limbs of Secession. "Had General Scott," said Mr. Floyd, in 1861, "been enabled to get all the forts in the South, in the condition he desired them to be, the Southern Confederacy would not now exist."

Mr. Floyd was the first to take alarm at the news from Sumter. "He resigned," as a newspaper expressed it, "with a clap of thunder." The Southern leaders met in sudden and irregular conferences; it was a holiday season of the year and formal deliberations had to be delayed for a day or two; but Mr. Floyd in his resignation from the Cabinet had already suggested the measure of the opportunity and how adroitly the whole controversy might be turned on the single specification of the facts concerning Sumter. The conspirators awoke to a sense of their position, saw the danger on one side and the opportunity on the other. If they gave a week's respite to a plot actually in course of execution, they might be hopelessly lost. The season of delay and uncertainty was past. From the day the news from Sumter reached Washington the question of disunion and war was practically decided; one of the most extraordinary councils in the history of the country was determined upon; a revolutionary body sat in the shadow of the Capitol at Washington; and in a few weeks this strange authority had sent over the country the order which led to the seizure of all the forts in the South except two.

The council summoned on this occasion at once assumed the powers of a revolutionary junta. It was composed of the Senators from seven Southern States:—Florida, Georgia, Alabama, Mississippi, Louisiana, Arkansas and Texas. It met in one of the rooms of the Capitol, on the night of the 5th January, 1861. The representation was full, two Senators from each of the States named being present;—but a body of fourteen Southern men, and those, too, properly acting in a very limited representative capacity, was certainly a small and extraordinary one to determine for the country the concern of peace or war, and to assume the destinies of the South. It was decided to "recommend" immediate Secession of their respective States, and the holding of a Convention at Montgomery, Alabama, on the 15th day of February. So much of the proceedings of this extraordinary council were published, and were perhaps legitimate. But it was not then published, and it is only fully known at this day, that this council assumed to themselves the political power of the South, and to control all political and military operations. They seized the telegraph, they controlled the press, they possessed themselves of all the avenues of information to the South, they dictated the plan of seizing the forts, arsenals and custom-houses, and they did the whole work of revolution at Washington, while public attention was drawn to the mere incidental movements that seconded the designs of these few men and concealed the true seat of operations. It was even doubted whether such a council had ever been held in Washington, and whether it was not a fiction of the newspapers. But in any case few had the least suspicion of the extent of their operations. It was a strange assumption of authority that, in the midst of the peaceful and ordinary transactions of public life, a body so small and so foreign to the purpose in hand, of a representative character at once so limited and so peculiar, composed of men who were every day in their accustomed seats in the Senate, who were to some extent privy-counsellors of the Executive, and thus acting under obligations of peculiar confidence, should have succeeded in erecting a revolutionary tribunal in a private committee-room, and been able to dictate from there, without detection or interruption, the plan of a great rebellion.

In the confusion and multitude of scenes which preface wars and other great events in history the mind naturally inquires for some particular body of men, some well-defined scene where the operation commences, and from which may be traced dramatically the succession of events. Such beginnings are often found in narrow circumstances. In the present instance the scenes of a great war properly open in the small room in Washington City, where fourteen men pledged themselves to overthrow the existing government. They assumed the direction of every affair of the South, and from the beginning it was evident that the people were to have no calm and deliberate voice in the matter. An *executive* committee was appointed, "to carry out the objects of the meeting." It consisted of three persons, and one of them was Jefferson Davis. That the council was not merely "advisory," that it represented the vigor and determination of a revolutionary purpose is proved from the fact that its programme was carried out with an exactness, a minute correspondence to every proposition that could only have proceeded from the force of command. Every thing was done that the council ordered. They did control "all political and military operations;" they did have forts and arsenals seized, as, one by one, the dispatches from Washington indicated them; they did effect a Convention at Montgomery arbitrarily appointed; and, in no instance, did the movements in the South towards Secession vary from the programme decided at Washington on the 5th of January. Never was a conspiracy more successful in all its designs and in every detail; and never could such a correspondence of events have been produced by mere councillors, so limited in numbers and in representative capacity, unless there had been concealed in the guise of "recommendations" the bold and imperious *fiat* of men who had resolved to rule the people rather than to counsel and then obey them.

The secret Senatorial council of the 5th of January can then only be historically known as a revolutionary body. It really dates the commencement of the war. To be sure after this there was a prolonged farce of a debate in Congress, and such affectations as might proceed from the tactics of parties; but war was practically determined when Anderson raised his flag at Sumter, and turned inland the frown of his guns.

The council of the 5th of January—as further evidence of the extent and force of its design—did not neglect the designation of a leader: that, indeed, was a matter of supreme concern, and one not likely to be overlooked in even a preliminary conference. The views of the council or caucus were naturally imperfect; they have never yet been correctly reported, or freely given to history; but there is no doubt of the remarkable fact that the programme of offices first designed for the new Confederacy was R. M. T. Hunter of Virginia, President, with Jefferson Davis, Secretary of War. There was, to be sure, no distinct expression of such a choice, no vote, no declaration; and yet that the affections of the Southern leaders at this time were for Hunter as President, that they hesitated, and that they were afterwards governed by a special circumstance do not admit of doubt.

The reasons which determined the early choice of Mr. Davis as Minister of War in the new republic, shadowed forth by the conspirators, were obvious enough. He was a graduate of West Point; he professed an aptitude for arms; he had gained considerable distinction in the Mexican war; and he had had large experience in the military committee of the Senate, and in the War Department.

Unfortunately for the pre-eminence of Mr. Hunter, as leader of the Secession movement, he fell into an act of imprudence, which lowered him in the estimation of his colleagues, and made him for a time an object of suspicion. The fact is, the staid and circumspect Virginian was not yet advanced enough in his notions; his heart was not yet in the scheme of Disunion; and not a week after the caucus in which he had sat and assented to its deliberations, he appears to have taken a sudden resolution, and was either bold or rash enough to propose a plan of peaceful adjustment.

This plan looked to the forts in the South—on which had hinged so much of secret anxiety in the minds of the conspirators. It proposed a resolution authorizing the *retrocession* of the forts within any State, upon the application of the Legislature, or of a Convention of the people of such State, the Federal authorities taking at the same time proper security for their safe-keeping and return, or payment for the same. Mr. Hunter knew the importance of the forts. He knew that on them trembled the heart of the controversy. It might not be too late to recall the *status quo* before the act of Major Anderson, to restore the confidence of the South, and for the Senator from Virginia, to pluck a higher honor than that to which he had been uncertainly appointed in the revolutionary council of the 5th of January. He said:—"To produce reunion it is essential that the Southern States should be allowed to take that position, which it is obvious they are going to take, in peace. You must give, too, all the time you can, and offer all the opportunities you may, to those who desire to make an effort for the reconstruction of this Confederacy."

The resolution cost Mr. Hunter the position which he had heretofore approached, of President of the New Confederacy. He was retired; he was assailed by reproaches; and Jefferson

Davis at once mounted to the unchallenged leadership of the Secession party, and from that moment became the arbiter of the destinies of the South. The circumstances which placed Mr. Davis in the position were, as we have seen, to some extent, accidental; and it was a question often occurring in the course of the war and in the progress of his administration, what other person in the South could have been found more capable of directing its affairs, and representing its character and cause. The question is a grave one, and has a supreme interest in history. It may be conceded at the outset, that Mr. Hunter was not the man to take precedence of Mr. Davis in a command so august, and in a care so various as that of the leader of a revolution. The Senator from Virginia had a superior intellect; he had a keen and worldly prudence; he had practical knowledge of men; but he lacked the qualities of leadership, the nervous temperament, the indispensable, personal enthusiasm that commands men. His manners were remarkable for stolidity. He was a heavy, impassive, studious statesman, rather than a brilliant partisan, or an ingenious conspirator. On the other hand, Mr. Davis had many of the elements of leadership. He had passion, brilliancy; there was a natural arrogance in his manners; his attitude in the Senate was authoritative, self-poised and commanding; he was as facile and powerful in conversation as in debate; he had an address at once erect and pleasing; with a face as imperious as that of Calhoun, and expressions as mobile as those of Clay, he appeared the impersonation of a popular leader, and wore easily and grandly the air of one born to command. It was a brilliant covering of great defects; yet no one can question the brightness and beauty of those colors in which Jefferson Davis first concealed his true character, and stood in the eyes of the South almost as the apparition of a divinely appointed leader.

CHAPTER V.

The Sectional Debate in the United States Senate—How Different from that in the House of Representatives—Intellectual Poverty of the Debate in Congress—Explanation of this—A Game of Pretences—A Class of Intermediate Politicians Sincerely Affected—References to Crittenden and Douglas—Andrew Johnson the Champion *Par Excellence* of the Union—His Extraordinary Life—Compared with Jefferson Davis—Johnson's Literary Style—What Senator Douglas Thought of Him—His Extraordinary Courage—Mr. Davis's Singular Criticism of Johnson—Reticence of the Former in the Debate in the Senate—His Explanation of the Secession Sentiment—Sinister Conduct—He offers an Amendment to the Constitution—Andrew Johnson's Appeals for the Union—A Curious History of the Vote on the Crittenden Resolutions—Colloquy of Johnson and Benjamin—Mr. Davis makes His Farewell Speech in the Senate—Wigfall's Picture of the Dead Union—Last Effort in the Senate to Save the Peace of the Country—A Memorable Scene.

THE debate in Congress which preceded the war is historical, and is a necessary part of the biography of Jefferson Davis. His place was in the Senate; and it is, therefore, to that branch of the national legislature that we shall confine our notice, assembling around the subject of our work the persons and circumstances necessary to explain his part in the drama. In the House the debate was naturally larger in volume and more excited than in the Senate; the former was a body more sensitive of the public impulses and convictions, and its tone of debate, if more immoderate, was yet, in some sense, more significant. The discussions in the Senate, prefacing the war, were more tame and partial than among the immediate representatives of the people, and yet scarcely superior, to the degree that might have been expected, in respect of deliberation or of dignity.

Indeed, this whole debate in Congress, was one of the most extraordinary in history, on one especial account, namely:—its lack of sincerity; and this fact will, perhaps, explain its comparative intellectual poverty, and the want, generally speaking, of a sublime and impassioned eloquence in a historical crisis so vast and fearful. Whatever brilliant episodes there were in this debate, whatever flashes of true eloquence, there is no doubt that, on the whole, it was below the occasion; and, lacking the element of earnestness, it fell into the commonplaces of affectation and routine. The Southern Senators, generally, had really no heart in the discussion; they had resolved, in secret caucus, to secede, despite whatever might ensue of persuasions or propositions to compromise; they did not really desire the pacification of the country, although determined to keep up a pretence of such disposition in order to affect public opinion; and thus, while professing an attempt for a peaceful settlement, they secretly intrigued against the possibility of such a conclusion. It was a shallow affectation, and was managed with but little adroitness. On the other hand, the majority of Republican Senators were also deficient in sincerity. The extreme men of that party had secretly resolved that there should be no compromise; and thus the two elements in debate were about equally engaged in a game of pretences, and a controversy that appeared so imposing in the highest council of the nation, was, in reality, very destitute of earnestness, almost barren of genuine emotion.

In such a condition, the few Senators who truly and deeply felt the magnitude of the crisis, and were sincerely affected in the debate, were naturally those who stood midway between the malcontents of the South and the extreme Republicans of the North, and who had not committed themselves to the secret schemes of either. The solicitude of these men was real. But they were few who thus stood in true patriotic concern between the two affectations that dulled and degraded a debate which was to these few a matter of life and death for the country. There was probably no member of the Senate more sincerely affected than Mr. Crittenden, of Kentucky, and it is said that he shed tears when his resolutions of com promise were voted down, mourning in the dignity of age, as an ancient Roman might have done, over the fall of the republic. But Mr. Crittenden lacked vigor as a debater; his powers, as an orator, had never been great, and were now impaired by years; and he was not the man to assume a dramatic figure in a debate that required much more of the impassioned and aggressive than the paternal style of eloquence. Mr. Douglas, of Illinois, had ability enough to stand between the factions, and probably sincerity enough in his desire for peace; but unfortunately his position as a pacificator was vulnerable. He had lost whatever influence he had ever had in the South, and his part in the last Presidential election might easily be construed to accuse him as a promoter of the troubles that had befallen the nation. On one occasion, when he attempted to reprove Wigfall, of Texas, as a disunionist, the fierce and rugged Texan Senator turned upon him, and said: "Why, I tell the Senator that that great principle of his (non-intervention) disrupted the Democratic party, and has now disrupted the Union; and but for him and his great principle, this day a Democrat would have been President, and the Union saved. That is the fact about the matter; and when a Senator, who has contributed more than any other man in the Union, according to his ability, to the destruction of the country, comes here and charges me with complicity in dissolving the Union, and charges in terms that extremes meet, and that I and my friends, and the Free-Soilers on the other hand, are co-operating for the same purpose; that we are voting together; and that we take great comfort in all these exhibitions of the impossibility of saving the Union: I tell him that he is not the man to come here and preach to anybody!"

In this deficiency of the Senate, this want of a fitting champion of the Union, one whose sincerity was unquestionable, and whose position in politics betwen the two factions, might command influence with both, a single man arose as if almost providentially qualified to supply the occasion. This man, this brave knight in season, was Andrew Johnson, of Tennessee. His antecedents, his position, his character as a popular tribune, qualified him for his peculiar and dramatic mission against Secession. Whatever have since been the varied and august fortunes in the life of this man, he never occupied a prouder position, or one of more historical sublimity than when he confronted the disunionists sprung from his own section, and stood against this important array of numerous and brilliant intellects, throwing in their very faces the rude but stalwart defiance of the patriot.

This remarkable man had already accomplished a life the most romantic in political annals, essentially *American* in its significance and interest, and replete with dramatic situations and surprises—a life which could only have been produced in the extraordinary growths of our peculiar political system, of which it was a most remarkable exponent. A boy of ten years who did not know his alphabet, apprenticed to a tailor; learning spelling and grammar by picking out words in an old volume of speeches by British statesmen; wandering as a journeyman tailor to Eastern Tennessee; obtaining a helpmate, whose wifely task was to read history and politics to him as he plied the needle on his work-bench, the man at last attracted attention, pleaded the rights of the working-classes, was despised by the aristocracy of the little town of Greenville, made his way through opposition, emerged from difficulties, climbed steadily the ladder of public promotion, and at last stood a peer in the highest council of the nation.

Scarcely have any two persons of equal rank in public life afforded a contrast in person and in character, so sharp and striking as Jefferson Davis, the leader of Secession, and Andrew Johnson, the especial champion of the Union. The former, a haughty and cultivated man, represented the traditional aristocrat of the South, and illustrated that type of scholarly statesmanship supposed to be nourished by the institution of Slavery, in the elegant leisure which it affords for literary culture and the improvement of the individual. He was a model of deportment in the social circle, a picture of graceful and well-poised dignity in the American Senate. He formed his speeches with classical severity and elegance; he spoke easily in measured and well-cut sentences; and the thought was always complete in his exact and well-rounded periods. Johnson, on the other hand, was the traditional democrat, a plain, earnest man; rough, but with a face too deeply engraved with character to be accounted plebeian; scorning the pretensions of aristocracy, and yet endowed with that medium and proper dignity in public life that invites access and yet easily sustains its official position of superiority. He was emphatically a man of the people, yet without the vulgar attributes of the demagogue. He had but few of the graces of the orator, and none of his virtues of language, but that of deep earnestness. He scorned literary flourishes, and valued chiefly the plain, coarse strength of argument. Once in the Senate he explained with more of pride than of humility: "I have not the power to con over and get by rote and memory handsomely rounded periods, and make a great display of rhetoric. I have to seize on fugitive thoughts as they pass through my mind, make the best application of them I can, and express them in my own crude way." He was an extempore speaker, and had the common affliction of that class in a habit of repetition of his thoughts and of straining for expression, quite unlike the literary style of Mr. Davis, who dropped his words perfect and rotund, one by one, moulding them with exquisite deliberation. As a writer, Mr. Johnson had considerable finish and elevation; but in his speeches he exhibited but few literary ornaments; yet in real intellectual force he had scarcely his equal in the Senate. A member of Congress, who sat with him in the memorable session of 1860–1, has described excellently his style as a speaker: "His elocution was more forcible than fine—more discursive than excellent; he *hammered* away with stalwart strength upon his thought, until he brought it into shape. He rarely failed to produce the impression he intended." He suffered from the poverty of language, which is so often remarked in self-educated men; he had the common misfortune of that class, frequent self-betrayal in historical and literary allusions; but his strong and courageous sense was not ashamed to make successive trials of expression, until at last it carried conviction home to the minds of his hearers. When his blundering blows did hit they told like those of a giant.

How effective they were in the hot conflict of ideas in which he engaged Mr. Davis and his followers may be judged from the fact—which has been frequently attested to the author—that Senator Douglas deplored to the day of his death that Mr. Johnson had not commenced the fight against Secession a little earlier, as he relied upon him and Crittenden repelling from a Southern stand-point the aggressive debate of the disunionists of the Senate, and giving the *coup de grace* to their schemes of ambition. But the opposition was—as Mr. Douglas might not have known—against a foregone conclusion. The conspiracy had ripened before Mr. Johnson spoke in the Senate; and the only effect of his anti-secession speeches there was to involve him in a severe personal controversy.

In this controversy, however, he showed striking and memorable courage. Indeed there was one trait of the man which always obtained for him a certain respect from the Southern people, even when in the heat of the war he was deemed their worst enemy. It was his high, personal courage —a quality which never fails of the admiration of the people of the South in any shape of man. The truest courage is not that which is constitutional; it is the fruit of the harsh experience of life, the education of self-confidence, the inspiration which comes from the memories of dangers tried, misfortunes conquered, and obstacles overcome. The remarkable courage of Andrew Johnson, now conceded by the world, was the product of a harsh, aggressive life, at war with fortune from infancy, and animated with the recollections of triumph. It was no ordinary spirit that could meet the Southern Senators who by concert set upon him for his opposition, to their schemes of Secession, made him an especial mark for their hostility, and hunted him with every weapon admitted in parliamentary strife. He answered them with defiance. Once driven almost to extremity by their threats and taunts, he turned upon them a face not to be forgotten, and said: "There are men who talk about cowardice, cowards, courage, and all that kind of thing; and in this connection I will say, once for all, not boastingly, with no anger in my bosom, that these two eyes never looked upon any being, in the shape of mortal man, that this heart of mine feared!"

In some recent recollections of his old antagonist in the Senate, Mr. Davis is reported to have said:

"The position of Mr. Johnson with his associates of the South had never been pleasant, not from any fault or superciliousness on their side, but solely due to the intense, almost morbidly sensitive, pride of Mr. Johnson. Sitting with associates, many of whom he knew pretended to aristocracy, Mr. Johnson seemed to set up before his own mind, and keep ever present with him, his democratic or plebeian origin as a bar to warm social relations."

But Mr. Davis has probably misinterpreted the separation of Johnson from those who "pretended to aristocracy," as a paltry matter of personal pride. It was the constitutional genius of the true democrat that thus divided him from associates like Mr. Davis. The key-note to the politics of the former was the rights of the working-class, the virtue of the popular masses; and, perhaps, no public man of equal station in America had so hated and defied the false and insolent aristocracy, which would have strangled his early aspirations, and, indeed, had hunted him to the summit of his career.

"What do you mean by 'the laboring-classes?'" was asked of Andrew Johnson, tailor and statesman, standing upon the floor of the United States Senate.

"I mean," replied Johnson, "those who earn their bread by the sweat of their face, and not by fatiguing their ingenuity." At another time: "Sir, I do not forget that I am a mechanic. I am proud to own it."

Such were the two men who met in the Senate of the United States at the threshold of the war, and who, more than any two other men of their day, were representatives of the ideas that struggled there for domination. They never met immediately in debate. Johnson did not make his most powerful and elaborate speech for the Union until Jefferson Davis had taken farewell of the Senate. As for Mr. Davis, he was singularly sparing of speech in the debate that preceded the war; he spoke but little in the questions before the Senate, and that only incidentally. His remarkable reticence may, perhaps, be explained from a sentiment of delicacy on account of his selection as president of the new Confederacy, which his Southern associates had already determined, and, therefore, his immediate profit in Secession; or more probably it may be ascribed to the supposition that he was really ashamed to play the part of a hypocrite, making fulsome rhetorical endeavors for pacification, well knowing that an opposite conclusion had been determined in secret caucus, and that he had accepted, if not already the position of leader of a rebellion, the place of one of the committee to carry out the design of disunion. Whatever the explanation, he did not make his accustomed figure in debate, and he assumed an appearance of singular impassiveness, whatever might have been the hopes and fears that swayed his breast, or the ambition that consumed him.

Before the Senatorial caucus, in the first week of January, and when the coercion of South Carolina was debated, Mr. Davis had spoken more freely, and in a very unequivocal style. Referring to the common threat to reclaim a sovereign State by force, he had declared: "I would have this Union severed into thirty-three fragments sooner than have that great evil befall constitutional liberty, and republican government." He freely asserted that the South had long meditated Secession, endorsing in effect those confessions to which we have already referred in the South Carolina Convention, that the secession of that State was the aspiration of years, and not a sudden indisposition to Federal rule. He said:—"We have warned you for years that you would drive us to the alternative of going out of the government, and you would not heed. I believe you still look upon it as a mere passing political move, as a desire to secure party ends, knowing little of the deep struggle with which we have contemplated this as a necessity, not as a choice, when we have brought to stand before the alternative—the destruction of our community independence, or the destruction of that Union which our fathers made. * * * You have believed—not looking to the great end to which our aims are directed—that it was a mere political resort, by which we would intimidate some of your own voters."

But in later stages of the debate, when the Southern Senators had actually determined on the programme of Secession, Mr. Davis's freedom of speech was suddenly checked, and he subsided into an almost sinister silence. He secretly knew that the period for argument was passed, and any pretence he made thereafter of it was very slight and brief. In his brief speech of the 8th of January, 1861, commenting merely on events, and vindicating the seizure of the Southern forts, he had said:—"Abstract argument had become among the things that are past."

Had the effort for pacification been sincere on the part of the Southern Senators, Mr. Davis of all men considering the position he had been assigned of chief representative, should have come forward in the debate, and should have framed the demands of the South. He was the man, of all others to do this, if the controversy had been real. Again and again it was asked by the Republican leaders in the Senate, who affected to depreciate the crisis, and to twit the anxiety of others, that the South should exhibit her bill of grievances and make a distinct ultimatum. "What do you want?" said Mr. Wade, of Ohio. "Many of those who supposed themselves aggrieved have spoken; but I confess that I am totally unable to understand precisely what it is of which they complain." Mr. Davis answered, with brief declamation. "After forty years of debate," he said, "you have asked us what was the matter." But it was necessary that the record should be made up for history, and to save appearances, Mr. Davis could scarcely do less than frame some measure which should indicate the wrongs of the South and express her demands.

A few days before his retirement from the Senate, Mr. Davis moved the following resolution:—

> "That it shall be declared by amendment to the Constitution, that property in slaves, recognized as such by the local law of any of the States of the Union, shall stand on the same footing in all constitutional and Federal relations as any other species of property so recognized; and, like other property, shall not be subject to be divested or impaired by the local law of any other State, either in escape thereto, or of transit or sojourn of the owner therein; and in no case whatever shall such property be subject to be divested or impaired by any legislative act of the United States, or of any territory thereof."

This proposition was never considered, discussed, or taken from the table. It was undoubtedly intended for appearances, and Mr. Davis had secretly determined to take no active part in any scheme of pacification. Indeed he had given evidence enough of his disposition of inactivity. When at an early period of the session he had been appointed one of the Committee of Thirteen to report a plan of settlement, he had asked to be excused, and had explained:—"The position which I am known to occupy, and the position in which the State I represent now stands, render it altogether impossible for me to serve upon that committee with any prospect of advantage."

Meanwhile Andrew Johnson, although not yet fully aroused to the danger of the country, and not yet knowing the extent and arrogance of the conspiracy against the Union had fully defined his position. As early as the 18th of December, 1860, although recognizing the just fears of the South in the election of Abraham Lincoln, and resenting the reluctance of the Republican party to offer new guaranties suggested by that event, he had given an advice to his Southern associates that possibly might have averted the war, when in manful and noble phrase he exhorted them to "fight for their Constitutional rights on the battlements of the Constitution." He entreated Mr. Davis and other Southern Senators to remain in their places, assuring them that if they thus remained firm and unshaken, Mr. Lincoln could not even organize his administration unless by their permission; and much less could he or his party do any direct injury to the Southern interests. With prophetic vision, he told them that Secession would be the death of Slavery, that in the blast of a sectional conflict it would be swept away with the sword of destruction. He gave his opinions clearly and impressively; he thought the tones of exhortation those best to be used before the movement of disunion had advanced very far; and raising his hands to heaven, he uttered that invocation which has since appeared to have been the inspiration of his life, and which deserves to be inscribed in golden letters beneath his place in history:—"Duties are mine; consequences are God's."

It was a remarkable speech. There was no finer burst of eloquence heard in the Senate Chamber, no loftier picture of the Union than what occurred in a passage of this speech, when Mr. Johnson aptly drew a figure from the scenery of his own home in Tennessee. "Who dare appropriate," he said, "to the exclusion of any part of the country the capital founded by Washington, and bearing his immortal name? It is within the borders of the States I have enumerated, in whose limits are found the graves of Washington, of Jackson, of Polk, of Clay. From them is it supposed we will be torn away? No sir; we will cherish these endearing associations with the hope, if this Republic shall be broken, that we may speak words of peace and reconciliation to a distracted, a divided, I may add a maddened people. Angry waves may be lashed into fury on the one hand; on the other blustering winds may rage; but we stand immovable upon our basis, as on our own native mountains—presenting their craggy brows, their unexplored caverns, their summits, 'rocked-ribbed and ancient as the sun'—we stand speaking peace, association and concert to a distracted Republic."

It would be useless and tedious to give the mere legislative form of a debate, which resulted in no measures, and to give *seriatim* the various and technical propositions on which it proceeded. The most of these propositions were, as we have insisted, mere affectations and shams. We have designed rather to produce the true spirit of the debate, and to confront in it the two most important characters—Jefferson Davis and Andrew Johnson. The Crittenden Resolutions—really the only seprate proposition of peace—may be taken as the only important text of the debate, and the originator of this measure was not conspicuous in discussing it.

These resolutions which lingered for many weeks in the Senate, and on which a vote was ominously avoided, came up at last for decisive action on the 16th of January, 1861. They were to the effect of re-affirming Slavery as against the authority of Congress or a Territorial Legislature south of the Missouri line of compromise; denying the power of Congress over Slavery in the District of Columbia, and in the forts, arsenals, dock-yards, or wherever else the Federal Government had exclusive jurisdiction; and strengthening the Fugitive Slave Law by additional enactments. The antithesis of the plan of settlement was resolutions offered by Mr. Clark of New Hampshire. These resolutions declared that the provisions of the Constitution were already ample enough for any emergencies; that it was to be obeyed rather than amended; and that an extrication from present dangers was to be looked for in strenuous efforts to preserve the peace, protect the public property, and enforce the laws, rather than in new guaranties for peculiar interests, compromises for particular difficulties, or concessions to unreasonable demands.

It has been said that Mr. Davis was in favor of the Crittenden Resolutions, and would have accepted them as a settlement of the grievances of the South, and that other Southern Senators were similarly disposed. In a speech of Mr. Breckinridge of Kentucky in the Senate, 16th of July, 1861, he said: "I happened personally to know the fact myself that the leading statesmen of the lower Southern States were willing to accept the terms of settlement which were proposed by the venerable Senator from Kentucky, my predecessor." But in face of the facts it is impossible to accept this explanation, or to consider it as other than a dishonest afterthought of the Southern leaders, an attempt to forge in the record a historical vindication of themselves. The Crittenden Resolutions came to a vote on the 16th of January, 1861. There were fifty-five Senators at that time upon the floor. The vote to supplant these resolutions by the proposition of Mr. Clark was yeas, 25; nays, 23. Six Southern Senators, Mr. Benjamin, of Louisiana; Mr. Hemphill and Mr. Wigfall, of Texas; Mr. Iverson, of Georgia; Mr. Johnson, of Arkansas, and Mr. Slidell, of Louisiana, were in their seats, but refused to cast their votes. Mr. Davis was detained in his room by a convenient sickness. But, as the records show, there were Southern Senators enough to have carried the resolutions and to have submitted the subject, as designed, to the people, "who," as Andrew Johnson, in his characteristic faith, remarked, "have never yet, after consideration, refused justice, for any length of time, to any portion of the country."

Mr. Johnson saw the balance suspended between peace and war. Watchful, brave, alert, he made the effort which patriotism suggested even at the expense of personal feeling. Although he had been rebuffed by the Secession leaders, who had haughtily and insolently surveyed him whenever he rose to speak, although he could not expect the commonest civilities from them, he was not the man to shrink from public duty, either from timidity or personal delicacy. When the vote was being taken on the Crittenden Resolutions, he moved near to Mr. Benjamin, of Louisiana, and said, with earnestness: "Let us save this proposition and see if we cannot bring the country to it. Mr. Benjamin, vote, and show yourself an honest man." He got only a scornful answer. The Crittenden Resolutions were lost; telegrams flew to all parts of the South that all hopes of compromise were gone; and Mr. Johnson, crossing the floor of the Senate to where Mr. Crittenden sat, wounded, pale, in the very agony of disappointment, has since remarked:—"Well do I remember the sadness, the gloom, the anguish that played over his venerable face."

True, the passage of the Crittenden Resolutions in the Senate might not have been decisive of the question of peace or war. Indeed, all the plans of compromise suggested might have been, as Mr. Hale, of New Hampshire, expressed it, "the mere daubing of the wall with untempered mortar." But partial and tentative as these resolutions were, they were yet to the Senate, to the extent of their effect, the question of peace and war, and thus a sufficient test of the dispositions of its members. The main effort of the Union men—as of Andrew Johnson, of Tennessee—was to get a distinct proposition of peace before the people trusting to their sense of justice and committing the responsibility to them; and thus the motion on the Crittenden proposition, whatever might be its ultimate results, was, as far as the action of the Senate could command, the complete and distinct issue of union or disunion.

The farewell speech of Mr. Davis in the Senate was memorable. The State of Mississippi seceded from the Union on the 9th of January, 1861, but her Senators lingered at Washington until the 21st before they withdrew. At that time the debate in Congress on the sectional question had, as we have seen, very much degenerated, and was, on both sides, an affectation. It had now really become an idle ceremony, a waste of words, and no one knew it better than Mr. Davis. Senator Hale, of New Hampshire, one of the most candid members of the Republican party of that day, has since testified, that on the 18th of December, 1860—the day the Crittenden Compromise was introduced—it was determined the controversy *should not be settled in Congress.* The season of debate, when Mr. Davis bade farewell to the Senate and announced another public career, had justly passed. The temper of the opposing party was well expressed in the savage witticism of one of its most truculent members. Owen Lovejoy was asked what he thought of Senator Seward's speech, noted somewhat for its conciliatory tone. "We want," said Lovejoy, "no Melancthons now; we want Martin Luthers.

We want no one to write essays upon the Union and the sin and disasters of Secession, but some one to throw the inkstand right at the devil's head!"

In these circumstances of useless and affected speech in Congress—knowing well that debate there had become a mere ceremony, and, what is worse, a deception of the public —Mr. Davis took leave of the councils of Washington in a speech of remarkable brevity. This explanation perhaps accounts for the comparative abstinence of this address from argument and historical illustration, and its literary barrenness in a great conjuncture, which it might be thought would have been adorned with the highest efforts of eloquence. There is a brief historical vindication of the South in this speech, an argument limited to the fewest words, and then a fit and dignified inspiration in an appeal to Providence, "invoking the God of our fathers who delivered them from the power of the lion, to protect us from the ravages of the bear." But the language was very fine, the spirit of the address dignified; and those who witnessed its delivery by Mr. Davis, will recollect how the Senate hung on the slow and unimpassioned words, and how tears even were shed when he walked forth from the chamber, "released from obligation, disencumbered of the memory of any injury he had received," prepared for a new career, the most important and dramatic of modern times. In the close of his speech he showed an unbounded personal generosity, begged pardon of all whom he had ever offended, and directing his attention to the Republican Senators, declared that he carried away no hostile feelings, and sincerely apologized for whatever of personal displeasure had ever been occasioned in debate. It is remarkable that after such a noble tender of personal reconciliation, only two Republican Senators approached him and shook his hand at parting. They were Messrs. Hale and Cameron.

When Mr. Davis took leave of the Senate, he left there but little to record of controversy or debate. A few Southern Senators, whose States had not yet seceded, still lingered in their seats, but only to insult what they supposed to be the last hours of the Union. It was already dead, said Senator Wigfall of Texas. The object of so many hopes, the Union that had emerged from the mist and blood of the Revolution, the traditional love of the American people, was, as the Texan Senator expressed it, only a corpse lying in state; and the whole government at Washington drawing around it a few tawdry ceremonies, and holding feebly the glorious memories of the past, was but nursing a distempered fancy in the cold sweat of death. The ghastly figure was not without significance. It appeared, indeed, as if the Government had lost all vitality and resolution; it had, indeed, sunk to a most abject and pitiful condition; and the Secession leaders might well brandish their contempt in the face of an authority that they had already openly defied, and that they had left, as they imagined, on the confines of dissolution.

"What is the condition?" said Mr. Polk, of Missouri. "Universal panic, prostration of credit, public and private. Our government has just advertised for a loan of five millions. and she could only get half of it bid for, nor even that except at usurious rates of interest, running up to the extreme of thirty per cent. per annum!"

It is notable that a government threatened by one of the fiercest revolutions of modern times, had yet made not the least provision for war. Not only was the debate we have described entirely fruitless, but it is remarkable that the Congress—of one branch of which we have treated here—had absolutely not passed a single act to increase or strengthen the military power of the government. The bills having that object in view—known as "force bills"—had all been defeated. The appropriations which were made were only ordinary ones. The troubles of the country received no solution at the hands of Congress, not even a temporary arrangement, not the slightest or remotest provision. It was a singular blank, indicating that weak and almost dumb expectation, in which the public mind of the North for a long time hung vaguely on the issues of the impending conflict.

One last effort in the Senate to save the peace of the country remains to be mentioned, and fitly concludes the chapter. Through the earnest endeavors of the friends of Mr. Crittenden, his proposition, once defeated, was taken up for reconsideration, although Mr. Pugh, of Ohio, had, when the vote was first announced, moved to lay the whole subject on the table, as in despair of reconciliation. Finally, on motion of Mr. Cameron, of Pennsylvania, a motion to reconsider was carried. On the 3d day of March, it was announced that the vote would be finally taken. It was the last day of the session; the next sun would bring in a new Administration, and might dash forever the hopes of those who had so long struggled to preserve the peace of the country. It was a critical day. A vast crowd pressed into and around the Senate Chamber; with difficulty the officers drove them from the floor; they surged in the galleries; there was great confusion there, but something was pardoned to the anxieties of the hour; many stood in spaces scarcely affording breath, until night descended on the debate. They were there to witness the tragedy of a nation's extremity. A few hours more and the curtain might fall on all that there had been of the glory and prosperity of a great country. The future was uncertain, alarming, hidden. Mr. Crittenden spoke in subdued tones; the galleries scarcely heard him; even the finest rhetoric would have been lost on the exhausted emotions of men who had come to hear simply "yes" or "no" to the hopes and fears that had agitated them for months. It was near midnight when the vote was taken: 19 to 20; the Crittenden Resolutions finally lost by one vote! Its announcement was made without impressiveness. Bewildered, stricken, speaking only in low murmurs, the vast crowd wandered out into the night, and separated to meet again in front of the bayonets that glittered the next noon before the new President of the United States, as, in the presence of the people, and in the sight of heaven, he swore to support the Constitution and assumed an office that was to be disfigured by four years of war.

CHAPTER VI.

Organization of the Confederate Government, at Montgomery—Mississippi Proposes a Southern Confederacy—Singular Instance of Rebellion Unchallenged—Explanation of the Remissness of the North—The Error of Mr. Lincoln—Secession as a Popular Sentiment, and Secession as an Organized Fact—Failure of the North to Distinguish between the Two—Rapid Action of the Montgomery Government—Interesting Historical Problem as to the Extent of the Idea of "Reconstruction" in the Southern Mind—Mr. Davis had no such Idea—Why not—His Defiant Speeches at Montgomery—Evidence of a Popular Sentiment in the South for "Reconstruction"—Why it was Ineffectual—Extraordinary and remarkable Exclusion of the Popular Element from the Southern Confederacy—A Usurpation Almost Unparalleled in History.

WHEN Mr. Lincoln delivered his inaugural speech from the portico of the Washington Capitol, he stood no longer in front only of a hostile and disorderly popular sentiment in the South, but in front of a government organized there, an actual structure of state discharging all political functions, furnished for war, and inspired for a desperate encounter. It was a singular and imposing spectacle—a government of insurgents quietly assuming power and organization without a struggle, and continuing for the space of months unchallenged and uninterrupted in its operations. It had come quietly into existence in the month of February. The secret revolutionary junta had proposed a convention of the seceding S ates on the 15th of this month. It assembled some days earlier. Mississippi—the State of Jefferson Davis—was the first to propose distinctly the idea of a Southern Confederacy, while in the other States the call for a convention was variously interpreted and communicated from the ambush of equivocal language. There could be no doubt of the intention of Mississippi. In the Legislature of that State, on the 19th of January, a committee reported resolutions to provide for a Southern Confederacy, and establish a Provisional Government. The State had already seceded—on the 9th of January. On the 11th of the same month, Alabama and Florida followed; on the 26th, Louisiana; and on the 1st of February, Texas. On the 4th of February, delegates from these States met at Montgomery, Alabama, organized a Provisional Government, framed a "permanent" Constitution; and on the 18th Jefferson Davis was inaugurated President of "the Confederate States of North America."

The Union at Montgomery represented six Southern States, from which had disappeared, in the strangest manner, not only every semblance of Federal authority, but almost every vestige of Federal power. All the Federal forts in these States but two (Sumter and Pickens) had been taken; all the property of the United States, whether arsenals, custom-house or light-houses, had been appropriated; and not a vestige of authority of the Government at Washington was suffered to remain, excepting the Post-office department, which the insurgents might have been considered to have arrogantly kept for their convenience. These amazing results which had swept a government from the face of so large a territory, had been accomplished with supreme ease. All had been done without a drop of blood having been shed, or even an arm persistently raised to oppose the progress of the rebellion. It had gone on without any counteraction on the part of the North, and even without any preparation of the Washington Government, in the shape of any act or appropriation by Congress, to overthrow or check the movement.

This remissness of the government yet claiming to be

supreme, its utter lack of preparation—an instance of stark improvidence almost without parallel in history—was fast bringing it into contempt; and it was, perhaps, the first occasion of that fatal tendency in the South to undervalue the power and spirit of the North in case of war. The explanation commonly formed of this remissness is that the North was not seriously apprehensive of war, and that it looked for Secession to disappear at last through peaceful agencies, or in the natural course of events. Mr. Lincoln did not expect war. He believed, as he declared on his way to Washington, that "behind the cloud the sun was shining still;" that the fervid sentiment of Union in the hearts of the people of the South would dispel all serious trouble.

There might have been a time when this belief in the natural dispersion of Secession could have been reasonably entertained; but it is strange that Mr. Lincoln and thoughtful men in the North did not distinguish between this time and that in which he spoke—that they failed to estimate the great difference between Secession as a diffuse popular sentiment, and Secession as an organized fact. When it was in the first condition, there was some hope that it might be overcome or scattered by peaceful means; but from the moment it became organized; from the moment a government was framed at Montgomery, it acquired that certain force which comes from organization; and how, thereafter, the North—and even reflecting men there—could have continued in the same calculations of peace, is not easy to be explained. The difference of the two conditions seems never to have been estimated. People generally, in the North, thought peace quite as probable after the Montgomery Convention as before it—that is, without regard to other events, considering that which had taken place at Montgomery as indifferent. And yet it was that event which should have determined for the North whether to treat Secession as a subject for peaceful dispersion, or one for violent destruction. An idea or even a purpose may be easily banished from the public mind; but when it once assumes *organization*, there is an actual power to be disbanded, while new interests too are brought into the conflict. Secession might possibly have died out in the South as any other public opinion; but when it took the form of a government at Montgomery, it passed that boundary whence it was not likely to be reclaimed but by violence. That government could not go down without carrying with it the hopes and aspirations of the Southern leaders, without consigning them to public shame; and although Jefferson Davis and his associates might have quitted Secession when it was a mere idea, and survived the sacrifice, it was obvious that they could not retract what they had done at Montgomery without consigning themselves to ruin.

But the distinction between Secession as an idea and as an organized fact was scarcely perceived by the North. The Government at Washington continued to lose time which that at Montgomery was persistent to improve. In four days the latter adopted a provisional Constitution, and immediately thereafter announced as its choice for President, Jefferson Davis, of Mississippi. He travelled rapidly from his home; he was inaugurated the day after his arrival at Montgomery, the 10th of February; and on the 28th of this month he was empowered by act of Congress to assume control of all the military operations of the Confederate States. He was thus swiftly advanced to the summit of authority; he was seated in apparent security at Montgomery, before Mr. Lincoln had been inaugurated at Washington; and two days after the latter had gone through this doubtful ceremony and was yet trembling for his personal safety, Jefferson Davis experienced the sense of power in dictating a call for one hundred thousand men to take the field under his unquestioned and supreme command.

The question has often been seriously asked whether the leaders and agents of the South at Montgomery did not really entertain some prospect of going back into the Union, and to what extent the problem of reunion or "reconstruction" was mixed with their plans. The answers given to this question have been as various as the stand-points from which they have been delivered. To treat the matter with historical accuracy, it is necessary to observe a distinction of which we have already availed ourselves in the progress of our work—that between the people and the politicians of the South; and yet further to distinguish between the time when the latter were acting in disguise or playing an insincere part, and that when they no longer thought it necessary to wear the mask and found occasion to publish freely their opinions.

In the Senate of the United States, Jefferson Davis had practised either equivocation or reserve on the question of re-union. He was part of a conspiracy there; and although that conspiracy hesitated to alarm the people of the South with the idea of *irrevocable* separation, there is abundant evidence that this conclusion was first and firm in their designs. Mr. Davis knew very well that Mr. Hunter, of Virginia, had lost his place in the conspiracy, and hazarded its confidence by a proposition looking to "reconstruction" after the Southern States had disbanded from the Union. He was not in danger of falling into the same error—one so disastrous to his ambition. Indeed, as we have already suggested, the fact of the personal ambition of the leaders of the South being so identified with the scheme of Secession, forbids the supposition that they could ever have had any serious thought of undoing their work at Montgomery, and returning into a Union where thenceforth they would have to take degraded seats, and endure much more than the obloquy of the old Hartford Convention.

On arriving at Montgomery, Mr. Davis broke the restraints he had worn at Washington. He threw his former prudence to the winds, and declared for separation from the North as eternal as human force could make it. He spoke with a burst of temper that suggested how much he had suffered from his continence in the Senate. In a speech to a crowd in the streets, he declared that "the South would make those who opposed her smell Southern powder and feel Southern steel;" but perhaps there was some soreness of the reporter in this language. Yet there was no doubt of his more deliberate words. He said: "The time for compromise has now passed, and the South is determined to maintain her position. We will maintain our rights and government at all hazards. We ask nothing, we want nothing; we will have no complications. If the other States join our Confederation they can freely come in on our terms. Our separation from the old Union is now complete. No compromise, no reconstruction is now to be entertained." Again, speaking from the balcony of his hotel: "If war should come, if we must again baptize in blood the principles for which our fathers bled in the Revolution, we shall show that we are not degenerate sons."

Such language is sufficient to disprove a theory or hypothesis which has obtained some color of history:—namely that Mr. Davis and his associates at Montgomery had in reserve some thought of peaceful reconstruction, but that they were driven from it into the gulf of the war by the further acts of the Federal Government. There can be no truth in such a theory. The Southern leaders had resolved from the first on final separation, even with the added consequence of war; they had used any other pretence simply as a stepping-stone to power; and from the moment they met at Montgomery they were prepared to put the heel on every hope of reconciliation.

It was different with the *people* of the South. The evidence is as abundant as that we have just quoted to show that the politicians at Montgomery were resolved on irrevocable separation, to establish that the people of the South on the contrary—indeed up to the moment of actual bloodshed—cherished the design of reconstruction, either hoping for a return to the old Union, or inclusion in another of the same dimensions. The Montgomery Convention did not represent them; it represented the States, and only the States so far as the Secession Conventions had assumed the political control of each. It is a significant fact that even the call for the Montgomery Convention had been made on an equivocation, as if in distrust of the temper of the people for separation and war. When Mississippi, after South Carolina, seceded, Governor Pickens of the latter State had telegraphed that delegates should be sent to Montgomery "to form immediately a strong Provisional Government, as *the only thing to prevent war.*" The State of Louisiana looked openly to a reunion, and published the assurance that as long as the Border States remained in the Union, she might be received back through their mediation.

Nor was the action of the Montgomery Convention—when it was seen to be driving the South into war—unattended by popular protests. The people became sensible of the rapid movement of the wheels of revolution under them; they were hurried along in a state of bewilderment; but there were those who loudly proclaimed their alarm, and cried out against the precipitancy. Why should not the Montgomery Convention try at least some demand, some possible expedient before the ultimatum of war? Why go so far at a single step? "Posterity," said a member from Georgia, "will condemn the advocates of Secession for the single reason that the seceding States in their several Conventions, made no demand for the redress of grievances, but madly—yea, blindly—precipitated a revolution."

But such protests were voices against the wind. The Montgomery Convention carried every thing with swift and irresistible force, and gave neither time for the popular alarm to take effect nor the slightest opportunity for the popular judgment to recover control of its affairs. In truth what the thoughtful historian must most deeply meditate of the causes and origin of the late war is the extent to which the popular element of the South was excluded from its inception. It was in constant subjection from the moment a conspiracy of Southern Senators at Washington held at arm's-length the States and dictated their course. Indeed there were cases where it was ignored to the extent of States passing ordinances of Secession, even after the Legislatures calling the Conventions had forbid the effect of such ordinances until ratified by the vote of the masses. It had no direct representation in the Convention at Montgomery. It did not confirm their work.* It had nothing to do with the early acts of the war; and briefly the astounding fact appears that the first time the *people* of the South had direct action on their affairs since the

* The only confirmation which the Montgomery Government ever received was by the State Conventions; and that only to the extent of approving the Provisional Constitution, which was to remain in force for one year, then to be supplanted by a regular Constitution, and officers duly elected under it.

election of Abraham Lincoln was to vote for a President, *after* Mr. Davis had been "provisional" chief or practical dictator, one whole year, counting from his inauguration at Montgomery. Whether the war was right or wrong is logically not involved in the question whether it was determined by the many or by the few; but certainly history has had few instances of such daring and strident usurpation as that commenced by fourteen men plotting revolution in a committee-room at Washington, and consummated by an irresponsible Convention proclaiming a war, electing a leader, and organizing a government, without let or hindrance!

CHAPTER VII.

Causes which determined Mr. Davis' Election as President of the Confederate States—The claims of Howell Cobb Secretly considered at Montgomery—Davis' Resentment of Cobb as a Possible Rival—Popular Congratulations on the Selection of Mr. Davis as Leader—His Qualifications for such a Position—Steady Line of Distinction between Davis and the South—A Fatal Weakness of the New President—An Attempt to Define the Objects of the War—Mr. Davis as a "Mixed" Character—A Remarkable Presentiment at Montgomery—A Criticism of Mr. Davis in Anticipation of His Administration.

THE election of Mr. Davis to the Presidential office at Montgomery was not publicly contested; but that he was the unanimous choice of the Southern people is by no means so clear as has been generally supposed. The Charleston *Mercury* contended that the Montgomery Convention had no authority to elect a President, and intimated that a "snap-judgment" had been taken on the public. A party in Georgia was malcontent, and the Augusta *Chronicle* insisted that Alexander H. Stephens should have led the movement for constitutional liberty and Southern independence, because he bore no "stain of the prevalent corruption." But these opinions were not brought to the test of the popular verdict, and whatever their significance or value, it is unquestionable that Mr. Davis had many qualities to constitute him the representative man of the South in this crisis of her destiny, and to signalize him as the leader of her movement to independence.

A Northern member of Congress, familiar with much of Mr. Davis's public and private life, and partially sympathizing with his politics, has thus drawn his picture as leader and hero of "the lost cause:"—"Every revolution has a fabulous or actual hero conformable to the local situation, manner, and character of the people who rise. To a rustic people like the Swiss, William Tell, with his cross-bow and the apple; to an aspiring race like the Americans, Washington, with his sword and the law, are, as Lamartine once said, the symbols standing erect at the cradles of these two distinct liberties! Jefferson Davis, haughty, self-willed, and persistent, full of martial ardor and defiant eloquence, is the symbol, both in his character and in his present situation, of the proud and impulsive, but suppressed ardors and hopes of the Southern mind."

The causes which determined the elevation of Mr. Davis to the office of President of the Southern Confederacy have already been briefly referred to. He had been chosen as chief by the revolutionary cabal at Washington. In some personal reminiscences of this period related after the war, and when he might have been supposed to speak with humiliation, Mr. Davis has explained that "one of his chief recommendations for the chief office of the Confederacy lay in the fact that after the removal of Calhoun and General Quitman by death, he became the chief exponent or representative of those principles of State Sovereignty which the South cherished, and of which, as he claimed, the Fathers of the country had been the founders, Thomas Jefferson the inspired prophet, and they the eloquent apostles." But there is an egotism and conceit in this scarcely tolerable. Mr. Davis, whatever his other qualifications for the preference of the South, was no more the representative of State Sovereignty than were Hunter, of Virginia; Yancey of Alabama, or Toombs, of Georgia—certainly not more than Alexander H. Stephens, whose friends for a time disputed for him the claim of eminence in the fortunes of a new government founded on the peculiar principles of a Southern Democracy. It is not generally known that there was even another person who disputed not slightly, at Montgomery with Mr. Davis, the office of leader and chief magistrate. This person was already in the conspicuous place of presiding officer of the Montgomery Congress; it was an office next to that of President and naturally suggested promotion to it. It thus happened that in the secret conferences of the committee on Military Affairs the name of Howell Cobb was for some time considered in connection with the chief office in the gift of the South, and in competition with that of Jefferson Davis.

It was a competition not canvassed in public, not brought to the test of a vote and perhaps but a brief and speculative suggestion in the secret conferences at Montgomery; but that there was such a consideration of Howell Cobb has been testified to the author in the subsequent regrets of some of the most influential members of the Provisional Congress that they had neglected the man who, after all, was best qualified for the office of the President of the Confederacy, and whose strong practical judgment might have been a saving substitute for the showy qualities and shallow brilliancy of Mr. Davis. The statesman in time of peace, and the leader of a revolution have missions more distinct than the vulgar opinion regards them; and who can doubt that history has more often shown the latter successful in the person of plain men of robust character than in that of cultivated scholars and "admirable Crichtons." But Mr. Cobb was not uncultivated; and those who knew him well claim that he added to the accomplishments of the statesman natural virtues which summed a character the most estimable and complete among his cotemporaries in public life. He had none of the unhealthy fancies or refinements of an over-cultivated mind; he was not deficient in the information and accomplishments necessary to found any great success in life; he was plain without coarseness and learned without affectation. He had that most uncommon of gifts—common sense; a nice and rotund adjustment of the faculties; a practical and ready judgment; and—not least among the qualities of great and successful men—that strong, complacent physique suggested by the "*mens sana in corpore sano*"—exactly that type of man which, not brilliant, is yet especially powerful, dexterous and conservative in revolutionary times.

Mr. Davis must have had some early intimation of the suggestion—imperfect as it was—of Mr. Cobb's name in opposition to his own; and he appears to have resented it with characteristic temper. The latter had not been presiding officer of the Provisional Congress many weeks before he mentioned to his friends that Mr. Davis's conduct had been cold and repellant to him for some unexplained reason; he had naturally visited the President to suggest some consultation on public affairs; Mr. Davis had each time replied, "I have no communication to make," and at last had done so with such disdain that Mr. Cobb broke off all intercourse with him. For the space of a year the two never exchanged a word, Mr. Cobb explaining to his friends that he had been wounded by the manner of the President when he approached him at Montgomery. It was the first instance of that fatal temper of Mr. Davis which repelled every one who might possibly share with him the public regard, and stand between him and the eyes of the world.

But really in the early days of the Confederacy he had but little to fear that any other man in the South, either in position of rival or counsellor, could intercept the public admiration of himself; and the alarm which his vanity might have taken from Mr. Cobb was unreasonable. The latter had all the merit we have described. But it was a type of leadership that had but little to dazzle the multitude, and it only stood in momentary competition with the brilliant and diseased character of Jefferson Davis. The first general impression of the people of the South on the selection of Mr. Davis as President was lively satisfaction and a disposition to congratulate themselves as on the striking natural fitness of their leader. The adjustment of affairs at Montgomery had so far been apparently easy, and every thing seemed to have fallen in its proper place, with a President to fit exactly the mission he was to undertake. The popular congratulation was a plausible one, and not without some foundation in fact. Mr. Davis we repeat was in many striking respects a fit and lofty representative of the proud and chivalrous people of the South; he had many good qualities as a leader; he was a fair and adequate exponent of the best civilization of the South; he illustrated in just and equal measures the political scholarship and social refinement of the land that had now imposed upon him its supreme representation in sight of the world. He represented the best culture of the South; he was undoubtedly one of its first gentlemen; he was a master of ceremonies in social life; and yet, after all, he was a person but thinly qualified to conduct any great enterprise, or to make a conspicuous and determined mark in the history of his times.

And here at the very outset of our narrative of the arms of the South, we may make a brief estimate of its leader, and denounce, at the start, that vulgar error which mistakes any intellectual superiority for universal genius, which thinks that the accomplished orator or the ingenious politician must also be the wise statesman, and which constantly indulges the vague notion that the man who excels in one career must be capable of equal things in other callings. This, indeed, is true of genius—exceptionally true; but there is no error more dangerous in the practical conduct of affairs as that which estimates men as alike able and excellent in whatever cause they may choose for themselves, or circumstances determine for them. In some respects, Jefferson Davis was an admirable man; in other respects, we shall be prepared to denounce him as a failure, a reproach and an abomination.

And here, again, we must draw a steady line of distinction between Mr. Davis and the South—between the delinquencies of the leader and the merits of his cause. We do it here, because this distinction runs through the whole of our narrative; because it is of the very spirit of our work, and because, with this idea adjusted to some extent in advance, we shall not be under the necessity of repeatedly asserting and proclaiming it on particular questions.

The author, in other works, has incurred the penalty of much popular misrepresentation in insisting on the virtues of the South in the past war, and yet persistently holding the opinion that Jefferson Davis was not a great man; that he lacked the essential requisites of such a character; that he was merely a narrow-brained person possessed of much address, and some very agreeable literary accomplishments which dazzled vulgar criticism and betrayed the admiration of the populace. This notion, to be sure, has been greatly resented by certain declamatory eulogists of Mr. Davis, men who have violently associated the virtues of his person with the merits of the Confederate cause. But such an association, we insist, is not proper or logical. Mr. Davis was to a great degree, an *accident* of the war, thrust into importance by fictitious influences; he added nothing to its inspiration, and he mixed with a great cause a game of selfishness and an experiment of vanity.

The most striking quality, the most constant and significant event of Mr. Davis' administration, will be found to be his jealous repulsion of advisers and assistants, and his descent to rivalry in popularity with his subordinates and lieutenants. He had, as we shall see, a puerile eagerness to appropriate all the honors of the Confederate cause, and to wear them conspicuously in the sight of the world. In this he departed from the true line of greatness, and fell from the summit to which fortune raised him. It is the unfailing characteristic of the great man that he never descends to competition with his subordinates, but ingeniously takes every success of theirs as the source and sustenance of his own greatness. Napoleon I. had marshals whom some critics have thought superior to himself in military genius; but he understood that so long as he was the central historical figure, history and the common opinion of mankind would naturally and logically refer their successes to himself, and bestow upon him the crowning glory. This, indeed, is the true art of the great man—the art of utilizing those around him, on the principle that the successes of his subordinates eventually recur to himself as the centre, magnifying him and filling up the measure of his fame, rather than the weak, jealous attempt of self-assertion, which drives from itself all necessary aid and counsel, and choosing a naked eminence, finds only a vanishing point. Such was the attempt of Jefferson Davis which we shall follow in our narrative, and display as the essential weakness of a little mind. He descended to competition with his lieutenants, instead of exciting among them a generous rivalry to serve his own central and crowning fame; he grasped at all public honors for himself; and so weak was his vanity, that it is remarkable it might be disturbed by the successes of his smallest subordinate.

But we are not going through here with an analysis of Mr. Davis's character. We are only saying so much as we may properly say in advance of our narrative—designing only, in this place, to appropriate to him that single characteristic of egotism or excessive self-assertion which is necessary to be understood just here as separating him in a severe and remarkable manner from the cause which he served, without representing, and which he lost, without illustrating either its dignity or virtue. We have thought it proper to introduce this explanation here; to say so much of the character of the man, at the date of his appointment as supreme leader of the South. We have ventured to indicate the spirit of our work, the basis of our narrative, without anticipating its interest, or prejudicing whatever future opinions we may advance in their due order of time and circumstance.

The Southern people had in the late war a great and noble cause—rightly understood—a cause of constitutional liberty, one of national and traditional import. No cause ever commanded braver men, and no men ever served a better cause. It perished, but only after it had run an honorable career, only after its arms had been crowned with glory, and its nimble lance had tried every link in the mail of an adverse fortune. However those who take afterthought of fortune may now despise and deride this cause—however they may use the flippant and easy libel of a false nomenclature, and call by the name of "rebellion" a struggle for what was permanent and traditional in American history, there is no doubt it carried its arms with courage, and surrendered them with dignity.

It is this cause which we shall find Jefferson Davis misrepresenting and degrading. With him the past war might have been an unworthy personal ambition, or an interest in Negro Slavery, the eagerness of an old decayed aristocracy to maintain its insolence and execute its menaces; but in the estimation of the just and the intelligent, the struggle had the dignity of a higher and nobler cause, and was maintained in the spirit of a great constitutional contest. It has been called a "rebellion;" but that is only a name, a vile word, the hiss of a weak and toothless argument. It has been called a "slaveholders' war;" but there fought in it men of the South who never owned a slave, or hoped to own one. It has been called "Secession," the rent of the Union, the diminution of its glories; but the separation of the States was only the incident of the war, and it might possibly have been overcome and repaired by the force of subsequent events. Indeed every explanation of the struggle fails—but this: that it was a manifestation of a traditional conflict in American politics, which continues to the present time, and is to-day vital, erect, critical, and dramatic.

Jefferson Davis was not the man to act as leader of a cause so broad and august. He might have represented excellently well some of its externals, some of its accidents or surroundings, but he fell illimitably below an occasion so great. The influences that elected him at Montgomery were accidental; they were happy in some respects; there were conspicuous and apparently fortunate coincidences in them; but they were fatal at the last.—A great cause was committed to an incompetent leader. The fatal error of the Southern Confederacy befell it at the moment that a man, perverse enough to ruin all that was committed to him, and yet plausible enough to hold for a long time the public confidence, became, by a strange fatality, the man best calculated and best able to wreck and betray the cause in which he was appointed. Indeed if a single individual had been sought within the limits of the South of such various character and temper as most effectually to seduce public confidence, to dazzle it, and at last to bring it to ruin, the most certain and complete, he could not have been found more exactly than in the person of Jefferson Davis. For such a brilliant and unequal career he had really no competitors.

On one of the first pages of this work we referred to the "mixed" character of Mr. Davis, and suggested what valuable and vivid subjects for biography have been found in characters of this description. Indeed our best and most interesting biographical literature is to be found in the lives of those remarkable men, who have been apparent contradictions, who have been held in estimations the most opposite, who have been admired and detested by turns, not so much from the fickleness of the populace or the uncertainty of criticism, as from the variableness of their own characters. The popular opinion is not disposed to put faith in these contradictions, to accept them as facts, or to regard them as other than misapprehensions—the man must be either great or mean, a hero or an imposter; and yet history is constantly telling us of men of great force and merit, who have yet had vices the most atrocious and frailties the most detestable, of those who have been at once "the wisest and meanest of mankind." A shallow criticism generally resents such estimates of men; and he who treats justly and independently of characters so remarkable is embarrassed between the enthusiasm of their friends and the extravagance of their enemies. A more thoughtful review however recognizes the possible reality of mixed and apparently inconsistent characters, appreciates the task of their analysis, and is satisfied to see justly distributed in the biographical work their virtues and their vices.

It is thus that we shall attempt to divide the good and the evil in the career of Jefferson Davis, and thus that we assert in the very beginning a rule of criticism which has been often neglected, and which is yet drawn from the depths of nature and some traces of which are in our commonest experience. It is only the base and diseased sensitiveness of partisans, on one side or the other, that resents the discriminations of history, and that would substitute for "skilled commendation" the vulgar eulogium, and for qualified censure the rage of passion and the unmeasured words of denunciation.

When Mr. Davis commenced the career which resulted so disastrously to himself and "his people"—in his address at the inauguration ceremonies at Montgomery in 1861—he spoke with more than the customary self-distrust in the acceptance of high public office. He said: "Experience in public stations of a subordinate grade to this which your kindness has conferred, has taught me that care and toil and disappointments are the price of official elevation. You will see many errors to forgive, many deficiencies to tolerate; but you shall not find in me either want of zeal or fidelity to the cause that is to me the highest in hope, and of most enduring affection." The presentiment and the pledge of this speech were alike fulfilled. Mr. Davis *did,* as the author firmly believes, commit numerous and grievous errors in the administration of public affairs; but his worst enemy could never question his zeal or devotion, and no hostile partisan was ever adventurous enough to cast a breath of suspicion on his fidelity to the cause of which he was so truly enamored, and in which he was so deeply interested.

We shall see, as our narrative progresses, that he did much to adorn the cause of the Confederacy by the purity of his life, his accomplishments, his eloquence, his dignity, the marked contrast of his mind and manners to the uncouth representative of the North at Washington. We shall see that in many respects he greatly honored his countrymen. We shall see that in the entire progress of the war, the educated opinion of Europe was inclined to the South by a strong personal admiration of Mr. Davis, as one of the first scholars and orators of America; that it could not fail to compare his learning, his polish, his eloquence with the rude conceits and cranks, the tangled English and the literary peculiarities of the Northern President. We shall see that he represented some of the best virtues and accomplishments of his countrymen; that he raised, in some respects, the standard of Southern character in the eyes of the world; that he decorated the Confederate name with many noble literary images, and that he served the Confederate cause with distinguished personal devotion. But we shall also see that he—of all men in the South—ruined this cause; that he mixed with his devotion to it, animosities the most unworthy; that he carried along and bound up with his public career a secret history of spiteful and mean jealousies. We shall see that his mind was unbalanced; that his judgment was at once shallow and perverse, that though his life was not stained with dishonor, it was often steeped in petty meannesses; that an obstacle to wise counsellors, he was yet an easy prey to flatterers; that overtaxing his time and almost wearing out his life by incessant labors, he had yet no faculty of business; that zealous and impertinently busy in public affairs, he was yet trifling and whimsical, a creator of nothing; that haughty, persistent, repellant of advice, the approach to his vanity was always open, and the avenues of his patronage beset by a conceit as easily bribed as by an obstinacy that was inexorable. Finally, we shall see how a nature, capable of better things in another and quieter career, was wholly unequal to the trials of a leader of a great revolution; how an ambition intoxicated by great opportunities, became at last malign and paltry; and how Jefferson Davis, who might have continued a distinguished man in a lesser cause, or, at least, not have had occasion there to unmask his weaknesses, fell under an accumulation of fortune, and ended his career in unequalled ruin and degradation.

CHAPTER VIII.

The Fire on Fort Sumter—The First Shot of the War—Congratulations in President Davis's Cabinet—The Second Secessionary Movement—Fatal mistake of Mr. Lincoln—He Adds a new Breadth to the War—Preparations at Montgomery—Mr. Davis and an Office-Seeker—Secret Design of Mr. Davis in his Display of Military Preparations—Sudden Disappearance of the Union Party Accounted for—Secession of Virginia—A Torch-Light Procession in Richmond—Robert E. Lee Appointed Commander-in-Chief of the Virginia Forces—His Character—His Motives in Leaving the Federal Service—His Political Opinions—The Fallacy of "Petitio Principii"—General Lee Accepting a Sword in the State-House—The Confederate States Government Removed to Richmond—Howell Cobb's Pledge for the Congressmen—Arrival of President Davis in Richmond—Popular Raptures—Eloquent Speeches of the President—"No Surrender."

THE fire on Fort Sumter opened the war; and from this octagonal work, the main post of defence in Charleston Harbor, rolled off the panoramic scene of four years of armed and bloody conflict. But a day before this baleful fire, Roger A. Pryor, in a speech to the citizens of Charleston, had said: "I will tell you what will put Virginia in the Southern Confederation in less than an hour by Shrewsbury clock. Strike a blow!" The blow was struck; and not only Virginia was added to the new Union, but there came trooping, in a *second secessionary movement,* the States of North Carolina, Tennessee and Arkansas; and not only such accession of territory and means to the government at Montgomery, but another breadth to the issues of the war, an added significance to the contest, and a new inspiration for the South.

The question has been made by some juvenile minds, which party fired the first shot in the war. But the true responsibility for the commencement of hostilities is not to be found in a circumstance so paltry and external. The question is rather which party first indicated the purpose of hostility, which made the fatal menace, which *drew* rather than which delivered the fire at Sumter. If Jefferson Davis signed the order for the reduction of the fort, Abraham Lincoln had, before, signed the order to reinforce it. Under a pretence of relieving a starving garrison he had thrust in the face of the South the menace of an expedition, consisting of eleven vessels, with two hundred and eighty-five guns and twenty-four hundred men. The reply to this was the blow that reduced Fort Sumter, and cleared the way of the South to the sea.

The South *did* fire the first shot. "We opened fire at 4.30 A. M." dispatched General Beauregard to the Secretary of War of the Confederate States on the 12th of April. The historic shot was a shell from a howitzer battery on James' Island. It pursued its way to a silent fortification. A white smoke floated after it, parted from its upmost curve, and melted in the higher air of heaven, like a departing angel of peace, as the missile sped on its errand of ruin and affright. It was the messenger of war in the cloudless sky of a Spring day. Alas, with what fortunes was fraught this missile describing its beautiful curve through the balmy air. A moment more, and that air was filled and smitten with the fiery wings of death; the ear was torn by fearful sounds; several miles of batteries were sending forth their wrath at the grim fortress that rose so defiantly from the sea. The shrill scream, the dull boom, the explosion now sharp and now spluttering, wrought an expression of war to which many of those assembled in contest were utter strangers, having never heard before of terrific sounds but "heaven's artillery" in their native mountains.

The grand auditorium of war was succeeded by a scene to which the darkness of the night was needed to give effect. The fort had held out, replying only at measured intervals, and the Stars and Stripes were seen floating in the breeze at twilight. When the night had descended, the Confederate batteries were still in full play. The skies were darkened by rain-clouds; a wind blew in shore, and repeated with distinctness in the streets of Charleston the regular boom of the guns. The horizon appeared, now and then, to lift from a sheet of flame, and the trails of the shells were now plainly seen along the black skies. It was a tracery of the heavens more near and more fearful than that of astronomic vision. Thousands watched it from the wharves of Charleston. The fire was kept up until near midnight; and those in the city who laid down to sleep before that time heard the sounds that told them that war had come on the land, and that a day memorable to them and their children's children was being numbered, by the measured strokes of battle, in the history of the world.

The next day the Confederates fired with more accuracy; and before its close, the Stars and Stripes were lowered from the post where they had so long been a taunting spectacle to Charleston, and a defiance to the South. The fort surrendered after a contest which had continued through thirty-four hours; its interior a heap of ruins, but its walls still standing with the marks of six hundred shot on them. Major Anderson notified the authorities at Washington that "on the afternoon of the 14th of April, he marched out of the fort, with colors flying and drums beating, bringing away company and private property and saluting his flag with fifty guns." But if his colors flew and his drums beat, it was but a sorry affectation; for he had been driven out of a defence that the

North had declared impregnable, and the South, in the eyes of the world, had plucked the first laurel of the war.

Nothing could exceed the transport at Montgomery, when it was known that Sumter had surrendered, and there swiftly followed the news that Mr. Lincoln had thereupon called for seventy-five thousand men, and made a virtual proclamation of war. President Davis showed all the joy that could be expected from one afflicted with neuralgia and dyspepsia; too unwell to appear before the crowd that clamored around his hotel for a speech of congratulation, but not too feeble to indulge his triumph in his Cabinet. The call of Mr. Lincoln for troops was treated there with derisive laughter. Mr. Benjamin, the Secretary of State, sat at a table, and wrote in verse a travesty of the call which afterwards found its way into the newspapers. Mr. Davis had reason to be well pleased at the turn events had taken; he saw at once the great mistake which the rival President at Washington had committed in usurping powers, and in broadly translating the war of Secession into a war for Liberty.

The added force and inspiration given to the war by the second secessionary movement of the States, impelled by Mr. Lincoln's proclamation, was the true significance of the affair of Sumter. It was not only that it added so many new States to the Southern Confederation; but it superinduced a new issue, and afforded a new appeal in the interest of the South. It was thus that the second movement of Secession took place on a basis higher than the first, on a broader issue and on better principles. It answered a call to the defence of liberty rather than the former feeble outcry of a complaint not substantiated, the mere fear of aggression. It furnished the "overt act" in an open breach of the Constitution of the United States. The proclamation of Mr. Lincoln was fuel cast on the flame of Sumter. From the time he put his foot on the Constitution and proclaimed a war, without the action of Congress, from that moment he appeared in the character of a dictator and despot, and from that moment the war in the South acquired a new inspiration. It grew, as it were, in one day, into the character and dimensions of a great popular revolution; it threw off the bad name of "rebellion;" it rid itself of much that had been odious in the early history of Secession; and disencumbered of the arguments and reproaches of those who had clung to the Union only as a guaranty of peace—and even gathering many of these former protestants in its ranks—it henceforth unfurled its banners as those of a contest for constitutional liberty.*

---

* It may be scarcely necessary to repeat here a thought which the reader should have already recognized in previous pages, viz. :—that no matter how the North and South got into the war—and even, if the latter was immediately impelled into it by a narrow and ambitious conspiracy—the question is not affected as to the real merit of the South in the contest. Every thoughtful historian must recognize that as the war widened and as its true volume and significance were developed the South rose higher and higher in the moral estimation of her cause ;—and if any one at this day questions that that cause was truly one of *liberty* the sequel of the war is perhaps the best test and argument to apply to such a doubt. If the cause of Secession became ultimately pregnant with the cause of the Constitution, the North made it so by her violence in the war. The fact is that at the last the South fought for her institutions, and fought for them under cover of a contest for the constitutional and traditional liberties of the country.

The distinction referred to is thus powerfully indicated in an article of the *Old Guard* (1866) :—

"Here is a torn and bleeding and lacerated thing—an aggregation of all fierce antagonisms—a great pot of conflicting passions, interests and prejudices, simmering, and boiling, and bubbling with injustice

Mr. Davis saw this new breadth of the war as an increase of his triumph. It was the signal for enlarged military preparations. There was already a force of nearly 35,000 men in the field, chiefly distributed at Charleston and Pensacola; and the rage for volunteering was furnishing troops faster than the government could organize them. The requisition for fifteen hundred troops from the President's State—Mississippi—was answered by more than three thousand

---

and hate—which madmen and fools would have us call a *Union.* But we, for one, will not so call it, because we will not lie. Union is *concord;* it is harmony. But there never can be concord, harmony or Union on the basis of fanaticism, intolerance, or injustice. And we pray Almighty God there never may be! We never wish to see our country fall so low as to exhibit a universal acquiescence in despotism and tyranny. Better eternal strife than an hour of cowardice and unmanly surrender of self-government and liberty! Better eternal strife than peace in injustice! We are told that there was a great, and radical, and necessary antagonism between the North and South. Who is to blame for that antagonism? Did the South start it? When? where? how? The North answers that she had an institution which we could not endure. Was the South to blame for our prejudice? She held her institutions by a charter beyond our right to meddle with, and guarantied even by the Constitution that made the Union. The whole controversy is in a nut-shell, thus: The North says to the South, we have prejudices against your institutions, and you must give them up. The South replies, we hold our institutions by organic and statute laws, your prejudices are the vagaries of the brain, and if any thing ought to be given up for the sake of peace, it is your prejudices. So it came simply to this:—that the South must give up its *rights*, or the North its *prejudices*, and as the North preferred to fight rather than give up its prejudices, the conflict came. The North were fighting for its *prejudices*, the South for its *rights*. Both parties may have gotten into the strife unwisely, but, being in, this is the simple and ineffaceable truth of the whole matter."

volunteers; and those who had the good fortune to be accepted were offered bonuses by those eager to take their places in the honors and hazards of war. A Navy Department was organized. Two steamers were fitted out at New Orleans; contracts were made for the casting of ordnance; and it was boasted that a single mill in South Carolina was then manufacturing fifty kegs of gunpowder a day. Another proclamation of President Davis was issued two days after that of Lincoln. It offered letters of marque to all persons who might desire, by service in private armed vessels, to aid the government; and it was exultingly said that Mr. Davis had produced by this proclamation a new arm of the South, more powerful than the navies of the North, and that might scourge the oceans of both hemispheres.

But even in the midst of these preparations it is wonderful how little was conceived at Montgomery of the prospect of an extended and elaborate war. It is now known that these preparations—and especially the large levies of troops—were designed to over-awe the North, to strike its imagination by a display of superior force, rather than to conduct real operations. It was supposed that the commercial necessities of that section would make an early suit for peace. "I apprehend," said a member of the Montgomery Congress, "that we are conscious of the power we hold in our hands by reason of our producing that staple so necessary to the world. I doubt not that power will exert an influence mightier than armies and navies. We know that by an embargo we could soon place, not only the United States, but many of the European Powers, under the necessity of electing between such a recognition of our independence as we require, or domestic convulsions at home." Such visions of the power of "King Cotton" were the familiar imaginations at Montgomery. There would be no war, or scarcely one of more than a few fields, which would determine the superior manhood of the South and dismay the North from a prolonged contest of arms. Mr. Davis was never done expressing this opinion in secret council at Montgomery, however much he might have publicly exhorted the South to display her utmost strength, designing such display as a menace to the enemy, or, perhaps, to some extent, as a dramatic effect of his own vanity of power. A favored candidate for office applied to him a few days after the fall of Sumter, for a situation in the War Department, suggesting that there would be an accumulation of business in that branch of the government. Mr. Davis smiled significantly, and remarked that "the work in that Department would be light—so light that he recommended the candidate to apply rather for a place in the Confederate Treasury, as there he would be likely to have a longer tenure of office.

Yet whether or not there was to be a serious war, and no matter to what length it might go, it is remarkable that scarcely one intelligent man in the South—and least of all Mr. Davis—doubted the issue of success. It is true, that since the opposite conclusion of the contest, many persons in the South, illustrating that common dishonesty which makes men declare that they foresaw whatever has happened, and impelled in many instances by a mean desire to repair the past and to conciliate present opinion, have declared that they expected from the first the overthrow of the Southern Confederacy, and prophesied in their hearts the triumph of the North. But this is the bald and detestable falsehood of time-service. Scarcely an intelligent person in the South, at the period of which we write, doubted that the Secession of the Southern States was equivalent to their independence; that the latter was only a question of time and effort; and the singular proof of the breadth of this delusion is the almost complete disappearance of the Union party in the South—a disappearance which continued precisely up to that time when the disasters of the Confederate arms did produce a feeling of uncertainty.* But there was no such feeling in

* "And here we have the opportunity of introducing an account of one of the most curious phenomena of the war—the sudden exit and entire disappearance of the Union party in the South on the declaration of Secession. Immediately before this event, that party had been numerous and formidable; it had a compact organization; it contained many men who, from principle and affection, were strongly attached to the Union, and who were incapable of changing their opinions at the mere bidding of expediency. And yet never did a political party more quickly and entirely vanish from the scene after an untoward election, than did the Unionists of the South after the proclamation of Secession. The explanation of this extraordinary disappearance is to be found not so much in the easy virtue of political parties, as in the especial fact of a foregone conclusion, which seemed to have taken possession of the whole mind of the South, that the impending conflict would necessarily result in its favor, and that the mere declaration of Secession was quite as decisive of the fate of the Union as would be the last battle of the war. The Union party in the South had contended for the Union up to the question of Secession; and that decided, it considered the controversy practically determined, and prepared to accommodate itself to what it regarded as the inevitable fact of assured separation. The mass of the Southern people, both Secessionists and Unionists, appears at this time never to have admitted even the possibility of an overthrow of the Southern arms, and defeat of the Confederate cause; and the few minds that did entertain such an event were so few as only to constitute the exception which proves the rule. When the Union members of the Virginia Convention sobbed at their desks, and exchanged tearful sympathies as the vote for Secession was announced, it was because they deemed that it was all over, and that by the mere will

the commencement of the war. The Union party in the South had nothing to build on; it sunk out of sight with a suddenness that only a conviction of its despair can explain, and it left the field to the foregone conclusion of the independence of the South. "None but the demented can doubt the issue," wrote General Beauregard a few days after the affair of Sumter. "Obstacles may retard," explained Mr. Davis, in his inaugural address, "they cannot long prevent the progress of a movement sanctified by its justice and sustained by a virtuous people." Nor were these boasts, nor assurances of the success of the Confederacy and consummations of Disunion yet opinions of but individual force: they were the expressions of the best intelligence of the South, and the echoes of the common thought of the people—even where that thought was not fathered by wishes, and was an unwelcome conclusion rather than a glad anticipation.

---

of the South the dissolution of the Union was irrevocably decreed. It is astonishing how universal and supreme was a conviction in the South, which subsequent events were so signally to belie. If we are to find an explanation for such a delusion, we perhaps need go no further than that popular vanity which, embracing for once the intelligent with the vulgar, appears to be the common sin of all communities in America. But whatever the cause, there is no doubt that the Southern public was so generally assured of the termination of the war in favor of a Southern Confederacy, that the Union party within the limits of the seceded States considered that the rôle of controversy was ended, and that nothing was left them but to submit to the *fiat*, and accommodate themselves to the change. Had there been in the early periods of the war any considerable doubt in the South of the issue of the war, it is more than probable that the Union party would have maintained its organization, asserted itself much sooner than it did, and seriously disturbed the first years of the government."—*Lee and his Lieutenants*. Pp. 238, 239.

While Mr. Davis and his associates were making their rather scenic preparations for war, events were taking place on a side theatre, smaller in dimensions, but for a time more important and vivid than that at Montgomery. This theatre was the State of Virginia. The logical course of the story of the war takes us there after Sumter. Virginia had long hesitated to go out of the Union and to erect a government in opposition to it; but the proclamation of Mr. Lincoln offered a provocation which she could no longer withstand, and extended a challenge which she could not afford to waive and which she was not content to brook. The *Examiner* had a quaint and impressive figure of the secession of Virginia. "She turned around, and walked out of the Union, with the step of an old QUEEN." There were thousands to hail her in her royal wandering and to shout "Excelsior" as she went, bearing the insignia of her sovereignty from the shadow of a trailing flag and turned her face, lofty and sorrowful, upon the path of a new fortune. That flag was stricken down in an instant; and as if by magic a new flag, the symbol of the Southern Confederacy, appeared on the Capitol, appeared on all the hills of Richmond, in the windows of houses, in the hands of passengers on the street. Cannon were fired around it; giddy crowds saluted it. The capital of Virginia gave itself up to the intoxication of a general joy. A torch-light procession illuminated the night of the 19th of April. A track of transparencies gleamed from Church Hill to the Exchange Hotel, and ended there in a vast crowd which hung n the speeches of orators speaking from balconies, imparting words of fire to the head of the column that toiled for a mile in one of the main thoroughfares of Richmond. Not quite four years later through that same thoroughfare reaching from hill to hill, following step by step, the route of the torch-light procession of 1861, passed the Federal Army, the line of conquering bayonets; and at that same convenient standpoint of the Exchange Hotel, where orators had inflamed the bearers of "the Southern Cross" and pointed to flags that "would float over Washington in thirty days," was collected the thickest of the mob that shouted welcome to the enemy, and cheered their way to the easy slopes of the Capitol.

The popular rapture on the Secession of Virginia was something peculiar; its sudden extent showed how repressive of the true sentiment of her people had been the Convention that had so long hesitated to take the course dictated at Montgomery. A correspondent of a Richmond paper wrote:—"I can give you no idea of the military spirit of the State. Augusta County, a strong Whig Union county, and Rockingham, an equally strong Democratic Union county, lying side by side with Augusta, each, contribute fifteen hundred men to the war. The war spirit is not confined to the men, or to the white population. The ladies are not only preparing comforts for the soldiers, but arming and practising themselves. Companies of boys, also, from ten to fourteen years of age, fully armed and well drilled, are preparing for the fray. In Petersburg three hundred free negroes offered their services, either to fight under white officers, or to ditch and dig."

In estimating the contributions of Virginia to the war, it is not only the spirit and resources she gave to it we have to calculate, but there is place here to mention one single gift she made to the South worth more than all her other princely cessions. She gave to the Confederate service Robert E. Lee. Of this man, more than any other the military leader of the South, and more than any other—far more than Jefferson Davis, its ornament—we may say something here—and that too without decline of our narrative to a slight event. In fact the resignation of Lee from the United States army was the signal of that defection from the Federal service which contributed to the Southern Confederacy nearly all it had of military talents, which did more than any thing else to sustain its arms, and which gave the severest blow to the Federal Government, as it was arming on the threshold of the war. In resigning his commission in the Federal Army and offering his sword to his native State, Lee was, both the herald of a great event and the representative of a great principle.

Robert E. Lee was one of the few characters in the past war that obtained admiration or favor on both sides. Indeed, in a war which proved to be so vast and exasperated, and in which the combatants became so widely and so oppositely separated, it required either a transcendent genius, or a large and generous breadth of character to draw from both sides a common tribute of admiration, and to win a joint encomium. In the case of General Lee, we are persuaded it was this second quality rather than any rare gift of genius, that has obtained for him a certain community of praise, and that distinguished him in the estimation of the North, as well as raised him to the pinnacle of admiration in the regards of his Southern countrymen. It was only a great man who could achieve any thing like a common reputation in the excessive heat and recrimination of the war, where there were so few points of agreement in either opinion or feeling; but "greatness" is the broadest of encomiastic terms, and the interesting and difficult question remains, after having conferred the term, in what respect and in what degree the individual was great? This question, with reference to Robert E. Lee, is not one of much intricacy, and we believe that history will adjust his reputation, and settle the proportions of his figure in the war, with more than usual justice and exactness.

In the progress of our narrative there will be found some fruitful and peculiar studies concerning the character of General Lee. Whatever the works of his life, they were accumulated under that *sense of duty* which even more than ambition taxes the public man, and fills his measure of usefulness.

The "sense of duty" is one of those virtues which partakes largely of the temperament of the individual. With some it is an over-delicacy of conscience; with others a plaguing and unhappy casuistry. General Lee appears, however, to have had that healthful and robust sense of duty which acts with decision, and marches straight to its work, which fortifies the soul in all circumstances, and inculcate the virtues of self-possession and readiness. His severest illustration of a sense of duty, he gave, in resigning from the Federal Army, and turning his sword upon the government which, for twenty-five years he had served with honor and satisfaction.

Since the war General Lee has given a distinct explanation of the motives which determined his action, and of the political theory on which he yet maintains the justification of the South. Resenting a report in the newspapers, that he had been "wheedled into the war," he said:—"So far as I know, the people of the South looked upon the action of the State in withdrawing itself from the Government of the United States as carrying the individuals of the State along with it; that the State was responsible for the act, not the individuals, and that the ordinance of Secession so-called, or those acts of the State which recognized a condition of war between the State and the General Government stood as their justification for bearing arms against the Government of the United States."

In the estimation of many, it is a slender and technical

theory on which General Lee holds his justification; but no one can doubt the sincerity of the allegation. He has, also, since the war, explained that he thought it was "unnecessary, and might have been avoided, if forbearance and wisdom had been exercised on both sides;" but he denies that his own individual action was at all determined by the persuasions and intrigues of politicians. This is the true historical explanation given by General Lee himself of the vexed story of his choice in the war—a story which has had so many apocryphal versions and additions; and the reader will probably make the commentary on it, suggested from his own standpoint in the traditional controversy of State Rights, and drawn from his own chosen school of political opinion.

In any view it must be confessed that, with respect to selfish consideration or worldly prudence, Lee's declination of the Federal service was undoubtedly pure. He spurned ambition, the bribes of office, personal interest; and while he appeared to hesitate at the outset of hostilities, it was only that his conscientious and introspective mind was anxious to discover the line of duty, as events developed it. The Secession of Virginia left him, as he considered, no choice but to obey her commands and to assure her solicitations. In most of the Northern criticisms of his decision in this juncture, the fallacy of the *petitio principii*, ("begging the question") has been ingeniously inserted in the charge that he showed a narrowness of mind in pleading a partiality for his State against his duty to the General Government, a mere local affection opposed to "loyalty." We certainly do not propose here to discuss the vexed subject of State Rights; and yet we must perceive that the criticism referred to, is logically unfair in ignoring that school of politics to which General Lee belonged, and in which he had been taught, that the Union was the creature of the States, that it had no mission apart from their convenience, and no virtue but in representing their interests. If this was an error it was yet an honest and traditional error, one which, for three generations, had included the best minds of the South, and had been illustrated by its most distinguished names. Admit that Lee was misled, and yet his error was not only unstained by selfishness, but a more generous one than his severe censors have been willing to admit.

He had been taught in his slight political education that the State was superior to the Federal Government in its claims upon the affections of the intelligent; that it was the peculiar object of patriotism; that it was the symbol of the love of country, rather than the Union which, in the estimation of the school of politics referred to, was the mere geographical designation of a league created by the States, and designed for the benefit and pleasure of each. Thus thinking, he went with Virginia in the war, and to her side of the contest. However he valued the Union, and saw no necessity for the Secession of his State, he felt bound to recognize it as that political community to which, as the original and only permanent element in the American system, his allegiance belonged; as his home, around which the affections of the man naturally cling; as the abode of family and friends, where the protection of his arm and sword was due at the approach of danger. When standing in the State-house, he accepted the sword which the Convention of Virginia placed in his hand, he said, with memorable solemnity: "Trusting in Almighty God, an approving conscience, and the aid of my fellow-citizens, I devote myself to the service of my native State, *in whose behalf alone* will I ever again draw the sword."

The person of the commander-in-chief of Virginia was

singularly noble, and at once inspired emotions. It has been thus described by this author, witnessing the scene of bestowing on him, in the State-house at Richmond, his first command in Virginia: "Every spectator admired the personal appearance of the man, his dignified figure, his air of self-poised strength, and features in which shone the steady animation of a consciousness of power, purpose, and position. He was in the full and hardy flush of ripe years and vigorous health. His figure was tall, its constituents well knit together; his head, well shaped and squarely built, gave indications of a powerful intellect; a face not yet interlined by age, still remarkable for its personal beauty, was lighted up by eyes black in the shade, but brown in the full light, clear, benignant, but with a deep recess of light, a curtained fire in them that blazed in moments of excitement; a countenance, the natural expression of which was gentle and benevolent, yet struck the beholder as masking an iron will. His manners were at once grave and kindly; without gayety or abandon, he was also without the affectation of dignity. Such was the man whose stately figure, in the Capitol at Richmond, brought to mind the old race of Virginians, and who was thereafter to win the reputation, not only as the first commander, but also as the first gentleman of the South, the most perfect and beautiful model of manhood in the war.

The first task imposed upon General Lee, after accepting a commission in the service of Virginia, was to organize the State forces, and that before President Davis had brought up the effulgent front of the war from Montgomery to Richmond. He performed this task most successfully. It has been well said of him, that he made the reputation of a skilful organizer of armies before he commenced the career of active commander in the field. He sat almost daily in the

Advisory Council of Virginia—a body, the secret history of which was, that it had been raised by the Secessionists in the Convention to keep watch and check on Governor Letcher, and which was now translated to the concern of equipping and preparing the State for war. So effectually was it done, that nearly fifty thousand men were in arms in Virginia to meet Mr. Davis in the month of May, 1861, and to shelter his government on its removal to Richmond.

That removal had been resolved upon by President Davis almost from the day it was known that Virginia had seceded. It has been said that he was secretly opposed to it, that he thought the seat of the government should not be so risked so near the enemy; but, in his public expressions at least, he passionately advised it, and was eager to display the advance line of the Confederacy on the banks of the Potomac. On the 21st May, the Montgomery Congress adjourned to meet in Richmond. Mr. Cobb, its presiding officer, gave a curious explanation of its desire to advance to Richmond, and one ludicrous enough in the sequel. He said—"We have sent our soldiers on to the posts of danger, and we wanted to be there to aid and counsel our brave 'boys.' In the progress of the war, further legislation may be necessary, and we will be there, that, when the hour of danger comes, we may lay aside the robes of legislation, buckle on the armor of the soldier, and do battle beside the brave ones who have volunteered for the defence of our beloved South." What proofs ensued of this flatulent patriotism and martial ardor of the Confederate legislators, remain to be told.

The Confederate Government came to Richmond in a storm of popular applause, and with an exaltation of spirits almost indescribable. President Davis travelled through scenes of ovation. Every thing wore for him now the color of the rose. None of those unhappy personal animosities that afterwards degraded his administration, had yet been developed; and even Vice-President Stephens, who had not yet been involved in that quarrel with him which gave so much scandal to the Confederacy, thus spoke of the "coming man": "His flag never yet trailed in the dust. This noble and true son of the South goes to Richmond to take command, in person, of our soldiers there, and to lead them upon the battle-field." On the 20th of May, Mr. Davis was receiving the congratulations of his friends in Richmond, and haranguing a crowd from the balcony of the Spotswood Hotel. "The President of the Six Nations," as he had been called at Montgomery, was now welcomed to accept an Empire extending from the Potomac to the Rio Grande. His first days in Richmond were devoted to ovations, to patriotic exhortations, to reviews, and other animating displays. Some of the speeches were the finest of his life. He exhorted his hearers to remember the dignity of the contest, and, leaving to the enemy the resources of plunderers and ruffians, to "smite the smiter with manly arms, as did our fathers before us." To the soldiers, he declared he would lay down his civil office, and take command of the armies, should the extremity of the cause ever demand his sword; and, on one occasion, speaking in an encampment at Rockett's, and turning his face to a regiment of South Carolina troops, he said, with grand emotion, "When the last line of bayonets is levelled, I will be with you!" The public had not yet conceived the length and breadth of the contest—the great figure it was to make in history. Their notions of the war appeared to be circumscribed by the memories of Mexico; and the crowd interrupted the august speaker, exclaiming, "Tell us something of Buena Vista!" Mr. Davis replied, "I can only say, we will make the battle-fields in Virginia another Buena Vista, and drench them with blood more precious than that which flowed there. We will make a history for ourselves. We do not ask that the past shall shed our lustre upon us, bright as our past has been—for we can achieve our own destiny. We may point to many a field, over which has floated the flag of our country, when we were of the United States, upon which Southern soldiers and Southern officers reflected their brave spirits in their deeds of daring; and without intending to cast a shadow upon the courage of any portion of the United States, let me call it to your remembrance, that no man who went from these Confederate States has ever yet, as a general officer, surrendered to an enemy."

CHAPTER IX.

Some Account of the City of Richmond—A Provincial City before the War—What its Decoration as Capital of the Confederacy cost it—Early Scenes of the War in Richmond—Brilliant and Picturesque Days—A Confederate Soldier and a Little Lady—The Red River Men—Early Clamor for Aggressive Warfare—Why it was Impossible at This Time—"On-to-Washington"—Horace Greeley wants the War Limited to a Single Battle—The Great Victory of Manassas—The Three Stages of the Battle—President Davis on the Field—A Curious *Contretemps*—How Mr. Davis was disappointed by General Beauregard—Instance of his Personal Courage on the Field—A Night Scene at General Beauregard's Quarters—Singular Figure of the President.

BEFORE the war, Richmond was a very quiet city, of only inland importance, and of simple provincial manners. It had neither the extent, nor the variety of a metropolis; and if it was at all deplorable that it had but few of the displays and excitements of such places, it was more than comforting that it had none of their vices. Rowdyism was almost unknown in it, and its whole police establishment consisted of about a dozen so-called "Watchmen," who had scarcely any other occupation than to confine the few belated negroes, who were found on its streets after nine o'clock at night, in a decayed wooden building—a terror to truants and evil-doers—under the name of "The Cage." There were no Police items for the newspapers, except what was furnished in the Mayor's Court, by the fine of a few minor malefactors collected in "The Cage," or a dreary list of negro vagabonds sent to the whipping-post. Richmond had no sensations—no fashionable dissipations—no alarming vices; it lived in an even, healthy atmosphere—perhaps the quietest of American cities—yet charming the traveller by the simplicity of its life, and detaining him by the abundant hospitality that circulated in its homes. It was often noticed as a city which was as remarkable for its quiet enjoyments as for its public order. To the countryman of Virginia, who visited the chief city of his State perhaps once a year, to sell his crop, it was a wonderful metropolis; and, after having dined at Zetelle's, and beheld, as he believed, the summit of civilization and luxury in Ballard's Exchange, he returned home to recount its sights and his adventures to circles of simple listeners. It is, indeed, curious and amusing, what pride of this sort a rude and untravelled people take in their large inland towns. It is one of the traditions of provincial cities. And thus, if one had said, some years back, in Virginia, that Richmond was but a large, comfortable village, compared with New York, Boston, or Philadelphia, he would perhaps have incurred the serious resentment alike of the Lords and Commons of the Old Dominion.

But, better for Richmond had it never aspired to metropolitan dignity, or quitted its good old habits of Virginia provincialism. The late war forced upon it an unhappy importance. It brought into a place, that had only conveniently held about forty thousand people, a population of at least one hundred and forty thousand. It revolutionized its manners, to an extent that only an observer of the contrast could realize—made of a healthful inland town, a brilliant, wicked metropolis—and turned its quiet, shady streets, hitherto unvexed of crowds, into the throbbing, tumultuous avenues of a crowded capital. It made this beautiful city, as by a single word of command, the unhappy capital of the Southern Confederacy, and the bloody hatchblock of the war! The Richmond of 1861, could no longer be recognized as the Richmond of other days. It was as if there had been suddenly called into existence, on the banks of the island dotted James, a new, monstrous, garish city of fable, decked with camps, and arsenals, and furnaces—full of the bustle and picturesqueness of preparations for war—and teeming with the new and strange life that had taken possession, as by magic, of the old land-marks and borders of a former period. Many of the old residents of Richmond would have regarded the change with dismay and resentment, had they not been consoled by the thought that their city was decorated by the choice of it as the capital of the new Confederacy, and the gateway to the war.

In the advent of Mr. Davis and his government, the quiet capital of Virginia was quick to put on the aspects of military life, the brilliant but harshly significant ornaments of war. The hills on which it rested, from the gentle swells north of the capital to the scarred and stone-decked acclivities about Rockett's, gashed with streaks of red clay, the topmost of them newly named "Chimborazo" by the troops which occupied it, were dotted with tents of soldiers; and these new and strange features of the scene, flecked the more distant landscape, stretched away on the table-lands, where the green corn already waved, or glanced in the thick foliage of the dells. The streets of the city were alive with new spectacles. Cavaliers, with severe looks, paced through them—picturesque couriers dashed to and fro—the blare of military music smote the ear, or died sweetly in the distance—the click of artillery wagons—the tramp of regiments, moving compactly through the thoroughfares—mingled with the clatter and voice of trade. For miles around the city—in the forests of the young oak which gird Richmond, where formerly nothing was heard but the twitter of birds, or the wheezing of the squirrel, or perchance the dull chant of the Negro moping through the underbrush for firewood—were now the camps and bivouacs of the new soldiers, the woods alive with horses and men, and vocal with the blast of the bugle, the shrill neigh of the tethered charger, and the shout of the recruits, amusing themselves with games, not yet having commenced the terrible one of life and death in battle.

These were brilliant and picturesque days for Richmond. None knew yet the dire realities, the sickness, the mutilation, the sufferings, and the injuries of war. They saw only its ornaments, its brilliant embroidery, its dancing plumes, and its bright arms. But the Confederate capital was yet serious in its joy; it had to pass through another stage, hereafter noticed, to become the most corrupt and licentious city south of the Potomac. For the present, there were no social diversions, none of those interludes of fashion and frivolity which happen in all great historical epochs—and even the common vices and dissipations which attend armies, had not caught up with the quick movement of the front into Virginia. The ladies were busy in sewing societies making garments for soldiers; and even the most frivolous of them found their time sufficiently occupied in manufacturing needle-cases, thread-bags, and forget-me-nots, for the sons of Mars. A lady of fashion, but a most estimable one, happened to propose, at one of the hotels, a dance to promote sociability, when she was silenced by exclamations of horror from her companions—"What, dance!" they cried, "when our brothers and husbands are courting death!" Yet, a few months later, there were balls enough in Richmond, besides worse festive occasions.

At the time of which we write, an earnest pre-occupation with the war was the feature of society in Richmond. The garb of the civilian had become unfamiliar in the streets. These were filled with troops. On each night was heard the tramp of new arrivals; and nearly every sun glanced on bayonets in the thoroughfare, many of these bayonets bearing on them flowers bestowed by women, a garnish dress for that murderous steel which in all language is the symbol of war. The soldiers were welcomed, and fêted, and lionized. The finest ladies in Richmond affected the dainty charity of baking bread in the camp of a South Carolina regiment. The reviews were attended by the most fashionable persons, and seldom a day passed, in the early summer of 1861, when the ladies were not called to the windows to wave their handkerchiefs amid the huzzas of some newly-arrived regiment, making the streets gay with music and banners, and the new gilt equipage of war not yet tried or tarnished in the furnace of battle.

The intermingling of the best ladies in Richmond with the soldiers was something curious. The usual routine of social life was abandoned, and a universal interest in the war broke down the barriers of sex as well as of class. Even those ladies most exclusively reared, who had formerly bristled with punctilios of propriety, admitted the right of any soldier to address them, to offer them attentions, and to escort them in the street. The ceremony of an introduction was not required; the uniform was sufficient as such; it became a pledge of gallantry—and woe, in female estimation, to the unlucky wight who yet tarried in citizens' habiliments. It is an honor to these early soldiers of the Confederacy that not a single instance is known of their freedom of accosting the ladies of Richmond—a most dangerous liberty surely—being abused by an insult, or an indignity, or one improper word. On the other hand, the author knew of but one instance of displeasure at such liberty on the part of a lady—and that a very little lady. A child of eight years, who had already learned something of the usual manners of society, was shocked at the familiarity of a soldier who had presumed to caress her. Turning to her elderly companion, she exclaimed:—"Why, Aunt! any man that wears a stripe on his pantaloons thinks he can speak to any lady!" The little lady had not yet learned the significance of the soldier's uniform, and, considering the circumstances in which it was donned, its persuasive power in the eyes of her sex.

In the first collection of troops in and around Richmond it was interesting to notice some of the early peculiarities of the Confederate soldier. Nearly every State of the South was represented by a regiment or more. The Hampton Legion from South Carolina, generally esteemed the flower of this first Army of Virginia, was remarkable for aristocratic material, and the luxurious habits of their camp. It is ludicrous now—and especially in memory of the tatterdemallions of another period of the war, who walked barefoot through the snow and slush in front of the War Department—to think of privates going to the battle-field with trunks in the army baggage, and attended by body servants. The dress-parades of this regiment of gentlemen were the admiration and delight of Richmond; and the elegant carriages that crowded the skirts of the manœuvres were as gay and numerous as on a fashionable race-course. Ranged not far from this envied regiment were the hardier sons of Southern Chivalry, presenting, indeed, every variety of the Southern man. There were the Louisiana Zouaves, Wheat's command, small tough men with gleaming eyes—fierce-looking warriors from the soldier State of Mississippi—quaint and sinewy Arkansas riflemen—soldierly-looking Virginians and Georgians, singularly alike in their physical characteristics—grotesque and drawling North Carolina "tar-heels," who did not need this recommendation to *stick*—rude and dashing

Texan Rangers, who had taken as a compliment General Taylor's remark in the Mexican war, that they were *any thing but gentlemen or cowards!* To look at these various men, one would have been completely disabused of an idea then somewhat prevalent in the North, that the Southern soldier was deficient in physique. The caricature of *Harpers' Magazine* of a sickly-looking Southerner carrying his musket under an umbrella and attended by a Negro with a cock-tail to replenish his strength, did not far outdo the popular notion. But probably in the Northern army it would have been impossible to match the Red River men—a singular body of soldiers distinguished by this name in the early war, and coming from the northern portion of Louisiana and southern portion of Arkansas, in the neighborhood of the Red River. These men were easily singled out by their resemblance to each other, in extraordinary stature, in brawny and muscular development, and in evident powers of endurance. In a regiment of these men there was scarcely one under six feet, and with their massive shoulders and chests bearing not an ounce of superfluous flesh, they appeared, indeed, to stand as a living wall to test the shocks of battle.

In view of such a numerous and brilliant soldiery, it was natural that there should have sprung up a popular passion for warfare of the most aggressive kind. The first clamor in Richmond was for a war of invasion—a plan of campaign which should capture Washington, "the wallow of Lincoln and Scott," and plant its standards of defiance on the territory of the North. The Richmond *Examiner* exclaimed: "From mountain top and valleys to the shores of the sea, there is one wild shout of fierce resolution to capture Washington City, at all and every human hazard!"

But President Davis did well to set his face against that

shout. For once at least his government was entirely right in quelling the popular sentiment. It was not a mean and timid prudence that dictated a defensive warfare; and looking back now, in the light of history, upon that early clamor for a war of invasion, we can understand how irrational it was, and how wise the government was in its efforts to contain the impatience of a people suddenly called to arms, and having but little idea of what they had to encounter. The South had already done wonders. It was an agricultural people; and that a people thus confined should in three months after their organization as a nation been able to put such armies in the field was a remarkable event; but that they should be able in this time to enter upon a war of invasion against a commercial and manufacturing people, greatly superior in numbers and resources, would have been an almost miraculous achievement. It takes the greatest and best equipped nations some time to get into actual war after they have declared it; and when that war is one of invasion, the task of preparation becomes greatly more arduous and extended. The North with every facility to raise and equip an army, and, indeed, possessing the army and navy of the nation when undivided, was yet unable to commence a movement of invasion until weeks after such a movement was asked on the part of the Confederate Government by the popular impatience at Richmond; and even then the afterthought of the experiment was that it had been hasty and premature. How then could the South, requiring an especial length of time to allow of concentration and national organization, fettered by agricultural pursuits, and destitute of all facilities for a strong and sustained effort have undertaken a war of invasion at the time the cry of "On-to-Washington" saluted the ears of a government not yet warm in its seat in Richmond?

It was a most senseless cry. Circumstances, and not Jefferson Davis, determined the character of the war on the part of the Confederacy, and decided that it should be, in the main, a defensive one. When, in his first message to Congress, he had said, "All we ask is to be let alone," he had spoken instinctively the present and immediate want of the South. Time in that emergency was the only source of life to the Confederacy; and to extend the season of preparation was the care of reflecting minds in opposition to the headlong passion of the multitude. The new government had actually nothing with which to clothe, equip or move an army, unless it had been bought abroad and imported within its territory. How, in the face of such stark necessities, could it have been expected in so short a time to not only put a great war on foot, but to carry into the territory of an enemy thickly planted with military resources, and superior in every respect of means and material?

The cry of "On-to-Washington" found no serious response in the government at Richmond. It was probably scarcely more than the popular expression of a certain contemptuous spirit towards the enemy. Mr. Davis wanted all the time he could get for preparation; General Lee was near him to advise that the war-spirit needed rather to be quieted and regulated than to be further inflamed; and when, at last, it was decided to give up Alexandria and Harper's Ferry, and to withdraw the line of defence twenty or thirty miles south of the Potomac, the wise thought the new government had ventured far enough, although the troops showed something of dispirit and the newspapers had something to say of "the hateful current of retreat."

But if there was such a current of retreat, it was soon to turn with a brilliant crest. The surprise at Philippi, the affair of Bethel, the operations of General Wise on Scary Creek, the bombardment of Pig's Point, and the disaster of Rich Mountain, made great figures in the newspapers when war was novel; but they were, in fact, the slightest preludes to the contest that was to ensue, and scarcely deserved a breath of exclamation. On both sides there was great popular anxiety for a general battle, to determine the question of relative manhood; and especially on the side of the South, from an impression that one distinct and large combat resulting in its favor, and showing conspicuously its superior valor would alarm the North sufficiently to make it abandon the war. This impression had been especially given from the New York *Tribune*, which was supposed to represent at that time, more than any other journal, the temper of the North. The readers of this paper at this day appear scarcely to recollect a remarkable, studious article in which in the month of July, 1861, Mr. Horace Greeley wrote or dictated to the effect that the North was averse to any thing like prolonged war, that it would not tolerate such a supposition, that it desired an early determination of the contest, to such an extent that if its troops were fairly defeated in one open field, man to man, he would pledge it to retire with good grace and to surrender the contest!*

A field for the grand *duello* was soon found; the question

---

* Thus the *Tribune* of the 19th of July, 1861, says:—"We have been most anxious that this struggle should be submitted at the earliest moment to the ordeal of a fair decisive battle. Give the Unionists a fair field, equal weapons and equal numbers, and we ask no more. Should the Rebel forces at all justify the vaunts of their journalistic trumpeters we shall candidly admit the fact. If they can beat double the number of Unionists, they can end the struggle on their own terms."

of relative manhood was brought fairly to the test; the battle of Manassas was fought—with what sequel, in contradiction of Mr. Greeley's pledge, the world now knows.

Here the South won the first great victory of her arms; and although varying fortunes followed this event, and disasters, which *never* came from lack of Southern valor lurked in the sequel—although the South afterwards sunk under vast accumulations of the enemy's power, but not until the courage of her soldiers, which blood had never quenched, had been beaten down by the iron heel of numbers—yet it is a grand consolation that the glory of Manassas is her "possession forever," that it can never be expunged from the page of history, or diminished by the utmost ingenuity or zeal of falsehood. The whole world knows this day; and although it may have kept blurred and indistinct recollections of other periods and scenes of the war, it is remarkable how full and faithful and vivid is the memory it has retained of the drama of Manassas.

There is less perhaps of confusion, and conflict of evidence, as to the numbers displayed on the field, and the incidents of the combat, than in the case of any other battle of the war. It is agreed that McDowell attempted his plan of battle with a force in motion of forty thousand, regulars and volunteers, against a force actually engaged of only fifteen thousand volunteers. We mean to say, that only fifteen thousand Confederate troops were *at any one time* engaged in the battle. When the column of attack first descended from Sudley Ford, only five Confederate regiments and six guns breasted it; and it was here that Jackson raised his crest, as the bristling Federal battalions came on, and, like Coleridge's Ancient Mariner, "held with glittering eye" the maddened retreat. Again the scene shifts, to the plateau of the Henry House; and here (we speak exactly from General Beauregard's official report,) 6500 withstood the onset. "It was then," says General Beauregard, "I urged the men to the resolution of victory, or death on the field,"—a modest report of the speech he made when leaping from his foaming horse; his spirit blazed out in words of remembered eloquence, and he pointed his shining sword to the path where he had "come to die." "Then," continues Beauregard, "I felt assured of the unconquerable spirit of that army, which would enable us to wrench victory from the host then threatening us with destruction." The plateau is won, and the third and final scene rises in succession. Here, with the reinforcements of Kirby Smith and Elzey, with the line of the Confederates fully developed, less than fifteen thousand men prepare for the final action of the day, while the enemy makes his second grand sweep by a still greater circuit. Just as he makes the bend to envelop the Confederate left, the command "Forward!" runs along its whole line. The field is swept as by a tempest—a great army is broken into a confused mass—its organization, its life, gone in a moment! And half an hour later, Jackson, rising in his stirrups, and looking over fields where there is nothing but herds of fugitives, mutters, "Give me ten thousand men, and I will be in Washington to-night!"

Such is the brief, dramatic story of the battle—at every point of it, in each of its three critical stages, great superiority of the enemy's force; a victory gained after the Confederate troops had been twice driven to the most desperate extremity: a crowning evidence of what valor may accomplish against the weight of numbers and the dispositions of science.

In the morning of the eventful day, President Davis had left Richmond for the field of battle. What carried him there was never explained. It was not—as President Lincoln, and other civil magistrates, often did in the course of the war—to visit a field already decided, and to review or meditate upon it. There was, indeed, a carping commentary in Richmond, that President Davis should have been present at Manassas on this day, and should have left his office at the capital to thrust himself into a scene of actual battle, and perhaps to interfere with the Confederate commanders. It was known only to those very intimate with him that he had left Richmond that morning to command, in person, the army; and hence the curious mistake which appeared in all the newspapers of the South next day, and which the agent of the Associated Press had predicated on what had been whispered to him of the intentions of Mr. Davis, that "the President commanded the centre" in the action of the day. Mr. Davis did not command the centre; he arrived too late for the battle, and only when the enemy was flying. It is said that he never forgave General Beauregard for this *contretemps*, in which his vanity was so disappointed, and that in this circumstance originated his first disaffection towards that commander, which was afterwards carried to every extremity of enraged persecution. However this may be, it is certain that General Beauregard had never notified the President of the time when he proposed to give battle; he was under no obligation to do so, and perhaps he suspected the intention of Mr. Davis to lead his army into action. All he was compelled to do was to apply to the President for authority for the army corps of General Johnston to join him, and it is positively known that this was the only intimation Mr. Davis had that a battle was to be delivered. He arrived too late to take part in it, or to gather the military laurel of which he had dreamed the night before. But he did not arrive too late to make some display of personal heroism.

He rode from the cars towards the sublime scene in which the battle had culminated and broken on the horizon of evening. A cloud of smoke and dust had lifted from the plain and hung sullenly in the sky; there was the distant clamor of battle; the strokes of artillery, slow and ponderous, smote the air; black masses of men, wavering, indistinguishable, bounded the strained vision and perplexed it. It was impossible to tell from a distance which army had won the day, or what flags rode in the mixed scene. The President galloped forward to learn the state of the field. No one could tell him amid the roar and confusion. As he rode swiftly through a stream of stragglers, it seemed as if he was in the midst of a retreat, breasting its bad and dusty current. At that moment his brother, Joseph Davis, galloped to his side, and said, "the day is lost; let us go no further." "No," said the President grandly, "if the army is defeated so much the greater reason that I should be with my brave men and share their fate." They were the words of a personal courage which nothing in his life ever turned or daunted;—and they were perhaps remembered when a distinguished son of Virginia recently reviewing the leader of "the lost cause," declared briefly that he was a man who had had many favorable chances and who had attained greatness only from comparison with a race of political pigmies in Mississippi and the Southwest, and who, with all the advantages of fortune, had shown but two virtues —a devoted espousal of his cause and "*indomitable pluck.*"

The scene changes from the grandeur and tumult of battle. The night has fallen and the stars have risen above the combs of the Blue Ridge, now a dusky boundary of the wide plain. Jackson has gone to his tent, gloomy and reluctant, muttering "it is not my office to advise the commander-in-chief to pursue." Before another tent, larger and more pretentious, above which float in the night air the emblems of the Southern Confederacy, a quiet, elderly gentleman is seated, clad in simple grey, his brows shaded by a felt hat of light color and ample dimensions, his mouth garnished with a fragrant cigar, evidently a person taking his ease and indulging self-complacency. This man is Jefferson Davis. There is a group of laced officers around him; General Beauregard sits among them; and General Johnston comes and goes, sharing the light and desultory conversation, and anon retiring to perform some duty. Not a man speaks of pursuit of the enemy; not one has conceived it. They speak of some incidents of the field; Mr. Davis inquires of some of his Mississippi friends; the conversation becomes general, of politics, of persons in Washington, of any thing else but the fugitive enemy; there is an abandonment in the scene, and every one is disposed to be well pleased and sociable. A few miles further from this light recreation, there are great, broken masses of men in mad retreat, the hum of their flight rising in the black hollowness of the night, panting, struggling, pressing on in inextricable disorder, and yet with nothing at their heels but their own terrors. This is the Federal Army, the "Grand Army." It flies through the night; it makes its escape; it is already shivering on the banks of the Potomac; while Jefferson Davis picturesquely smokes his cigar, strokes his neuralgic parts, and tells anecdotes at the door of General Beauregard's tent.

CHAPTER X.

The South Intoxicated by the Victory of Manassas—Who was Responsible for not Pursuing the Enemy to Washington—A Larger and more Important Question than that—The True History of a Secret and Notable Council of War—President Davis Rejects the Advice of his Three Principal Generals—He Decides for the Policy of Dispersion or Frontier-Defence—A Glance at the Character of General Johnston—President Davis's Quarrel with General Beauregard—An Interval of Infamous Intrigues at Richmond—How Mr. Hunter was Driven from the Cabinet—Conceit of the President—"Waiting for Europe"—Demoralization of Inactive Armies—Rapid Corruption of Society in Richmond—"The Wickedest City"—Mr. Davis at a Fancy Dress Ball—Unpopular Conduct of his Wife—Anecdote of the President—Criticism of a "Tar Heel"—Mr. Davis and the Faithful Sentinel of the Libby Prison—A Historical Parallel—Connubial Fondness of Mr. Davis—His Collection of Small and Mean Favorites—A Curious Sort of Obstinacy, and some Reflections thereon.

THE victory of Manassas was an intoxicating fruit for the South. It occasioned an excessive sense of false security on the part of the Confederacy, and was followed by a period of neglect and supineness in the military administration of the South, wherein it lost, not only all the advantages of this field, but nearly all the spirit and means it had for the contest.

An over-busy attempt has been made to defend President Davis against the charge, once popular, that he, by his superior orders, had prevented his Generals from pursuing the enemy to Washington, or from making a forward movement immediately after the battle of Manassas. But this question as to what took place so shortly after the battle, is a narrow and particular one we scarcely need discuss; it certainly does not cover the responsibility for that period of inaction and listlessness extending through several months, and in which the Confederacy lapsed to the disastrous close of the first year of the war. The true inquiry is as to the responsibility for a period of supine administration so long, in which the South came nigh to ruin, rather than as to the delinquency of a few days in which it lost the fruits of a single field.

Months passed, in which the main army of Virginia remained without any general action or movement, rusting in idleness, a huge victim of ennui, occupying a filthy and unhealthy camp, and sacrificing more men to disease than had fallen by the bullets of Manassas. Nothing was done practically to replenish it; nothing was done to restore its animation; it was fast sinking into demoralization, and was wasting to a skeleton organization, as destitute of spirit as of substance. There were no preparations even to match the sounding and elaborate ones of the enemy for a renewed campaign. In vain, the newspapers clamored for some action, or sought to awake the Government either from a lethargic indifference, or the stupid joys of a blind and excessive confidence. The golden days of autumn passed without any improvement of the military situation. Besides some partial affairs of arms and a brilliant campaign in Missouri, the latter too exceptional and distant to affect the general fortunes of the war—the main armies of the Confederacy remained idle to the close of the year, and appeared to rest on the idea that the main task of fighting was over, and that the fruit of Southern independence was to drop with the snows of winter.

It has been said, that President Davis was in favor of an advance movement; was not a willing party to the fatal inaction of the Confederate troops, that ensued for months after Manassas. There has been much recrimination on the subject as between him and his Generals, and much has been written, in a confused and disputatious way, of the causes which compelled the military barrenness of the latter half of the first year of the war. But the truth of this matter, we are persuaded, is to be found in the secret history of a certain notable council of war, accounts of which never appeared in the newspapers, and the existence of which was, for a long time, unknown. If President Davis was really in favor of an active campaign after Manassas, he had but a poor way of showing it. If he really did favor a forward movement, he yet wantonly and deliberately destroyed the conditions in which such a movement might take place; and it is but a poor rule of responsibility that does not impose upon a person the foreseen, necessary, and obvious results of his own action.

The council referred to, was held some weeks after the battle of Manassas, when President Davis was on a visit to the headquarters of the army. General Johnston then submitted a plan illustrating the value of concentration, and proposing it as a preliminary for an aggressive campaign. He was sustained in his views by Generals Beauregard and G. W. Smith. These Generals urged the immediate concentration in that quarter of the greater part of the forces dispersed along the sea-coast at Pensacola, Savannah, Norfolk, Yorktown, and Fredericksburg, with which, added to the troops already in hand, a campaign across the Potomac should be initiated, before Gen. McClellan had completed the organization of his grand army. This, they believed, might be done without risk to the positions weakened by the measure—though, in fact, the principles of the art of war prescribed that places of such relative military unimportance should be sacrificed or hazarded for the sake of the vital advantage anticipated. A very considerable army could have been thus assembled—larger, perhaps, than either of those which subsequently General Lee was able to lead across the border under much less favorable military conditions. But the President could not be induced to sanction the measure, or to give up a conceit with which he commenced the war, and which was only wrung from him many months later by the force of fearful disasters.

That conceit which he placed in opposition to General Johnston's policy of *concentration*—a policy that would have afforded an aggressive campaign and an immediate forward movement across the Potomac—was to defend the entire frontier of the Southern Confederacy, and to give up no foot of its soil to the invader. There was something high-sounding in such a resolution; it was a bravado to affect the masses, a rhetorical *afflatus* about the integrity of "sacred soil," and the "polluting steps" of invading armies; and it was that idea which might be expected from one who was more a politician than a General, and who calculated that if he uncovered any part of the South he would provoke, from that quarter, a clamor against his administration, and that to have all the people of the Confederacy satisfied he must protect them all alike. But it was the wretched policy of *dispersion*—that policy that strung the armies of the Confederacy on every imaginable line of defence, that wasted the resources of the South in the attempted defence of every threatened position, and that was abandoned by President Davis only when, after a trial of six months to cover the "sacred soil" of the South, he was forced to confess that "events have demonstrated that the Government had attempted more than it had power successfully to achieve." But this was the slow lesson coming only after disaster, and only when the Confederacy was trembling under a catastrophe which the President's policy of dispersion had precipitated. In the council referred to, it was impossible to bring him to reason, and all the arguments of General Johnston had no effect. This commander pointed to clear and firm principles of military science. He argued the value of the *concentration* of forces in war; that such concentration was, indeed, the condition of vigorous war, the necessary means of striking the enemy with effect, and making decisive fields. The President heard him with impatience, dismissed the council, adhered to the military situation, as it then existed, and declined, as he suggested to a friend, to wound any further the sensibilities of the States further South, by bringing any more troops to Virginia.

If, afterwards, he did expect General Johnston to move across the Potomac, that commander did right to disappoint him, and was even excusable for something of sullen reticence which he ever afterwards maintained concerning his plans. The President's policy of *dispersion* decided against an aggressive campaign for 1861. It was the true logical cause of that inaction which ensued after the battle of Manassas, and in which the spirit of the army declined; in which the resources of the South rotted in idleness; and in which the false idea was insinuated in the public mind, that the war had been virtually decided, and that nothing remained but such scattered and desultory affairs as were then taking place in Western Virginia and Southern Missouri.

The radical disagreement between Mr. Davis and the Generals at Manassas, appears to have founded his first dislike of Johnston, and to have developed his tendency to imperious and envious command. Johnston was never a very popular commander in the South; he was not understood by the masses, and even to this day, his reputation is severely canvassed. He had not that turbulence and passion remarkable among the most popular leaders in the early stages of the war; he was disposed to chasten the confidence of the South; and although his severe and cold military judgment and his sedate calculations gained for him the appreciation of the intelligent few, there were many people in the Confederacy who condemned him as tame, who interpreted his precision as timidity, and who treated with suspicion and innuendo his opposition to Mr. Davis's policy of frontier defence. In his aversion to Johnston, the President was for a long time sustained by an ignorant populace. They did not care to inquire how much there was of personal malice in the quarrel, as long as the President did not offend one of their favorites, and as long as the victim was a patient, silent man, who cared nothing for popular sympathy or support, and did nothing to excite or entreat them. But when Mr. Davis went further, gave additional proofs of his temper, and broke with General Beauregard, a commander who was then prime military favorite of the South, who had a temper of his own, and who had such a sensitive regard for public opinion as to commit the un-officerlike act of writing letters in the newspapers, the quarrel attracted attention through the length and breadth of the South, was carried into Congress, actually created two parties in the Confederacy, and occasioned, indeed, the first serious fluctuation of public confidence in the administration of Mr. Davis.

The people were suddenly awakened to the regard of a trait of character in the President which had heretofore been concealed by the lacquer of his fine accomplishments, and which now gaped to view at the first strain put on his vanity. It was seen that he had an enormous conceit from the moment he became inflated with the victory of Manassas, and considered his tenure of office secure from that day. The fact is, that that victory became the signal for political intrigues, in which all care for the war seemed to be dismissed for an anxiety to secure the offices and patronage of a government as already firmly seated. It was the most indecent interlude of the war. Already politicians commenced to fish for nominations under the "permanent" Constitution which was shortly to be inaugurated, and it was whispered to Mr. Davis that General Beauregard was courting the vote of the army for the office of President, and was undermining him in popularity. To the alarm and grieved surprise of all his judicious friends, Mr. Davis suddenly undertook a series of political proscriptions in the midst of war, planted his quarrel with General Beauregard in Congress, drove Mr. Hunter, the man of greatest weight in his administration, from his Cabinet, and stocked the public offices with creatures of his favor, who were rather calculated to support him on some issue of political party than to render any service in the prosecution of the war. It seemed for weeks and even months that the war was forgotten, or had sunk to the mere ordinary concern of the adjustment by politicians of a new government. The topic in Richmond was no longer battles and movements of armies, but the doings of politicians and the latest gossip about the President's quarrels. It was reported to the disadvantage of Mr. Hunter that he had voluntarily left the Cabinet to disembarrass himself for a nomination for President, as against Mr. Davis; but he replied unequivocally enough that he had resigned because he had wished to be Secretary of State, and was not content to be "the clerk of Jefferson Davis." The truth was, there had been a disgraceful quarrel in the Cabinet, and when Mr. Hunter had offered some advice about the conduct of the war, Mr. Davis had said with a flushed and almost insolent manner: "Mr. Hunter, you are Secretary of State, and when information is wanted of that particular department, it will be time for you to speak." The spirited Virginian next day sent in his resignation. Almost in the very outset of his career, and at what should have been the sharpest crisis of the war, President Davis found himself in the situation of having quarreled with his principal General in the field, of having dismissed the premier of his Administration, and of having risked a trial of public confidence greater than other Presidents, even in times of peace, and after a considerable term of popularity, have been willing to undertake.

The interval after Manassas in which took place these political intrigues and these displays of the President's temper, appears almost as one of insanity when we consider the thoughtless and arrogant security with which Mr. Davis asserted his power, and counted the victims of his offended vanity. He either folded his arms idly in the face of the war—"waiting for Europe" as Mr. Benjamin expressed it, with the perpetual smile that basked on his Jewish lips—or he did worse in inspiring from his official position the popular sentiment of security, with a contemptuous regard for the enemy. It was a luxurious conceit. It not only impaired all the true interests of the Confederacy, but it bred the innumerable evils which exist where there is a state of war, without the action of troops, where armies are kept in ostentatious idleness, and where society in such unnatural and excited condition unemployed by the interest which grows out of active campaigns, finds its passions turned upon itself, and becomes infested with a thousand vices.

Such results were seen in the South. After Manassas, the capital of the Confederacy was given up to a licentious joy and dissipation. These, although the President might not have shared, he yet promoted by his own disposition to triumph in the present, and to be indifferent of the future. It was in this time that Richmond made that reputation of moral infamy, which marred whatever military glories it afterwards won—a reputation which has not only lasted, but has accumulated since the war, which in fact has suggested the title of "*the wickedest city*" in America for a place where the houses on the best streets are shops of female infamy, and where in nearly every court there is kept behind the drapery of justice an auction-block for bribes. In the early months of the war Richmond won the bad eminence that has since made it a name of scorn in the world. The decoration of being the capital of the Confederacy—which its citizens had at first so highly valued—cost it dearly enough. It was the convenient cloak by which entered into a formerly quiet and moral city all the vices which follow in the train of war. The vultures were soon gathered at the carcass. With the imposing and grand displays of war came vices and dissipations heretofore unknown in Richmond; various flocks of villains, adventurers, gamblers, harlots, thieves in uniform, thugs, "tigers," and nondescripts. The city was soon overrun with rowdyism. The coarse vices of the street, however, were even less deplorable than those which affected a certain refinement, and invaded the higher ranks of society with that style of immoral and fantastic luxury bred out of the vast expenditures, the reckless passions, and the heedless self-gratifications in a state of war. The sobriety of Old Virginia society gave way completely to a new order of reckless, social amusements in which money was spent with a lavishness that taxed fancy, and a recklessness that scorned the morrow. As the war advanced, poverty and suffering, of course, came into many doors, and the world has heard much historically of the distress in Richmond; but it is remarkable of this city that, even to the last extremity of the war, when there were hundreds of people on its streets wanting bread, there yet constantly resided in it a wild fantastic luxury, pouring out money in every extravagant fancy of wickedness and vice.

The gamblers reaped a harvest that will probably never be told. A few months after the commencement of the war, a Richmond newspaper stated that twenty gambling-houses might be counted in three or four blocks on Main street. There was abundant gossip of almost fabulous sums lost in these places, by quartermasters, commissaries, and pay-agents. And in these "hells" were, doubtless, concealed the traces of that immense amount of defalcation in the Confederate administration, which has never yet been told of but in broken and imperfect whispers. In every war, the frauds and peculations of disbursing officers make a large amount; and it is curious, that no reference to this loss—busily investigated as it was by the North, on her side, in the late contest—was ever made, in any public manner, in the case of the Southern Confederacy. There was a vague impression of the people of the South, that there was an enormous amount to be credited to this account; and towards the end of the war there was an uneasy report that the proportions of such fraud would stagger belief, and that the discovery would terminate the last breath of popular confidence in the Davis government.

While the war lagged, Richmond enjoyed high carnival. There were extravagant social diversions—balls, parties, tableaus, and nondescript revels of wanton and excessive luxury. Curiously enough, considering the historical want of clothing in the Confederacy, fancy-dress balls were the social rage in Richmond. At one of these, a beautiful blonde, from Baltimore, impersonated "My Maryland," her slender wrists bound behind her back with miniature chains; and at the height of the festive excitement, the President of the Confederacy essayed a historical tableau, approaching the lady and relieving her of her bonds, amid the acclamations of the revellers. The old staid society of Richmond was overrun; and mad, wild, social diversions in the Confederate capital recked nothing, and reflected nothing of the sufferings, and toils, and mutilations of war.

Amid the frivolities and vicissitudes of Richmond society, so early in the war, Mrs. Jefferson Davis was conspicuous for an attempt to introduce into them something of the manners and etiquette she had imported from certain circles in Washington; but it proved not only an ignominious failure, but an unpleasant scandal. The Confederate President himself, although recluse and haughty in his government, was democratic enough in his personal habits, simple in his social tastes, and plain, and accessible to the populace. But Mr. Davis was the most uxorious of men; and it was surprising, indeed, that a man of his fine nervous organism, a very type of social *dilletantism*, should have fallen so much under the dominion of a woman, who was excessively coarse and physical in her person, and in whom the defects of nature had been repaired neither by the grace of manners nor the charms of conversation. Mrs. Davis was a brawny, able-bodied woman, who had much more of masculine mettle than of feminine grace. Her complexion was tawny, even to the point of mulattoism; a woman loud and coarse in her manners; full of social self-assertion; not the one of her sex who would have been supposed to win the deference of a delicate man like Mr. Davis, whimsical in his health, a victim of "nerves," nice and morbid in his social tastes, although she might well have conquered the submission of such a creature by the force of her character. Mr. Davis deferred to her in the social regulations she would impose upon Richmond. She demanded the etiquette of Washington, that the President's lady should return no calls. She introduced what were unknown in Richmond, liveried servants; and, when every horse was impressed in the military service, the citizens, forced to go afoot, remarked, with some disdain, the elegant equipage of Mrs. Davis, that paused much more before the shops of Main street, than the aristocratic residences of Grace and Franklin.

Mr. Davis himself was simple and democratic in his habits. His figure, habitually clothed in Confederate grey, was familiar on the streets, or might be seen almost every evening mounted on the rather mean horse on which he took regular exercise. He invited the approach and freedom of the commonest men, but sometimes to the disadvantage of his dignity.

A number of stories were told in Richmond of his curiously free intercourse with his soldiers, although they lacked something of the Napoleonic tradition. Once, when he was crossing the Capitol Square, a drunken North Carolina soldier stopped him, and inquired, "Say, mister, be'ent you Jefferson Davis?" "Sir," returned the President, "that is my name." "I thought so," replied tar-heel, "you look so much like a Confederate postage stamp." Another occasion was more dramatic. The President was returning with Mrs. Davis from one of the customary festivities on a flag of truce boat that had come up the James; walking the street in the night, unattended by his staff, and with no indications of his importance, he had to pass the front of the Libby Prison, where a sentinel paced, and, according to his orders, forced passengers from the sidewalk to take the middle of the street. As the President, with his wife on his arm, approached him, he ordered them off the pavement. "I am the President," replied Mr. Davis; "allow us to pass." "None of your gammon," replied the soldier, bringing his musket to his shoulder; "if you don't get into the street I'll blow the top of your head off." "But I am Jefferson Davis, man—I am your President—no more of your insolence;" and the President pressed forward. He was rudely thrust back, and in a moment he had drawn a sword or dagger concealed in his cane, and was about to rush on the insolent sentinel, when Mrs. Davis flung herself between the strange combatants, and by her screams aroused the officer of the guard. Explanations were made and the President went safely home. But, instead of the traditional reward to the faithful sentry, that has usually graced such romantic adventures, came an order next day to the Libby to degrade the soldier, and give him a taste of bread and water for his unwitting insult of the commander-in-chief of the Confederate armies.

The connubial fondness of President Davis suggests the story of Rienzi the Last of the Roman Tribunes; only the Nina of the Southern Tribune was a very plain and unqueenly body. The strong resemblance of the character of Jefferson Davis to that drawn by Gibbon of the man who attempted to restore the glories of Rome—the elegant orator, the weak statesman, the doting and sentimental husband, the ruler haughty and authoritative, yet governed by woman and small favorites, the man eloquent and gaudy in the forum, yet consenting to escape from the ruins of his capital in the disguise of a baker, blessed by every fortune, and yet blindfolded, misguided and ruined by a conceit that affected humility and an obstinacy that was really the disguise of weakness. It is not the place here to fill the parallel. The suggestion is only of that singular weakness to be observed in the ingenious history of many notable rulers, who, obstinate to the general public, flinty and imperious, have yet been secretly governed by women, jesters and fools. No one could be apparently firmer than Mr. Davis in his public intercourse; no one could resent advice with greater disdain, or chill it with colder courtesy, when offered by the best and wisest men in the South; and yet this man who could set his face as flint against the counsels of the intelligent, was as wax in the hands of his wife, and the easy prey of the most unworthy adventurers who understood the approaches to his favor. It is a curious fact that the harshest and most tyrannical rulers have generally been controlled by a few mean favorites, the intriguers of a seraglio or the parasites of a court. Such weakness Mr. Davis sadly illustrated. Inflexible to the counsels of Congress and his Cabinet, lofty and cold in his public intercourse, he was yet ready to make a quarrel of State for the whim or distemper of his wife, or to take into his political household the most contemptible of lickspittles. He was constantly imposed upon by "confidence-men;" he was susceptible to women, preachers and adventurers; he had for a long time as chief-of-staff a newspaper-reporter who had flattered him in Washington, and who boasted that he was the fruit of the liason of a member of the English nobility; and the immediate patronage of his office was eat up by small and unprofitable knaves who knew how to amuse his vanity and seduce his favors. The man who could remove the most important officer in his government—his Quartermaster-General—because a female member of the family of the latter had presumed to criticise Mrs. Davis's figure; who was pleased with the veriest jacks-in-office, and would take tribute to his vanity in the smallest coin; who gave himself up to social frivolities in the midst of a great war, and amused himself with intrigues and shows in Richmond when the enemy was making his vastest preparations, was clearly not the one to rule and direct the struggle of eight millions of people in a cause of life or death.

CHAPTER XI.

President Davis playing the Adorned Conqueror—Decay of the Confederacy—Review of the Military Situation—Share of Congress in the Maladministration of Mr. Davis—Weak and Infamous Character of that Body—How it Expelled the Best Intellect of the South—A Notable Rule against Military Officers—How the Political Affairs of the Confederacy were Entirely Surrendered to Mr. Davis and his Party—Two Measures that Brought the South to the Brink of Ruin—The Army of Virginia almost Disbanded—Protests of Generals Johnston and Beauregard—The Civil or Internal Administration of Mr. Davis—Its Intellectual Barrenness—Not One Act of Statesmanship in the Whole History of the Confederacy—Richmond a Reflex of Washington—A New Rule by which to Measure Mr. Davis's Responsibility—A Literary Dyspeptic, with more Ink than Blood in his Veins—Complaints Breaking Out Against Mr. Davis—His Vaunt of the Blockade as a Blessing in Disguise—Dethronement of King Cotton—Extreme Scarcity of Arms at the South.

WHILE Richmond was captivated by social diversions, while the South basked in a false security, and while Mr. Davis was intoxicated with the sweets of power, and playing the adorned conqueror in his capital, the real interests of the Confederacy were going fast to wreck and ruin. Not only was nothing done to meet the vast preparations upon which the enemy had visibly entered, but the means of the Confederacy were not even kept up to the standard which they had attained before the battle of Manassas. Mr. Davis's policy of dispersion had kept the whole frontier of the war dull and almost barren, until the blows of the enemy, in the opening months of 1862, carried away two thin sections of defence—one on the seacoast, and the other in the West—and showed how false was the system that relied on the length, rather than the breadth of its defences. To the close of the year 1861, the Confederacy was in a rapid decline, and only when the disease passed its stage of flushed concealment, was the discovery made that it was almost in the agonies of death

The campaign in Western Virginia, had ended in disaster, and had surrendered an important territory. All that Price had achieved in Missouri had been given up at the last, and an army, in which there was no discipline, was rapidly passing through his fingers. The action of Leesburg, or Ball's Bluff, had been but a brilliant episode and a fruitless glory. There were, really, no military results for the South at the end of the year, no positive acquisitions; while, on the other hand, her means had been diminished, her *morale* impaired, and her resolution relaxed in that interval of negligent repose into which the public confidence had been drugged after the battle of Manassas.

In writing of the dereliction of the Confederate Government within the period referred to in the preceding chapter, it may be thought strange that we have not drawn into the account some notice of Congress, and distributed upon it some of the responsibility for the decay of Confederate affairs in the first year of the war. But, an especial explanation attaches here. We may, at once, remark upon the utter inanity of that body which made a pretence of performing legislative duties during the war; and if the Confederate Congress has been sunk nearly out of sight in all historical notices of the contest, it is because of the meagre and unimportant part it performed in it. What was known as the Provisional Congress, was really the most inane, unimportant, incompetent and barren of public assemblies. It was composed of delegates sent to Montgomery, and afterwards to Richmond, by the different State Conventions, as they respectively passed ordinances of secession. It had been designed as a revolutionary council, rather than as a regular legislative body. It was a national assembly, but with the defect, that, instead of being the fresh and immediate representatives of the popular will, it was the secondary and weak creature of conventions.

Yet, it contained some distinguished names; and, when first organized, there was considerable weight of character in it. Howell Cobb, of Georgia, was its President. All the Heads of the Executive Departments had seats in it, and participated in its debates. Among its members, were naturally those politicians who had formerly distinguished themselves at Washington, in leading, from there, the first movements of Secession—such as Toombs, Wigfall, Pryor, and Keitt. But, a single measure expelled from Congress nearly all it had of worth and talents, and, in a day, reduced it to an inane body of mediocrities. Its most distinguished members had also military commissions; they were Generals, colonels, etc., as well as legislators. It was a time when the most brilliant and ambitious men of the South sought the field, and preferred its honors; and when, a few weeks after the first session of Congress in Richmond, the objection was raised, that the two careers were incompatible, and that members of Congress could not hold military commissions, the decision drove from it nearly every man of merit or note. Military men, who had come down from Manassas to take their places in Congress, and who proposed to fill the pauses of the war with legislative duties, were excluded, and compelled to rejoin their commands—leaving the work of legislation to be done by common, ignorant men, who were satisfied to remain in seats which soon came to be considered, as even dishonorable, in comparison with the places of glory and danger in the field.

The decision that excluded military officers from Congress, was probably just, but, in many respects, unfortunate. It accounts for that extreme intellectual degradation, which made the Confederate Congress a peculiar stock of shame in the war—actually one of the weakest and most inane bodies that ever met under the title of a legislative assembly in historical times. It came, at last, to be composed chiefly of two classes—men who were never before publicly known, or old politicians, too far broken down in their fortunes to attempt new careers or to be invited by the prospect of military honors. This prospect, unfortunately for the South, drew from its political councils too much of its best mind, and may be said to have abandoned the whole government to Mr. Davis and a few weak creatures surrounding him; although, in later periods of the war, some of the distinguished politicians who had sought the field, either from disappointment there, or from resentment of what they supposed Mr. Davis's disfavor, returned to plague him and to assail his administration—but, unhappily, only after it had sunk almost beneath reproach. Beyond this brief and exceptional animation, the history of the Confederate Congress is scarcely more than that of the reflection of the will and temper of President Davis—a mere servile appendage to an autocracy the most supreme of modern times.

It is difficult to understand how, at one time of the war, the political concerns of the Southern Confederacy were almost entirely abandoned to Mr. Davis, and a Congress which was scarcely more than a figure-head, unless we take into account a peculiar passion in the South for military service that marked the first years of hostilities. There was nothing like it in the North; there the ambition for military honors was not so absorbing, and the labors and aspirations of public men were divided with singular fairness between the political council and the field. But, to the prizes of the latter, the ambition of the South seems to have been almost exclusively directed. Scarcely any thing was attempted in that career of statesmanship, which, in such great historical periods, should run even with that of arms. The best men of the South neglected all former fields of political ambition; they were no longer anxious to be known as statesmen, or legislators, or orators, when they might be known as successful generals. It was not only that the South, probably from its natural temper, placed a higher value on martial prowess than did the North, but the former had a peculiar estimation of the war—it was *pro aris et focis;* and there was a public sentiment that drove men into the army from every occupation in life, and from every seat of public office, until, at last, civil office was held in disrepute, and the government was denuded almost to the point of stark incapacity. This inflated desire for the military field, might have been admirable in some respects; but none, except those who witnessed its wild and sweeping operations in the South, can imagine how it stripped the political arena, or estimate the injury it wrought in surrendering the civil affairs of the Southern Confederacy to incompetent men, and securing an easy and blind toleration of Mr. Davis, and the servile Congress that waited on and executed his decrees.

Indeed, for the first year of the war Mr. Davis was actually the legislator of the Confederacy, and laws, framed in the Executive Office, were as regularly sent into the dingy room in which Congress sat in secret session, as the common communications of information from the departments. Unfortunately, Mr. Davis had an excessive conceit that he was born under the star of Mars, and that he was excellently qualified to legislate on military subjects; and Congress was weak enough to indulge his foolish and pragmatical fancy. He was really responsible (as he had not used his authority to check, although busy enough with the *veto* in other instances,) for two notable military measures, in the first year of the war, which brought the Confederacy to the brink of ruin, and, indeed, would have delivered her an easy prey to the enemy, had the hesitating and unready McClellan known the extent of his opportunity.

One of these measures was a law passed in December, 1861, of which it has been well remarked, its true title would have been, "To disband the armies of the Confederacy." It was the fruit of the lowest demagogism. It permitted the men to change their arm of the service, to elect new officers, and to reorganize throughout the army. It was said that the soldiers claimed the letter of their contract—to leave the service at the expiration of one year; and the weak legislators at Richmond thought it necessary to indulge what was called their democratic sense of individuality, by allowing them to reduce the organization and discipline of the army to whatever standards would content them, and to convert their camps into a carnival of misrule, and into the vilest scenes of electioneering for commissions. This so-called "reorganization" had gone on in the face of an enemy who, if he had taken timely advantage of it, would have found little else than demoralized men, disgracing the uniform of soldiers, covering the most vital points of the Confederacy. Every candidate who was anxious to serve his country with braid on his shoulders, plied the men with the lowest arts of the cross-roads politician, even to the argument of whiskey, and contributed to the general demoralization—until the men, feeling the power to dethrone their present officers, lost all respect for their authority, and became the miserable tools of every adventurer and charlatan who imposed upon their confidence.

Not satisfied with demoralizing the army, another legislative measure was passed, some months later, under the inspiration of Mr. Davis, to deplete it. With the professed purpose of inciting re-enlistments, it was provided that furloughs for sixty days should be granted all those soldiers who would re-enlist for three years or the war—said furloughs to be dealt out in lots drawn from each company. The consequence was, the Southern armies wasted away in front of the enemy, and at a most critical period, when he was completing his own elaborate and imposing preparations for the spring campaign of 1862. Those who lived in Richmond in those times, will remember the flocks of soldiers passing through its streets to their homes, in magnitude of numbers almost an army—sometimes, in a single day, an unbroken throng stretching from the depot on Broad street to the bridge over the James. It appeared as if the army in Northern Virginia had disbanded. The newspapers could not use remonstrance; and, how narrow was their field for critical discussion, may be understood from the fact that they were enjoined to make no reference that could possibly be construed as revealing any weakness in the Confederacy, so as "to give information to the enemy." This absurd rule was practised on the press sometimes to the point of puerility; and once, it is known, that Secretary Benjamin prepared an order to suppress the Richmond *Examiner*, because its criticisms of public affairs gave information to the enemy. Mr. Davis prudently declined to sign the order, and Mr. Benjamin, or his successors, never dared to repeat the experiment on a free and virile press. But though, in the instance of public danger referred to, the press was dumb, the Generals commanding in the field were not. They took the alarm before it was too late. Generals Johnston and Beauregard united in letters of protest, and it was only when they intimated that they would resign their commands, before their forces should be spirited away by foolish legislation, that Congress repealed the disastrous law; or, rather, unwilling to incur the appearance of concession, suffered its operations to be withheld by military orders.

In the civil or internal administration of Confederate affairs, Mr. Davis was not more happy than in the conduct of the war. He had created a great scandal in his Cabinet; the support of the public was slipping from him; his government was weak and insecure of the confidence of the people. It is remarkable of the civil administration of the Confederacy that in the entire history of it there is not to be pointed out one *act of statesmanship.* There was no breadth in any of its measures; they were partial and halting, make-shifts and afterthoughts; and he who writes truly of the war, whatever he may have to commemorate of the valor of Southern soldiers or of the devotion of Southern leaders, must yet note the sad absence of enterprise, genius and energy in the conduct of public affairs.

Before the war the Southern mind was supposed to have peculiarly the gift of *statesmanship.* It had contributed most of the political literature of the country; it had reigned in the councils of the old government. But it was a speculative statesmanship that achieved these honors; the Southern mind lacked the faculty of *business;* and in the practical art of government, just that talent in which the South was supposed to be superior to the North, it was beaten at every point. No politician of his day could split hairs between State

Rights and the Constitution with more skill and dexterity than Jefferson Davis; but when it came to the practical cares of administering the affairs of eight millions of people he was as ignorant as a child, and had nothing to offer but weak and blundering imitations of the government from which he had professed to depart. The summary description of his administration is that it was a pale reflex of what was taking place at Washington. He copied the Constitution of the United States with all its patches of departments and bureaus; he reproduced all the old routine of Washington, and he even imported men from there to assist him in various branches of his government. There was no political invention in Richmond. A government in the position of a seceder, if not of a rebel, was so utterly destitute of statesmanship, so devoid of intellectual force and originality, as to follow with halting and apish imitations upon the government it had forsaken and denounced.

Mr. Davis produced not one good invention of political management; and submitting that the war was a question of political management as well as of arms, we have a new measure of the responsibility of this single man for the loss of the Southern cause. He had no talent for government. This defect alone would have turned the balance of the war, without the conspiracy of other causes. He had every thing at command: a willing and docile people, brave soldiers, competent officers, a territory large and difficult to conquer. It is against all these we must measure his responsibility. As we enumerate advantage after advantage of the South, we narrow the hypothesis as to the cause of its failure, until at last it must come down by logical reduction to one man—he the ruler who permitted these advantages to be conquered through an imbecile and barren administration. The South did not need men or means: it needed statesmanship to direct and employ them. The definition of what was needed at Richmond was thus given in one of its journals:—"the foresight that perceives, but is not appalled by coming misfortunes; the hard sense, the vigorous command, the courage that flames up from defeat and rebounds unhurt from disaster, the manly confidence in others, the strength of body, as well as of mind, which supports and renews them all." But here was a man who had no foresight; who was blind to the preparations of the enemy; who had refused fortune when it had been thrust upon him at Manassas; who had allowed magnificent armies that rushed forward in the first months of the war to dwindle into insignificance; who scorned common sense; who was vigorous only in his obstinacy; who was jealous of all intellect that had already been marked by the public judgment; who had a broken physical constitution and a querulous disease; an accomplished scholar who knew much more of the hieroglyphs of Egypt than of the art of government, a literary dyspeptic who had more ink than blood in his veins, and an intriguer who, busy with private enmities, and encircled by the fire they kindled, was stinging himself to death! No wonder the South was doomed to early failure under such a leader!

Complaints were already breaking out against the administration of Mr. Davis as the people began to feel the actual distress of the war and thus to have their eyes turned to the improvidence of the government. It was seen that clothing and arms were deficient for the army, when they might have been easily imported before the blockade had been confirmed. At Montgomery the Government had thought it quite sufficient to order eight thousand stand of small-arms from Europe. When the blockade became binding, it was said that the commercial enterprise of England would at once be excited by the high prices it would establish to send forward cargoes of arms, munitions, medicines and other stores most needed; but this calculation had proved delusive, and such was the distress for arms that the Governors of several of the States were obliged to issue appeals to the citizens to contribute their shot guns and fowling-pieces to arm the Confederate troops. In some cases appropriations were made to manufacture pikes, and there were regiments who had no weapon but shafts of tough wood pointed with steel. But besides this scantiness of the very implements of war, there were other complaints to be ascribed to the stupidity of the government, its want of foresight and its deception of the people.

Not only had the opportunity not been taken to bring in supplies from Europe when the ports of the Confederacy were open, but Mr. Davis had actually welcomed the blockade, and vaunted it as a blessing in disguise. He had hoped that the manufacturing necessities of England and France would force them to a speedy recognition of the Confederacy, and to an interference with the blockade. But there was no evidence of these manufacturing necessities at the end of the year. The supply of cotton was as large in Liverpool at the beginning of 1862 as at the beginning of 1861, although the blockade of the Southern ports had then existed more than six months. "King Cotton" was already dethroned. Meanwhile an agricultural people who had always relied on the sale of the year's crops had found no market; and the complaints of crippled planters were added to the volume of recrimination against the government.

The financial embarrassment of the Confederacy had already commenced. There could be no greater cause of alarm to those intelligent persons who understood that war required money as well as men, that it could not be carried on by a mere sentiment. Indeed the finance of the Confederacy was a vital element of the situation, and is a distinct part of the political life of Mr. Davis not to be omitted. But the subject is large and distinct enough for a separate treatment, and it may well fill another chapter.

CHAPTER XII.

The Finances of the Southern Confederacy—Early Measures of Taxation at Montgomery—A Civil List Voted of a Million and a half Dollars—The Five Million Loan—Deficiency of American Politicians in Finance—Extreme and Grotesque Ignorance of Mr. Davis on this Subject—Secretary Memminger a Curiosity in his Cabinet—A Race of Absurd Fancies—History of the Produce Loan—Extravagant Expectations from it—Its Complete and Ludicrous Failure—Mr. DeBow's Office "To Let"—The Confederate Government Abandons its First Proposition of Finance—How the Commissariat was Relieved—History of a Grand Financial Scheme—Proposition for the Government to Buy all the Cotton in the South—Extraordinary Virtues of this Scheme—It might have Decided the War—How Mr. Memminger Derided the Scheme—Mr. Davis's After-thought in the Prison at Fortress Monroe—A Shallow and Miserable Subterfuge—Supplements of the Financial Policy of the Confederacy—Conversion of Private Debts Due in the North—The Sequestration Law—The Administration of Mr. Davis Challenged on it—A Scathing Denunciation by Mr. Pettigru, of South Carolina—Mr. Davis Attempts to Use the Credit of the States—He Fails in this Recourse—His Government Thrown Back to the Beginning of its Financial Policy—He Proposes Paper Money as a Panacea—Distinction Between Currency and Revenue—Stupidity of Mr. Davis in Financial Matters—The First Seeds of Corruption Sown in the Confederate Finance—Mr. Memminger's Funding Juggle—"Flush Times" in Richmond—Silly Self-Congratulations of the President—The Road to Ruin.

THE Confederate Government had commenced its career with but small concern for its finances. When established at Montgomery, it had, mistaking the resolution of the North, scarcely entertained a thought of actual war—at least, the anticipation of such was at once too limited and too light to have founded upon it much legislation. And, besides, the authorities then were naturally anxious not to alarm, by a too early apparition of taxation (perhaps the severest test of the popular courage and devotion in any cause) the people then being brought under the experiment of a new government. Indeed, we may remark by the way, that the constitutional dread of taxation inseparable from the public mind, was somewhat adroitly turned by the Montgomery Congress, to decide the border States, then hesitating to enter the new Confederacy, and to suggest to the North a new argument against war, and a special inducement to contract early relations of friendship and reciprocity with the new Republic. As early as April, 1861, a stringent law had been passed, exacting heavy duties on all goods coming into the then six federated States from coterminous territory; and among the first serious duties of Mr. Memminger, Secretary of the Treasury, was to prepare elaborate circulars establishing "Revenue stations" on the land frontier, where the duties and tolls were to be collected, and the railroad trains halted and visited. The freedom of trade, was a concession which the new government reserved, for political effect, and it was undoubtedly used with some advantage in persuading the reluctant Border States to throw their commercial interests, as well as their political destinies, with the Confederacy.

It is in curious contrast with later experiences of the war, to observe with what hesitation and closeness the Confederate Government commenced, in the article of expenditures. The whole civil list voted at Montgomery was but $1,468,196. The first military appropriation, to be added to this, was $1,323,767, for the equipment and support of *three thousand* troops for twelve months! This was before Mr. Lincoln's inauguration. But only two days had elapsed after he had appeared officially in Washington and made that equivocal speech, which the South generally interpreted as war, when the Montgomery Congress, opening its eyes somewhat to the width of the prospect before it, voted to raise one hundred thousand volunteers. From this point the appreciation of the impending crisis may be said to have enlarged, the scale of finance keeping even pace with it, and thus affording a curious measure of the growing volume of public expectation concerning the war.

The first notable financial measure of the new government was to advertise for a loan of five millions of dollars. Three millions were subscribed in excess, and the whole amount was taken, represented by bonds bearing eight per cent. interest. When the war had become flagrant, and the Government had removed to Richmond, with a larger representation, and an appreciation comparatively heightened of the struggle in which it had now actually engaged, it became necessary to found a permanent scheme of finance; and the Provisional Congress was early perplexed with this, at once the most difficult and delicate problem of new governments.

There is nothing in which the Confederate Government halted and blundered worse, even from the first stages in its career, and wherein it more strongly illustrated its puerility of device, than its financial policy. It has been generally remarked, how sadly deficient the public men of America are in finance—a branch of statesmanship which the European politician is taught to consider the most important part of his education, and his most available fund of popularity. The fact is, that in our government, preceding the war, so little did it know of pecuniary necessities—a distress common to European governments—with a revenue generally in excess of its expenditures, and with an almost nominal public debt, that our politicians were satisfied to be ignorant of finance, and scarcely ever felt such want of knowledge in their speeches and canvasses of popular favor. The single phase of this subject in our politics, was the tariff; and that was exceptional, and scarcely ever treated as an independent measure of finance, outside of its sectional relations as between North and South. Its significance was sectional rather than financial. Among our most accomplished politicians, before the war, it was rare to find one who had a head for figures, or who would venture before a popular audience on a subject which he esteemed so dry, and so incapable of rhetorical effects. Jefferson Davis was not only no exception to this rule, but he was a most remarkable example of it. He had more than usual breadth of cultivation for an American politician. His fund of historical illustration was large and facile; he had an extensive acquaintance with general literature; and his habits were those of a student. And yet, as the war showed him, he was ignorant of finance, even to the point of grotesqueness, and on that subject full of childish devices, which can only be related now to amuse the world. Unhappily, he added to his own deficiencies in this respect by an absurd, almost inexplicable choice of his Secretary of the Treasury. Instead of calling to his aid, in that department, one having some former experience in, or particular knowledge of financial matters, who might supply his own defect of education therein, he selected a man who knew even less of these matters than himself—who competed with him in ignorance—who encouraged his tendency to vagaries—and who redoubled that fondness of inventions and reforms, in which the smatterer is characteristically bold. It was a most unfortunate trait of Mr. Davis to imagine that his abilities laid precisely in that direction in which he had none; and the fruit of this dangerous conceit, was a shallow and whimsical character of inventions, nowhere more remarkably displayed than in his various suggestions on the subject of finance. Mr. Memminger had very much the same order of mind, which mistakes its vocation; and through the joined conceits of the two, the field of Confederate finance was populated with grotesque and absurd fancies. What could have determined Mr. Davis to make this man Secretary of the Treasury, has not been discovered to the author. He had been known in South Carolina only as a lawyer. He had the hard, unsympathizing face of that profession, manners almost rude, and an unpleasant eccentricity—a curious man—a zealot in religion, who had an almost insane passion for controversial theology—and who appeared much more in character, poking among the bookstores of Richmond and hunting recondite works on the religious beliefs of a former age, than performing the duties of financier of the Confederate States, and supplying its vulgar needs of money.

The first fruit of the financial consultations in Richmond was what was popularly known as "the Produce Loan." Mr. Davis, with an effort at modesty, has referred to this measure as "one happily devised by the superior wisdom of Congress;" but it is certain that he inspired it, accepting the consummation by Congress of his wishes on this subject with unusual affability. The scheme was a singular one, ingeniously partaking both of the character of a patriotic contribution and a thrifty loan. It was proposed that the producers of the Confederacy, particularly those of cotton and tobacco, should subscribe portions of their annual crops to the government, not in the sense of segregating it in kind, or of actual delivery, but on condition that when the crop was sold in regular way—a particular day designated for the sale so as to give certainty to the contract—the factor or commission merchant should invest a part of the proceeds corresponding to the amount of subscription, in bonds of the government bearing eight per cent. interest. The plan looked excellent on paper. The planter was not to part with his crop; there was to be no inconvenience of delivery in kind; the whole scheme rested on the assumption that the subscriptions might be used by the government as credits, and thus sustain the value of its promises to pay in shape of currency. The government regarded it as a model of financial wisdom, appealing to the patriotism of the producer, as well as consulting his selfishness, by offering him a good investment; and, for some time, it appeared, indeed, to have reason to congratulate itself on its ingenuity.

Commissioners were appointed to canvass every square mile of territory in the Confederacy. A separate bureau to manage the loan was organized in Richmond, the lamented J. D. B. De Bow being its head. The progress of subscriptions was watched with the greatest solicitude by the public; the reporters of the newspapers visited almost every day the office of the chief commissioner and published the list of subscriptions to excite the competition of particular districts. On the 20th of July, 1861, it was announced by the government with ill-restrained delight, and to the lively gratification of the public, that the Produce Loan, estimated by values, had already reached fifty millions of dollars, and by the close of the year might be expected to touch the magnificent sum of one hundred millions.

When the year did close, the Produce Loan had disappeared; no one knew of it, no one inquired of it, no one cared for it. In reality it had ceased to exist; it had already passed into history as one of the most complete failures and notable absurdities of the Confederacy. The bureau, which had been so ostentatiously constructed was discontinued; the office-rooms which Mr. De Bow had so handsomely furnished, and which had been the rendezvous of politicians and reporters, were closed and "to let;" and actually all that remained of this magnificent loan were the dead leaves of paper on which its figures had been marshalled.

What had become of it? It had died strangely, quietly but surely, of defects inherent in the scheme. Of these defects the dull government had, after its usual fashion of discovery, been convinced only on experiment; and its first important proposition of finance it uterly abandoned without explanation or excuses to the public. It had failed to perceive until experience demonstrated the obvious consideration that without markets the cotton and tobacco were not available as it had designed them; and that in proportion as they were not so available, the credits founded solely on the prospect of sale, represented in the planters' subscriptions, were of no account. There were other fatal difficulties. The essential virtue of the contract between the government and the planter was that the crop should be sold at some *certain*—even if distant—day; the certainty of the sale founding the credit, the time in which an obligation is to run rather improving than impairing it in financial estimation as long as it is sure of performance. But it was impossible to guaranty such certainty, and thus obtain credit for the transaction. The crop might be burned, or otherwise destroyed, in the ravages of the war; the planter might become bankrupt; if he refused to sell on a falling or disadvantageous market, the government had practically no power to compel him, and, indeed it would have incurred a great moral guilt and shame in forcing a sale in circumstances which might be ruinous to a patriotic citizen standing in the light of its benefactor and creditor. A scheme hedged with such uncertainties could, of course, not be used as a source of credit; it was defective in almost every particular; and the government, after a short trial, abandoned it, but not until it had displayed that disposition for nice and paltry empiricisms which was hereafter to afflict nearly all the public affairs of the Confederacy.

But while the Produce Loan was thus essentially a failure —even to the point, as we have seen of utter abandonment— it was incidentally not without benefits. Where the crops were other than cotton or tobacco, such as grain, meat, etc., special arrangements were effected to take the subscriptions in kind, and they were made immediately available as army supplies. In this way the Confederate commissariat was considerably relieved, and the greater part of the subsistence of the army was obtained at first hand without the intervention of purchasers. This, to some extent was an advantage; but a more considerable benefit of the Produce Loan was its suggestion of a much larger scheme in which what there was of virtue in this loan was logically extended to a wider conclusion, and whereon might have been founded one of the most admirable financial systems of modern times. This imperfect loan was the germ in fact of an idea which might have saved the financial integrity of the Confederacy, and not remotely turned the balance of the war.

The subscriptions of the planters to the Produce Loan naturally furnished, in their estimation, some ground for reclamation on the government. Those men, in want of a market, soon became distressed for ready means; they applied to the government for assistance in the nature of advances; this was properly refused as invidious to others of the public; and out of these embarrassments, ultimately and naturally grew the proposition that the government should take absolute possession and control of the whole cotton crop of the South, at a stipulated price, the minimum of the market. It was to employ and control the crop in its own right, as purchaser, unfettered, as in the Produce Loan, by uncertain and speculative agreements with the planter.

A grand scheme was offered the government thus to utilize

the main bulk of the wealth of the South; and under this arrangement cotton, indeed, instead of remaining an idle hoard in the war, might have asserted something of that regal influence, which the early politicians of the Confederacy had ascribed to it. The newspaper press enlarged upon the idea thrown out by the necessities of the planters, but commensurate with the interests of the country, and discovered in it the breadth of a financial scheme, which would have answered all the exigencies and expectations of the war. The Richmond *Dispatch* calculated, that with the cotton crop, purchased and deposited in England, the government, at the then prevailing prices for this staple, might make a clear profit of six hundred millions of dollars, even allowing twenty cents a pound to the planter, and supposing that one-fifth of the cargoes was captured by the enemy—a balance in favor of the Confederacy that would have enabled it to drain every bank in Europe of specie, or if drawn upon as its need required, would have made its treasury notes equal to gold.

But the planters were willing to sell at seven cents a pound, and the blockade being yet unadjusted, and most of the ports of the Confederacy being actually open, the proportion of captures would have been slight; and the correct basis of estimate was three million and a half bales of cotton, at the maximum price, as the government could have held it in Europe for the highest rise of the market, which, even in the second year of the war had advanced to seventy or eighty cents a pound. The imagination is dazzled contemplating the financial consequences in reach of the Confederate rulers. The government commenced in such narrow pecuniary fortunes, and ultimately squandered in make-shifts, had really the elements of one of the most successful and elastic schemes of finance that the world had seen. In its cotton it had a store of wealth that might have been easily mobilized, and a basis of credit which, extending as the price of the staple advanced, would thus have kept progress with the war, supplied all its necessities, and furnished an evidence of Southern prosperity and stability, that, acting powerfully on the opinion of the world and the avarice of the enemy, might have terminated the contest.

It is absolutely painful to review the argument and temper with which the Confederate Administration treated a proposition of finance that had really so many merits; to observe how it rejected and disdained a means of safety, that circumstances had, as if providentially, thrust upon it, aided, too, by reinforcements of public opinion. Mr. Memminger derided the scheme. In his private conversation he spoke of it as "soup-house legislation," charity to a class, which entailed expense to the whole community. In an official circular on the subject, dated the 17th October, 1861, he said: "No clause in the Constitution can be found which would sanction so stupendous a scheme as purchasing the entire crop of cotton." He objected that the government might "hazard its entire credit and stability. The experiment was too dangerous." The argument he used against the scheme deserves a conspicuous place among the curiosities of financial literature. He contended, that "the cotton would do the government no good, and that it would receive no benefit whatever from this advance. The money is paid to each individual planter; and in exchange the government receives only his bond or note; or, if the cotton be purchased, the government receives only certain bales of cotton, that is to say, the government pays out money which is needful to its very existence, and receives in exchange, planters' notes or produce, which it does not need, and cannot in any way make use of."

But the mind of the Secretary, so juvenile in financial matters, failed in this estimate to understand the simple idea of values, in the shape of credit, and he leaves out of account—what he appears never to have conceived in his whole financial career—the necessity of some basis for all forms and designs of currency. The cotton, even if held in Europe and not sold, would have served all the purposes of the Confederacy for credit, and would have kept its notes at par, while the "money," which Mr. Memminger regretted to see go out of the Treasury for what he considered a useless acquisition, was comparatively worthless, as long as it represented a promise to pay without anything to support it.

We are aware that in that convenient commentary which Mr. Davis is reported to have made in prison on Confederate affairs, and wherein he is as wise as the most foolish may be on retrospect, he has attempted to throw the discredit of the rejection of the Cotton Purchase wholly on his subordinate, Mr. Memminger, and to acquit himself of what he now perceives to have been an almost criminal absurdity. It is the invariable resort of weak men to attempt to cure their reputation by asserting prophetic visions of the event after it has happened; and Mr. Davis appears to have been busy with this work in the reflections of his prison at Fortress Monroe. He is there reported to have declared that Mr. Memminger defeated the financial plan referred to in opposition to his wishes; that he, the President, "*privately* approved it, but had not time to study and take the responsibility of directing it."

But this explanation of Mr. Davis is a dishonest afterthought—a shallow and miserable subterfuge from which he may be easily driven. He was the President of the Confederacy, and he was responsible for his agents, by every known rule of American Administration. Indeed this rule may be urged against him with exceptional force, considering how much he was disposed to assert his individuality in his Administration, in how many instances he removed subordinates even more important than Mr. Memminger and for even comparatively trifling opposition to his wishes, and how little likely he was to be controlled by any man in ordinary matters, much less in one that he has since protested to have felt at the time as of vital moment. It is not to be believed that the Confederate President, with his known habit or temper, would have allowed himself to be controlled by a man like Memminger remarkable for his servility, and that too in a matter which in his conversation since the war as a prisoner he declares "in itself would have insured victory." The attempt of Mr. Davis thus to shift responsibility for his misgovernment in an issue so important, is as weak as it is ungenerous. He summed the financial history of the Confederacy plainly enough, saying: "When we might have put silver in the purse, we did not put it there; when we had only silver on the tongue, our promises were found to become excessive." But unhappily this ingenious contrast had never occurred to him in Richmond; he appreciated the financial situation only after it had lapsed to ruin; and, like many another unfortunate, he lamented lost opportunities only at the end of his career, and within the walls that reduced him to imprisonment and reflection.

In addition to the Produce Loan and Cotton Purchase there were some other proposed measures to bring money into the Confederate Treasury. They were feeble supplements of the financial policy, and are chiefly remarkable for their large promises on paper and the small sums they realized. These financial aids—the measures were designed too, somewhat in a political or general sense—were a charge to all those owing money in the North to pay their debts into the Confederate

Treasury and thus acquit themselves, and the sequestration of the property of alien enemies, as were designated not only the people of the North, but all those who, since the war, had left the Confederacy as malcontents. The most dazzling estimates were made of these two singular sources of revenue. It was said the debts due the North amounted at least to two hundred millions of dollars, so accumulated had been the credits between the two sections before the war; and it was hoped that at least a large portion of this sum would be converted into the Confederate Treasury under the prospect of debtors thus escaping their obligations. The results of the sequestration law were calculated at scarcely less; and the writer recollects a careful estimate made in Congress, that the property and interests of Northern men in the city of New Orleans alone falling under the operations of this law, would amount to some thirty millions of dollars.

But these irregular schemes of finance, on which were entertained such visions of gain, broke down miserably and not without some dishonor. But few reputable persons in the South could make up their minds to compound debts, in which their honor was to some extent involved, and with which perhaps were mixed personal obligations and sentiments, by paying them into the Confederate Treasury to the deprivation and disowning of their creditors. The results of the sequestration law were yet more meagre. At the close of the year 1863, the fruits of this measure of large expectations were considerably less than two millions of dollars. Worse than this, provisions of this law for discovering Northern property by writs of "garnisheeing," and by interrogatories running into inquisitions of the private affairs of any man suspected by the officers of the law, were resented as a breach of the constitutional and traditional rights of the people, and raised perhaps the first signal of serious opposition to the new government with respect to the republican character of its measures. The cries of this opposition were numerous enough at another period of the war; but probably the administration of Mr. Davis on its inroad into the liberties of the people, never received a severer challenge than at this first stage of his experiment on the popular submission. The challenge in this instance was given by one of the most important citizens of the Confederacy—a declared Secessionist—and happily from the elevation and purity of his character, a man whose motives of opposition could not be misunderstood. This man was J. S. Pettigru, a distinguished lawyer of Charleston. In a case in which he was interested, he went into open court, defied the sequestration law, spoke with surpassing eloquence for hours against it, and denounced it as "an act borrowed from the darkest period of tyranny, and a relic of the past dug up from the quarries of despotism." These were stinging words for the hitherto soothed ear of Mr. Davis, where had entered yet scarcely anything but the competing voices of flattery or the pleasing tones of submission. The newspapers published the speech of Mr. Pettigru with hesitation, but not without a secret sympathy with its expressions, or at least some ardor of admiration for the courage that could speak thus boldy and scorn every advantage but that of truth.

Meanwhile the Confederate Government was plunging further into financial confusion and embarassment and on this subject was actually at the end of its wits. With the abandonment of the Produce Loan, the rejection of the Cotton Purchase, and the failure of other measures to replenish the treasury, the government was now completely at sea in its financial policy. The serious question was to obtain means to carry on a war which was constantly enlarging. The Confederate Government, having rejected the plan, referred to, of utilizing the cotton had really no credit but what was dependent on the fortune of the war. The States of course as permanent political bodies which were expected to survive any event of the war had their credit comparatively unimpaired; and Mr. Davis earnestly recommended that they should aid the general government in the war to the extent of equipping and paying their respective troops in the field. But here again the argument which moved the President to this appeal, though ingenious, was weak and contained a fatal fallacy. The aid thus given by the State Governments to that extent enfeebled the resources of the whole people of the Confederacy; it was only a devious process where the results did not differ, and which only made more certain the conclusion of general bankruptcy. As it was, the "war-debts" of the States contracted by this use of their credit were inconsiderable, and amounted only to a few millions of dollars.

The Confederate Government was thrown back to the beginning of its financial policy. In its bewilderment it had recourse to a policy always attractive from its simplicity, but universally fatal—the vice of making paper money illimitably; the mistake of using currency as revenue. Mr. Davis's Administration, we repeat, was ignorant of the most primitive truths of finance; and it never showed that ignorance more recklessly than when it relied upon the manufacture of a revenue out of naked paper obligations. Indeed, the science of political economy on this subject is not difficult. The proper use of paper money is only as a currency, a means to facilitate exchanges; it is limited by the wants of the community for a circulating medium; and all issues in excess of this, in the vain illusion of creating values, is quite as fatal as the empiricism which debases the coin of a country to increase the revenue of the government. There are briefly no royal ways of making money out of nothing; governments must raise money in the legitimate way of taxation, loans, etc.; its paper currency is not money except as limited by the necessities of exchange, and based upon values commensurate in the shape of credits.

In the month of July, 1861, the Provisional Congress passed a law authorizing the issue of one hundred millions of Treasury notes. At the same time it enacted a tax-bill—the first attempt at direct burdens on the people;—but it was calculated to raise only fifteen millions of dollars, leaving all the expenditures of the war in excess of this sum to be provided for by issues of paper money, which, of course, to this extent were translated from currency into revenue, and put on the inevitable road to depreciation. Thus was the financial doom of the Confederacy early pronounced. The door, once opened to paper issues, was not easily closed; other issues than that just mentioned followed; when the Confederacy entered the second year of the war, it was already carrying a volume of currency four times what were the wants of the community for a circulating medium; and from this time, Treasury notes fell rapidly—first 20 per cent. less than gold; 50 per cent. three months later; 225 per cent. in December, 1862; 400 per cent. in the spring of 1863, and thereafter, until 6,000 per cent. was the last measure of its value, at which Mr. Memminger exchanged it at his counters.

But we cannot anticipate here so much of the history of the Confederate currency. We are writing now only of that period in which the first design of paper became fixed in the mind of Mr. Davis's Administration, and referring to the law which sowed the first seed of corruption. This law was afterwards aggravated by another invention of Mr. Memminger—that of funding the Treasury notes by a certain compulsion, making arbitrary reductions of interest in case they remained unfunded after certain dates. It can be described only as the very multiplication of ignorance.

It was easy to see that slight differences in rates of interest would afford but feeble inducements for the conversion of the treasury note into a bond, when money was easily doubled or quadrupled in the active commercial speculations peculiar to the condition of the South in the war, unless the bond could be readily used as a medium of exchange; and in that event there would only be a change in the form of the paper, the volume of the currency would be undiminished, and its depreciation therefore remain the same. But while the analysis of this system of funding showed it to be a transparent juggle, it was by no means certain that it did not contain the germ of many positive evils. The right of a government to make arbitrary changes in any of the terms of its obligations which affect their value, is questionable, and the commercial honor of such an expedient is more than doubtful. Thus, with the first issues of paper money, came the shadow of repudiation, as if the Government had determined to make double assurance of the financial wreck of the country.

There could be no doubt of the final event of ruin. The Government had nothing, owned nothing; it had laid only inconsiderable taxes; it had fallen upon the mistake, fatal in all financial experience—of confounding the two distinct topics of currency and revenue. The history of the paper money of the Confederacy is briefly that of all schemes of redundant currency—commencing with a great show of factitious prosperity, and thus cheating for a time the imagination, but invariably ending in universal bankruptcy and ruin.

For the present Mr. Davis saw only the first of these conditions. He was delighted, and even gleeful, at the easy way of making money.* The printers and the engravers, and the five hundred women who clipped the notes, were kept busy in Richmond; all business appeared to improve, activity was everywhere visible; the fever of a redundant currency was mistaken for high health, and Mr. Davis congratulating himself on his experiment, pointed with derision to the slow and painful financial tasks of the North. What extravagances he uttered on this subject, when he officially summed the events of the first year of the war, we shall elsewhere notice. It is unnecessary to anticipate. There could be but one end to the system of Confederate finance; its final condition of collapse was as certain as the first of inflation. The law of supply and demand is as applicable to money as to anything else; it punishes all who violate it, and, however it may operate unseen by the tyro or empiric, it is as certain, as supreme, and as inexorable as the law of gravitation.

---

* If any one doubts the financial ignorance of Mr. Davis, or questions the extent of his responsibility for the excessive paper money of the Confederacy, let him read his Message as late as August, 1862, advising Congress to issue yet more Treasury notes, without fear of their depreciation, viz.:—"The legislation of the last session provided for the purchase of supplies with the bonds of the government, but the preference of the people for Treasury notes has been so marked, that legislation is recommended to authorize an increase in the issue of Treasury notes, which the public service seems to require. No grave inconvenience need be apprehended from this increased issue, as the provision of law by which these notes are convertible into eight per cent. bonds, forms an efficient and permanent safeguard against any serious depreciation of the currency."

CHAPTER XIII.

John M. Daniel's New Year's Article—A Philosopher's Mourn for the Union—No Thought yet of the Subjugation of the South—Analysis of the Popular Sentiment, concerning President Davis—Description of the Military Lines of the Confederacy—Reflections on the Spirit and Character of the Southern People—Their Conceit about the War—The "Raccoon Roughs," and Mr. Lincoln's Hair—Why Mr. Davis was not Excusable for his Short Vision in the War—A Train of Disasters—Alarm and Demoralization of the People—A Cruel Mistake concerning General A. S. Johnston—Inauguration of Mr. Davis as Permanent President—A Gloomy Scene in the Public Square at Richmond—Piteous Prayer of the President—Significance of the Change from a Provisional to a Permanent Form of Government—Some Account of a Secret Debate at Montgomery—Why the Adoption of a Permanent Constitution was a Mistake—The New Congress at Richmond—Significant Speech of Speaker Bocock—Who was the author of the Conscription Law?—How Narrowly it Saved the Confederacy—A Statement of President Davis Shamelessly False—Two Remarkable Men in the Confederate Congress—Mr. Foote ("*Gubernator Pes*,") of Mississippi—Mr. Boyce of South Carolina—A Remarkable Effort of these Two Men to Impel the Confederate Armies into the North—The Effort is Defeated—Traces of a Remarkable Conspiracy.

JOHN M. DANIEL, the famous editor of Virgiana, wrote but seldom in the columns of the Richmond *Examiner*, and was the actual author of but few of the articles in his paper. He always insisted, however, on writing a New Year's article, summing events in an historical tone, and bestowing on them some reflections of philosophy. That which he wrote on the 1st of January, 1862, we have always thought the finest composition of his pen, an example of lofty and elaborate style; yet most remarkable for its thoughtful sorrow on the events of the past year. It was the mourn of a philosopher, on what he imagined to be the ruins of a once great and happy government.

He wrote:—" The end of the year just passed fills the mind " with melancholy reflections on the vanity of human wishes, "the instability of human creations, and the frivolity of all the "thoughts of man. Where now is that wonderful country "which realized the political dream of philosophers and "patriots;—that grand temple of liberty, built for eternal "duration; that perfect commonwealth, which gave the lie to "all the ages, and proved the self-government of nations to be "something more than the fable of a noble, but irrational, "imagination? What has become of that splendid illusion "which shed its lustre on the opening mind of the American "youth—the lofty thought, that he was born and would live "in a glorious republic of heroic States and free citizens, "whose title was above the royal rank, and whose birth-right "was the envy of the world? One short year has ended both "alike. The 'star-pointing-pyramid' has proven a tower of "Babel; that noble faith in the virtue and intelligence of the "soil's sons has given place to a disgust and indignation, too "deep for utterance in words; and on the plains where per-"petual peace was supposed to have made her settled seat, "war, with all its original savagery, reigns undisputed. The "catastrophe, brought by the year that ended yesterday, leaves "us not even the sombre consolation of the grandeur that has "attended the ruin of other empires. The majestic fabric fell "not beneath the giant hand of an invading race, or before "the blazing ambition of a secular genius. Enfeebled by the "cankers of inaction, and gnawed by the teeth of vermin, it "has gone down like a ship, whose timbers have been the un-"suspected prey of worms and mice. Few, who meditated 'yesterday on these things, have not felt the justice of that "contempt for the conceited animal called man, his pursuits "and his projects, which religion and philosophy inculcate, "but few have realized before."

The paragraph quoted, expressed the almost universal

thought of the South, to the effect that the Union was hopelessly gone, irrevocably destroyed—that this fabric of government, once esteemed so fair, had fallen to shapeless ruin, and that it remained only to construct out of the foregone conclusion of the war, a new political experiment. But few persons yet doubted the ultimate conclusion of the contest in the independence and separate government of the South. So far all that was feared or complained of in the Administration of Mr. Davis, was that it delayed the inevitable result of the war, and that it might unnecessarily increase the price that the South was to pay for her independence. This was the extent of uneasiness in the Confederacy. The ultimate faith in its successful emergence from the war was not yet seriously diminished; the popular outcry was only that the Richmond Administration was making the war harder than was necessary; was exasperating its evils, by errors in its policy, and was enlarging its sufferings and sacrifices, by trials of its own creation. The thought of subjugation and of a re-affirmation of the Union had not yet, to any considerable extent, entered the Southern mind; and this, although the Confederacy had not made any visible progress since the victory of Manassas, and although the enemy was making vast preparations for the second year of the war. But it must be remembered that these preparations had not yet been unveiled, and even the rumors of these were subjects of equivocation in the press. On the other hand, the Confederate extreme line of defence was, as yet, unbroken, had not yet been assailed; and Mr. Davis's policy of dispersion, while it really weakened the substance of Confederate defence, yet made a very imposing and extravagant spectacle to the populace. It was a grand task for the eye to sweep a line of posts from the Atlantic ocean to the Mississippi river; a magnificent thing to be plotted on paper: a brilliant meretricious display, vastly pleasing to the vulgar observation, however offensive to military calculation. Here was a line of defence extending from Columbus, Kentucky, eastward through Bowling Green, the Cumberland river post, with advances on the Big Sandy and Kanawha rivers, Staunton, Winchester, Leesburg, Centreville, Aquia Creek, and the Potomac. This line yet rested near the verge of the enemy's territory. With what force it was threatened, and what powers it had to resist, were but little thought of by the many persons in the South, who were imposed upon by such geographical magnificence of defence; who calculated on their maps that if the Confederacy was to be conquered by square miles, it would be an endless labor; and who thus assured themselves that, however Mr. Davis, or his unworthy favorites might misconduct the war, they could only add to its term, they could not endanger its final result. The public mind of the Confederacy had, indeed, been disturbed by the maladministration of Mr. Davis, but it had not yet taken any serious alarm as to the possibility of subjugation.

It is convenient here to reflect on an excuse frequently made by the partisans of Mr. Davis, as to his alleged over-confidence in the success of the South, and his short-sighted regard of the enemy. It is plausibly said that if such was his fault, nearly the whole popular sentiment of the South shared in it, and that in this he did nothing more than reflect the prevalent opinion of the Confederate public. What is here suggested of the imperfect and conceited vision of the people of the South, concerning the war, is unquestionably true; but the excuse it would prefer for Mr. Davis and his Administration, is, as we shall presently see, of but little avail, and of an essentially fallacious nature.

The character of the Southern people is but little understood by the world, and it has so long been a show-stock to mankind in the matter of slavery that it is difficult to exhibit it unless through mists of prejudice. There are great defects in that character—peculiar defects of accident; but there is also in it the sum of many virtues. The people of the South are brave to a fault, they are generous to credulity, polite, hospitable, cherishing many noble virtues which the commercial spirit of the age has elsewhere outgrown; but they have all the peculiar faults of an *untravelled* people—a people who pass their lives in local neighborhoods, and who having but little idea of how large and various the world is, easily take conceit of their own powers and virtues. The worst faults of the Southern mind are to be traced to the isolation of agricultural pursuits and to peculiar habits of local attachment added to that. A people untravelled have high ideas of their own importance, are morbidly sensitive to criticism, and are remarkable for a certain puerility measured by the standards of the world. Men for whom the sun rises or sets in a particular county or State are not apt to take just views of the extent and variety of the world beyond them. It may thus at least in a measure be explained why the South was so long in obtaining an idea of the immense resources of the North against which she had to contend in the war, and with what extravagent conceit she commenced the contest. The soldiers who at the commencement of the war thought their flags would be flying in Washington in a few weeks, and the "Raccoon Roughs" who had promised the sweet-hearts they had left in their native mountains, to bring them back a lock of Abraham Lincoln's hair were really honest, sincere fellows. They saw the hills and valleys pouring out men; many of them had never been in a Northern city; they were unaccustomed to see large collections of people, unused to multitudes and in the simplicity of their hearts they believed the South was making a display of force that could sweep the continent, and that in a month would be able to exhibit Abraham Lincoln in the cage that popular imagination had designed for him.

But Jefferson Davis knew better. He had facilities of knowledge which the public did not have; he knew the exact amount of the enemy's resources; he had secret agents and emissaries in the North, and its preparations for the next campaign were dinned into his ears. But even omitting his official facilities for information as to the strength and temper of the enemy, the argument that he is to be held excusable for short vision and imperfect judgments of the war, because the public was alike defective, is impudently fallacious, would destroy the responsibility of all rulers, and would deny the existence of such a thing as the science of government. It is the business and education of rulers to be superior to the masses in public affairs; else government is nothing but the lowest demagogism, the *alter ego* of the populace. The specialty of the statesman is prescience; he is supposed to be able to advise and warn the common people, to see what they do not see, and to direct what they do not understand. Not that a miraculous gift is expected from him; only a special accomplishment within the limits of human power. If the person called to preside over the destinies of several millions of people, and standing on the chief eminence of authority, his vision increased by all possible artificial aids, could yet see no more than they did, and if his ignorance is to be excused by whatever of popular ignorance was extant at the same time, then Jefferson Davis was a supernumerary, and had no right to be in the place he had assumed. It is impossible by such arguments as that referred to, to refine away the responsibility of great historical actors, or to distribute it through the multitude. Mr. Davis is to be judged as President of the Southern Confederacy, and not as a single distinguished citizen. As the latter, he might have pardonably erred with the majority of the people; but as the President, he is to be judged as the head of every other government is judged in history, not forgetting that responsibility is the correlative of trust, as duty is that of power.

The alarm with which the heart of the South was smitten in the beginning of 1862, came with sudden and terrible effect. It was a series of disasters, the force of which the newspapers could not break by their stories of "blessings in disguise" and the happy losses of barren positions; a blow to the hopes of the South which could not be muffled by equivocal dispatches from the War Department. The truth could no longer be avoided by official circumlocution. Even the few persons in the South who had foreseen and calculated the preparations of the enemy were taken by surprise; they had expected demonstrations only in the next spring or summer; they had scarcely imagined that in mid-winter, when the season proclaimed truce, the enemy would dare to have given a command of advance, sweeping across what was almost half a continent.

First came the fall of New Orleans, an event which staggered all the hopes of European recognition. Mr. Slidell wrote from Paris privately to Mr. Davis: "If New Orleans had not fallen, our recognition could not have been much longer delayed." The disaster at Fishing Creek broke the Confederate line in Kentucky. Then followed the capture of Forts Henry and Donelson, the evacuation of Bowling Green and Columbus, and the surrender of Nashville; the entire line of defence in the West was swept away, and the next array of the Confederates was formed on the lagoons of Mississippi. Roanoke

Island was captured with the army on it, and after a handfull of loss on the part of the enemy. It was silly of newspapers to speak of these losses as those only of mud forts and barren places; war is an affair of lines—a problem in geometry; and it was obvious to men of calculation and reflection, that with two sections of defence broken down, the enemy had got not only a new breadth of territory, but positions of the greatest value—and it is curious that the Confederates never recaptured anything, and that an important post once lost, was lost for ever. Meanwhile the army of McClellan hung like an ominous cloud on the horizon.

There was a general alarm and demoralization of the people west of the Alleghanies. It is not generally known that after the retreat of the Western army from Nashville, the Congressional delegation of Tennessee called on President Davis, and asked him to transfer the command of General Albert Sidney Johnston to some other person. It was a cruel mistake; for the protestants did not then know—as Mr. Davis was conveniently dumb—that the wide distribution of troops in the trans-Alleghany ordered by the President, had left Johnston with only 11,000 effective men to oppose Buell's column of 40,000 troops, while Grant's army of 60,000 had nothing to prevent them from ascending the Cumberland, leaving to the Confederate commander no alternative but to evacuate Nashville, or sacrifice his army.

In the midst of these disasters, Jefferson Davis was inaugurated President of the Confederate States, to continue in office for six years! A worse day than the 22d of February, 1862, could not have been selected for a ceremony so important. Mr. Davis delivered his inaugural speech at the statue of Washington, in the public square. It was the weakest and most unsatisfactory speech he ever made; and the crowd—if four or five hundred persons might be called such—listened gloomily to the imperfect tones of his voice. He dared not draw a presage from the skies of this day. At his first inauguration at Montgomery, he had spoken under smiling skies; and there he had said, with his rare aptitude to draw from circumstances:—"It may be that as this morning opened with clouds, rain and mist, we shall have to encounter inconveniences at the beginning; but as the sun rose and lifted the mist, it dispersed the clouds and left us to the pure sunshine of heaven." But the day of the second and more important inauguration was clothed with sable. There was a mean, hateful rain; the patterings on the hundred umbrellas held over the crowd drowned the voice of the speaker; people, sullen, damp, and drenched, did not care to stretch their ears to catch the voice of the President, and only pitied his bare head in the damp atmosphere. Not a single cheer broke the current of his speech; not a movement of the crowd betokened its emotion. It was a piteous address. The President stretched his arms towards the dark sky, and cried:—"To Thee, O God! I trustingly commit myself, and prayerfully invoke Thy blessing on my country and its cause." There was nothing of practical human comfort in his speech; he was forced to admit the disasters that had occurred, although "the final result in our favor was not doubtful;" he had not a word to kindle inspiration, not a reproof with which to flog the failing heart of the South; he had only this wretched nonsense to offer:—"*The period is near at hand, when our foes must sink under the immense load of debt they have incurred!*" The slouched and gloomy crowd heard him sullenly; and no sooner had he concluded, than from brutal curiosity, or from a desire to save themselves from the weather, they rushed to the halls of Congress to see the next dull feature of the programme.

The "provisional" government of the Confederacy was now displaced. It had been nothing more than a political structure, designed merely for carrying on a war, which it was supposed would continue for only a few months; and it is a fact not generally noticed or estimated, that it was designed at Montgomery to determine a *permanent* system of government for the South, only after the war had concluded, and to accommodate its results. The length and pre-occupation of the war defeated the detail of this design, and so busy was the South in its regards of the enemy in February, 1862—the period appointed for a permanent organization of the government—that there was no time for the political after-thought, no time to execute a design, which possibly lurked in the minds of some of the Southern leaders, to change the form of government; and thus the provisional passed into the permanent government with slight ceremony, with only the affirmation of a Constitution copied from Washington, and without even a canvass or an opposing candidate to question the succession of Mr. Davis to the Presidency, or to disturb his authority. He ascended from the mere provisional chief of a rebellion to the office of President of the Confederate States, for the term of six years, without question, without effort or concession, making no change whatever in his cabinet, or in the executive branches of his government.

But this curious political translation—the event of a day, marked only by a tawdry ceremony in the public square at Richmond—had a significance which the public did not perceive. It was not known how vexed in secret council had been the leaders at Montgomery, in the very outset of the war, as to this single point of the time of adopting a *permanent* government for the South; and it is not yet appreciated how vital was this question. It is only lately that one of the principal actors at Montgomery confessed to the author, that the adoption of a permanent form of Constitution by the South, while the war continued, was its fatal mistake, the main source of controversy that enfeebled and ruined it. At Montgomery there had been a prolonged secret debate as to the relative terms of the provisional and permanent governments. The arguments on each side were singularly balanced. On one side it was urged that a provisional form of government was necessary in a state of war, on account of its elasticity; that a strict definition of powers was impossible at such a time, and that certain margins had to be allowed to each department of the government; and that if a permanent Constitution was adopted while the war was still flagrant, it would embarrass the government with political parties that would inevitably spring up, as making various interpretations of a fixed organic law. On the other side it was argued that the leaders at Montgomery would confess a want of confidence in the result of the war, to delay too long the adoption of a permanent Constitution; that such a Constitution would be a signal to the people of faith in the cause, and would afford them that immediate guaranty they desired of the permanancy of their institutions. The result of the secret deliberation was to displace the provisional form of government one year from date, and to rely thereafter on permanent tenures of office. The extent and grief of this mistake will be understood in the course of our narrative. It not only inflicted upon the South a permanent President, who could not be removed unless by resolution; but it was the immediate source of those parties which embarrassed the conduct of the war, which raised the most untimely political questions in the midst of hostilities, and which, once having adjusted the Procrustean bed of constitutional scruples, insisted on measuring upon it every act of the government, and compelling to its test every necessity and exigency of the war. It was certainly a great error. If the history of the late war proved anything clearly, it is that in the vigorous proseoution of arms, the measures of constitutional organic law, provided in a time of peace, must be relaxed; and although much has been heard of that superficial platitude, that one Constitution will serve for war as well as for peace, that the powers of government are to be the same in all cases, the experience of mankind has almost invariably avowed to the contrary. The fact is, that Jefferson Davis, in presuming to accept the office of President, as one of permanent nature, and in allowing himself to be fettered by the fixed and unelastic law of a Constitution, stiffly copied from the United States, did, in his eagerness for the gauds of official title, make a mistake that he rued to the end of his career, that at once beset him with political parties, and that created an embarrassment of his government, from which he was never relieved. What door was opened to political controversy in the midst of war, by the adoption of a permanent form of Constitution at Richmond, and the declaration, as it were, of a fixed model of government, remains to be seen.

In this event, however, there was one subject of congratulation—one change in the political constituents at Richmond that promised some improvement. It was the assemblage of a Congress of new fashion and material, after the Provisional Congress that had meanly expired on the 22d of February. The latter had been but one house—possibly from the idea that a single legislative body was most efficient in time of war. Now the Confederate Legislature was divided into a Senate and House of Representatives, after the fashion of the old government at Washington.

Thomas S. Bocock was elected Speaker of the House, and

on taking the chair he made a suggestive speech, indicating the hard experiment of a change of organic law in the midst of war, and calling Congress up to an elevated standard of duty. He declared that the gaze of the world was fixed upon Richmond, in another interest than that of military campaigns. "Nations," he said, "look on, curious to see how this new system of government will move off, and what manner of men have been chosen to guide its earliest movements. It is, indeed, a new system, for, though coinciding in many particulars with that under which we lived so long, it yet differs from it in many essentials. When the Constitution of 1787 was put in operation, the war of the Revolution had been successfully closed. Peaçe prevailed throughout the whole land, and hallowed all its borders. The case with our Constitution is very different. It is put into operation in time of war, and its first movements are disturbed by the shock of battle. Its trial is one created by the urgencies of this contest. The question to be decided is, whether, without injury to its own integrity, it can supply the machinery, and afford the means requisite to conduct this war to that successful conclusion which the people, in their heart of hearts, have resolved on, and which, I trust, has been decreed in that higher court from whose decisions there is no appeal. The solution of this question is in the bosom of the future . . . . . Can our political system legitimately afford the means to carry the war to a successful conclusion? If not, it must perish; but a successful result must be achieved. But it must be destroyed, not by the hand of violence, or by the taint of perjury; it must go out peacefully, and in pursuance of its own provisions. Better submit to momentary inconvenience than to injure representative honor, or violate public faith. In the whole book of expedients there is no place for falsehood or perjury."

It was a brave manly voice in Congress. There was hope now that there would be an infusion of new blood and vigor in this withered branch of the Government. It commenced well, with the passage of a conscription law, in place of the old system of volunteers. The critical value of this law may be estimated from the fact that nearly two-thirds of the forces with which General Lee, some months later, saved Richmond from the hosts of McClellan, were gathered under its operations. It saved the Confederacy for the time, and gave a new lease to the war. But it is to be remarked that the conscription law was not properly produced by Congress, but had been prepared for it before it met, by the press, even to details, Congress only adopting it from the columns of the newspapers, and only after the latter had carefully brought public opinion up to the necessary point of sacrifice. If any one is to stand as author of this law, it is the Richmond *Examiner*. When it first proposed such a measure, another journal, popularly known as Mr. Davis's organ, opposed it, and actually scoffed it as a reflection on the patriotism of the South. Mr. Davis—who had that wretched and dangerous vanity which resents the tone of suggestion, no matter what the value of the counsel it would impart, and who, besides, had his own reasons to hate the *Examiner*—was long in being brought to the conscription; and he at last ungracefully and imperfectly yielded the recommendation which the necessity of the case extorted from his pride of opinion. He referred to it only in weak and partial phrases, but with a remarkable jesuitism, having at once the shamelessness and the shallowness to pretend that the conscription, instead of testifying to any necessity in the South for troops, was really intended to moderate the rage for volunteering. He wrote a paltry and detestable falsehood rather than an ingenious statement. In his message to Congress he declared: "The operation of the various laws now in force for raising armies has exhibited the necessity for reform. . . . The vast preparations made by the enemy for a combined assault at numerous points on our frontier and seaboard, have produced results that might have been expected. They have animated the people with a spirit of resistance so general, so resolute, and so self-sacrificing, that *it requires rather to be regulated than stimulated!*"

In the conscription law, Congress demanded from the people the greatest of sacrifices; and it followed the act by resolutions, offered by Mr. Rawles, of Alabama, and *unanimously* adopted, announcing to the world that "it is the unalterable determination of the people of the Confederate States to suffer all the calamities of the most protracted war, but that they will never, on any terms, politically affiliate with a people who are guilty of an invasion of their soil and the butchery of their citizens." Would it be believed that after such testimonies, this Congress would, a few weeks later, give, in the person of its own members, an exhibition of the most arrant cowardice and the meanest selfishness—an exhibition almost incredible, and unparalleled, perhaps, in similar historical circumstances in modern times!

But we reserve this exhibition for the course of time; and we turn for a moment to a most remarkable incident in this Congress—on which the reader may build all the romantic speculations he pleases.

There were two notable men returned to the Congress meeting at the inauguration of President Davis. One of them was Mr. Foote of Mississippi, a man who had been for a long time a curiosity in the politics of the country. Mr. Davis is reported to have described his fellow-citizen, as "a man of no account or credit;"—and here we may remark that whatever the truth of his estimate in this instance, his freedom of animadversion on the character of persons around his administration, as illustrated in the "Prison Conversations," lately published, does not suggest that abstinence of criticism for the President himself, which his friends would plead for him, as a broken old man who had outlived the resentments of his life, and who harbored nothing but a desire to die in peace. Mr. Davis since the war has spoken with great bitterness of other characters in the Confederacy; yet his partisans are ever ready to raise their hands sensitively against any historical inquest of himself, and to say that nothing but what is good and merciful should be spoken of a man who is no more dead than Johnston, Beauregard, or even the redoubtable Foote himself. But to return to the curiosity of Mississippi—the *Gubernator Pes*. He was a man of learning, even erudite in historical illustrations; he was remarkable for the *Latinity* of his style; but he had the most indecent itch for notoriety; he was constantly grasping at everything that promised sensation; his fidgets in Congress, his sudden apparitions as jack-in-the-box, his lofty combativeness (once taken down a peg by a challenge from John Mitchel) made him the amusement of the wiser members, the terror of timid country delegates, and the stock of the newspaper reporters. He had had an old quarrel with Mr. Davis in the local politics of Mississippi; but he came to the Congress at Richmond, professing that the quarrel had been completely cured, and exhibiting much more than was necessary an autograph letter from Mr. Davis, tendering reconciliation and expressing the highest consideration, regard, and friendship, for the gentleman who had so happily returned from a political adventure in California, to support

Douglas for the Presidency, next to declaim against Buchanan for not crushing South Carolina, and now to offer his estimable service to the cause of the Southern Confederacy! "I'm on excellent terms with Mr. Davis, excellent terms, sir: only see what he says of me in his letter," were words with which Foote bored all comers, and the proclamation with which he took his seat in Congress.

The other of the notable *duo* of this body, to be introduced to the reader on a special occasion, was Mr. Boyce of South Carolina. Apparently a cold, ascetic man; but one who had a larger record of gallantries than any other Congressman in Richmond; a person without ambition, without any desire for public distinction (and in abilities, he was really second to no member of Congress) yet full of the passion of intrigue, sinister, devious, amusing himself with masks and puppets, a man who would make a conspiracy to relieve his ennui, if for nothing else.

These two men became afterwards notorious in the South, for having morally deserted the Confederate cause at a certain period; and since the war they are remembered as having shown an especial aptitude for "reconstruction." Mr. Foote fled from the Confederacy before the war had concluded; and at the period of this excursion, Mr. Boyce was earnestly advocating a peace convention in Congress. It is in view of the subsequent histories of these two particular men that what we are about to relate becomes significant.

No sooner had the new Congress of the Confederacy met than Messrs. Foote and Boyce commenced a violent clamor for an immediate movement from every point on the enemy's lines. These two men were the only members who spoke to this effect, and they spoke in evident concert. On the very day the President's Message was sent in, Mr. Foote sprung to his feet in great heat, declared that Judge Harris of Mississippi had declared that Mr. Davis was willing to take the military aggressive, if Congress would signify its pleasure to this effect; and in a speech, which had evidently been prepared, he exhorted members to accept a resolution that "it will be the duty of the government of the Confederate States to impart all possible activity to our military forces everywhere, and to assail the forces of the enemy wherever they are to be found, whether upon the land or water." He said that he was in favor of a vigorous onward movement of the Confederate armies; he desired that the Yankees should be made to pay the whole expenses of the war, that the commercial magnates of New York, Boston, and Philadelphia, should be compelled to unlock their strong boxes, and to indemnify the South for losses which they had imposed upon her. He desired above all things to drive the enemy beyond the Southern borders. All this he would have, and nothing less. The Confederate armies should pass into Maryland—heroic Maryland—rescue Baltimore and Annapolis, cut off the railroad communication with the North; and if this had been done months before, the independence, which the South had now to purchase with a vast expenditure of blood and treasure, could have been secured at less than one-fourth of what the war had already cost.

Not five minutes after Mr. Foote had ceased this rhetorical bravado and taken his seat, Mr. Boyce succeeded him in a yet more singular speech, urging an advance upon the enemy's lines. He said:—" We should have pursued from the first more of an aggressive policy, which would have given a position to the Southern States; it would have encouraged our friends and discouraged our enemies, and such a policy had been indicated by our distinguished President from Mississippi when on his way to be inaugurated as President of the Provisional Government, that we should wage war on the enemy's own ground. Mr. L. P. Walker, the former Secretary of War, had said, at an early day, that the flag of the South should float shortly over the Capitol at Washington. He, the speaker, had thought the expression unwise at that time. We should have talked peace and acted war; used peaceful terms, but prepared for active war. Audacity! audacity! audacity! is the key to success. Make no show of fear; prosecute the war with great vigor. Talk of risk! have we not risked a resolution? and shall we see it fail?"

It is remarkable of this strenuous advice delivered by Foote and Boyce—by only these two members in the whole body of Congress—that it would inevitably have sacrificed the South, and been a short cut to its ruin. Why this sudden anxiety that the Confederate lines should be advanced, expressed by these two particular men in Congress? Must they not have known that an aggressive movement of the South at this time would have been to consign it to certain destruction, to have thrown it into the jaws of an enemy six times its superior in strength? They must have known the obvious facts of the military situation. They must have known that the enlistments of the Confederate soldiers for twelve months, commencing immediately upon the secession of the States to which they belonged, were about expiring; they must have known that Johnston's army in Northern Virginia had dwindled to thirty-odd thousand men; they must have known that the operations in the West had swept the Confederate line of defence from near Cumberland Gap to the Mississippi, and raising the blockade of the upper portions of that river, had even passed into Arkansas; they must have known that it was the period of greatest weakness in the South, when the vital concern was to recruit and to re-organize; and at such a time, and in such an exigency, to have taken advantage of the vulgar flatulence, about carrying the war into the enemy's country, and to have urged that the South should throw all that remained of its armies on an enemy, who had brought his troops into camp during the latter part of 1861; who had already organized and drilled them; who had prepared the immense materials necessary for an active campaign; who in such preparations was, at least, four months in advance of the Confederate Government, and who already outnumbered them in the field, six to one, was, to say the least, a suspicious counsel, and one which could scarcely have been made in the sincere interest of an endangered and critical government.

But if Foote and Boyce designed the early destruction of the Southern Confederacy, they were disappointed. The resolution offered by the former was laid on the table. It was the episode of a day; but it preserves the curious remembrance, that these two men, who subsequently made such indecent haste to submission, were the loudest and brazenest champions for vengeance upon the North (even to the robbery of banks in its cities) at a memorable period, in which the severe alternative is, that they must have been either miserable time-servers, or deep and infamous conspirators.

CHAPTER XIV.

Military Condition of the Southern Confederacy—Immense Political Significance of the Conscription Law—It necessarily Changed the Character of the Government—First Appearance of Political Parties against President Davis—Some Account of Governor Jo. Brown of Georgia—An Infamous Underplot against the Confederacy—The Conscription Law Unconstitutional, but Justifiable—Mr. Davis's Boast of Superior Liberty in the South Exploded—How he had to Swallow his Words—A Military Despotism at Richmond—Two Notable Sequels to the Conscription Law—A Terrible Reproof from Mr. Hunter in the Senate—Outrages of Winder's Police—A Description of the Fouché of the Southern Confederacy—Anecdote of Winder—Alarm in Richmond at McClellan's Advance—The Federal Commander up a Tree—Shameful and Cowardly Flight of the Confederate Congress—President Davis Secretly Resolves to Evacuate Richmond—He Changes his Resolution—A Witticism of General Lee—Excitement in Richmond on account of the Destruction of the Virginia-Merrimac—A Littleness of Expedients as Characteristic of the Confederate Administration—It Advertises for Scrap Iron and Old Brass—Anecdote of Secretary Memminger—Appeal of "The Old Lady"—A Notable Assembly in Richmond—"The Ladies' Gun-Boat" and an Oyster Supper.

If the Southern Confederacy had moved on the enemy, when Messrs. Foote and Boyce urged aggression, it would have been dashed to pieces. Indeed, even if it had been content to wait for the attack of the enemy at this time, without a new effort to recruit and to re-organize, it would have been the easy prey of overwhelming numbers. The calculation was thus made in a Richmond paper: "Had the Confederacy lain still two months more, with the army dwindling daily under the furlough system, disgusted with the inaction of stationary camps, while the government was quarreling with the Generals, and the people sinking under indifference, we would have been overrun between the 15th of April and the 15th of May."

The Conscription Law undoubtedly saved the Confederacy from the armies of the enemy, and it is so far to be commended. But while such was its military beneficence, its moral and political effects were certainly disastrous. If it saved the arms of the Confederacy, it yet, of necessity, established at Richmond a *despotism*—a rule, which, however it might claim to be just and kindly in its views, was yet essentially a despotism, according to every test which distinguishes forms of government. In the first place, the moral import of the law was unfavorable; it was a confession that the ardor of the people of the South had ceased to be a safe medium of reliance in the conduct of the war, and it was the first marked occasion of those desertions from the Confederate armies, which afterwards became the crying evil and shame of the South. Its political significance was immense and unavoidable. It necessarily established a consolidated government, founded on military principles; it was a departure from all the constitutional precedents known in the country, a direct assault upon State Rights, a declaration that the powers of Mr. Davis, and his Congress, were henceforward to be measured by military necessities, instead of being contained in a written Constitution.

And here we are recommitted to the thought suggested in the preceding chapter:—that the adoption of a permanent Constitution in the midst of the war was a mistake, that it threw an untimely fetter on its operations, and that it was likely to produce political parties that would embarrass the government. In striking illustration of this thought, we find that almost the first act of the government at Richmond, after adopting such a Constitution, was to break it in its most vital part, under the pressure of a great necessity; and that this act, of itself, created a moral distemper in the Confederacy, and was, indeed, the signal of the first appearance of organized parties in opposition to the government of Mr. Davis.

The conscription law was at once seized as political capital, and by men who had a much deeper design than that of contesting a particular measure, and who had the opportunity thrust into their hands of kindling popular dissatisfaction and undermining the Confederate cause. Governor Joseph Brown of Georgia, came out against the measure in flaming proclamations and speeches; he defied the conscript officers commissioned at Richmond to touch the militia of his State; he opened a correspondence with President Davis that lasted for months, had it printed in a pamphlet and hawked through the streets of every city in the South. His suspicious industry in this respect drew upon him the attention of the whole South; and it was asked what were really the motives of this person in thus sowing the seeds of political controversy, while the enemy was thundering at the gates of Richmond, and while his own State, whose troops he wished to remain at home as militia for its protection, basked in security with not an enemy within a hundred miles of it. The point of controversy was, that Governor Brown insisted that under the Constitution, the President could use the military forces of Georgia only as militia and through the forms of a call on the State authorities "to repel invasion." Mr. Davis replied: "If this Government cannot call on its arms-bearing population more than as militia, and if the militia can only be called forth to repel invasion, we should be utterly helpless to vindicate our honor or protect our rights. War has been styled 'the terrible litigation of nations.' Have we formed our government that in litigation we may never be plaintiffs?"

It was obvious that Governor Brown had the written provisions of the Constitution on his side. He had the advantage of appealing not only to the letter of the law, but to old political prejudices against a centralization of power; it was an excellent chance for vapor; he wrote long letters on constitutional law and the love of liberty; and he even challenged the Legislature of the State to pronounce that the conscription law was of no effect, and not to be obeyed within the limits of Georgia.

Whatever may have been the technical merits of the position of this opponent of President Davis, enough is now known of his subsequent conduct to support the explanation that he had merely raised a false clamor with the ultimate design of weakening and betraying the Confederacy. He was fulsome in his declarations of devotion to the success of the war; he vied with Mr. Davis in his expressions of hostility towards the North; and yet this vile person, under the plea for the integrity of State Rights, was secretly trying to pave the way for the success of the centralized government of the North, and under the color of an excessively pure and hypercritical Southern party, was really marshalling the old elements of the Union faction distributed through Georgia, Tennessee and North Carolina, and was compassing the conspiracy of a traitor. It was one of the most shameful underplots of the war. Something may be said here of its infamous chief, whom President Davis having first cozened and perhaps misunderstood, afterward pronounced a "scoundrel" on the soil of his State, whom the South has since disowned as an infliction upon her honor, and with whom the country has been recently amused as an unmasked hypocrite and superfluous trifler on the stage of public life.

Joe Brown, as he was popularly named, made a great noise in the war from the first time he resisted the conscription, and was adroit enough to get Mr. Davis into a printed controversy with him. He was the coarse, obese prince of Southern demagogues. There were various accounts of his low origin, and of the vulgar associations of his life before he had been elevated to the Governorship of Georgia; but the most that is certainly known of this period of his existence is that he had been a "sand-hill cracker" in South Carolina, where he was born, scratching a piece of poor land for subsistence, and trading on the skirts of the large plantations. The person who made this wonderful ascent in political life, found a notoriety and advantage in the war by indulging a controversial mood, and opening issues of old parties. His game with President Davis was to "out-herod Herod" in the matter of State Rights. In this pretence, he kept up a constant exclamation of his earnest and passionate desire, even in excess of Mr. Davis, to whip the enemy and accomplish independence; he excelled in "Yankeephobia," and in all the incandescent sentiments of the original Secession party; but under cover of these cries of excessive Southern fervor, he was doing his best to embarrass the government and to disband its armies. It was not without reason that Mr. Davis dictated a dispatch sent to him and signed by the Secretary of War:—"I think we might as well drive out our common enemy before we make war on each other."

In our commentary on the constitutionality of the conscription law, we are not to be mistaken. It did transcend the Constitution adopted at Richmond; it was essentially a revolutionary measure; but we are persuaded that the true distinction as to the assumption of irregular and extraordinary powers in a state of war is a moral one, to be decided by good or bad effects; and as this law certainly did save the Confederacy, we must consider it as a beneficent stretch of power, and account opposition to it as a single measure, untenable, unwise, and unpatriotic. We respect the thought that we have elsewhere suggested, that organic laws in time of war must be stretched; the true question becomes whether the enlargement of power in the government is really turned to just purposes and good results. The conscription law accomplished its own justification. But what was unfortunate of it was that it necessarily placed the government on the basis of military necessity, that it thus essentially revolutionized its whole character, and that it was naturally followed by breaches of the Constitution, which became successively larger, and for which there was no adequate justification. When a section of constitutional law is once broken down, the citadel of liberty is soon taken.

And so it swiftly proved at Richmond. Heretofore Mr. Davis in all his public addresses had declared that the Confederate Government was established to preserve their "ancient institutions;" he constantly pointed to the disregard which the North had shown of civil liberty, to its suspension of *habeas corpus,* to bastiles filled with prisoners, arrested without legal process or indictment; and no later than the day of his second inauguration, he had congratulated the South that "through all the necessities of an unequal struggle there has been no act on our part, to impair personal liberty, or the freedom of speech, of thought, or of the press." This argument of superior liberty in the Confederacy, had been advanced on every occasion; the preservation of the civil routine in a time of war, had been the habitual boast of Mr. Davis. Now he was compelled to swallow this bit of glittering stereotype. For in a few weeks there was exhibited in Richmond a military tyranny that outdid "the strong government" at Washington, that committed outrages of which the newspapers spared accounts, and of which subsequent narratives of the war have only given imperfect glimpses, but which were unexcelled in the history of sudden and violent usurpations.

To the conscription law there were two notable sequels:—one an attempt to prescribe the production of the country—the *ultima thule* of despotism; the other the establishment of a military police, of the most frightful and odious description. The first usurpation failed, at least to the extent it designed, but only by a slender majority in the Confederate Senate. It had been at first proposed there to "advise" the planters of the South to abstain from raising cotton and tobacco, so as to increase the product of grain and provisions in the country. For this proposition Mr. Brown, of Mississippi, offered a substitute, to curtail the cotton crop; providing in detail that no planter or head of a family should sow more cotton seed than would produce three bales of the staple for himself, and one bale for each of the hands employed in the culture during the year 1862, and that he should be sworn to the extent of his crop under a penalty for perjury. It is an illustration of the rapid advance of despotic ideas in Richmond, that such a proposition should have been even entertained. The Government, protested Mr. Hunter of Virginia, had not the shadow of a right to go to any of the States, and say, how much cotton should be produced. The sovereignty of the States themselves hardly dare do this, much less the delegated power of the Confederacy. If he believed that Congress would pass any such act, or the Government possessed any such power, he would pronounce it a most notorious despotism, "worse even than that from which the people of the South had just escaped." The infamous bill failed through only three votes in the Senate; but Mr. Hunter's denunciation of it and of the tendency it exhibited to despotic rule was conveniently omitted from the newspapers, while it smarted in the ears of Mr. Davis.

The worst despotism however into which the President

plunged, alarmed by the military disasters that had occurred and by the now visible approach of McClellan's army to Richmond was to declare martial law for ten miles around the capital, and to supplant all the civil authorities by a military police, of the vilest materials that could be raked from the dens, or fished from the slums of his dissolute capital. Every one who lived in Richmond in those days has cause to remember "Winder's Police." The excuse which Mr. Davis made for fastening on the city the atrocious curse of these creatures was that a Union sentiment was being developed as McClellan advanced, that summary arrests of suspected persons might become necessary, and that a new vigilance was necessary to guard against political conspiracies. There was, indeed, a great uneasiness in Richmond as the Federal army gathered around it; the air was poisoned by rumors and suspicions; there was a necessity for vigilance and vigor. But a police composed of rowdies and gamblers imported from Baltimore as non-conscripts, the vilest of adventurers, who might without legal process tear any citizen from his home, who made domiciliary visits at pleasures, who could write anonymous denunciations, who trafficked in bribes, from whom no man was safe, and against whom there was no protection of sex or condition, was not a measure calculated to re-assure the anxiety of the public, or to improve its confidence in, or affection for Mr. Davis. It introduced a new and terrible distrust in the community. There were two hundred spies employed in Richmond, and no man's conversation was safe from them. The newspapers did not publish the arrests, or only as the scantiest items; and although but few persons were actually imprisoned on account of their political sentiments, the cases were many where respectable citizens, among them ladies, were conveyed to certain tribunals held in drinking-shops and the "pens" of negro-traders and "warned" by police magnates of the President.*

At the head of this wretched police business, which in some form or other continued through the administration of Mr. Davis, he placed a man than whom a fitter exponent of despotism and cruelty could not be found within the limits of the South. This person was General Winder, of Maryland, —a name that thousands of living persons yet recall with horror; and a character that deserves an especial study in

---

* An incident illustrating the outrages and effrontery of this political police, is recollected by the author. In a boarding-house in Richmond was an estimable lady, a native of Virginia, who owned a large estate of negroes in Culpeper county. She had been very much annoyed by the desertion of her slaves; and hearing of the flight of one of the most valuable of them, she exclaimed to a company assembled in the parlor, "I do wish the Yankees would come and take away all the negroes." It was nothing more than a petulant remark—such as one living in the South might hear a hundred times, when the mistress of the house was disposed to describe her slaves as pests and sources of annoyance. The remark through some channel, was reported to General Winder, "Commanding the Department of Henrico." The next day, the lady was called to the door by a shabby stranger; she came back running into the parlor, weeping, and praying some gentleman in the house to protect her. She had received the dread summons to attend before General Winder, on a charge of uttering treasonable sentiments! There could be no opposition or escape; the detective was at the door, importunate for his victim. It was only when this accomplished and delicately nurtured lady had been compelled to walk nearly a mile through the street, to enter a mean building recently used as a drinking-shop, to press through a throng of rumsellers and rowdies to the dirty throne of Winder, and to humbly protest there, that her offence had been temper and not treason, that she was allowed to depart on the brutal injunction to "hold her tongue in future."

the moral history of the war. At first sight this person was not unpleasant. Mr. Ely, the memorable State prisoner of the Libby, speaks of General Winder, then his principal jailor, as an agreeable grey-headed officer, a little stiff and disposed to stand on his dignity, prim and neat to scrupulousness, but having no traits of harshness in his manner or countenance. But this impression was not that of a close study. This man whom President Davis had found in some obscure place in the old army, and kept to the end of his Administration as his chief of military police, and head-jailor of the Confederacy, was near sixty years of age; his hair was white and tufty; and at a distance he had a patriarchal appearance. But his face was a picture of cruelty, a study for an artist; a harsh dry face; cruel eyes, not muddy as from temper, but with a clear cold light in them; a faded, poisonous mouth on which a smile seemed mockery.

Under martial law proclaimed in Richmond, this creature held in his hands the powers of a viceroy. He was responsible to no one but Mr. Davis. He ordered what arrests he pleased; he regulated trade; he gave permits for the transportation of goods; he hunted conscripts through the streets. As a curious specimen of his authority, we may quote a single order:—"The obtaining by conscripts of substitutes through the medium of agents is strictly forbidden. When such agents are employed, the principal, the substitute, and the agent, will be impressed into the military service, and the money paid for the substitute, and as a reward to the agent, will be confiscated to the government!" It is almost incredible that such despotic edicts could be issued in the capital of the Southern Confederacy; but here they were, written under the eye of Mr. Davis, and put in the hands of his creature for execution. Winder carried the interests of Richmond in his pocket. If a citizen wished to commute for military duty, if a merchant desired to secure the sacrifice of his flour and bacon from the tariff of prices under martial law, if a liquor-dealer wished to bring into the city a lot of apple-brandy, Winder had to be seen, and his favor had to be secured. He was courted, caressed; people of all sorts sent him presents; and when an acquaintance suggested to him that it was imprudent to receive such testimonies of regard, and that they might be coarsely interpreted as bribes, the reply was:—"If the devil himself chooses to send me presents, I don't see why I should not accept them." He had a curious habit about these offerings; they seldom availed to obtain any return from him. His peculiarity in this respect suggests a description in Macaulay of the infamous Jeffreys, to the effect that he would often carouse with the meanest men; but when he was sober on the bench, and his companions of the night before would presume on the maudlin affection they had contracted in their cups, he would pretend not to know them, and would drown their attempts at familiarity in volleys of wrath and imprecation. There was a striking analogy to such behavior in the relations of Winder and his gift-bearers. He invariably accepted anything sent him in the shape of a present; the ingenious wretch who had sent it, perhaps to escape the conscription, or to get a permit to traffic in liquors, would felicitate himself that he had secured his concession, that the business was done; but the next day would come an order to clap him in the conscript camp, or to impound all the whiskey on his premises. It was a feline way the General had of playing with his victims, and must have been intensely gratifying to a nature like his. The unhappy bearer of gifts seldom escaped from his clutches—the gifts never.

Meanwhile McClellan continued to advance, and his white tents already gleamed on the rank banks of the Chickahominy. His toilsome marches up the Peninsula had brought him within sight of the house-tops of Richmond; and he had approached what appeared to be the grand consummation of his hopes. As his army took its position near Richmond, he climbed a lofty tree—it was too near his adversary's lines to send up a balloon;—from his leafy perch he saw bending around the devoted city the long line of his troops, the array of blue and gilt glittering in the sun, the black fangs of the batteries in the forest; beyond them patches of "grey-backs" half-concealed in the underbrush or peering out from sodden marshes, the slovenly semblance of the army which he imagined he had driven to its last imperfect cover, all that was between him and victory. The commander descended from the tree. It was not a dignified post of observation; but it must have afforded him a charming prospect, for, having reached the ground, he threw his arms around a subordinate officer, and exclaimed, "We've got them."

And there were thousands of persons in Richmond who then believed that the grand army had "got" them, and who already seemed to feel the weight of arrest on their shoulders. No assurance had yet been given by President Davis that the capital was to be defended to extremity. It was a memorable season of popular alarm; there were uneasy whispers in Richmond; a panic was threatened; and it was just that critical period when the authorities were required and called upon to do everything to nourish and sustain public confidence. We have seen a few pages back, what declarations of desperate courage the Confederate Congress had made. Now the infamous response of this body to the popular alarm was to exceed it, to adjourn precipitately, and to break up in confusion, its members fleeing to the safety of their obscure homes, amid the execrations of the press, the hootings of the populace, and with even the contempt of the women thrown after them. The shame of the fugacious Congress was in the mouth of every one in Richmond. It was one of the most contemptible and ludicrous incidents of the war. The shop-windows were filled with caricatures of it—one of the most popular, and which might be considered to have originated the tradition of the *carpet-bag*, representing a fat and terrified Congressman, with his slight baggage in hand, pursued by a gun-boat, the apparition of a magnified insect mounted on spindle legs. The cowardice of the Congress in this flight from McClellan was so extravagant that the people of Richmond actually took heart from its contrast to their own reasonable fears, in which they had not yet lost their self-possession, and amused themselves in ridiculing and lampooning it.*

The true history of this uneasiness in Richmond is, that President Davis had secretly resolved to evacuate Richmond. What was at that time an angry suspicion is now ascertained to have been an actual fact. It is a remarkable circumstance that up to the time General Johnston fell wounded in the

---

* The Richmond "*Whig*" announced the hasty adjournment and its consequences in the following paragraph:

For fear of accident on the railroad, the stampeded Congress left in a number of the strongest and newest canal-boats. These boats are drawn by mules of approved sweetness of temper. To protect the stampeders from the snakes and bull-frogs that abound along the line of the canal, General Winder has detailed a regiment of ladies to march in advance of the mules, and clear the tow-path of the pirates. The ladies will accompany the stampeders to a secluded cave in the mountains of Hepsidan, and leave them there in charge of the children of the vicinage, until McClellan thinks proper to let them come forth. The ladies return to the defence of their country.

battle of Seven Pines, Mr. Davis had obstinately refused the recommendations of this commander (with whom he seemed determined never to act in concert) to draw in any considerable forces from other parts of the South to defend Richmond —a condition which Johnston had named as essential to the safety of the capital. He had sent his wife to a country retreat in North Carolina; he had bestowed the most important papers of the government in boxes ticketed for Columbia, South Carolina; and whenever approached on the subject of the defence of Richmond, he had shown an equivocation and an anxiety from which no assurance was derived, and from which the most distressful rumors were bred. A day for public fasting and prayer was appointed; the President betook himself to the consolations of religion. He was "confirmed" in the Episcopal Church; and a circumstance ordinarily so solemn and delicate, was interpreted in a curious way by the fears and superstitions of the public impressed by the coincidence of Mr. Davis's religious conversion and the extremity of his Government. The President was represented as "standing in a corner telling his beads and relying on a miracle to save the country, instead of mounting his horse and putting forth every human power to defeat the enemy." His indecision, his religious melancholy, his equivocal speeches were texts of almost savage complaint in the newspapers.

For once Mr. Davis bowed to popular opinion; and after a visit of a committee of the Virginia Legislature, it became generally known that the *fiat* had been distinctly written out that Richmond was to be defended, and that a new disposition of the Confederate forces was to be made to assure its safety. It was the summons of a new spirit in the army, and an occasion of congratulations among the citizens. The President was for once conquered by public opinion. Looking at the after events of the war, it may perhaps be regretted that he was so conquered, and that he did not adhere to his first resolution to evacuate the city, and thus disembarrass the main army of the Confederacy which was so long tied to the one object of the safety of Richmond. True, it would have excited great popular complaint; it would have risked a great alarm; but the moral spirit of the Confederacy would at that time probably have sustained a misfortune which, resulting three years later, was then a fatal blow to its spirit. In 1862 the Confederacy might have survived the fall of Richmond; in 1865 it perished under it. Further, in military estimation, the defence of Richmond proved a constant fetter on the army of Virginia; for years it embarrassed all the operations of General Lee on the border, and this commander once complained in his quaint way, that "*he had got a creak in his neck from constantly looking over his shoulder after Richmond.*" But these calculations were remote, hid in the future; and when Mr. Davis determined and announced that the city was to be defended, the resolution was taken as the wisest and most heroic thing that could be done in the circumstances. Happily there was time to effect the change thus determined upon, and the capital of the Confederacy, at the last, was more saved through the unreadiness of McClellan, than through the spirit and providence of its defenders. While this commander, formerly the superintendent of a Northern railroad, had, as Mr. Aylett, one of the Richmond wits, expressed it, "accustomed in peace to the indecent haste of railroad travelling, adopted in war the sedate tactics of the mud-turtle," Richmond was being filled with soldiers; and the city into which he might once have cut his way through the army he had driven from Williamsburg, now interposed the most numerous force the South ever put in a single field.

But while these consultations and preparations of Mr. Davis were taking place, and while popular confidence trembled on his decision, whether the Confederate capital should be evacuated or defended, there came a single incident which, of itself, nearly surrendered Richmond, and which claims here a curious notice. In fact, it created a public grief, so wild and bitter, that at one time it was feared the building, in which were collected the departments of the government, might be stormed by a mob. This event was the destruction of the iron-clad "Virginia-Merrimac," in the tidewater of the James. It was the most important naval structure that defended the water approach to Richmond; it had cost nearly a year to complete it; it had won the only important naval victory which the Confederates ever gained;* it had been fondly and gloriously named "the iron diadem of the South," and it was accounted the equivalent of an army of fifty thousand men in the defence of the Confederate capital. It was fired by its own crew, and blown to the four winds of heaven at a time when its destruction left the water avenue to Richmond so nearly open, that only four guns defended it, in an unfinished work on the upper part of the river. It has been said that

* We make no account of the deeds of the *Alabama*, as naval triumphs, for she went down in the first regular battle which Captain Semmes, whetted by the persuasions of his friends in England, fought for the especial purpose of getting a prestige on the sea for the Confederacy. The destruction of merchant vessels, however effective it may be in war, does not constitute exploits to boast of. When Captain Semmes was presented with a sword for them, by some of his English admirers, the London *Punch* had a witticism on the appropriateness of the gift to the hero who "*cuts away*." In brief, the Confederate navy was an arm so vastly inferior in the war, that it will scarcely claim the attention of the just historian—except for records of weakness and folly.

this vessel was destroyed without the orders of the Government, and through the alarm of the commander, Commodore Tatnall, who had never once fought it since its victory, under another commander, in Hampton Roads, and who now, instead of riding it into, at least, one grand final action, that it might perish gloriously, had carried it under the shelter of an island and blown it into the air of midnight.

But what was most notable of this astounding shame is, that at the time there was thus cleanly destroyed an iron-clad, which had cost the government of Mr. Davis one year to build, and not a bolt saved from the wreck—at a time when a structure so immense and elaborate was given to the winds, the same Government was advertising through the length and breadth of the South for scrap-iron, old brass, saucepans, and even clock-weights, in its scarcity of metal for naval armor and ordnance. It was a ludicrous apposition of expedients, but one, characteristic of the administration of Mr. Davis. The puerility of these metal contributions was ridiculous enough. Here was an Ordnance Bureau advertising for church bells, out of which to make light artillery; here were ladies sending preserving kettles to assist in the defence of their beloved Confederacy. One woman in Mobile wrote that she sent her "mite of old brass;" another patriotic lady wrote from Charleston, "I send you, as a contribution to the Confederacy, the lead weight which was attached to the striking part of my clock." These things are not mentioned for amusement; they were solemnly published in the country newspapers, from which we copy them. They are, indeed, profoundly significant of that littleness of expedients in the South, that paltriness of device in great necessities, which runs as a singular and curious characteristic through the whole of Mr. Davis's administration in the war. When the most elaborate iron-clad the world had yet seen was wantonly blown to useless atoms; when blockade-runners, from Europe, instead of importing ordnance, were laying in cargoes of champagne, and special consignments of cigars for Mr. Davis and Mr. Benjamin; and when the armories and work-shops were suffering for material, the Government of Mr. Davis was performing the silly romance of collecting scrap-iron, and publishing lists of lady-contributors of kettles and pans. Some of these lists, printed for emulative excitement, are yet to be found in Southern newspapers of that time. They were quite on a par with a later advice of Secretary Memminger, to relieve the needs of the Confederate Treasury, by patriotic contributions of sugar-pots and finger rings—a device, by the way, which provoked Senator Wigfall to tell the anecdote of Mr. Davis's wise financier, that he had at first proposed that the expenses of the war should be paid by collection bags in the churches. Seriously, the public necessities of a government require large measures, acts of provident statesmanship, and Mr. Davis's idea of patching them up with such contributions as we have mentioned, was one of those silly, juvenile thoughts, worthy perhaps of the minds of women, but absurdities to statesmen.

And, indeed, this paltriness of "patriotic contributions" was a little romance for the female population of the South, in which Mr. Davis, of course, was the hero. It was so pleasant to think of building what should be called "The Ladies' Gunboat," to take the place of the Virginia-Merrimac; and so, on the destruction of this vessel, the ladies of Richmond were called to meet in one of the churches, and Mrs. Judge Clopton—an estimable Virginia matron, who had given some noble sons to her country's service, "The Old Lady" who wrote in the newspapers diatribes against Governor

Letcher—was solemnly authorized to send circulars through the country to collect old iron, even to the extremity of nails and broken horse-shoes. It was a cheerful assembly, under the circumstances; letters were read from Mr. Davis; speeches were made, and for once Richmond had a dim perception of "woman's rights." A lady president delivered a long oration, but unfortunately she died a few days thereafter from the effects of a supper, which the warlike sisterhood had given in honor of their enterprise. It was one of those ludicrous and grotesque episodes which sometimes happen in great popular excitements—and yet it reflected, not a little, that juvenile mind of the South, its want of commensurate appreciation and just provision, so remarkable in the war, and so characteristic of a people who have been always deficient in the practical application of means to an end.

CHAPTER XV.

The City of Richmond Saved—General Lee Appointed to Command before it—Incidents and Anecdotes of his previous Military Career—A Private Understanding between Generals Johnston and Lee—The Latter Promises to Resign—Changes of Military Policy of the Confederacy—Great Influence of Lee over President Davis—How the Latter was Managed—The "Seven Days'" Battles—Terrible scenes in Richmond—Refusal of the Southern People to Mourn their Dead—Some Reminiscences of Richmond Hospitals—Significant Address of President Davis—The First Experiment by the Confederacy of an Aggressive Campaign—Plans of the Campaign on both sides of the Alleghany—The period of Greatest Effulgence of the Confederate arms—Results of Bragg's Campaign in Kentucky—The Dramatic Battle of Sharpsburgh—A Secret Agent of the Confederacy Prepared to Visit Washington—Mr. Foote's Confidences with President Davis—Romance of "The Lost Dispatch"—Review of the Autumnal Campaign of 1862—A Brilliant Record on the Valor of the Confederate Troops—Why was this Valor so Unavailing—The Outcry of Wasted Blood against Jefferson Davis—Silly Transports of the Confederate President—His Fulsome Address to the Mississippi Legislature—A Remarkable Private Letter from General Floyd—Two Notable Views of the War in Contrast.

Richmond was saved—saved for a lingering death, a postponed catastrophe. It was saved by a new spirit in the army that defended it, and by a change in the military policy of Mr. Davis. This change was fairly inaugurated on placing before Richmond a new commander, whose name was hereafter to illustrate the brightest pages of Southern history, and to be borne through all the brilliant battles of Virginia, from those of the "Seven Days" to those which gilded the last efforts of the Southern Confederacy.

General Lee had commenced his military career in the Confederate service, by a campaign in the mountains of Western Virginia, in a field narrow and difficult, where he obtained but scant laurels. He had returned to Richmond with a sadly diminished reputation, and for months he lan guished in obscurity, in nominal command of the span of seacoast from Charleston to Savannah where there was yet no considerable enemy. Mr. Davis has since justly remarked, that under the Northern system of retiring unsuccessful commanders, Lee would have been sacrificed and the genius that was to illuminate so many fields in the South would have been lost to the Confederacy. But happily the disasters of the Confederacy had not yet become so alarming as to require such sacrifices of officers to the passion and ignorance of an unwarlike people; there was as yet no demand for scape-goats, and when General Lee was appointed to take command of the forces around Richmond, beleaguered by McClellan, although some of the newspapers twitted him as "Letcher's pet," and the Richmond *Examiner* thought to discover in the appointment, a paltry game of politicians, and jeered the report that a spawn of West Point, was arrogant enough to aspire to be next Governor of Virginia, there was no more violent expression of dissatisfaction, and even if there had been a disposition to raise a popular clamor against the appointment, the condition of Confederate affairs was then too extreme to support criticism.

General Lee accepted the appointment modestly enough, and, as is known to the author, with the private intention of relinquishing the command of the Army of Virginia to Johnston, as soon as the latter should recover from the wound that prostrated him at Seven Pines. A message to this effect was conveyed by one of Lee's family to Johnston lying on his sick bed, and fretting under his wound; but, although he might have been consoled by it, he responded generously that he rejoiced that General Lee had command of the army, since he observed that he had obtained the confidence and aid of Mr. Davis's government more than he

(Johnston) had been able to do. "I thus regard my wound as a good providence," said the stricken and suffering commander; "the Government will now draw in troops to Lee that it refused me, and Richmond will be saved." Richmond was saved; but if General Lee remembered his promise to resign, events moved too fast to enable him to gratify his inclinations to a less important command, and to disembarrass himself of public opinion that already hailed him as a hero. When Johnston had recovered from his wound, Lee had mounted to the zenith of his fame at second Manassas; had closed an important campaign, with lively satisfaction to the public, and had already so possessed the affections and confidence of his army, that his separation from it could no longer be thought of, and indeed, if attempted, would have risked the mutiny of his soldiers, and aroused the resentment of the whole South. The man who a few months ago had been held in mediocre estimation at best—of whom an officer in the Army of Virginia had said at the time Lee had been banished to the "coast service" in 1861, "General Beauregard thinks well of him"—was already the first favorite of the South, and had far outridden in fame the heroes of an earlier period of the war who had assumed to patronize and praise faintly his struggling genius.

The change of the military policy of the Confederacy from that of dispersion to that of concentration—a change which General Johnston had been the first to propose, but which General Lee, who had greater arts of persuasion, had alone been able to effect—saved its capital. The contraction of the line of defence produced, of course, a greater capacity of resistance, and made a successful defence of Richmond almost in its last extremity. Whatever General Lee's reputation for independence and directness of conduct, it is remarkable of him that he had rare insight into character, and understood how to use men for his purposes, accommodating himself readily to the peculiarities of the persons with whom he had to deal. He must have been sensible of the peculiar weakness of Mr. Davis, to judge from his adroit interpolation in his official report of the operations around Richmond, of the remark that they had been conducted under the "approving presence" of the President, notwithstanding the fact that the latter had never done more than ride out curiously two or three miles to the battle-fields, and had had no more to do with the operations than those conducted hundreds of miles from the capital. But it was just such stuff as caught Mr. Davis, and he was as pliant as a child to those who chose to manage him with a few plums of compliment. In his whole military career General Lee made it a point always to recognize an advisory relation as subsisting between him and the President, and the consequence was, that he had more absolutely a *carte blanche* as to his operations and movements than any other Confederate commander in the war.

The "seven days" of battle around Richmond were days of well-remembered glory for the South. It is not our design here to enter into the military details of this, or of any other battle of the war; these do not properly belong to our work. In a week the enemy was fought down to the James river, twenty miles below Richmond, a circuit of victories was achieved, and although McClellan's army was not destroyed or captured, there was no disposition of the Southern people to carp at the extent of the results accomplished, but on the contrary, a general concurrence in the sentiment of General Lee, who wrote with pious moderation in his official report: "Regret that more was not accomplished gives way to gratitude to the Sovereign Ruler of the universe, for the results achieved." The victory of Richmond was an encouragement bestowed on the whole South; it illuminated the entire Confederacy; but it exhibited to the capital city itself that reverse side of the picture of the war, from which men lift the embroidery to stand face to face with the stark horrors of Death.

Richmond was filled with wounded, dying men; the death agony might be seen at any time by the passenger on the street, who would pause to look, with horrifying curiosity, through the plates of glass of some large store on the thoroughfares, now converted into a temporary hospital, a hundred pallets arranged where once had been the counters of trade, and where Death was now busy in his ghastly traffic. Ambulances in long lines were being driven through the streets, every hour of the day. It was heart-rending to hear the screams, the groans, or the peculiar chants of pain from bloody and disfigured men, to whom every jolt on the rough stones was as a new wound. Nearly every building in Richmond was a house of mourning, or a private hospital. Death became familiar. A half-dozen corpses were often put in a single cart, and hurried to the burial ground, where they had to await the turn of the grave-digger, it not being unusual for the bodies to swell from exposure, and to burst the frail shell of boards, called a coffin, while exposed for nights in the cemetery, before the final resting-place was prepared for them. The air was poisoned with sickening odors. The hospitals were loathsome with bloated, disfigured, bodies, for gangrene and erysipelas attacked many of the wounded in the heat of the midsummer, and hurried them to graves from which timely medical attention might have saved them. And in these charnel-houses, where women attended and prayed—where tender ladies supplied with their ministrations the neglect and improvidence of the government—each beat of artillery in the distance that came through the windows, smote the imagination of the watchers with the thought that at that moment their own loved ones might be stretched on the bloody and cheerless sod of the battle-field, and might be giving up their lives in the unattended and unsoothed agonies of lingering death.

But private griefs are soon swallowed up in a great public joy; and it is remarkable how readily and cheerfully the people of the South accepted for their dead the consolations of patriotism. Indeed regrets should be slight for men fallen in any good cause; and, considering the pain and emptiness of all human life, the thought has often occurred that scarcely more than the decent semblances of grief, or the tributes of a tender and submissive melancholy are due to those who die in the peace of God or on the path of duty. There were voices of mourning in Richmond; yet they were but slight, compared with the acclamations of public triumph over the great victory which, though it had filled its houses with the dead, had saved it from a hated enemy, and girded its adjacent fields with an imperishable glory. But few persons in the South wore, during the war, mourning for their dead. Nor was this omission of dress due only to poverty; for immediately after the battle of Manassas an appeal had been published in the newspapers, and especially to the ladies of the South, that they should forbear from wearing mourning for relatives fallen in the war, as such a spectacle would become painful from the multitude of display, and was really an inappropriate tribute to those who had freely given their lives to their country's cause of liberty and honor. Of Richmond the general aspect was that of joy and animation, even while its hospitals groaned with the wounded and the dying; and although there might have been no impropriety in raising to some extent the voice of a great public congratulation above that of private and domestic griefs, yet it was sometimes painful to find in this vile city, peculiarly accursed by the war, so many festive and dissolute entertainments so close to scenes of suffering and death. The hotels were filled with gay companies; the crash of festive music might be heard a few doors from hospitals; and there is even a notorious scandal to this day in Richmond, that one of these abodes of suffering was actually turned into a shop of the worst female characters, and afforded its social dinners as regularly and as sumptuously as the finest "hells" in the city.

The popular elation on the delivery of Richmond from an enemy who had come so near to possessing it, was naturally great. In the shallow mind of the populace, the tumult of alarm and the extravagance of hope are perhaps in the same proportion easily excited; and thus Richmond passed suddenly from the most depressing anxiety to the most exalted expectations. Mr. Davis did more than share the general elation; he gave it increased volume in a fulsome address to the soldiers. This address is copied below for the literary interest of its style, as well as for the significance of the appeal with which it concludes:—

RICHMOND, July 5, 1862.

"*To the Army in Eastern Virginia:*

SOLDIERS: I congratulate you on the series of brilliant victories which, under the favor of Divine Providence, you have lately won, and as the President of the Confederate States, do hereby tender to you the thanks of the country, whose just cause you have so skillfully and heroically served. Ten days ago, an invading army, vastly superior to you in numbers and the material of war, closely beleagured your capital and vauntingly proclaimed its speedy conquest; you marched to attack the enemy in his intrenchments; with well-directed movements and death-defying valor you charged upon him in his strong positions, drove him from field to field over a distance of more than thirty-five miles, and despite his reinforcements, compelled him to seek safety under the cover of his gun-boats, where he now lies cowering before the army so lately derided and threatened with entire subjugation. The fortitude with which you have borne toil and privation, the gallantry with which you have entered into each successive battle, must have been witnessed to be fully appreciated; but a grateful people will not fail to recognize you and to bear you in loved remembrance. Well may it be said of you that you have "done enough for glory;" but duty to a suffering country and to the cause of constitutional liberty claims from you yet further effort. Let it be your pride to relax in nothing which can promote your future efficiency; your one great object being to drive the invader from your soil, and, carrying your standards beyond the outer boundaries of the Confederacy, to wring from an unscrupulous foe the recognition of your birthright, community, and independence."

This address of Mr. Davis indicated clearly enough a change of military policy, and announced (even with imprudent freedom to the enemy) that the Confederacy was resolved and prepared to essay for the first time an aggressive campaign. The policy of concentration, which had at last been undertaken, furnished Mr. Davis with two compact powerful armies on each side of the Alleghanies—the Army of Tennessee, now commanded by Bragg, and that called the Army of Northern Virginia, from the day it marched away from Richmond under the command of Lee. With these two armies there was now undertaken the grandest and widest campaign of the war, stretching from the Mississippi to the Atlantic; Lee to carry the war to the foreground of Washington, and Bragg to penetrate the heart of Kentucky, sweeping a tract of country bounded by the enemy's posts in Alabama and Tennessee and the cities of Louisville and Cincinnati. It was an instance of strategy remarkable for its comprehension and unity; the object being to carry the war to the enemy's frontier by combined movements, to relieve for purposes of subsistence large sections of country which had been overrun, and possibly to wreak upon the enemy some punishment for his own crimes of invasion, and make the people of the North taste some of the bitterness of the war which had so far been to them a military entertainment and a distant show. It was undoubtedly the period of the greatest effulgence of the Confederate arms; and the latter half of the year 1862 must take its place in the history of the war as the span of greatest glory for the South.

The results of this most magnificent enterprise of the war fell below public expectation in the South; and yet a great glory was achieved, vast acquisitions of subsistence were made, and the sum of the campaign is, that it showed to the world that a Confederacy which a few months before had had its capital beleaguered, had been able to take its great and powerful adversary at a disadvantage, and that it had nearly demonstrated to civilized nations its own military strength and ability to win the independence it had proclaimed. General Bragg was at last forced to retire from Kentucky; and General Lee decided not to deliver a second battle in Maryland, even after the victory which he has ever claimed to have borne from the banks of the Antietam. The results of Bragg's campaign, although it abandoned Kentucky, were yet large and visible. He relieved considerable sections of Tennessee and Alabama from the presence of the enemy; he recovered Cumberland Gap, the main avenue from Richmond to the heart of the Confederacy; and although he had not fulfilled the hopes that he might permanently occupy Kentucky, he brought from it subsistence that supported his army during the whole ensuing winter; he gained the brilliant victory of Perryville; he came back with the record of having killed, wounded and captured of the enemy a number equal to half the force of his army, and he exhibited as consequences of his campaign, the recovery of the country between Nashville and Chattanooga and a securer hold on a section of two hundred miles of the Mississippi River, extending from Vicksburg to Port Hudson. The Virginia correspondent of this campaign was even more successful. But Sharpsburg was a more dramatic termination than Perryville; the avenue of conflict to it more brilliant and interesting, and the final disappointment there as keen in proportion as the expectations had been high, that mounted to this the most important field in the second year of the war. The victory of the Second Manassas had raised the hopes of the South to the highest pitch; and there were men in Richmond who had expected that General Lee would be dictating peace from Washington the day the news came that he was struggling back across the fords of the Potomac.

It was not generally known to the Southern public at the time of which we write—and indeed a question is yet made of the incident by those who believe that Mr. Davis was always calm, well-advised and prescient, a perfection and a sciolist—that such was the exaltation of the President at the prospect of Lee's advance into Maryland, that even before the battle of Sharpsburg he had prepared a mission to propose terms of peace at Washington. Hereafter we shall find the same experiment repeated on the disposition and temper of the enemy, in circumstances somewhat similar; but what is remarkable of each occasion is, that the mission was disguised as the mere negotiation of a question as to the humanities of the war. The design of these missions was really for a certain moral effect. Mr. Davis had been persuaded that at the moment the Confederate armies were so visibly superior as to carry the war into the enemy's country, if he would then make any propositions showing the moderation of the designs of the South, it would furnish capital to the Democratic party in the North, widen the divisions of party there, and excite a political diversion in favor of the South, besides making a moral exhibition to the world of great advantage to its cause. He was thus always hasty to send peace messengers to Washington on every possible occasion; but in convenient disguise, so that they might not convey any confession of weakness or of over-anxiety for the termination of hostilities. It was no sooner known that Lee's army was across the Potomac, than Mr. Foote of Tennessee—a person who was always prompt to catch at any sensation, and ready to ride whatever hobby was in career, offered a resolution in Congress for the "terms of a just and honorable peace," considering how Providence had "continually blessed" the arms of the Confederacy. But Mr. Foote, then in relations of intimate friendship with Mr. Davis, overdid the desires of the latter, and another friend of the President (Mr. Holt, of Georgia,) immediately rose to his feet in the House of Representatives, and moved to modify the resolution to the effect that a commissioner should be sent to Washington to protest that "the war should be conducted in the sense established by the rules of Christian and civilized nations." It was privately explained that the design was only to lay a foundation for negotiations to the extent of experimenting on the Democratic party of the North; and that while the South had already sufficiently offered terms of peace in Mr. Davis's first manifesto at Montgomery, to the effect that eight millions of people, in the right to pursue their own happiness, should be "let alone," it would be an ingenious thing, and have the appearance of great magnanimity, to offer to ameliorate the war at the time that the South was manifestly superior in the contest and her armies actually on the enemy's soil. It was for these reasons that Mr. Davis proposed a mission to Washington, and gave, besides, the most positive and stringent orders that Lee's army was to protect every right of private property in the North, to abstain from retaliation, and to show the utmost regard for the humanities of war. It was not so much to sentimentalism of "Christian warfare" as the calculation of political effect—the demonstration of that idea which Mr. Davis cherished throughout the war, and yet feebly executed, of operating on the division of parties in the North, and thus weakening its resolution and temper in the contest.

But the design in this instance fell through almost at the time it was meditated. While the Commissioner for Washington was being prepared and clothed at Richmond, news came that Lee's army had fallen back across the Potomac, after having fought the unhappy battle of Sharpsburg. This battle General Lee has always claimed as a victory for his army. But its true story is a peculiar one: that of a jaded army; outnumbered, 33,000 against 90,000 (taking the figures from the official reports of each commander, respectively); its plan of campaign betrayed; suffering no defeat; offering battle the day after the main conflict; compelled at last to retire since there was no prospect of reinforcements to balance against the quick reorganization of the enemy; and conducting its retreat so skilfully that not a gun or a single material of war was left behind, and so bravely that (as General A. P. Hill wrote in his official report) "the broad surface of the Potomac was blue with the floating bodies of our foe!" General Lee had designed to hold not only what Mr. Davis called "heroic Maryland," but to plant the war—where Mr. Davis, when speaking in the Senate of the United States, had declared it would be found—in the wheat-fields of Pennsylvania. The steps of the campaign were distinctly marked out:—to capture Harper's Ferry, and then to enter Pennsylvania by the Cumberland Valley.

A single incident was perhaps more fatal to Lee's campaign than the circumstance that he had been compelled to leave ten thousand bare-foot or ill-shod stragglers on the other side of the Potomac. The entire plan of his movement drawn out to detail had been prepared by him at Frederick (Maryland) and been communicated to the different corps commanders. One of the latter—D. H. Hill, a man of coarse and brutal eccentricities—had in a fit of displeasure at the place assigned him, thrown the paper to the ground; it was found by a private in McClellan's army, when it occupied the town and it at once made that commander master of the situation.

The romance of "The Lost Dispatch" was long a subject of painful gossip in the South, and it appears to have founded some strong personal recriminations. It is, indeed, one of these melancholy, familiar romances, where, an apparent trifle has decided the most momentous fate, defeated the most elaborate hopes, and turned the balance of history. A little piece of paper, neglected, given to the winds, becomes the most sorrowful accident of the late war, reveals to a Federal General the entire plan of a campaign, just at the crisis of execution, and plucks from the commander of the Confederates a victory that might have ultimately decided the immense issue of Southern independence. This is not a strained imagination. It is reasonable that if D. H. Hill had not been the instrument of a revelation to McClellan of General Lee's designs in Maryland, the latter succeeding at Harper's Ferry, might have fully collected his forces from that dash, and precipitating them upon the enemy, might have won a complete success, instead of being forced through Hill's disclosures to deliver a battle, with his forces not up, and to cover a retreat where he had hoped to gain a victory.

Since the war Mr. Davis is reported to have referred to this strange incident as an explanation of Lee's defeat in Maryland; but to have added: "I hear that General Hill protests that he never lost or misplaced the order, and that in proof of this he has it yet in his possession among his papers at home. If this is so, that is the end of the matter, and I have no more to say of it." But it is proper to say that in the explanation to which Mr. Davis refers, recently developed in a controversy in the newspapers, General Hill has only been able to assert that he retains a copy of the the order referred to—and thus "The Lost Dispatch" yet remains among the myteries of the war.*

---

* In the controversy referred to, as of a historical question, the author may place here for the interest and curiosity of the reader some parts of a printed reply which he was recently constrained to make to a criticism of D. H. Hill on the now notorious statement of "The Lost Dispatch:"—

* * * * The whole issue is as to the loss of a certain diapatch, by which D. H. Hill became the instrument of a revelation to the enemy, that defeated General Lee's first campaign in Maryland in 1862. Here is the statement which the author made of the extraordinary accident, and here hinge the twenty pages of D. H. Hill's criticism:

"A copy of the order directing the movement of the army from Frederick had been sent to D. H. Hill; and this vain and petulant officer, in a moment of passion, had thrown the paper on the ground. It was picked up by a Federal soldier, and McClellan thus strangely became possessed of the exact detail of his adversary's plan of operations."—*Lost Cause*, p. 314.

* * * * We have the evidence in our hands that, before the light obtained from the "The Lost Dispatch," McClellan was completely

The last winter months of 1862 found Lee reorganizing his army in the neighborhood of Winchester, Virginia, and Bragg fronting Rosecrans on the lines of Nashville, Tennes-

---

bewildered as to General Lee's designs; that he was in doubt whether he was progressing to Pennsylvania or aiming at Baltimore; that he knew nothing of the disposition of the Confederate forces beyond a vague idea that they were in the vicinity of Frederick, and that "the unready Athelstane" was never less prepared to do battle than he was until Hill's disclosure came to his information and relief. Here is McClellan's own account of the event, and his implied estimation of its importance:

"On the 13th of September an order fell into my hands, issued by General Lee, *which fully disclosed his plans*, and I *immediately* gave orders for a rapid and vigorous forward movement."—*Report of the Organization and Campaigns of the Army of the Potomac. McClellan*, p. 352.

The author prepared his account of "The Lost Dispatch," and of D. H. Hill's carelessness, productive, as it was, of the defeat of the Maryland campaign, from persons singularly intelligent and disinterested, and whose commentaries were far severer than that to which the irate General has chosen to respond. He should turn his pen to these commentators who have spread the disgraceful story over half the globe, instead of making a partial recourse, or an ingenious diversion to this writer.

First we have the account of an English writer, Lieutenant-Colonel Fletcher, of Scots Fusileer Guards, who has recently written a most just and admirable history of the Confederate war, published by Bentley, London. This intelligent officer will be remembered as having travelled both North and South during the war; as having had excellent opportunities of observation; as having resided for some time in the Confederate camps, and as, therefore, possessing unusual claims to credit, on the score both of correct information and of impartial justice. Here is his account of "The Lost Dispatch:"

"General Lee directed D. Hill, with his division, to guard the passes through South Mountain, and to cover the siege of Harper's

see. It was not the situation that the South had hoped for when the command "forward" had rung from Richmond to the lagoons of Mississippi; and yet we repeat there were

---

Ferry. To insure a distinct understanding of the plan of operations, he sent written orders, to D. Hill; and this document, detailing with exactitude the proposed movements of the several portions of the army, fell into the hands of General McClellan. It had been conveyed to D. Hill, who, after reading it, either through a feeling of impatience at its contents, or through carelessness, threw or let it fall on the ground, and, lying there forgotten, it was picked up by a soldier of the Federal army, and forwarded at once to McClellan, who thus became possessed of his adversary's plan of operations. This knowledge enabled General McClellan to direct the movements of his army with certainty."—*Fletcher's History.* Bentley, London. Vol. 2, p. 157.

We have a yet more detailed account of this unhappy disclosure to the enemy, again from a foreigner, supposed to write with no partiality for the North, and certainly with no personal animosity toward D. H. Hill. We quote from an article in the *Quarterly Review*, composed from various testimonies concerning the war:

"But before D. H. Hill fell back upon South Mountain, it is now notorious that a momentous incident had happened. It will be necessary to give a few words of the character of this General. It should be premised that the wives of D. H. Hill and Stonewall Jackson are sisters, and it is generally believed (we know not with what truth) that Mrs. Hill had long urged her husband to do something whereby some portion of Jackson's lustrous fame might be acquired by, and accrue to D. H. Hill. * * The orders of General Lee respecting the battle, which was now imminent, were placed in General Hill's hands. These orders, according to General Lee's invariable practice, were full, precise and unreserved. It was, according to General Lee's views, very desirable to gain a few days, in order to permit General Jackson to finish his task at Harper's Ferry, and to allow some of the many stragglers to get to the front. General Hill was, therefore, instructed to take up a strong position at South Mountain. These orders, as it happened, were displeasing to Gene-

lively and visible causes of congratulation, and that the Confederacy had won the highest honors for its arms in this most memorable period of the war.

---

ral Hill. He flung them after reading them, indignantly from him, in the belief (as has been urged in his defence) that they would be picked up by one of his staff, and carried safely to his quarters. Be this as it may, they were left lying where they fell; the ground was shortly afterward evacuated by the Confederates, and occupied by the Federals; General Lee's orders were picked up by a Federal soldier, and their value being recognized, quickly carried to McClellan. No wonder that McClellan, commanding, according to his own statement, 87,164, and according to the other Federal statements, 110,000 men, promised himself an assured and easy victory over the worn and weary troops which he knew to be before him, and as to whose movements and intentions he now had full information." —*Quarterly Review*, April Number, 1864, pp. 303, 304.

It will doubtless surprise the reader that in face of these multiplied, vivid and detailed evidences, D. H. Hill should deny that he lost the dispatch referred to, and that it ever passed through his hands! The denial is unfortunately argumentative. He admits: "There can be no doubt that such a dispatch was lost; but it is obviously unfair to assume that a paper with my name on the envelope was necessarily lost by me in person." He argues that he carefully preserved a *copy* of said dispatch, and now has it in red tape among his military remains. This is not evidence, it is trash. But the worst part of D. H. Hill's explanation is that he argues with suspicious industry that, *if* such dispatch was lost by him, it was really of no value to McClellan; that "the loss of the order was a benefit, and not an injury to the Confederate arms!"

It is a most suspicious *if*, and an absurdity so bald and insolent that we scarcely know how to comment on it. Certainly, it will occur to the reader that McClellan himself was the best judge of the value of such a paper as a revelation; and we have seen him in the quotation from his official report made above, admitting, unwillingly, and at the expense of his own penetration and genius, that the discovery of the dispatch was decisive, that it "fully disclosed" Lee's

Thus although the campaigns directed against the Potomac and the Ohio fell short of their prizes, they secured a military prestige for the South, almost unequalled in modern times.

---

plans, and enabled himself to make the movement that decided the battle of Antietam, or Sharpsburg.

As if in profound ignorance of all historical record of this matter, and without the least reference of McClellan's own report, D. H. Hill goes on complacently to argue that the Federal commander might have obtained from his scouts, etc., all the information that the dispatch furnished, and that, therefore, the discovery of it was harmless. He says: "McClellan would have been the most inefficient of Generals, could he not have gained that information in a friendly country from his own scouts and spies."

Is it possible that this innocence of D. H. Hill is unfeigned, that he never read a document so important to this whole question as McClellan's official report! The dispatch, as we have seen, came into the hands of the Federal commander on the 13th of September. Now, let us see what he says of the state of his information previous to this:

"On the 10th of September I received *from my scouts* information which rendered it quite *probable* that General Lee's army was in the vicinity of Frederick, but *whether his intention was to move forward toward Baltimore or Pennsylvania was not then known.*"—*Report of the Organization and Campaigns of the Army of the Potomac. McClellan*, p. 352.

He does not refer to any other source of information of General Lee's movements, until he records, with sudden vivacity, the discovery of the all-important dispatch, and his "immediate" movement thereupon. Before this he was almost completely in the dark; he had not the smallest suspicion of the leaguer of Harper's Ferry; he had no plan of campaign until that dispatch, betraying not only Stonewall Jackson's diversion, but the movements of every corps of Lee's army, illuminated the whole field and put in his hands the means of victory!

This is the whole sorrowful story, and argument ends with McClellan's own admissions.

They were luminous tracks of glory; it was the period of the world's greatest admiration of the arms of the South; they had already secured a reputation, which without the recognition of the Confederacy at the council-board of nations, yet placed it in the front rank of heroic peoples. And here we may pause to consider that one thing so remarkable in the war which the enemies of the South in all their busy and daring misrepresentations have never been able to deny—the one thread of gold which no web of invention ventures to omit—the exceeding valor of those devoted men who carried on their bayonets the hopes of the South and the fortunes of Jefferson Davis.

No matter how defective was the government of the Southern Confederacy, no matter what of weakness or dishonor there was at Richmond, the armies of that Confederacy won a renown as imperishable as history; and no reflections on any political questions can diminish or disturb the tribute to the Southern soldier. Indeed that tribute is best defended on the hypothesis of the unworthiness of the Confederate Government; for how can we explain that a people so brave, occupying such breadth of territory, in fact superior to the North in the advantages of the contest when we come to balance against the larger numbers and resources of the latter the aggregate of circumstances, that the South was on the defensive, that she had a superior cause and better inspiration, that she did not suffer as the North did from political divisions, and that she occupied an extent of territory such as the world has never seen conquered, except through some decay of the spirit of its defenders—should have been subjugated, and subjugated so thoroughly, unless we take the supposition that the merits of the Southern army and all the advantages nature had given it were outweighed by the faults of its government. It is the theory most honorable to the Southern soldier, although the one most unpleasant to Jefferson Davis.*

---

* There has been a very superficial, and to some people a very pleasant way of accounting for the downfall of the Southern Confederacy, by simply ascribing it to the great superiority of the North in numbers and resources. This argument has had a great career in the newspapers and in small publications; and the vulgar mind is easily imposed upon by the statistical parallel and the arithmetical statement, inclined as it is to limit its comprehension of great historical problems to mere material views of the question. There is no doubt that this superiority of the North in numbers had great weight; that it contributed much to the discomfiture of the Confederacy; that it must be taken largely into any explanation of the results of the war—but the great question, at last, remains—Was this numerical inequality, of itself, sufficient to determine the war in favor of the North, considering the great compensation which the South had in superior animation, in the circumstance of fighting on the defensive, and, above all, in the great extent of her territory? We fear that the lessons and examples of history are to the contrary, and we search in vain for one instance where a country of such extent as the Confederacy has been so thoroughly subdued by any amount of military force, *unless where popular demoralization has supervened.* If war was a contest on an open plain, where military forces fight a duel, of course that inferior in numbers must go under. But war is an intricate game, and there are elements in it far more decisive than that of numbers. At the beginning of the war in America all intelligent men in the world and the Southern leaders themselves knew the disparity of population and consequently of military force as between the North and South; but they did not on that account determine that the defeat of the South was a foregone conclusion, and the argument comes with a bad grace from leaders of the Confederacy to ascribe now its failure to what stared them in the face at the commencement of the contest, and was then so lightly and even insolently dismissed from their calculation. The judgment of men who reflected, was that the South would be ultimately the victor, mainly because it was impossible to conquer *space;* that her subjection was a "geo-

It is in contemplating the splendid martial valor of the South the bitterest thought of the war seizes us:—that it should after the campaign we have described have been so misdirected mainly through the errors and conceits of one man, and that it should have shed its blood so utterly in vain. It was, indeed, this extraordinary virtue of Southern soldiers that, alone, sustained for four years the unwise, capricious, and incoherent government of Mr. Davis, which, without this support, without this ornament, would have much sooner sunk into contempt and ruin. In view of the volume of lost blood and in view of the tens of thousands of human lives, many of which must have been sacrificed to the maladministration of Jefferson Davis, it is wonderful what self-complacency this person is reported to display in looking back upon the war, when it might be supposed that the retrospection would be enough to plunge him into melancholy, if not to torture him with self-reproaches for the remnant of his days. The cheerfulness which Mr. Davis has shown since the war, his habits of light conversation on it, and his lively assertions of satisfaction at his own part in it are not pleasant to those who look back upon one of the greatest stories of human sacrifice that has taken place in this age. If the thought of wasted blood

graphical impossibility"; that three millions of men could not garrison her territory; that a country so vast and of such peculiar features—not open as the European countries, and traversed everywhere by practicable roads, but wild and difficult with river, mountain, and swamp, equivalent to successive lines of military fortifications, welted, as it were, with natural mounds and barriers—could never be brought under subjection to the military power of the North. And these views were severely just; they are true forever, now as formerly; but they proceeded on the supposition that the *morale* of the Confederacy would be preserved, and when the hypothesis fell (mainly through maladministration in Richmond) the argument fell with it."—*The Lost Cause*, pp. 727, 728.

did not ride his dreams like a demon, it might at least have given a shadow to his countenance, or engraved there some lines of regret. It has done neither. The valor of the South is its immortal ornament in the war; but it is full of reproaches and of sad reflections for those who abused it by useless sacrifices, and at last betrayed it through an incompetent and wanton rule.

In some periods of the history of the war—and never more so than at the close of the campaign of 1862—it appeared as if the bravery of the soldiers of the South would accomplish its independence, despite the imperfect and slattern support it got from the government at Richmond, despite the shortcomings and misdeeds of Mr. Davis. This, indeed, was the only hope of thoughtful persons in the South. The spirit and efficiency of the soldiers, they considered, would be superior to the errors of the government. But these errors—as we shall hereafter see—were to become so large, so critical, that the bravest army in the world could no longer struggle against them with success. The blood it lost, wherever or in whatever proportion it can be traced to an unwise and dishonest administration, will forever cry from the ground; and it is one of the bitterest wails that has ever ascended the skies, accusing the folly and inhumanity of rulers.

But in the season of success there is unhappily but little place in the vulgar mind either for reflection or for criticism on what has happened. The popular elation in the South which ensued on the campaign of 1862, was impatient of the doubts and speculations of those who suggested that the war was to be considerably prolonged, and that its issue in the independence of the Confederacy was by no means yet secure. The criticism of the newspapers on Mr. Davis's administration was for once disarmed. The President was inflated with illimitable and unimaginable confidence. In his gale of spirits at what Lee and Bragg had accomplished, he proposed a pleasant visit to his native State, Mississippi, to indulge there his congratulations on the success of the war. He visited the Legislature of that State; he was received with unbounded acclamations; it was the occasion of rhetorical compliments; and the President, with eyes suffused, and placing his hand on his heart, declared that in all the brilliant array around his capital, he had looked upon Mississippi soldiers with a pride and emotion that no other had inspired. He ventured a memorable prophecy of the war. He had reason to believe that it would soon be closed; "in all respects, moral as well as physical, the Confederacy was better prepared than it was a year previous;" and, extending his arm in a theatrical manner, he declared that the star of peace would soon appear on the horizon of the West.

About the time the President was thus vividly prophesying the approaching termination of the war, a statesman of Virginia—John B. Floyd, then in obscurity, to which he had been consigned by Mr. Davis for the affair at Fort Donelson—wrote a private letter to Mr. Curry of Alabama. In that letter the retired statesman exhorted one of the most thoughtful and cultivated members of Congress to impress that body with the view that the war was to be continued for a long time yet, that it would demand enlarged sacrifices, and besought him, with an earnest solicitude not intended for the public eye, that he should urge increased means to meet the recovered spirit of the North, then re-organizing its armies, and accumulating its resources. The two views were in singular contrast. The Richmond *Examiner* published them in juxtaposition in its columns—and awaited the commentary of time on their relative truth and value.

CHAPTER XVI.

Some Account of the Secret Misgivings or Private Calculations of Mr. Davis concerning the War—His Delinquency on the Subject of Retaliation—A Record of Weak Threats—The Emancipation Proclamation of President Lincoln the Supreme Act of Outrage in the War—Excited Propositions in the Confederate Congress—Various Resolutions for Retaliation—The Response of Mr. Davis practically Nothing—His Infamous Subterfuge, Suggesting Retaliation by the States—How Mr. Yancey Ridiculed it—A Distinct Law of Retaliation Passed by the Confederate Congress—Mr. Davis Refuses to Execute it—Curious Explanation of Mr. Davis's Unwillingness to Retaliate on the Enemy—A Detestable Calculation for his Personal Safety—Singular Apology for Mr. Davis by South Carolina Ladies—Moral Cowardice of Mr. Davis—Some Reflections on the True Nature of Courage—Excessive Admiration in the South of Mere Physical Manhood—Bravado of Mr. Davis—The Emancipation Proclamation an Encouragement to the North—Review of the Military Situation at the Close of 1862—The South Retires to a Defensive Policy—Summary of its Military Plans.

If President Davis was so well assured as he professed to be in his speech in Mississippi, of the success of the Confederate cause, he had but a poor way of showing it in one remarkable line of conduct in his administration. With a faith so firm, it might have been supposed that the tone of his administration would have been high and unyielding, if not positively defiant. It was, indeed, excessively so in words; but when it came to acts, and especially to retaliatory measures for the outrages and atrocities of the enemy—a class of measures which might have given the best evidence of the true resolution and spirit of his government, the best test of the firm and sperate mind which he displayed in rhetorical declamations—he invariably blanched, broke down and fell into the weakest and most contemptible negativeness. It was this delinquency on a point where the sensitiveness of the Southern people was especially keen and exasperated, that showed on Mr. Davis's part an extreme moral timidity, or suggested his secret despair at times of a cause of which he yet made, publicly, such a boastful profession of confidence.

To the period of the war of which we are now treating, the enemy had committed a series of outrages that had raised an outcry for retaliation, or for some sort of retributive justice that, apart from the satisfaction of vengeance, would attest the dignity and firmness of the Confederate government. Mr. Davis had replied with pronunciamentos, gloomy appeals, and melodramatic threats with respect to retaliation; but it is remarkable that in not a single case had he executed the *lex talionis,* that he had made a record of bluster, without one solitary performance to sustain the position of the Southern Confederacy as an equal combatant, with the same recourse to extraordinary measures as the North might claim; that when brought face to face with the stern duties of retaliation, the imperious traits of his character had suddenly disappeared, and been replaced by halting timidity and weak hesitation. Mumford, the martyr of New Orleans, had been hung by General Butler. Mr. Davis had threatened retaliation, and yet dropped the whole subject after he had procured a letter of protest to be written by General Lee, which was returned to him by the Washington authorities, with the endorsement that it was "exceedingly insulting," and therefore dismissed. The "Palmyra massacre" had gone unavenged. Mr. Davis had ordered the execution in retaliation of ten Federal prisoners; but when the fatal day came the order was suspended, nothing was heard more of the threatened melodrama, and the President, having made an unworthy *show* of compliance with the demands of public sentiment in the South by ordering the execution of ten designated prisoners, secretly went back upon it, and wrote a private telegram to suspend the sentence he had publicly pronounced. In no case had an act of retaliation been performed; in no case had a single victim been demanded for the various murders committed by the enemy—until at last that enemy, encouraged by impunity, and having no fear of retribution before his eyes, ventured upon a supreme act of outrage, one that fairly crowned his unparalleled boldness and atrocity in the war.

This act was the Emancipation Proclamation of President Lincoln. It was to take effect on the 1st of January, 1863. Here was an act aimed to destroy three thousand millions of dollars of property in the South, designed to disorganize its whole society, and calculated to light the flames of servile insurrection in the midst of a civil war. If any thing could have kindled in Mr. Davis's breast a courageous resentment, and have laid a foundation for retaliatory measures, it might have been supposed that this huge wickedness would have done it. It occasioned an outburst of anger in the South; and proposition after proposition followed in the Confederate Congress to make some response of spirit to a measure so infamous and so cruel, to mark in some way the popular sense of this unsurpassed outrage of the war.

The first motion in the Confederate Congress, when, after the battle of Sharpsburg, the preliminary announcement was made of the design of the Northern Government to declare free, at a future day, the slaves of the South, was to condemn it in a formal resolution as "a gross violation of the usages of civilized warfare, an outrage on the rights of private property, and an invitation to an atrocious servile warfare." This resolution proceeded to declare that the proclamation of Abraham Lincoln "should be held up to the execration of mankind, and counteracted by such retaliatory measures as in the judgment of the President may be best calculated to secure its withdrawal or arrest its execution." Several members of Congress made speeches which even exceeded the strong language of the resolution. Mr. Clark, of Missouri, was in favor of declaring every citizen of the Southern Confederacy a soldier authorized to put to death every man caught on Southern soil in arms against the government. Mr. Henry, of Tennessee, said that the resolution did not go far enough. He favored the passage of a law providing that upon any attempt being made to execute the proclamation of Abraham Lincoln, the Confederates should immediately hoist the "black flag," and proclaim a war of extermination upon all invaders of their soil. Another member offered a resolution as a substitute for that referred to:—"That from this day forth, all rules of civilized warfare should be discarded in the future defence of our country, our liberties and our lives, against the fell design now openly avowed by the Government of the United States to annihilate or enslave us; and that a *war of extermination* should henceforth be waged against every invader whose hostile foot shall cross the boundaries of these Confederate States."

Such sentiments were undoubtedly extravagant and bad. They are significant, however, of the resentment aroused in the South by the Emancipation Proclamation, and of the popular demand for a measure of retaliation. Yet Congress was forced to perceive that the question of retaliation was exclusively an Executive one; and after indicating its own passions and desires in this matter, it was compelled for a time to commit it to the discretion and pleasure of President Davis. The convenient disposition of the matter, for some months at least, was the passage of a resolution, declaring that Congress would sustain the President in such retaliatory measures as he might adopt.

The response of Mr. Davis was practically nothing. He strained language to denounce the great act of spoliation and crime in the proclamation of Mr. Lincoln; he attempted to drown public indignation in a volume of furious words; but he ventured not upon a single measure of revenge upon the enemy, and could invent nothing in the way of retribution. To the greatest outrage in American annals Mr. Davis never had a single practical act of retribution in reply. The Emancipation Proclamation is truly an instance without parallel in the history of war of an outrage so large provoking no responsive measure, suffered without practical retort or remedy. It passed off after a brief rhetorical heat on the part of Mr. Davis. There could be nothing more contemptible in the career of the Confederate President, than the mean patience with which he submitted to an act of the enemy which despoiled a whole people of their property, and consigned them to a loss and ruin unequalled in all the penalties of modern war.

But there is yet something of infamous subterfuge to add to this record of omission of duty on the part of President Davis. At a date many months subsequent to that of the Emancipation Proclamation, Mr. Davis having done nothing to testify his resentment of it beyond rhetorical effusions, useless expenditures of words, and at last excited by the indignation of the people, who not only saw this proclamation going into effect without retaliation or check, but witnessed the enlargement of it in the enlistment of Negro troops, saw it carried to the consequences of employing the emancipated slave either as the agent of a servile insurrection or as a Federal soldier, his arms turned against his former master, the Confederate President, convinced at last that something should be done to appease popular clamor, invented a subterfuge, probably the meanest of all his stock of expedients, to escape the due responsibility of his office, and to captivate by pretences the sentiment of the vulgar. It was only when the consequences of Emancipation had been realized to the extent we have described, and when more than one battle-field had been disfigured by black brigades, that Mr. Davis, in the later months of 1863, made the infamous proposition to relieve the Confederate Government of all responsibility for retaliation, by bestowing it upon the States; suggesting that under the local laws of each State, and in their courts, Federal prisoners might be prosecuted as criminals, and be made amenable to the statutes on the subject of Negro insurrections. It was a most unworthy and superficial device; a silly and flagitious plot to relieve the Confederate Government of a proper responsibility, and to saddle on the States a duty growing out of the war, and belonging to the former government as the supreme power conducting the war, and bound to declare a general law in this respect for all the States. If the States might treat as criminals the soldiers armed under the Emancipation Proclamation, and punish the marauders as common malefactors, why might not the Confederate Government do the same? And if Mr. Davis was willing to remit the duty of retaliation to the States, why was he so exclusive and jealous and retentive with respect to all other faculties of his administration in the conduct of the war—why make an exception of this particular matter in which his powers were written so plainly, and in which the jurisdiction of the State was no more coincident than in any other affair of the war?

This mean proposition to abdicate to the State Governments retaliation upon the public enemy, was sharply reproved in Congress, which had, at least, sense and temper enough to refuse to be made a party to such a trick on the demands of public sentiment. In a secret session of this body it was roughly ridiculed. Mr. Yancey, Senator from Alabama, applied to it unsparingly the *reductio ad absurdum.* If the Federal soldier might be punished in a State Court, under the statute concerning Negro insurrections, then, one law of the State being no more sacred than another, he might be punished for equal reason under the law of trespass. If the Confederate Government might shift the responsibility of retaliation upon the local laws of the separate States in one case, the same responsibility might be assumed by the latter in all cases. The proposition of Mr. Davis, made in a special message, was rejected with emphasis. Congress declared plainly in joint resolutions passed near the close of the year 1863, that "the commissioned officers of the enemy ought not to be delivered to the authorities of the respective States, as suggested in the said message, but all captives taken by the Confederate forces ought to be dealt with and disposed of by the Confederate Government;" it re-committed the subject of retaliation to the President; it re-affirmed its declaration that the Emancipation Proclamation was "inconsistent with the spirit of those usages which in modern warfare prevail among civilized nations;" and it went further, and passed a distinct law, as if to impose upon the President the duty of retaliation, which heretofore it had been willing to leave to measures of his own direction. This law was as follows:

> "Every person being a commissioned officer, or acting as such in the service of the enemy, who shall, during the present war, excite, attempt, or cause to be excited, servile insurrection, or who shall incite, or cause to be incited, a slave to rebel, shall, if captured, be put to death, or be otherwise punished, at the discretion of the court."

This law was never executed in a single instance. It is

doubtful whether it was ever published, unless in a limited range of official documents. The President paid no attention to it, and never referred to its existence. He was only impressed by it to the extent that he ceased to write those gloomy and vaporing messages about taking vengeance upon the enemy, which he had been tolerably safe in doing, as long as retaliation was an abstract speculation, a text of sentimental rhetoric, and not, as now, the subject of a neglected law, and likely, if disturbed, to develope an ugly record and to show to the world his weakness and his infamy.

There have been many attempts to explain the remissness of retaliation on the part of Mr. Davis, not only in the instance of the Emancipation Proclamation and its incidents, but when the atrocities of the enemy were of the darkest kind, and when, from all parts of the South, the cries of anger, or the wails of despair, smote his ears. Why should he have been so considerate of humanity to an enemy, who constantly outraged all the rules of civilized warfare, and who even insulted his tenderness as the cowardice of the culprit in despair? The effect of the non-retaliation policy, so studiously preserved by Mr. Davis, was not only to give particular causes of complaint to those who suffered from the outrages of the enemy, but in its moral influence, it was to diminish the true inspiration of the war in the South, to an extent which we believe has never been justly accounted. It was to represent the South constantly in the position of a moral inferior; to create the idea that its people, instead of equal belligerents, were culprits, evading and postponing the penalty of their crimes; to interpret to the world the hostilities of the North as military execution and coercion; to concede to the enemy the great moral advantage and prestige which officers of the law have over malefactors.

Why Mr. Davis should have thus so greatly injured the inspiration of the war, and the dignity of his government, is a curious problem, and one that admits a number of hypotheses. There was long a painful suspicion in Richmond that the President was by no means so confident of the issue of the war as he publicly professed to be, that he had secret misgivings, and that in the event of failure he had plotted his own safety, and that he had, therefore, feared to exact any retribution from the public enemy, for which he might hereafter be called personally to account. This explanation of the non-retaliation policy was not without plausibility. If the war should fail it might be to the interest of Mr. Davis that he should come out of it without any blood on his hands, and in the character of one who had conducted a moderate warfare; while whatever vindictive measures the enemy might resolve upon, in case of success, might be ingeniously diverted to certain mean subordinates, for whose acts of cruelty and oppression he might easily claim that he was not personally responsible. It was a detestable calculation; but it has been so closely fulfilled by the actual sequel of the war, that we are not permitted to regard it as a mere imaginary supposition. Since the termination of the war, and when victims have been claimed of such inconsiderable agents of the Confederate Government, as Wirz and Braine and Surratt, it is remarkable that the plea has been busily made for a merciful consideration of Mr. Davis, that he was averse to any acts of even apparent cruelty upon the enemy, that no blood had ever been shed by his direct order, even in the way of retaliation, and that he had resisted the popular passion upon this point, keeping his hands scrupulously clean. This ground of mercy for the fallen chief of the Confederacy has appeared since the war in a petition sent to Washington, by some ladies of South

Carolina, and in terms so distinct and ingenious as to suggest that they were dictated from some quarter of calculation, such as we have described. These petitioners write thus of Mr. Davis:—"The same firmness and calm views of policy, which on repeated occasions he displayed in resisting the cries, which in his region were raised, for sanguinary retaliation, we hope will now be exhibited, in disregard of the unfeeling agitation which seeks his life."

John M. Daniel was accustomed to say that if the war resulted against the South, Jefferson Davis would be found safe in Europe. The ex-President could have no fear of any indictments for murder or cruelty; and having taken care not to inculpate himself directly in those affairs which might most excite the resentment of the enemy, and playing himself off as a humane and chivalric combatant, he might easily escape those passions likely to result should the North prove victorious after the exasperation of years of hard and expensive war.

It is not impossible that such calculations may have entered the mind of Mr. Davis. The suspicion increases when we find him constantly declining all acts of retaliation and yet doing so by devious processes, and all the time proclaiming an excessive fury of resentment for stated outrages of the enemy and yet forbearing from the very acts which such passion, if real, would naturally produce. There must have been a game of hypocrisy somewhere in a difference so wide between professions and acts—the professions serving to gratify the anger of the South and yet the acts (acts of omission) calculated to appease whatever might be the ultimate and practical complaints of the North. No man in the South could write or speak more strongly than Mr. Davis did of the outrages of the enemy; yet no man could be weaker or more derelict when he came to translate his words into acts. The contrast between the two is so sharp and wide that it is impossible not to admit in it some charge of insincerity, or some supposition of a dishonest and evil calculation.

But more than one reason may be adduced to explain Mr. Davis's delinquency in the matter of retaliation; and it is not unlikely that a composition of motives governed him in his declination of all harsh measures against the Washington Government as equivalents of its own outrages. His natural spirit was not firm enough for a policy of retaliation. He had a weak sentimentalism in his character which made him the prey of all artful petitioners; a man who wept easily, whose tears laid shallow, who was readily moved by appeals to mercy at variance with justice. He was accessible to all emotional influences. "If I ever had a point to make on President Davis," said a Richmond politician, "I always got his pastor, Dr. Minnigerode, to see him." A character so shallow and hesitating was not that to furnish those firm and severe measures in a state of war, where there is no place for the tender emotions, and where the man of iron is the type of wisdom and of courage.

It is true that we have heretofore written of the courage of Mr. Davis, in a certain sense—as exhibited on the field of Manassas and elsewhere—and we are not disposed to detract anything from that tribute. But the President of the Confederate States appears to us a striking example of that character, which those experienced in the world sometimes meet with, of persons physically brave, ready in a certain exaltation of spirits to put their lives at a pin's fee, and yet so utterly and woefully defective in moral courage, that the meanest temptations make them their victims, and the most unworthy weaknesses display them to the world. Mr. Davis was not a man who shirked physical dangers; and yet we find him the picture of shrinking timidity on every appeal to moral courage, a man who wore around his Administration a belt of preachers and women, who had no mind of his own, unless to display it in obstinacy to those who bluntly advised him, or to surrender it in weak acquiescences to those who ingeniously cajoled him. He had "pluck," combativeness; he might have fought on any trial of physical hardihood; he might have ridden grandly into the tides of battle with his life on his sleeve; and yet, after all, he might have had no moral courage, and been the man we have described as trembling at the vision of retribution, and afraid to undertake the tasks of justice which retaliation upon the enemy demanded.

There is an excess of admiration in the world for the courage that despises physical dangers. More than this there appears to be a certain indulgence for all the weaknesses of men accounted brave; and sometimes the very fact that these persons are weak in all other respects than that of facing a certain amount of physical peril; that they are slaves of paltry influences; that they are victims of the dram-shop; that they yield to the most unworthy temptations; that the man who can march to a cannon is yet, like one of Napoleon's marshals, afraid of the spider in his coach; that he who can draw his weapon in mortal conflict on the slightest provocation is yet the slave of vice and dissipation, the sport of every adventurer who practices on the weak side of his character, has been held as a sort of lively and interesting contrast to the bellicose virtue of the individual. The anecdotes of these contradictions of character have not unfrequently been taken as pleasant. The man who defies death on a battle-field, or who is willing to venture his life in a personal conflict, may be a sot, or the unworthiest wretch and coward in every moral relation of life, and yet a certain admiration clings to him as the brave man, with foibles that are curious, rather than with faults which are detestable. The reflection forces itself—has not the world attached too much value to the mere physical brawn which may despise danger in certain shapes, and is yet coupled with equivocation and disgrace in every true relation of moral courage. Especially does this reflection apply to the countrymen of Mr. Davis, where a coarse, untravelled people have formed an estimate of courage peculiarly rude; where the person who can give most proofs of physical manhood, the hero who can fight on call with bowie-knife or pistol, who can exhibit the longest list of adventures with women, who is the best shot, the best rider, the best in all contests and games of virility, is taken as the approved pattern of courage, and is allowed almost illimitable indulgences for every sort of moral cowardice that he may choose to couple with his mere physical prowess.

The people of the South are excessive in their admiration of a low physical courage. A certain amount of animal combativeness has been often vulgarly taken for a type of "Southern Chivalry"; but the thoughtful and manful spirit will always reject such estimates of courage, or rate them at their due, considering that this noble virtue is not the transport of a passion, or the accident of a physical constitution, but rather the balance of just and heroic resolutions in all the affairs of life. He who cannot say "No" to a temptation, who cannot rule his own spirit, who cannot put the opinion of men under his feet, and act in the secret light of his own convictions of right and duty—he who is the pallid instrument of other men's designs and influences—may be ready to risk his life on battle-fields, or to accept challenges to mortal conflict, or to give all the vulgar exhibitions of high spirit; yet he is not the brave man—neither in that sense in which the exalted sentences of the Christian religion have it written, nor in that wherein the cultivated voice of human civilization has decided the noblest title of humanity.

But we wander to reflections too distant and general, concerning the kind and degree of courage in the composition of Mr. Davis. The design has been only to show his lack of a real spirited response to the supreme outrage compassed in the Emancipation Proclamation of Abraham Lincoln, especially in view of his vapors of retaliation, as a remarkable evidence of the weakness and chicanery of the President of the Confederacy, and of his cowardly calculation of personal safety in a war, in which, on other occasions, he had breathed such expressions of confidence. The whole subject is intimately connected with the character of Mr. Davis; it illustrates his weakness, his moral cowardice, his habits of deception; and it gives the history of at least one of his principal games on the credulity of the South, and suggests a reflection on its easy confidence in its public men, and its absurd admiration of pretence and bravado, in forms the most plethoric, though in disguises the least ingenious.

To the mind of the North, the Emancipation Proclamation, uninterrupted by any retaliation on the part of the South, was the signal of renewed confidence and animation in the war. Its moral effect was thus vast. To be sure, coming after the autumn campaign of 1862, so splendid for the South, it did not suggest a military situation of much advantage to the North, one visibly calculated to support a measure which could only be interpreted as one of imperious, unscrupulous exaction on an adversary sure to be conquered. The results of that campaign we have already distributed. The South had been forced back to the defensive; Lee had been expelled from Maryland, and Bragg had retreated to Tennessee; but the balance of glory was on the side of the Confederate forces; their arms had acquired their greatest prestige, their marches had been tracked with brilliant victories, their retreats or retrogrades had been encumbered with rich spoils, and if the campaign had regained no political territory, it had yet recovered many districts of subsistence, and was able to display the visible fruits of success.

Yet the thoughtful mind easily discovered under these accumulations the fact that the Confederacy had strained itself in this memorable campaign, that it had put forth for the time, the utmost of its resources, that it had made exertions which it would not readily renew, and that a period of exhaustion was likely to ensue after such an extraordinary development of the strength of the South. The conscription had been taxed to the limits that the law allowed; the number of able-bodied men was becoming fatally reduced; the depreciation of the currency was near the verge beyond which it might be precipitated into worthlessness; and the condition of the South was precisely that which required time for recruitment, and in which the enemy might boastfully anticipate and amuse his own leisure with schemes, like the Emancipation Proclamation, predicated on his final success, or even with glimpses of "reconstruction."

It was thus that after the campaign of the summer and fall months of 1862, the South relapsed to a defensive policy. Its military plans for the remainder of the year may be generally described as a habitual, common attempt to annoy the enemy, a lookout for the preservation of Richmond, and the chief concern of keeping up the blockade of the Mississippi river by holding the strong positions of Vicksburg and Port Hudson. In such a situation, it was to prepare for the great contest of the summer of 1863, and from such extremity it was again to display its arms in another campaign—a campaign where we shall see raised again the balance of the war at almost equal arms;—so equal that we shall find the decision trembling on the edge of a battle-field, and cast by a single incident that fortune threw in the hesitating scale.

CHAPTER XVII

The Battles of Murfreesboro', of Fredericksburg, and of Chancellorsville—A Trio of Important Contests—A Singular and Romantic Incident of the Field of Fredericksburg—Stonewall Jackson Makes a Proposition to Massacre the Enemy in the Night—Parallel between the Battles of Fredericksburg and Chancellorsville—Death of Jackson—Mr. Davis's Tribute to Him—Character of Stonewall Jackson—Poverty of Genius in the War—Jackson and his Sophomorical Admirers—The Rag-Tag Style of Eulogistic Criticism—The Religious Character of Jackson not Admirable—Estimate of Him as a Commander—His Gloomy Ideas of War—He Proposes "the Black Flag"—His Enormous and Consuming Ambition—Description of His Person—In what Respects, he was the Representative of the South—A Particular Description of his Last Moments.

THE battles of Murfreesboro', of Fredericksburg and of Chancellorsville, occurring after the date to which we have brought down the general story of the war, do not claim extended notices, even in a purely military history of the Confederacy (which latter it is scarcely necessary to repeat is not within the limited design of our work). They were brilliant incidents of arms; they were large and bloody contests; but they are not connected with any great chain of movements, they left but little impression on the fortunes of the Confederacy, and the military era of greatest interest after that we have placed in the autumn of 1862, when the war was carried to the frontier by Lee and Bragg, may be taken as occurring not until the midsummer of 1863, when two important campaigns in the two great divisions of the Confederacy culminated at Gettysburg and Vicksburg. The military history of the Confederacy, so far, may be divided into eras: first, Manassas and its consequences; second, the autumn campaign of 1862; and third, the movements to which we have yet to refer, as the second experiment of the invasion of the enemy's country and the breaking of the line of the Mississippi. We have not yet reached in the just course of our narrative this third period of interest in the military fortunes of the Confederacy; but between it and the second period, as referred to in a former chapter, there is a space of only slight and desultory interest; for however great were the three battles we have named, they were only single incidents and left but shallow traces on the general military situation.

Fredericksburg and Chancellorsville are chiefly significant as defeats of the *fourth* and *fifth* attempts of the "On to Richmond" adventure of the enemy. But these two fields and that of Murfreesboro' are curiously alike in illustrating the barrenness of Confederate victories, and repeating the uniform story of successes not followed up, of glorious "first days" of contest with an invariable sequel of disappointment. After all, they were repetitions of the untimely halt at Manassas: a comparative estimate of mortality lists, a balance of carnage in favor of the South, the escape of the enemy, while the public waited to hear of the surrender or annihilation of an army, and the fruits of victory gathered only in the dust of a retreat.

The field of Fredericksburg had an interesting incident, which has not appeared in the common histories of the war. After night had fallen upon the contest and when the shattered remnants of Burnside's army were cowering under cover of the town, Stonewall Jackson—a commander who, whatever he might have had of pure and admirable elements of character, was fierce in his notions of war almost to savagery, who believed that "war meant fighting and fighting"—made the extraordinary and fearful proposition of stripping his men to the waist and hurling them in the darkness upon the enemy, trusting to paralyze his already demoralized forces by the terror and novelty of such an apparition. This story of Jackson has been doubted, and has excited some unpleasant criticism in the newspapers. But the incident has been related to the author as having occurred in a council of war in which Jackson dissented from the opinion of General Lee, that the enemy would make another attack, and then proposed that the artillery should be collected upon the hills directly in front of the town, and a heavy fire be opened upon it, and that the men of his corps be stripped to the waist to distinguish them from the enemy, and under cover of the artillery fire force their way into the town, and bayonet all who were not similarly attired. "My troops shall not be allowed to fire," stipulated the grim commander; "they shall use only the bayonet." There was only one pontoon at the town, which would not have afforded egress for one fifth of Burnside's army; the bridges at Deep Run could have been easily secured; and to the suggestion that his own men might suffer from the artillery fire, when mingled with the enemy, Jackson replied that it should cease when his troops were once in the town and that "their yells would tell when they were at work." The plan for one of the most horrible butcheries of the war seemed complete, and the imagination can scarcely conceive the scenes that might have ensued:—twenty thousand men stripped for the work of death—doing it in darkness—a fitful sheet of flame on the hills to light them to their task—an army pursued from street to street as from one slaughter-pen to another—a town choked with artillery and wagons—the sharp scream of death in every corner of it—the black womb of the night giving forth the strange and piercing cries of mortal agony, as untold horrors issue from it and travel in demon shapes, an air indistinct and poisonous with blood!

But these scenes were not to occur, however sure might be the destruction of the enemy. There was one suggestion to which Jackson had not a ready reply. There were some thousands of non-combatants yet in Fredericksburg, among them women and children; and General Lee was unwilling to risk their safety by firing on the town. He must reluctantly, however, have declined the proposition of Jackson, for the fact is that the infantry of the First Corps (it was the Second that was to strip for the attack) had been posted to defend the artillery and were waiting the signal for the bombardment, when the order came to them to retire within their breastworks. The next night—the 15th of December 1862—a Federal army yet numbering some sixty thousand men moved quietly out of the jaws of destruction, crossed the river without molestation, and left the Confederates to rejoice over another barren victory.*

* A Confederate officer, unknown to the author, and of course unsolicited by him, has recently published a communication in the newpapers in reply to an attempt of these to discredit the statement, which appears to have been first publicly made by this author, of General Jackson's novel proposition of a night attack, as related above, and in commentary on the yet more foolish attempt of some sensitive country editors in the South to represent the story as a slander on the memory of the illustrious dead. After testifying to nearly every incident related in the text above, he says:—"The writer of this communication has a most profound respect for the memory of General Stonewall Jackson, yet he does not believe with others that the assertion made by Mr. Pollard, that the illustrious hero desired to make a night attack upon the enemy with his troops stripped, is a slander upon his memory, but he does believe that if there had been more stripping to the waist, and night attacks, with fewer days of thanksgiving and fastings and prayers, the South would have less barren victories to rejoice over and less to mourn for now."

Chancellorsville was a repetition of Fredericksburg—the same story of the retreat of the enemy across the same river, the exact reproduction of the *status quo*, except so many men killed and wounded, the wonder of a few weeks. These two great battles were thus described in the Richmond *Examiner:* —"If this war was a tournament, we might desire nothing better than the manner in which it has been conducted by these two hosts up to the present time. The six months they have passed between Falmouth and Fredericksburg furnishes a fair specimen of their extensive intercourse. After long and careful preparation, the Grand Army crosses over, a hundred thousand strong; fifty or sixty thousand Confederates, well posted, fight with them; the Grand Army is prodigiously whipped—loses twenty thousand—and then marches back to camp. After a month or more of recruiting, it comes again—finds the same Confederates reposing in the same fields—is whipped again, loses more men, and marches back to camp in the same order. On the occurrence of these events, great praise is given to General Lee, and several Yankee Generals are dismissed the service, relieved of their commands, or sent away to torture old men, or fight women and little children, in some unfortunate district of the country subject to the striped flag. If we could import shiploads of Irish and Dutch, after each of these 'victories,' no way of carrying on this war more favorable could be desired. But, while our army kills a great many Yankees, Dutch, and Irish, on one of these splendid field days, it also loses a considerable number of brave men. One of these is a greater loss to us than three of the others to the enemy. If that loss were counterbalanced by some military advantage which might serve as the foundation for future hopes, it would not be a loss at all, but a wise expenditure. Unfortunately, such victories change nothing. The United States and the Confederacy preserve their proportions and attitudes. The war will last forty years on these terms. Take the last of them, Chancellorsville. What have we gained by that glorious battle? The poor lands of Spottsylvania have received a costly manure, and that is all. After the fight, the general order for both armies might have been the musician's command at the conclusion of a quadrille—'as you were!'—Hooker in Stafford, Lee in Spottsylvania, the Rappahannock between."

But Chancellorsville has a veiled place among the victories of the South. Here Stonewall Jackson gave up his life; an irreparable loss, one which the army wherein he had commanded felt to the end of the war. "He fell," said Mr. Davis, speaking rather sophomorically, "like the eagle, his own feather on the shaft that was dripping with his life-blood." He had been mortally wounded by the fire of his own men, who mistook him for an enemy. His death created a black day in the South that in distinctness and importance may be measured as an era; and the public mind was never divested of the imagination that with him expired the most heroic and fortunate spirit of the Army of Northern Virginia.

Some space should be taken here to say something of the character of this commander, in view of its elevation in the war, and in consideration of its exception to the general barrenness of subjects of biographical interest—true heroes—in a contest so large, so excited, and yet so destitute of apparitions of individual genius on the stage of action. It has been customary in the South to speak, and not without a mixture of vanity, of the great figure this war will make when the future historian comes to deal with it elaborately, and to explore its operations. Yet, how meagre the biographical interest of this struggle; how scant in its illustrations of any conspicuous virtues or novelties of personal character; how unfruitful of great or remarkable men! It is in the dominant feature of historical interest that the late war, of which we usually speak in so many superlative phrases, is singularly and fatally deficient. It is remarkable for immense physical phenomena, rather than for intellectual and moral display. What is wonderful in it is the extent of physical masses, the *cloaca populorum,* stupendous sums of money, monuments of carnage; but how paltry and flowerless its crops of men, how few its productions of genius, how slight those illustrations which make up the personal, heroic interest of history! It produced, of course, if only by the rule of comparison, some military celebrities—these even few, and one only of surpassing fame; but we look in vain for the intellectual contagion of a great excitement, for those tongues of fire with which men speak in a great war, for those thoughts of orator, poet, and priest, which burn along the opposing lines like signal-fires, and make of modern war a conflict of inspirations as well as of arms.

We do not propose to invite here invidious comparisons between the military leaders on either side in the late war, And yet, as we have already referred to one of them as of surpassing fame, we may take this name apart, as at least one conspicuous centre of biographical interest in the war. We refer to STONEWALL JACKSON—whose life, as we have seen, paid the price of the insignificant victory of Chancellorsville. Around this man, whose fame has already gone, on those quick messengers, the wings of battle, to the ends of the world, there must necessarily congregate, in the future, some of the most impressive memories of the war; and his biography especially the study of his peculiar character, becomes at once a dominant subject of historical interest, and a standpoint of narrative. Whoever may hereafter write profoundly and philosophically a history of the Southern Confederacy, must take Jackson as a central figure; and he must mingle his biography, at least the characterization of the man, with many parts of his story, thereby dramatizing, coloring it, and binding up the attention of the reader with personal sympathies and heroic aspirations.

There have been a number of sophomorical pens in the South which have been fleshed on the character of Stonewall Jackson; he is the easy subject of poetasters and silly young men, who have a fancy for fine writing. It is painful to witness how such characters suffer from the glare of eulogium; and it is humiliating to confess that we have had scarcely any estimate of this great commander in the South, more thoughtful than garish verses and stilted panegyrics. An example of this sort of tribute we have lately seen in a rag-tag of romance and the cheap poetry of literary encyclopedias published under the title of "The Character of Stonewall Jackson," one of the lowest and most wretched of its class of juvenile daubs, unworthy to be mentioned out of the college debating society, but significant of the manner in which great men are usually made to suffer from a style not above the composition of school boys, fulsome and silly transports proceeding from too free a use of Anthon's hand-books, and classical mythologies. It is the penalty of the great man to suffer from "the dunce's puff;" and the thoughtful and scholarly mind grieves at the infliction of the smatterer. The character of Stonewall Jackson, having sustained so much of excessive eulogy, demands indeed a sober and analytical review; it is a character rare, profound, and not to be dismissed on a tide of fine writing, composed of "elegant extracts," poetical quotations, and illustrations from the Hindoo mythologies and the *Viri Romæ.*

It will be the especial and exact task of the military historian, the expert critic, to adjust Jackson's peculiar fame in arms and to determine its details. It is just that his life should be regarded from a high and critical military point of view, for here is its excellent and almost exclusive interest; and, besides, it is remarkable how much he has already suffered from the inaccurate and overdrawn estimates of incompetent critics. His only considerable biographer (Dr. Dabney, a Presbyterian clergyman,) has fallen into the lamentable error of regarding the religious and even sectarian character of his hero as the chief interest of his life, and subordinating to it his wonderful military career and his character as a master of war. So far is this estimate in error, that we may even venture a remark—which will probably be novel and distasteful to many readers—that the religious element in General Jackson's life has come in for an undue share of public attention; that it was among the least admirable parts of his character; and that it was singularly and painfully deficient.

Of this aspect of the life of the great Southern commander, the author has had occasion, in some historical sketches of the war, to deliver an opinion, perhaps as unpopular as it is novel. He says: "There are considerations which make Jackson's piety of very partial interest. "It is true that he was an enthusiast in religion, that he was wonderfully attentive in his devotions, and that prayer was as the breath of his nostrils. To one of his friends he declared that he had cultivated the habit of 'praying without ceasing,' and connecting a silent testimony of devotion with every familiar act of the day. 'Thus,' he said, 'When I take my meals, there is the grace. When I take a draught of water I always pause, as my palate receives the refreshment, to lift up my heart to God in thanks and prayer for the water of life. Whenever I drop a letter in the box, I send a petition along with it for God's blessing upon its mission, and upon the person to whom it is sent. When I break the seal of a letter just received, I stop to pray to God that He may prepare me for its contents, and make it a messenger of good.' But, notwithstanding the extreme fervor of Jackson's religion, it is remarkable that he kept it for certain places and companies; that he was disposed to be solitary in its exercise; and that he was singularly innocent of that Cromwellian fanaticism that mixes religious invocations with orders and utterances on a battle-field. He prayed in his tent; he delighted in long talks with the many clergymen who visited him; he poured out the joys and aspirations of his faith in private correspondence; but he seldom introduced religion into the ordinary conversation of his military life; and he exhibited this side of his character in the army in scarcely any thing more than Sunday services in his camp, and a habitual brief line in all his official reports, acknowledging the divine favor. He was very attentive to these outward observances; but his religious habit was shy and solitary; he had none of the activity of the priest; we hear but little of his work in the hospitals, of private ministrations by the death-bed, and of walks and exercises of active charity."

Havelock distributed tracts in the British army; Vickers comforted the dying in the trenches, and held prayer-meetings within the range of the enemy's guns. We do not hear of such noble and amiable offices performed by Jackson. His religion lacked in active benevolence; it was a cold, introspective religion, subjective in its experiences, severe, no doubt, in its self-discipline, correct in its faith, but with few works, few visible testimonies of zeal in the usual rounds of Christian duty. His religion was in no way mixed with the administration of his command. In his military intercourse he was the military commander. On the field of battle he was the passionate, distinct, harsh commander, whose sharp and strident orders were inexorable as messengers of fate. He had no religious appeals or exhortations to make to his men; if he prayed in action, it was in invariable silence; he never dropped a word of regret on the conquered field, such as spectacles of death have often moved benevolent men to utter; he never comforted the dying, or visited the hospitals; he had no peculiar schemes of benevolence in his army (beyond the usual Sunday preaching); he was no winner of souls, no messenger of conversions and revivals; in brief, he was utterly deficient in those active and priestly offices which the popular mind associates with the Christian hero. He was warm enough in his self-communions, in prayer, and in intercourse with a few intimate friends; but his religion was essentially a selfish, intellectual fanaticism, that seldom appeared out of his meditations, where it was excessively nursed. It did not go forth on the divine errands of charity. It was a religion curious rather than lovable. There was probably but little of philanthropy in Jackson's composition. He did not have the charming amiability of Lee; he was disposed to recrimination with his officers, stern and exacting in his commands; he was naturally of an excessive temper, harsh and domineering; and we are disposed to think that it required all the grace of his Christian character and the severest discipline of his religion to keep within bounds his constitutional impulses of anger.

While we thus lessen (no doubt to the surprise of many

readers) the popular regards for Jackson as a Christian hero, it is yet to observe him in his supreme character of a master of war, the surpassing military genius of the South. It is here where the chief interest of his life resides; here where the biographer should have pointed and held attention. He was a "heaven-born General," said the *London Times*, a journal least accustomed to extravagant phrases, and almost historical in its deliberate measure of language. He was a born soldier —*natus est, non factus, nascitur non fit;* he had far more of the inspiration of war than Lee. He was undoubtedly superior to the latter, in the sense that genius is superior to the highest intellect, that it has more self-possession and readiness, that it acts with intuition and rapidity on instant combinations; thus having advantage of the latter, and executing while it has taken time to meditate. Jackson knew, as by intuition, when and where to strike the enemy; he had an almost infallible insight into his condition and temper; he marched to his purpose with that supreme self-confidence, that absolute certainty, which always designate the efforts of genius. He had the inspiration of war rather than its pedantry. He must have been really deficient in military learning, for, as a professor at the Institute of Virginia, he would have had abundant opportunities, unavoidable occasions, no matter how unfortunate and blundering he was as an instructor, to let out the contents of his mind, to blurt them in some way; but his reputation there was quite as remarkable for a blank mind as for a bad delivery. Yet he was not only the most brilliant of Confederate commanders, but the most uniformly successful. It is remarkable of him that he was never suprised; that he was never routed in battle; that he never had a train or any organized portion of his army captured by the enemy; and that he never made intrenchments.

A common error has prevailed that Jackson's military faculty was a partial one; that he was brilliant in executing the parts assigned him by his superiors, but that he was scarcely competent to plan and originate for himself. When he fell, General Lee deplored the loss as that of his "right arm," and the phrase has been too literally or narrowly taken, as meaning that Jackson was chiefly valuable in executing the plans of the commander-in-chief. This estimate does him great injustice, and ignores some of the most important parts of his career. Indeed, there was, on the Southern side in the war, no military genius more complete, more diversified in its accomplishments, more universal in the range of arms, and in its methods of illustration. His plans were as excellent as his executions. His famous campaign of 1862, in the Valley of Virginia, was of his own origination, further than that he had been placed there by Johnston to draw attention from Richmond; but it was not expected that he would act offensively, until the news electrified the country that he had defeated four separate armies, marched four hundred miles in forty days, neutralized a force of sixty thousand men designed to operate against Richmond, and was sweeping through the mountain-passes to the relief of the Confederate capital in a blaze of glory. The movements that constituted this campaign were as precise as were ever adjusted by military skill, and the diagram that describes them remains one of the nicest strategic studies of the war Again, the great event of Chancellorsville—the movement on Hooker's flank, when Jackson blazed from the Wilderness, sudden and consuming as the lightning—was his own conception, urged upon Lee; and the night before the great warrior fell, he had planned beneath the pines, and by the light of a camp-fire, this masterpiece of the most famous victory of the Confederates. It was the characteristic, crowning repetition of his favorite strategy on the enemy's flanks; dealing those sudden and mortal blows which show the nerve of a great commander, and illustrate the precision of genius.

Jackson had that rare and interesting test of genius—the support of a weak physique by the transports of the mind. In his campaigning he was as impervious to the elements, as strong and grim as Charles XII. of Sweden, the iron warrior of his age. At ordinary times he was weak and whimsical as to health; in the life of the professor he was dyspeptic and hypochondriac; but in the excitements of war he was equal to almost incredible hardships, and the animation of his genius alone seems to have made him a type of endurance. He was never absent a day from his command; he often slept without any thing but a blanket between him and the mud or the snow; he ate with almost mechanical indifference as to the quality of his food; vigilant, elastic, always in motion, he excelled all other Confederate commanders in activity and endurance, and made his "foot-calvary" the wonder of the country. When his brigade was making a forced march to the first Manassas, it bivouacked near the railroad, and the volunteers, unused to such fatigue, murmured at the necessity of setting guards for the night. Jackson pitied their weariness; he replied that he himself, alone, would do the guard duty for that night; and during all its lonely hours, when his men were stretched on the ground, worn out, the commander stalked on his rounds, disdaining the least refreshment of sleep, and wrapped in unknown meditations. At another time, when, in the harshest depths of winter, and through a raging, merciless storm, he marched towards the headwaters of the Potomac; when overwearied men sank by the way to die, or slipped down the precipices overlaid with ice; when the animals of his trains gave out, or stumbled along with bleeding muzzles; when many of his shelterless troops froze dead in the night-time, and their gloomy comrades murmured against their commander; on the toilsome and agonizing march through snow-fields and along the yawning precipices full of black, jagged rock and ghostly-frosted shapes, Jackson was yet the silent, grim, inexorable General, the only man in the command who never uttered a word of suffering, although sharing the hardships and privations of the commonest soldier, apparently having no thoughts, no feelings, beyond the victory, to which he toiled on the narrow mountain-path, through the wreck of winter, the ravages of death, and the defiances of nature. His constitution was naturally weak, but it was braced by an extraordinary will; and his endurance was probably an illustration of that very physical strength which comes from the transports of genius.

He had another remarkable trait, which has often been observed in great military commanders: a cold method, which has sometimes been taken for cruelty, but it is really nothing more than the expression of the severe and supreme idea of war. He had no weak sentimentalism, and he was even averse to much of the ostentation and refinement of arms. War for him had a gloomy, terrible meaning; it was the shedding of blood, wounds, death. Once an inferior officer was regretting that some Federal soldiers had been killed in a display of extraordinary courage when they might as readily have been captured. Jackson replied, curtly, "Shoot them all; I don't want them to be brave." He had a gloomy, fierce idea of war, which we are forced to confess was sometimes almost savage in its expressions. It was testified by Governor Letcher, in a distinct and authentic manner, during the life-time of Jackson, that, from the opening of the war, the latter favored the *black flag*, and thought that no prisoner should be taken in a war invading the homes of the South. The fact is, Jackson had no politics, not a particle of political animosity in the war, and, in this respect, represented many of his countrymen, who only realized that an issue of arms was made, and that they were called upon to defend their homes against invaders, whom the newspapers represented to be no better then marauders and incendiaries. Jackson had only the idea of the soldier—to fight, and to fight in the most terrible manner. It was not a natural cruelty, a constitutional harshness, but a stern conception of war and its dread realities—the soldier's disposition for quick, decisive, destructive work.

We are aware that we have disturbed some popular notions about the favorite hero of the South. But we are endeavoring to obtain the truth of a somewhat mysterious character; and we have yet to notice the most complete delusion that the common mind has attached to the name of Jackson. It is, that he was a cold figure in a round of duty, operated only by conscientious motives, deaf to praise and destitute of ambition. The author recollects, on one occasion, writing some encomium on Jackson, in a Richmond journal, and remarking thereupon that Jackson would probably never read it, and undoubtedly cared nothing for public opinion. "You are utterly mistaken," spoke up John M. Daniel, the editor; "he is to-day the most ambitious man within the limits of the Southern Confederacy."

A close inspection of Jackson's life, and especially of his peculiar and masking manners, shows that he really had an enormous, consuming ambition. It was an ambition that resided in the depths of his nature; that ate into and honeycombed his heart; that bounded and fluctuated in every pulse of his being. He was almost fierce in the confession of this secret feeling in the beginning of his military career. When once asked if he had felt no trepidation when he made most extraordinary exposures of his person in some of the famous battles of the Mexican war, he replied that the only anxiety of which he was conscious in any of these engagements was a fear lest he should not meet danger enough to make his conduct under it as conspicuous as he desired; and as the peril grew greater, he rejoiced in it as his opportunity for distinction. He courted the greatest amount of danger for the greatest amount of glory; and this sentiment of the true soldier survived to his last moments.

But it is to be observed that Jackson's ambition was of a true, lofty sort, quite unlike that vulgar passion which makes men itch for notoriety, and constantly place themselves in circumstances and attitudes to attract public attention. Such an ambition (if the term may be so profaned) is the quality of mean souls; and even its little, noisy prizes are worthless, for it is remarkable that mere notoriety generally recoils upon itself, and that those who make themselves notorious, at last tax public attention to find out something disreputable or ridiculous about them. Jackson's passion was that fine and lofty ambition which pursues *idealities,* which looks to a name in history, and which, averse to the mere noisy, evanescent gifts of popularity, actually shuns notoriety, is pained by all vulgar and meretricious displays, and is constantly maintaining a close and sensitive reserve. Such ambition is the property of grand and noble souls. It is most interesting to regard its reserves, its disguises, its taciturn moods, its apparent want of sympathy with immediate surroundings, and the common mistake the world makes in designating as emotionless, ascetic men, those who are daily and nightly consumed by grand aspirations. An ambition of this sort pursues only the ideal; it finds its happiness in self-culture and self-approval, in secret aspiration, in communion with the historical and universal; it is but the vulgar counterfeit, the low desire, that seeks the coarse rewards of popularity in offices, in applause, in newspaper paragraphs; that imagines mere noise is the acclamation of glory, and mistakes "a dunce's puff for fame." Jackson, no doubt, valued "skilled commendation," while he did not mistake the penny-a-lines of the newspaper for the inscriptions of history; he was not entirely insensible to the praise of his contemporaries; but what he mostly and chiefly prized was the name in history—an aspiration after the ideal, and not the vulgar hunt for notoriety and its gifts. Such an ambition is consonant with the most refined spirit of Christianity; it resides in the depths of great minds; and it easily escapes observation, because those moved by it are generally silent men, of mysterious air and mechanical manners, living within themselves, conscious that few can enter into sympathy with them, and constantly practicing the art of impenetrable reserve.

The very awkwardness of Jackson's manners, his taciturn habit, his constraint in company, the readiness with which he was put to embarrassment, were marks of sensitive ambition, with its supreme self-confidence, which is yet not vanity, its raw self-regard which is yet not conceit, rather than evidences of a strained and excessive modesty, blundering in its steps and painfully protesting its unworthiness. It is a superficial, common mistake of the world to designate as "modest" men, or as persons holding low opinions of themselves, those who are awkward and bashful in society, who blush easily when confronted in a general conversation, or are constrained and embarrassed in the conventionalism of social intercourse. But an observation more studious than that of the drawing-room, and general assembly, often discovers under such manners the very sensitiveness of a supreme self-appreciation, the chafe or reserve of a great, proud spirit, without opportunity to assert itself. It is thus we may explain how the shy and clumsy manners of Jackson, which made him the butt of social companies, yet covered an enormous self-regard, and masked the ambition which devoured him. Mr. John Esten Cooke, who was near his person in the war, declares: "The recollection is still preserved by many of his personal peculiarities; his simplicity and absence of supicion when all around were laughing at some of his odd ways, his grave expression and air of innocent inquiry when some jest excited general merriment, and he could not see the point; his solitary habits and self-contained deportment; his absence of mind, awkwardness of gait, and evident indifference to every species of amusement."

There is a common disposition to caricature great men, to exaggerate their peculiarities, and to discover eccentricities. It comes, probably, from a low literary adventure, a design to point paragraphs at the expense of truth. Jackson has suffered greatly from such caricature; he has been represented as uncouth and odd in the most various particulars, and the apocrypha of the Bohemians have given the most conflicting representations of his person and manners. There was nothing really very extraordinary in these; but it is surprising what different opinions have been held as to the comeliness of the man. We may quote here from some of our own personal recollections of Jackson, written on another occasion, what we yet think the most correct description of the hero:

"To the vulgar eye, he was a clumsy-looking man, and his roughly-cut features obtained for him the easy epithet of an ugly man. But to the eye that makes of the human face the *janua animi*, and examines in it the traces of character and spirit, the countenance of Jackson was superlatively noble and interesting. The outline was coarse; the reddish beard was scraggy; but he had a majestic brow, and in the blue eyes was an introverted expression, and just sufficient expression of melancholy to show the deeply-earnest man. But the most striking feature, the combative sign of the face, was the massive iron-bound jaw—that which Bulwer declares to be the mark of the conqueror, the facial characteristic of Cæsar and William of Normandy, the latter of whom he has brought before our eyes in one of his most splendid romances. In brief, while common curiosity saw nothing to admire in Jackson, a closer scrutiny discovered a rare and interesting study. It was not the popular picture of a *bizarre* and austere hero; it was that of a plain gentleman, of ordinary figure, but with a lordly face, in which serious and noble thoughts were written without effort or affectation."

The views the present author has taken of Jackson scarcely correspond to the beaten types of the man, and their novelty may be unpleasant, and provocative of criticism in some quarters. But we conceive the necessity of a profound exploration, a searching analysis of a character so central and dramatic in the war, that stands in so many important historical connections. Many of the most important events of the war must be grouped around Jackson, and the veins of his single dominant character must run through many pages of the general narrative. We cannot exaggerate the importance of a correct study of the man. In many respects he was the representative of his countrymen. His chaste and noble ambition represented the aspirations of the best and most cultivated men of the South, as opposed to a mania in the North for noisy and visible distinctions; his innocence of politics was extremely characteristic of perhaps a majority of the Southern soldiers, who fought more from martial instincts than from political convictions; and his superb valor illustrated the sentiment of the South that thinks personal courage a virtue and an ornament, and ranks it first among the titles of admiration. It is indispensable that an influence that contributed so much to the war should be carefully analyzed; that a person so conspicuous in it should be correctly portrayed; and that the character of Stonewall Jackson should be placed among its first historical studies.

The last moments of the great warrior have been variously described. The following statement is derived from the exact and literal accounts of his physician. Within two hours of his death, he was told distinctly that there was no hope, that he was dying; and he answered, feebly but firmly, "Very good; it is all right." A few moments before he died, he cried out in his delirium, "Order A. P. Hill to prepare for action! Pass the infantry to the front rapidly! Tell Major Hawks—" then stopped, leaving the sentence unfinished. Presently a smile of ineffable sweetness spread itself over his pale face, and he said, quietly, and with an expression as if of relief, "Let us cross over the river, and rest under the shade of the trees." And so, with these beautiful, typical words trembling on his lips, the soul of the great soldier, taxed with battle, and trial, ana weariness, passed through the deep waters of Death, and found sweet and eternal rest.

CHAPTER XVIII.

Increased Spirit of the Army of Northern Virginia—A Second Experiment of Invasion Originated by General Lee and Opposed by Mr. Davis—Some Accounts of a Secret Correspondence between the Commander and the President—A Curious and perhaps Fatal Misapprehension concerning the Campaign—Failure of Mr. Davis to Order General Beauregard to Virginia—The Battle of Gettysburg the Worst Error of General Lee's Military Life—He Makes a Disingenuous Account of it—True Theory of the Action—Reflections on the Military Character of Lee—Gettysburg, a Divided Name in the Calendar of Battles—Why there were No Popular Reproaches of Lee—The Disaster of Vicksburg, a Very Different Story—Lee and Johnston, "*Par Nobile Fratrum*" of the War—The "President's Pets"—John C. Pemberton, an Obscure Military Man Put in Command of Vicksburg—Extraordinary Protests against the Appointment—The Influence of a Woman Brought to Bear on Mr. Davis—An Infamous Imposture in the Command Given to Johnston—The President Cheats the Public Sentiment—Johnston Mere Figure-Head in the West—Proofs of a Dishonorable Private Correspondence of Mr. Davis in Derogation of Johnston's Command—The Secret Dispatch to Pemberton—Consequences of the Surrender of Vicksburg—The Most Aggravated Disaster of the War.

In midsummer of 1863, the Army of Northern Virginia reached its highest point of efficiency. The Confederacy had enjoyed a season for recruiting; its affairs again wore a brilliant color. There was a raw bloom of new hopes springing from the battle fields we have described in the preceding chapter. Recruits had flocked into camps where they might hope no longer to rust in idleness, and to waste from disease, but to enjoy the adventures of an active campaign, and to reap the glory of swift and decisive battles. The sympathy of the Confederate Army with the general public sentiment of the country was singularly delicate and exact; and it is remarkable that as the hopes of the people rose in the contest, as victories were won, the army was readily replenished, suffered but little from desertion, and drew in an abundance of recruits. Although the law to furnish troops was uniform the same in all cases, the Confederate army appeared to vary not only in spirit but in numbers with the fortunes of the contest, and was as sensitive to outside influences as any other congregation of people within the limits of the South.

In the month of June, 1863, General Lee found himself at the head of an army ninety thousand strong; and animated by the numbers and condition of his men, rather than for any other reason, he determined to make a second attempt to invade the territory of the enemy, and with a broader design than when in the preceding year, he had proposed rather to clear the frontiers of the Confederacy than to effect a permanent occupation of Northern soil. The project of the invasion of Pennsylvania was entirely his own. It has since been discovered that President Davis was averse to it; and an act of justice should be done in relieving him entirely from responsibility for one broad passage of disaster in the history of the war.

The Pennsylvania campaign furnishes the only instance of displeasure that ever took place between the President and General Lee. The troops of the latter were scarcely across the Potomac, when he was overtaken by a private letter from Mr. Davis, making a delicate, but studied protest against the movement of his army so far away from Richmond, and significantly committing to his own responsibility this second experiment of invasion. Worse than this, a misunderstanding had grown up between the President and General Lee, of which it is not saying too much that it materially spoiled the campaign, and contributed largely to the catastrophe at Gettysburg. General Lee had considered it of the utmost importance on the wide departure of his army from Richmond that General Beauregard should be placed in command at Culpepper Court House; he had thought that matter arranged, he had relied upon it as likely to produce a considerable division of the forces of the enemy, and calculated to distract his attention. Mr. Davis did not fulfil this part of the campaign from what was evidently a misapprehension; he supposed that General Lee desired an army of some magnitude to be assembled at Culpepper Court House; and the latter was across the Potomac, when he received dispatches from Richmond that there were no forces at the disposal of the President to constitute such an army. General Lee hastened to correct the mistake; he explained that he only required a *semblance* of an army at the point designated; he argued that if nothing more could be done, General Beauregard should, at least, make his headquarters at Culpepper Court House, and the fact be industriously reported in the newspapers, yet hoping to call off some of the overmatching forces of the enemy that hung on his flanks; but before the letter, freighted with such hope, and designed to correct the misapprehension of Mr. Davis, reached Richmond, the battle of Gettysburg had been delivered, the army of Northern Virginia had sustained an irretrievable defeat, and the Pennsylvania campaign had been decided, in a brief span of days, memorable for their disaster to the South.

It is wonderful, whatever the errors that led to the field of Gettysburg, and in the face of inequalities which nature exaggerated, placing the army of superior numbers in a position almost impregnable, how near the Confederacy came to winning what might have been the decisive victory of the war. The narrowness of the chance makes a dramatic picture—the Confederacy within a stone's throw of peace—nothing but the brows of brass and iron that frowned on Lee's army from Cemetery Ridge to dispute its inroad into the heart of the Northern territory, nothing but a line of guns between it and the prizes of Washington, Philadelphia and New York! On the 3d of July, 1863, occurred a single hour, fraught with the destinies of two countries. It was a crowded, sublime hour, stocked with scenes that make the history of years—when Pickett's Virginians marched on ground quivering under the concussion of three hundred cannon, and made the last effort to pluck the victory that for three days had trembled in the tangled brushwood of a mountain ridge. In vain! With ranks torn and shattered, most of its officers killed or wounded, no valor able to surmount impossibilities, annihilation or capture inevitable, Pickett's division slowly, reluctantly falls back, and the day ends.

The crest of Gettysburg was the knife balance of the war. The strained confidence, the elevated expectation at Richmond were cast to the ground in a single day. Mr. Davis was inconsolable, and for weeks he withdrew himself from public observation on the plea of a nervous disorder. He had not only been disappointed, but he had been insulted by the enemy. While Vice-President Stephens was on his way to sound the Northern Government on the subject of peace—a second coquettish mission of Mr. Davis on the heels of an army of invasion—a battle was fought that shut the gates of Washington in his face, and prompted the North to return an insulting message to Richmond. An enemy recovered from the grotesque alarms that had made it humble and ridiculous when Lee's Army first appeared across the Potomac, was now quick to resume its former stature and tone of insolent contempt.

At Gettysburg was committed the worst error of the military life of the favorite General of the South; and, although the peculiar generosity of the Southern people forgave him, and even to this day, is unwilling to tolerate criticism of him, history must judge him severely for his conduct on a field so critical. The worst reflection of the story of Gettysburg on General Lee's fame, is that here, for once, he has been disingenuous in his account of the field, giving false and trivial reasons to excuse his impulsion to a battle so unequal and disastrous. The fact was, General Lee shared too much the fault of his army in despising and underrating his enemy; and thus, when he had splendid opportunities in his hand, and when the fortunes of the South were mounting to the climacteric, he committed a risk, which could only have been pardonable in desperate circumstances, of attacking at odds and disadvantages such as had never before occurred in the war, urging his troops against a rocky fortress far stronger than that against which Burnside had so madly dashed his army at Fredericksburg. In the way of excuse, General Lee has weakly intimated that the battle was not of his own choice, that it was in a measure unavoidable, that it was "a matter of great difficulty to withdraw through the mountains with his large trains." The statement is unfair, and is unworthy of the great commander, whose reputation might well have supported a free and full confession of his error. He went into the fight against the protest of his Lieutenants, against his pledges at the outset of the campaign that he would invite the enemy's attack and not risk an aggressive movement, and with General Longstreet insisting that the road to Washington was open, and that an attack upon Frederick, Maryland, would withdraw Meade to ground of their own choosing. As to the difficulty of the Confederate trains, the fact was that the greater portion of them was still west of the mountains, and what of them had reached the field were safely withdrawn after the defeat of the Confederates, in circumstances more unfavorable, of course, than those in which General Lee debated whether he would deliver battle. There was not only no necessity for the battle, but there was even a broad and obvious alternative.. The fact has not been commonly known or esteemed that General Lee fought the battle of Gettysburg, not only when he had full opportunity of retreat, but after he had actually put the right wing of his army between Meade and Washington. He was probably carried away by a transport of temper to attack the enemy on his front, in almost impregnable position; and in this fatal action the historian will judge that he threw away the best of the opportunities of the war, and dated on a field blotched with useless carnage the decline of the fortunes of the Con federacy.

We find General Lee twice failing to carry the war into the enemy's country—at Sharpsburg and at Gettysburg. The thought occurs that he was unequal in aggressive warfare, and suggests a conception of his abilities as a commander more limited and thoughtful than the fulsome estimate of the populace. Probably the best opinion of General Lee is that he showed but little genius in offensive campaigns, and that his excellence as a commander was almost exclusively within the lines of defensive warfare. Here he was acute, prompt, resourceful; he never lost his self-possession, or the command of any of his faculties; he had an electric promptness in acting in sudden and extreme necessities; and what is probably the most remarkable feature of his campaigns, was his wonderful faculty of recovery when it was supposed that he had been pushed to the last extremity and was impending on the brink of ruin. Again and again, when the enemy congratulated themselves that they had given him a death-blow, he would astonish them by the readiness and dexterity of his resource; and when the North was vocal with exultant reports that Lee was retreating, or that his fortunes had been broken or lost, it would be suddenly known that he was again in the field with unabashed front, erect and plumed with new resolution.

And so it happened in a measure after Gettysburg. The spirit of the Army of Northern Virginia had declined, but it had not been broken; a great disaster had been suffered, but only the firmness of General Lee in retreat saved it from an irretrievable catastrophe; and what he preserved of the *morale* and efficiency of his troops even after the defeat we have described, was yet sufficient to check the pursuit of the enemy, and to hold, though with feebler array than formerly, the old defensive lines in Virginia.

But whatever was the amount of disaster at Gettysburg, and however severe was the shock which the hopes of the South suffered on this field, it is to be remarked peculiarly of this case of popular disappointment, that there was but little of recrimination mixed with it, but few traces of the bitterness of reproach. If Lee had fought unadvisedly, he had yet done so from a generous transport, and with such splendid bravery as to gild the page of disaster—to make the story of defeat one of tender regret and reverential memories, rather than one of despair and shame. It was thus that the people of the South accepted, and to this day maintain the memory of Gettysburg as of a field unhappy but adorned. In the calendar of the battles of the war, the name is yet a divided one for the Confederacy, mentioned perhaps as often with a noble and sorrowful pride by the Southerner for the valor displayed on it, as with keen regrets and tantalized reflections for the narrow loss upon it of a victory that might have been decisive of the war.

Far different was the story of another disaster in another part of the Confederacy, the news of which reached Richmond the same day as that from Gettysburg; a story replete with recrimination and full of bitterness and shame—one that piled reproaches upon the Confederate Government until popular indignation became fatigued with building the monument of infamy. This story was the surrender of Vicksburg. It coupled one of the worst records of unworthiness and shame on the part of the government. It was a disaster that nearly broke the heart of the Confederacy, as it did cut in twain its body. It was the clearest and most important complaint that had yet been made against President Davis; it inflicted upon him an indelible disgrace; and it is alone sufficient to determine any doubt which may yet linger on oúr pages so far of his unworthiness in the war.

Vicksburg was the strategic point in the Confederacy, second only to the capital. It was a post already adorned by four different successes of the Confederate arms, repulsing so many attempts of the enemy to capture it. It afforded the only firm line of communication between the cis-Mississippi and the trans-Mississippi. It might have been supposed that at a position so important, to which pointed so much of the hope and anxiety of the South, Mr. Davis would have appointed to command one of the best Generals of the Confederacy, one, indeed, whose reputation might have balanced that of Lee of Virginia, and one who might have inspired a confidence on the other side of the Alleghany that would have kept, to some extent, equal and uniform the fortunes of the war. Nor was such a man wanting. Public opinion in the South had long designated as the *par nobile fratrum* in the war, Robert E. Lee and Joseph E. Johnston, and had suggested the convenient decision between these two men of the two dominant departments lying on either side of the Alleghany. It was the natural and just division between the two greatest military geniuses of the war. The military record of Johnston was quiet; but it had great substantial merit, and in the estimation of the most thoughtful persons in the South, he was the superior of Lee as a *safe* General—just the man to command in the uncertain and chequered field of the West, where the fortunes of the war had hitherto been so various, and where prudent successes might have been the just balance of Lee's easier and more brilliant victories in Virginia. No one but Mr. Davis doubted that Johnston was a commander of first-class ability and knowledge. Manassas, Williamsburg, and Seven Pines, were all his battles; and it was notable of his career so far, that he had never incurred a single defeat, and never lost an army, not even a brigade, not a regiment.

Unfortunately Mr. Davis had an inveterate and stubborn dislike of Johnston. Perhaps the reader has been already brought to consider him as a ruler, whose private obstinacies were superior to all considerations of the public interest; a nervous, ill-tempered person, making his government a fretful distribution of his personal likes and dislikes. It is said that he hated Johnston for no other reason than his cold and sturdy manners. This commander was remarkable for his plain and business-like communications with the government; he scorned political influence; he had no arts to conciliate Mr. Davis; in manners he was the severe soldier, cold and reticent; he never gratified the vanity of the President by shows of deference, or even pleased popular passion by fulsome and rhetorical language about the war; and yet this stern, almost mute commander, illustrating the severity of military manners, had outlived a short term of unpopularity in the South, was generally esteemed the most sober and safe of Confederate Generals, and to-day is accounted, even beyond Lee, the most careful and judicious spirit in the war. But although Mr. Davis was secretly and deeply offended with Johnston, although he was the victim of prejudices, he was now about to carry these to a point almost incredible, and to actually confound and bewilder popular indignation with his excess of favoritism.

In all periods of the war there was a parcel of Confederate commanders known as "the President's Pets." The use of such a phrase shows how familiar was public sentiment in the South with the fact that the President was a man of prejudices, and how persistent he was in asserting them. One of these pets was John C. Pemberton. He was a native of Pennsylvania, and in the old Federal service had been a Captain without distinction. He had yet fought not a single battle in the Confederacy; he had not made one record of meritorious service therein; he had never commanded troops in action, not a regiment, not a company, not a man. By a single stroke of the pen Mr. Davis had made this man a Lieutenant-General, giving him one of the seven great commissions authorized by the Confederate Congress, over the heads of such men as Gustavus W. Smith, D. H. Hill, A. P. Hill, the brilliant young Southern Generals who had really done the fighting of the war. He was appointed to an independent post, no less than that of Charleston. Thence a great outcry of public opinion compelled the President to remove him; the story got out that General Pemberton had decided that this important city was untenable; he was accused of incompetency, treachery even was hinted, and Mr. Davis had to recall his favorite from a command barren of any action with the enemy, and fruitful only of disgraceful rumors. But the President had that evil temper which, forced to make some show of compliance to opposition, yet insults and defies it by making at the first opportunity an aggravation of the cause of complaint—actually defying public opinion, showing contempt for it, even taunting it by the very enlargement of the offence of which it has dared to complain. This unhappy temper, this mean and spiteful resentment of public opinion will be found running through the whole of Mr. Davis's administration. Pemberton was removed from Charleston, only to receive strident promotion. The country saw with astonishment and dismay this untried commander—a man who had absolutely nothing to support him but the personal affection of Mr. Davis—placed over the Department of Mississippi and Louisiana, and in the command at Vicksburg, the critical point of the Mississippi Valley, the Western correspondent to Richmond!

No explanations but that of sheer obstinacy, can be possibly afforded for this choice by Mr. Davis of a commander for a post the second in importance in the Confederacy. But it is almost unaccountable, the degree of tenacity with which he clung to his favorite in the midst of a storm of public indignation. Delegations visited him with protests from the people, and army alike; the Legislature of his own State, Mississippi, passed resolutions complaining of the appointment. Outside the forms of public dissension, other agencies were employed upon the President by those who understood how narrow were his resolutions, and how accessible he was to paltry and irregular influences in conducting the public business. It is shameful that in a matter of so great public concern as the appointment of a General to a vital point in the Confederacy, the influence of women and of relatives had to be sought to change the intentions of the President. Even this degraded access to him was not neglected. His brother

Joseph Davis was induced to travel to Richmond, and to attempt to dissuade him from Pemberton. A woman in Jackson, Mississippi, who was reported to have an extraordinary influence over the President was won to the side of the protestants against Pemberton, and was prevailed upon to write private letters to Mr. Davis. But all protests were unavailing, and the President had the invariable answer that he had discovered in Pemberton a great military genius; that his choice would be soon approved by brilliant victories; that the country had only to wait for the tests of his judgment. Mr. Davis might possibly have thought that he was acting for the public good; there is no bias which so easily eludes self-inspection, and at the same time is so patent to the world, as favoritism; yet even if the President had discovered a military jewel in this obscure man, even if Pemberton had been a mute Napoleon awaiting occasion, the thought should have occurred to Mr. Davis that the confidence of soldiers is an essential element in the success of a General, and that as long as his favorite lacked this he was not the man to command the second army of the Confederacy. It is a maxim in the science of military command that no matter what the cause of distrust of troops, the distrust itself is sufficient to disqualify the General for his position. And Pemberton's soldiers distrusted him from the moment he took command, to the time he marched them out to the field of surrender.

If Mr. Davis had strictly and literally adhered to the appointment of Pemberton to command Vicksburg, there would at least have been honesty in this conduct. But unfortunately the President had a curious way of double-dealing with public sentiment; he had a habit, when strongly urged, of making a show of compliance with it, yet cheating it, substantially. No stronger example can be given of this detestable cheat of the sentiment of the people, this unworthy subterfuge of the President, than after the translation of Pemberton to Vicksburg, the appointment of General Johnston to the visible nominal command of the Western Department, and yet without any practical power to conduct a campaign therein, or to control the armies within the limits of his military jurisdiction. The appointment was made to appease popular clamor; and to cover the President's unworthy affection for Pemberton. Johnston was too generous to expose the game on public opinion to which he was made an instrument; but at last under the pressure of recrimination after the fall of Vicksburg, the details came out stark and disgraceful, and they compose a story of dishonor for Mr. Davis, the like of which is scarcely to be found in all the crooked and sunken paths of his administration.

General Johnston was appointed to command in the West with scarcely any other powers than those of an Inspector-General. His appointment was a mission, not a military command. When it had at first been spoken of, he had a private conversation in the War Office in which he strongly urged that the entire Mississippi Valley should be one department, under one command; that the river did not affect its unity; and that the measures for its defence ought to comprehend the whole valley and both sides of the river. These views were overruled by Mr. Davis, even after the Secretary of war (Mr. Randolph) had assented to them. There was another "pet" of the President on the other side of the Mississippi, who was kept in command in Arkansas, despite the prayers of the State and the irrepressible complaints of the army. "If," said a journal of these times, "General Holmes be not in his dotage, the English language possesses no synonym to indicate his stupidity and inertia." Pemberton, Mr. Davis's protege No. 2, was at Vicksburg, and commanded the Department of Mississippi and Louisiana. Bragg, another "pet," who, at the beginning of the year, had telegraphed from the field of Murfreesboro', "God has given us a happy new year," was uneasily resting at Tullahoma. Thus General Johnston was misplaced among the "pets" of the President. He was nominally the superior officer of Maury at Mobile, of Bragg at Tullahoma, and of Pemberton at Vicksburg; but his real control was naught. He could not withdraw the armies from the points they defended; he could only reinforce one of them by detachments from another. They were commanded by the respective Generals placed over them by President Davis; and it is remarkable that each of them reported their actions, not through General Johnston, but directly to Richmond. Being favorites to whom the President was partial, they could, each, disobey Johnston's orders with impunity. The latter could not be ubiquitous. If he left General Bragg to himself, blunders were immediately committed; if he left General Pemberton with orders to collect provisions and ammunition, and sped to Tullahoma, Vicksburg might be starved out; if he ventured towards Mobile to examine its defences, he uncovered the larger part of his military district and left to nominal subordinates the fairest and most important portion of the Confederacy.

This disarrangement of military commands in the West, this confusion of authorities, it is now known, was calculated by President Davis to shield his appointment of Pemberton, and to hide a surreptitious and underhanded correspondence which he conducted with him in derogation of the views of Johnston and in diminution of his command. When the latter arrived at his post in the West, he saw at once the emptiness of his command. He wrote to a private friend in Richmond:—"I have no hope that Pemberton will regard a suggestion of mine." The anticipation was abundantly fulfilled. At the conclusion of the campaign on the fall of Vicksburg, General Johnston was constrained to write in his official report:—"General Pemberton made not a single movement in obedience to my orders, and regarded none of my instructions; and finally did not embrace the only opportunity to save his army—that given by my order to abandon Vicksburg."

The series of the acts of disobedience on the part of Pemberton was persistent and high-handed. When Grant crossed the river and invaded the State of Mississippi to make a detour upon Vicksburg, the constant idea of Johnston, his incessant order was that Pemberton should unite with him and fight for Vicksburg in the open field; that they should manœuvre to prevent a siege, that if such was once effected by the enemy the loss of the city would become only a question of time, with the Federal army in a position to receive reinforcements from all parts of the North, and with no Confederate force outside the town sufficient to break its rear. This was his plain, dominant idea of the campaign. It might have given a great victory to the Confederacy; it proposed the easy and obvious occasion of Grant brought to a great battle in the interior of Mississippi, where the united forces of Johnston and Pemberton could have matched his numbers, and where, if defeated, he would have no opportunity of retreat. It was a splendid chance. But Pemberton appears to have been afflicted with the morbid idea that Vicksburg was his base—from what inspiration we shall presently see; from first to last his chief anxiety seems to have been to avoid a junction with Johnston, and to keep a distance between them; and every order of the latter he disobeyed with a *sang froid* and insolent self-complacency unexampled in the relations of a commanding General and his subordinate, and inexplicable, unless on the supposition of some hidden assurance to support him.

When Grant first crossed the Mississippi, General Johnston telegraphed to Pemberton: "Unite all your troops to beat him; success will give back what was abandoned to win it." The response of Pemberton was the feeble adventure of a single division of 5,500 troops thrown upon the enemy's front at Port Gibson, and a disastrous battle there. The consequence of his vacillation and of his mere color of resistance on the river was that the town of Jackson was lost, and the way opened to Vicksburg. But again Johnston saw the chance of concentration, and the prospect of a great victory. No sooner had the enemy left Jackson, four of his divisions under Sherman deflected towards the west, than General Johnston hurried a dispatch to Pemberton on the night of the 13th of May, urging the importance of establishing communications, and ordering him to come upon Sherman's rear at once, and adding, "to beat such a detachment would be of immense value." "The troops here," wrote Johnston, speaking of his own command, "could co-operate. All the strength you can quickly assemble should be brought. Time is all important." The reply of Pemberton was again feeble; he could not cut loose from Vicksburg; that had been committed to him as the chief object of President Davis's solicitude; and the dull and shallow commander could not understand the advantage of fighting for a point at a distance from it, in preference to the puerile conceit of fighting on the immediate front of it. He preferred to be besieged, for a reason that at the time was locked in his breast. A few hours after Johnston's dispatch reached him, he was fighting the enemy on the immediate approaches to Vicksburg; and at the close of the next day, he was retreating with a shattered and demoralized army into the town, falling into the fatal trap of which Johnston had forewarned him. "Had the battle of Baker's Creek not been fought," wrote this commander, "Pemberton's belief that Vicksburg was his base rendered his ruin inevitable. He would still have been besieged and therefore captured. The larger force he would have carried into the lines would have added to and hastened this catastrophe. His disasters were due, not merely to his entangling himself with the advancing columns of a superior and unobserved enemy, but to his evident determination to be besieged in Vicksburg, instead of manœuvering to prevent a siege."

But why should General Pemberton thus have persevered against the orders of his superior; why allow himself to be shut up in Vicksburg with the determination to be besieged? It was very strange conduct, even on an excessive hypothesis of military incompetency. *The fact was that he bore on his person—even from the shameful field of Baker's Creek, the secret advices of President Davis in opposition to the orders of General Johnston!* From that field, where the shame of Bull Run was nearly reversed upon the South—he carried an army back into the streets of Vicksburg a profane, howling mob. It was a scene of disorder, of cowardice, of despair. "I was surprised," said an officer who rode near General Pemberton when he re-entered Vicksburg, "to notice his self-complacency, and to see how little he was disturbed by what to us was a woful retreat." But Pemberton had secret sources of consolation; he had lost a battle, he had disobeyed Johnston, he had defied his displeasure; but he knew very well that in betaking himself to a siege in Vicksburg, he was fulfilling the views of Mr. Davis at Richmond, as communicated to him in private telegrams, and that he might calculate on the support of the President in all he had done.

There has recently came to light, a *secret dispatch* that curiously supplements the story of Vicksburg. On the 7th of May, 1863, the very day on which General Johnston was writing from Tullahoma, by a remarkable intuition, that he had "no hope that General Pemberton would regard a suggestion" from him, President Davis telegraphed General Pemberton in these words:—"Want of transportation of supplies must compel the enemy to seek a junction with their fleet after a few days' absence from it. To hold both Vicksburg and Port Hudson is necessary to a connection with trans-Mississippi. You may expect whatever it is in my power to do." This order had doubtless been given to General Pemberton for the purpose of superseding that which General Johnston had sent him six days before, from Tullahoma, directing him "to concentrate and attack Grant immediately;" of which General Johnston had advised the War Department.

Here was a command superior to that of General Johnston, which General Pemberton was obliged to obey. He did so, in the spirit and in the letter. Whatever may have been the blunders that his inexperience in the field might have led him to commit, it cannot be said that he failed in fidelity to his trust; or that his disobedience to the orders of his immediate superior was not excused by the order which had come to him from the superior of both.

There was long an unpleasant suspicion in the Confederacy that President Davis had a secret and underhanded correspondence in the government of military campaigns, conducting such with subordinate commanders, and thus displacing or diminishing the authority of the commander-in-chief, whom he had nominally appointed. We shall see other remarkable instances of this disreputable interference with the conduct of armies in the field. But in the present case the proof is in black and white, that Pemberton was the creature of Mr. Davis; that he was receiving secret instructions from him when all orders to the latter should have passed through General Johnston; and the suggestion occurs that even the violation of this usual and respectful form, must have involved a sinister purpose, and a dishonorable confidence, if not a positive conspiracy against the authority of General Johnston. The latter was placed in the field to bear the responsibility of a campaign which he never ordered, and the secret history of which remained at Richmond, to be disclosed or to be retained, according as the result might make to the credit or discredit of the military genius of Mr. Davis.

When Pemberton had once retired to Vicksburg, Johnston saw well that the fate of that town was determined, and he had nothing more to beseech than that the army should be saved by a speedy evacuation. Pemberton replied: "I have decided to hold Vicksburg as long as possible. * * * I still conceive it to be the most important point in the Confederacy." Once besieged by an enemy whose communications were all open, without prospect of relief from the insufficent army of Johnston, without hope of reinforcement from other burdened parts of the Confederacy, time was soon called upon Vicksburg; and on the 4th of July, 1863, the South suffered the most aggravated disaster of the war. Pemberton had surrendered to the enemy a force of more than twenty-three thousand men, with three Major-Generals, and nine Brigadiers; upwards of ninety pieces of artillery, and about forty thousand small arms, large numbers of the latter having been taken from the enemy during the siege.* These, however, were only the immediate and visible losses of a day. There were great results, such as had not yet been weighed on a single field of the war. The fall of Vicksburg was the decisive event of the Mississippi Valley; the virtual surrender of the great river; and the severance of the Southern Confederacy. The natural consequences were numerous and mournful:—the attack on and defence of Jackson, and withdrawal of Johnston to Meridian; the brilliant but fruitless battle of Chickamauga; the misfortune of Missionary Ridge; the reinforcement and transfer of Sherman to Dalton; the Confederate retreat into Georgia; the fall of Atlanta; the desolation of Georgia and the Carolinas; the surrender at Chapel Hill; finally a lost Confederacy.

* General Grant in his official report claims thirty-seven thousand prisoners, but appears to speak of the results of the campaign, rather than of the immediate fruits of the surrender.

CHAPTER XIX.

A Pause in the Military History of the Confederacy, and a View thereupon of its Internal Administration—Reference to the Confederate Congress—Its Secret Sessions—The "College Debating Society" in the Capitol—Some of the Notable Members of Congress—Disgraceful Scenes in Secret Session—An Episode of the Bowie-Knife—Judge Dargan a Curiosity—A Hand-to-Hand Fight in the Senate—Other Scandals in Congress—The Newspapers and "Contraband Information"—Mr. Davis and his "Back-Door" Conferences—An Ill-natured Remark about General Beauregard—Bad Results of the Secret Sessions of Confederate Congress—Multitude of Rumors in the South—Comments of the Richmond *Examiner* and the Charleston *Mercury*—Newsmongers in Richmond—Two Notable Characters in the Capital—"Long Tom" and the Druggist—Reflections on the Birth and Flight of Rumors concerning the War—How Mr. Davis's Pastor was Deceived—An Anecdote of "Recognition"—The Demoralizing Consequences of False Rumors in the War—The Heart of the South Worn Out, Swinging from Hope to Fear—How Mr. Davis's Uncaged Rumors—How he Dulled and Destroyed Public Spirit.

THE disasters of Gettysburg and Vicksburg naturally give a pause for some reflections on the war. From these outward events we propose to look in upon the internal administration of Mr. Davis, and to describe something of official persons and manners in the Confederate capital.

This view first presents us the Congress, the last appearance of which on our pages was in its ignominious flight from McClellan's army. It had reassembled a few months after that army had been scattered. It entered thereafter upon a prolonged term of existence; the brief history of which is that of dreary servitude to Mr. Davis, broken only by intervals of weak and spasmodic protest.

For a long time the existence of this legislative body was almost unnoticed, except for some occasional foolish and empirical measure, with which it startled the public. It transacted all important business in secret session. It was a violent affectation of the concealed habits of a despotism, and its insolent withdrawal from public notice presented to the world the first example of a public body which claimed to represent the people of a country, and to be acting by their authority and in their behalf, sitting with closed doors, and withholding all its impo tant transactions from their knowledge. Such an exhibition illustrates that curious mixture in the Southern Confederacy, which made it such a strange and anomalous government, holding out to the world republican forms and yet practising in many things the recluseness and isolation and arrogance of the worst despotism.

Occasionally there would issue from these veiled mysteries of legislation the most unexpected and astounding measures, some of them expressing the most puerile conceits, and disarming criticism by the very excess of their absurdity. Nor was this secret legislation always without corrupt advantage to members. An instance was commonly related in Richmond, on an occasion where a law had been passed in secret to have future effect to repudiate partially Confederate notes above the denomination of five dollars, of a distinguished Senator buying up the small currency in every broker's shop in the capital, and making his millions by the operation. But such corruption was only a day's gossip. The Confederate Congress had long ceased to maintain anything of public respect. Its secret sessions were regarded only with slighting or suspicious interest; and when it did indulge in public some slight discussion, those who happened to attend the exhibition confessed themselves stricken with shame, and repeated the common bit of sarcasm in Richmond of "the college debating society" on Capitol Hill.

The appearance of the Congress was singularly plain and unimposing. It was mostly composed of men who were as ordinary in appearance as they were dull in mind. Its surroundings were excessively democratic, dingy, and dirty, and the poverty of the Confederacy scarcely afforded those conveniences and accessories, if not luxuries, which one is accustomed to see in the halls of our legislation. The Congress sat in the "State House," and such was the want of convenient room, that the Senate was forced to occupy a room in the third story, separated by a simple railing from the audience; the only apparent distinction between it and the rough crowd (for there was no accommodation for ladies) being that the Senators sat, while the listeners and loafers, having not even benches, were satisfied to find standing-room on the same floor, with the slight separation we have described. The House had a better chamber; but the bare walls, where there were no paintings, the uncushioned chairs, the dingy desks slashed with pocket-knives, and the attitudes of members, with their heels in air, or their bodies sprawled over two or three chairs, gave one but little idea of legislative dignity or decorum.

There were not more than a dozen men in both Houses who were before known to the country, or had enjoyed a reputation a hundred miles from home. There were Congressmen from districts overrun by the enemy, who had been elected by a few dozens of soldiers' votes cast in camp. It was absurd to find Senators and Representatives from Missouri, Arkansas, Louisiana, etc., holding their seats by virtue of a handful of votes cast by soldiers from their respective States in the camps of the Army of Northern Virginia. Among these unworthy members of Congress were some ridiculous figures, and not a few rustic curiosities who suggested the backwoods and the sedge-fields. The men who relieved something of the rude and ludicrous aspect of the body had generally served before in the old Congress at Washington; but it was often remarked that even these appeared to have lost their former force and dignity, and to have been belittled by the company in which they were misplaced. There were of remarkable members in the House, Mr. Foote, who spoke classical English, and dealt historical illustrations to the unappreciating homespun members, a voluble debater, but afflicted with extravagance and a colicky delivery; William Porcher Miles, of South Carolina, smooth, gentlemanly, scrupulously dressed, a master of deportment, and a type, indeed, of the truest cultivation, deprecating anything like violence in speech or manner; Barksdale, of Mississippi, the especial friend and champion of Mr. Davis, the leader of the Administration party in the House, a small, dark-featured man, who spoke so vehemently as sometimes to overrun the rules of grammar, but really forcible, dealing rude blows with facts and solid arguments; James Lyons, of Virginia, who was satisfied with the shallow reputation of "the handsome member," and who possessed little brains, showed very excellent large white teeth, and stood six feet three in his stockings, the elevated "Turveydrop" of the House. In the Senate were Yancey, of Alabama, the silver-tongued orator of the South, speaking a subdued but luxuriant language, quite unlike that of the American hustings, Wigfall, of Texas, fierce, impatient, incandescent, illustrating another school of eloquence; Orr, of South Carolina, an excellent man in the committee-room, but as heavy and blundering as a school-boy in his speeches; and Hill, of Georgia, the very picture of a smooth and plausible mediocrity, having much of address and of gentlemanly equivocations, inclining to the administration of the President, but at an angle nice and variable in its degrees.

In a body chiefly composed of uncultivated men—to which have been mentioned as exceptions, more or less partial, the names above—there might naturally be expected some breaches of decorum and some scenes of personal violence. Indeed, several most extraordinary scenes of this sort occurred in the Confederate Congress, which were either suppressed in the newspapers, or were but meagerly and tenderly mentioned in their columns. An occurrence at a certain time, by which the whole House of Representatives was thrown into a panic and into the most disgraceful disorder, was so carefully suppressed, that but few people in Richmond ever obtained any knowledge of it, or ever suspected that a scene of bloodshed was about to be enacted behind the convenient curtains of a secret legislative session.

The immediate parties to the disgraceful occurrence (which happened in the summer of 1863) were Mr. Foote, of Tennessee, and Judge Dargan, of Alabama, the latter an old man whose eccentric dress and whose soliloquies on the street were well known in Richmond, and whose habit in Congress of scratching his arms and saying "Mr. Cheer-man," had often brought him under the notice of the galleries. Some words of defiance had passed between the two members. While Judge Dargan was speaking, Mr. Foote sat near him, and muttered that he was a "d—d rascal." The member from Alabama immediately drew a bowie-knife, brandished it in the gas-light (it was a night session), amid the shouts and cries of the House, and made for the member from Tennessee. For a moment all was consternation, and members rushed to the scene of encounter. Several of them literally threw themselves upon Judge Dargan, and wrested from his grasp the murderous weapon; when, just at this moment, Dargan having been pinned to the floor, the whole scene was converted into one irresistibly ludicrous, shouts of laughter succeeding those of passion, as Mr. Foote, striking an attitude and smiting his expanded breast, exclaimed with peculiar melodramatic air, "I defy the steel of the assassin!"

Another memorable scene of personal violence was in the Senate, and was more tragical in its results. In a secret session of that body there occurred a hand-to-hand fight between Mr. Yancey and Mr. Hill, in which the latter, being greatly superior in strength, threw his antagonist across a desk, and bent him over it, continuing to strike him in the face. The consequence was a wrenching and severe injury to Mr. Yancey's spine. It was rumored that it caused his death a few months later; but there is at least no doubt that it hastened the decline of a constitution already feeble by years and disease.

There were other scenes of indecorum in the Congress, of which we may spare details, in one of which a member was flogged with a cowhide in his seat for some indignity or aspersion in social life. Half an hour after this dramatic display took place, messages were flying to all the newspapers in Richmond asking that their reporters should make no mention of it, putting the request on the ground that the publication would degrade the character of the Confederacy, and might be construed as "*giving information to the enemy!*" There is no intention of satire or extravagance in stating this explanation of "contraband" matter; it was actually given by sapient Congressmen, and accepted by complaisant journalists. The newspapers were generally taught an obligation to put all Confederate affairs in roseate color, and to dress them up in the stiffest garments of dignity. To relate anything prejudicial to the Confederacy, to mention even a derogatory social incident, was to incur in the minds of certain vain and paltry, but numerous persons in the South, the charge of publishing "contraband" matter, or of at least lacking in proofs of Southern patriotism. It was thus, to an extent, that the reader of this day can scarcely believe that public opinion in the Southern Confederacy was disarmed, and a wretched Congress passed almost unchallenged and unnoticed through a history of vile excesses and flagitious scenes.

A notable and not the least disgraceful incident of the secluded character of Congress was the shape of the intercourse between President Davis and it in the later periods of the war. It became a singularly devious intercourse, in which delegations composed of five or six Congressman would visit the President in a private way, and make remonstrances and protests to him on special subjects. The public was generally kept in ignorance of these *back-door* communications; it was a private sort of interlocution and catechism dishonorable to both parties, and the incidents of which would scarcely bear publication.

On one occasion Mr. Foote, with two or three other Congressmen, visited the President, to make some remonstrance about the military commands in the West, and abruptly retired from the room without finishing their mission, on the allegation of Mr. Foote that Mr. Davis had spies posted in or near the room to catch and retail the conversation!

On another occasion a Congressional delegation called on Mr. Davis to entreat his restoration of General Beauregard to the command of the army of Tennessee, representing that he had quitted it on a short sick furlough, not supposing that the advantage would be meanly taken of construing his furlough into a resignation, and forcing him into retirement. The President replied, in measured and memorable words: "If the whole world were to ask me to restore General Beauregard to the command which I have already given to General Bragg, I would refuse it."

The veiled government of the Southern Confederacy not only interrupted popular sympathy with it, but it created the most various evils. Making itself constantly the object of mystery it was likely soon to render itself the object of suspicion. It injured the patriotism and confidence of the people of the South in many more ways than that of sheltering itself from proper official responsibility.

And here we are called to regard a most curious subject in the history of the war—the number and volume of false rumors that circulated in it. To search the origin of these rumors, to describe their flight, to inquire how the falsehoods were fledged, and to trace their effects on the spirit and conduct of the belligerents, would constitute, we believe, a chapter of entertaining and even valuable speculation. Although the two powers at war were coterminous, and although there were varied and multiplied communications between the lines of military operations, it is wonderful to notice the multitude and prevalence of false rumors which obscured the true history of the war, and tantalized, provoked, and indeed, seriously embarrassed the combatants. The prevalence of these rumors was peculiar in the South. The comparative multitude of them was due not only to the characteristically lively disposition of the people, but to a special and exceptional cause. That cause was the affected mystery with which Mr. Davis imitated some of the worst examples of government, and in the mists of which he was anxious to enlarge his own figure to most undue proportions.

We have noticed, as a remarkable anomaly of the Confederate Government, the secrecy with which it invested its operations, not only including the conduct of the military field but extended to the administration of every public interest and concern. Here was a government professing to be one of the people created under the inspiration of an extreme republicanism, and yet preaching all the insolation, exclusiveness and mystery of an oriental despotism. This rule of secrecy was first commenced on the pretence, just enough to a certain extent, to exclude the enemy from information of Confederate affairs; but this pretence was capable of a very indefinite extension, and the authorities of Richmond carried it to the most puerile and trivial lengths. It was not only to condemn information generally esteemed contraband in a state of war, but to silence the discussion of almost every public topic by an absurd stretch of the plea that it might injure or disparage the Confederacy abroad. Criticism was not to be tolerated of Mr. Davis's administration, not because it might indicate its faults to the people of the South, but because it would exhibit its weakness to the enemy and improve his confidence. This absurd and unworthy argument was carried in the South to extravagances which will scarcely now be believed. The government was shrouded with a close and imposing mystery; the sessions of Congress even in debate of the commonest civil matter, were habitually secret; and the press was silenced more effectually than by the worst gag law of a despotism. Nearly every article of criticism in the newspapers might by an artful or violent construction be construed as giving information to the enemy, and might be condemned as unpatriotic, if not contraband, under the rule that no evil was to be spoken of the Confederacy, and all its affairs were to be written of in color of the rose.

The effect of this rule upon the newspapers was to silence

the pliant and to embarrass the boldest of them. One of them had spirit enough thus to comment and explain: "Nations will suffer just punishment whenever they intrust power to puny hands, puff up the conceit and encourage the passions of their rulers by fulsome flattery or silent submission. We have done so. The follies of the government are manifest to all, but if any one who pays their cost proposes opposition, or even a remonstrance, the amiable majority cry, 'Hush! oh, hush, hush! we can't get rid of him; and he will do thus and so, all the more if he is opposed. Don't say anything. We must have concord—unanimity—and there must be no opposition to government.' Therefore the only voice which is heard at all is the voice of flatterers—the voice of those who have neither head nor heart, neither knowledge nor principle. Hence the Executive is encouraged to pursue its fancies; and although every military misfortune of the country is palpably and confessedly due to the personal interference of Mr. Davis, the Congress continues at each session to be his subservient tool and to furnish new incentives to perversity, new means of mischief."

The consequences of this secrecy with which the Richmond Government invested itself were various, and, with respect to the responsibility of its rulers, were unjust, despotic and ruinous. In a recent reminiscence of the Confederacy, the Charleston *Mercury* thus writes in a style of just historical review: "There never was any people so completely kept in the dark, as the people of the Government of the Confederate States were under Mr. Davis's administration. His friends soon came to the conclusion, both in the Provisional and the Regular Congresses of the Confederate States, that the less the people knew of their President the better. Therefore, the doors of Congress were closed to publicity; and almost everything that was said or done in Congress was said and done in secret session. It was made a standing rule of the Provisional Congress, and of the Regular Congress we believe also, that the Congress was opened by prayer, and soon after went into secret session. From its impenetrable silence, not a voice of remonstrance or of opposition could be heard. To disclose anything which took place in secret session, was punishable by expulsion. The Government was thus practically, totally irresponsible to the people. Whatever they knew of their government, was by the special favor of those who originally concealed it. The Confederate Congress thus was made to appear to be a *caput mortuum*. Although speeches were delivered, and measures proposed in it, which would have commanded the deepest interest with the people, the only thing the people heard or saw, was Jefferson Davis—and of course Jefferson Davis, in the most imposing and advantageous attitudes. This irresponsibility, stimulated a thousand improprieties and lent countenance to grave and fatal follies both of omission and commission, which the press forebore to publish."

But our particular design here is to treat this extraordinary secrecy of the Confederate Government in a new light, and to portray a train of curious consequences. It was to populate the air of the South so thick with rumors that one could scarcely breathe in it, except at exclamation points. Each day, often each hour, had its rumors, and the country was delivered to the worse than Egyptian plague of these flying pests. The public heart was eat out by rumors. The Southern newspapers of these times, from their forced reticence, give no idea of the extent of this plague. When the doors of official information were closed to all enquirers, any one might presume to be the herald of secret intelligence, and the most foolish story, at any time of the day or night, might collect an audience.

In Richmond there was no end of "confidence men," pretenders, gossipers; and any man who sought a brief hour of self-importance had only to profess that he had been admitted to a back-door confidence with some General, Secretary, or even Department clerk. The most paltry individuals affected this confidence. A disreputable blockade-runner, accustomed to wait in the ante-rooms of head clerks for passports, or permits for whiskey and woolen goods, would, to gaping and ill-smelling audiences in bar rooms, tell stories of "behind the scenes," and offer explanations why General Lee fought the battle of Gettysburg, and what were President Davis's whispered words about Johnston.

It would be one of the most curious volumes of modern times, a collection of all the rumors circulated in Richmond alone during the war, leaving out none of their absurdities. It would be metaphysically interesting as showing how busy and various the human fancy is. There are but two persons now who could make such a collection, even approximately; and they, through this generation, will be graphically remembered in Richmond as the rival news-hunters of a historical period. In this character they were the most notorious men in the capital.

The first, a wealthy speculator and man of leisure, was popularly known as "Long Tom," from his thin and elongated figure. This man appeared to take a morbid delight in the sole occupation of hunting news day and night; it got to be a kind of insanity with him; he scarcely ate or slept, and, at almost every hour of the day, and far into the night, he might be seen haunting the telegraph office, wandering like a weary ghost in the passage way of the War Department, or holding his hand to his ear on the skirts of every crowd on the street corners. He had no particular purpose to serve in this eaves-dropping and ear-wigging; it was his entertainment, his occupation by choice, and he was never happier than when he obtained a piece of news, good or bad, with permission to retail it.

His rival in the rumor business was a little, ferrety, incoherent man, a druggist by profession, but a "sensationist" by real occupation. He dealt only in the largest sensations. He had a habit of speaking with infinite gesture; would sometimes be lost in a perfect splutter of exclamation, when he had important news to convey; and was so dense and unintelligible in his communications, that he generally had to tell his story twice to be understood. He would sometimes break into the newspaper offices, pale and incoherent, with the most dreadful stories, nigh to bursting with news, and in such tremor from his emotions that the reporters would find it a task to calm him, and were wont to compose his nerves by a strengthening draught as a preface to his recital. Once the author recollects to have been called across the street by this little man making the most eager and dramatic gestures, and actually quivering with excitement. "Great God, have you heard the news, Mr. P.," he exclaimed thickly; "Jeff. Davis has just committed suicide!" An hour later, this news of the tragic end of the Confederate Chief had circulated all through Richmond, was wafted across the lines, and was given to the wings of the telegraph from James River to the Penobscot.

To recount even the most important of the false rumors which possessed Richmond during the war, would occupy more space than we can command. Let those who then resided in the Confederate capital but attempt to recall to memory how often Ministers from England and France had arrived with news of recognition ; how often peace commissioners had come by devious ways to Richmond, with protocols and treaties ; how often Beauregard crossed the Potomac in 1861 ; how often Washington had been captured ; how often Grant's army had been defeated before Vicksburg—the stench of its dead being such that fires had to be kindled on the lines and in the streets of the town, to purify the atmosphere (so said the telegraph) ; in short, how often great victories were won and great defeats suffered, which never happened, or existed out of imagination !

The rumors we have described were not the least of the demoralizing consequences of Mr. Davis's unrepublican style of government. They were saps of the public spirit of the South. What is most remarkable of these rumors is that they frequently came from reputable and even semi-official sources They did not always come from obscure authors. There were, of course, the common, paltry classes of news retailers: —the man who had just came through the lines, the "intelligent gentleman," the interesting lady refugee, and the person who mysteriously had it from "good authority." These might be listened to with contempt, or with a degree of skepticism. But in many instances in Richmond, rumors grossly false were circulated from sources so well calculated to obtain belief, that for days and weeks they would possess the public mind, and compel even the credence of newspaper men, a class which, though ambitious of news, is characteristically skeptical, and trained to estimate its probability. The fact is, the Confederate Government was so close in its confidences so absolutely secret and secluse, that even those otherwise in close relations with it were imposed upon by false beliefs, and gave impressive endorsement to the wildest rumors. Thus, on one occasion, the excellent Doctor Minnigerode, pastor of Mr. Davis, and supposed to have confidences which the President would not give even to his Cabinet, related in the streets of Richmond, that a French envoy had landed on the North Carolina coast, and was making his way to the capital. Coming from such a source, the story was religiously, almost universally believed in Richmond, for several days; but it turned out that Doctor M. had been somehow imposed upon, and had innocently raised the hopes of the Confederacy to a height that increased the shock and cruelty of the fall.

An explanation of the birth of rumors is very difficult. We have often wondered and speculated where all the falsehoods came from which make history. Many false rumors may be accounted for in interested inventions; many may be traced to motives; many originate in mistake and misrepresentation; many come from the excess of hope or fear, "the wish the father of the thought," and dread the parent of the apparition. But this does not account for all of them. How shall we explain those many rumors to which no conceivable motive attaches, causelessly originated, in cold blood, having no imaginable object? We sometimes find worthy and respectable persons who by no means can be put in the degraded class of liars giving currency to gross falsehoods, and even professing to have been witnesses of what they relate. These men are to some extent honest. Their conduct is not entirely beyond explanation, or inadmissible of some charitable construction. It often happens that they themselves have become absolutely convinced of some fact or occurrence; they meet hearers who are disposed to be skeptical, and who insist upon doubting; and, in a zeal to overcome what they consider the obstinacy of disbelief, they will make additions to the story, or supply circumstances which never occurred, to increase its credibility, believing, as long as the main statement is true, it will do no harm to add means to compel belief. This sophism in narrative is much more common than supposed, disreputable as it is. It accounts for a peculiar and large class of false rumors, and we remember some remarkable instances of it in the war.

One instance may be given as characteristic. Towards the close of 1863, an "intelligent gentleman" arrived on the Mississippi, related that he had travelled through a great part of the State of Texas with an envoy from England, who had come through Mexico on his way to Richmond, and had actually exhibited to him both his credentials and his letters of authority to recognize the Confederacy. What was most notable of the story was that its bearer was well known to many of the Western newspapers, which, in relating the agreable news, vouched for him as a gentleman whose honor, veracity and intelligence were absolutely indisputable. So there was an uproar of joyful excitement from one end to the other of the Confederacy. Unfortunately, however, for the sequel, the envoy never arrived at Richmond, or put in an appearance in the cis-Mississippi. The truth of the story is probably that the "intelligent gentleman" had been imposed upon by an adventurer, and was so sure of his news that he thought himself safe in adding the circumstance of having seen his papers, bearing the royal seal, thus persuading the public to believe a fact of which he himself entertained no misgivings or doubts.

The effect of this multitude of rumors on the public mind of the South could not but be to strain and distress, and ultimately to demoralize it. It could not end otherwise than in blunting the sensibilities of the people. Mr. Davis did not have practical sense enough to appreciate this disastrous effect ot the secrecy and exclusiveness in which hé insisted upon conducting the public affairs; he could not understand how the country suffered from his feverish fancies of imperialism, and how, at last, overburdened with anxieties, and dulled by excessive excitement, it was losing its emotions and thus its inspiration in the war. It was significant how the public mind of the Confederacy in the last periods of its career descended to a condition of dull expectation. Its heart was worn out by the pendulous swing in which it oscillated from hope to fear. The very extent of rumors diminished the sensibilities with which they were received, and disheartened the Confederacy to a degree which many perceived without the least suspicion of its cause.

In the North there could be no equal to the demoralization of the South from excessive rumors. There false statements of the war were plentiful; but, with the doors of Congress open, and with public curiosity having its usual access to the Government, barring only operations strictly military, the field for rumors was, of course, partial and contracted. In the South this field was illimitable.

Mr. Davis bolted every door of the government, and every time he turned the key on a public measure, he uncaged, on the other hand, a flock of rumors. They darkened the air; they preyed on the hearts of the people. Many of these rumors were of the most cruel description, heartless cheats of the little that remained to the people of hope. Like the Indian bats which are said to fan with their pinions the wound they make in the body of the sleeper, so as to soothe and not disturb him, while they drink from his veins, so these insidoius winged creatures of the imagination fed on the life-blood of the Confederacy, dying while it indulged in dreams.

CHAPTER XX.

Decay of the Patriotism of the South—No Possible Explanation of it, but the Maladministration of Mr. Davis—Condition of the Confederate Armies—Aversion to Military Service—Mr. Davis's Appeal to Absentees—False Praise of the South for Devotion in the War—Eighteen Hundred *Habeas Corpuses* in Richmond—How the Conscription was Dodged—Humors of the *Habeas Corpus*—The Public Spirit of the South, Mean and Decayed—Senator Wigfall Scathes the Farmers—Utter Loss of Moral Influence by President Davis—Enlargement of the Conscription—A Thorough Military Despotism at Richmond—Conscription and Impressment Twin Measures—The Scarcity of Food in the South, the Result of Mismanagement—A Notable Law in the Depreciation of a Currency—An Interesting Incident of the First Battle of Manassas—The Errors of the Impressment Law—The War, a Choice of Despots, One at Washington, and One at Richmond—Fearful Attack of Senator Toombs on Mr. Davis's Administration—The South "Already Conquered."

IT would be difficult and perhaps unnecessary to enumerate all the causes which conspired to decay the patriotism of the South, and to produce such manifest disaffection in the Confederacy as the war advanced to the limits of the period where our narrative has paused. For certainly and obviously the chief and sufficient cause of this must have been the maladministration of Mr. Davis, in whatever particulars it occurred, and the loss of that influence which had formerly commanded the unmeasured devotion of the South. There had been no increase of the hardships of the war, commensurate with the decline of spirit in it; there was no diminution of the desire for independence; the sense of the enemy's wrongs had been exasperated; there existed all the original motives and inspirations which had formerly commanded the efforts of the South; and there is no other explanation for the falling off and delinquency of these than a dissatisfaction, wide-spread and profound, concerning the conduct of the war and the administration of affairs summed in Mr. Davis's hands.

In the early periods of the war there had been an excessive rage of volunteering. The care of the government had been not to raise but to reduce it; and the zeal of patriotic contributions of all sorts had been unlimited. Now the army had become a name of terror; everything was done to avoid the conscription which instead of being accepted as formerly with alacrity was shunned as the gates of death; in the midsummer of 1863, it was estimated that a half or three-fourths of the Confederate forces were in the condition of desertion, straggling and absenteeism; and as a further evidence of the aversion to military service, the curious statistic was furnished in a secret session of Congress that 10,000 fraudulent substitute papers had been discovered in the archives of conscription. In vain Mr. Davis tried appeals to patriotism; publishing:—"The victory is within your reach; you need but stretch forth your hand to grasp it; * * * * * the men now absent from their posts would, if present in the field, suffice to create numerical equality between our force and that of the invaders." The absentees did not return; and thousands of men subject to military duty fled the conscription, or exhausted all the means and arts of their lives to avoid its demands.

Much has been written boastfully of the patriotic devotion of the South in the late war. But we think judicious history will declare that although there might have been such a fervor in the commencement of the contest, all the later efforts of the South were compelled only by the harshest measures, and instead of being the free contributions of a public spirit, were the forced results of a military despotism.

Certainly the claim of patriotic devotion of the South cannot be maintained in the face of the facts, that only the utmost rigor of conscription forced a majority of its troops in the field; that half of these were disposed to desert on the first opportunities; and that the demands for military service were cheated in a way and to an extent unexampled in the case of any brave and honorable nation engaged in a war for its own existence. We have the remarkable fact that in one year the Confederate States Attorney in Richmond tried *eighteen hundred* cases in that city on writs of *habeas corpus* for relief from conscription! This honored writ in fact became the vilest instrument of the most undeserving men; and there is attached to it a record of shame for the South that we would willingly spare. Mr. Humphrey Marshall, a member of the Confederate Congress who recited woman's poetry in that body, about all sorts of death being preferable to submission, added to his pay as a legislator the fees of an attorney to get men out of the army; he became the famous advocate in Richmond in cases of *habeas corpus;* and he is reported to have boasted that this practice alone yielded him an average of two thousand dollars a day!

It has occurred to us that a book might be written of the experiences, in Richmond alone, of efforts to escape the dreaded conscription, and of the various dodges and artifices to which resort was had for exemption from service in a war which the newspapers were constantly declaiming as the most glorious of the age, and as illustrated with acts of universal and unmeasured devotion on the part of the people. Such devotion was only the imagination of editors, or the affectation of Mr. Davis's partizans. How to escape the conscription was for months in Richmond the unceasing concern of a population of one hundred and fifty thousand souls. The various dodges of this dreadful measure would be curious as examples of the general ingenuity of the human mind, if they were not also entertaining and humorous as incidents of character. The courts were sonorous with *habeas corpus.* Family Bibles were brought in to determine uncertainties of ages as within the boundaries of conscription. There were romances of perjury. One of the attorneys in such a case tells of an amusing instance where an old maid living in the country, anxious to diminish her own record of years, had tampered with the Bible of the family, and to make her reduced age consistent, had ventured to dock a number of years from the lives of two or three brothers recorded on the same page. When the men came to claim their exemption on the score of age, the Bible was produced, and to their dismay they found they had been made several years younger on the record, bringing them within the fateful terms of the conscript age. Explanations had to be made, not the most delicate or pleasant;—but any thing was to be suffered rather than to step into the ranks of those whom the journals represented as the glorious and happy defenders of their country. If conscription seized the shrinking victim there was yet hope. There were marts for substitutes in every alley-way of Richmond; and even, at the last, there was hope of a "detail," if there was money or influence to command this last extremity of relief. The application for details was the side-show of the *habeas corpus.* It burdened all the routines of the War Department, and claimed a "bureau" for its convenience. Merchants and bankers were willing to be detailed as mechanics and laboring men, to work on army supplies. Rich men applied for positions as railroad men, telegraphers, and miners, at the pay of thirteen dollars a month, equal to fifteen cents in gold. Offices were invented by a convenient Secretary of War to shield fugitives from the conscription; a person was relieved by him from military duty to write a "history of the war;" and two notorious lawyers of Richmond, who had been busy at *habeas corpus* and who affected literary pastimes, were sheltered by the Macænas of the War Department, one as a sinecure in the Treasury and the other as *custos rutulorum* in the scholastic dominions of Mr. Seddon.

If such facts, concerning the evasion of military duty, signify any thing, it is that the patriotism of the South had become mean and decayed—that there was an amount of unwillingness in the war, which had to be constantly chastised and compelled by despotic laws. A few public men in the Confederacy were bold enough to confess its loss of public spirit, in opposition to all the cheap eulogiums and the self-complacency which has come down to our day of the noble devotion and generous sacrifices of the South in the war. Mr. Wigfall of Texas told the story plainly in the Senate, of the mean and grudging spirit that had taken possession of the people of the South concerning every contribution to the war. He said:—"It was the fashion to talk about the bone and sinew of the country, and to speak of the planters and farmers as having all of the religion, cultivation, education and patriotism of the country. Talk of speculators, extortioners, and Dutch Jews! The farmers have been the worst speculators, extortioners, and Dutch Jews of this war. Has the population of the South changed? No. Have the Yankees driven out the people from their lands, and put in their places the Dutch and Irish with whom they have threatened to colonize the conquered States? No. These are the people of the South who are fighting for their liberties or getting other people to fight for them."

It is remarkable that to those who make a boast of the patriotic devotion of the South in the war, and are intent to display it as an ornament of a lost cause, the thought has never occurred how this claim can consist with the necessities of conscription and impressment, the amount of force necessary to raise armies in the Confederacy, the amount of fraud by which the public service was cheated of men and material, the extent of desertions and of evasions of military duty, and all the other peculiar incidents we have mentioned of unwilling service and forced contribution in the war. We may not be able to establish fully the consistency of facts so opposite, but we have an explanation that may go a great way to redeem a contradiction that impeaches seriously the honor and spirit of the South. The only possible hypothesis on which that honor can be saved is that the people of the South acted in the manner we have described, grudging the demands of the war from the conviction of the unworthiness and misdirection of their government, rather than from that of any demerit or decline of their cause. It is certain that they had a great and noble cause to fight for, and that in the first part of the contest they had displayed unbounded devotion and courage, the admiration of the world. The cause had lost none of its merits, the war none of its just inspiration; these rather had been increased; and yet at a time when the people of the South had in no degree diminished their desire for independence, and long before they thought the war for any natural reason hopeless, and when all that was thought necessary for its success was well-directed effort—when the disasters that had occurred were considered only of that measure which reinspires and strengthens the courageous spirit rather than reduces it—we find them yielding the war an uncertain and niggardly support, displaying nothing of a former devotion, and disposed to deny or to cheat every contribution which the government required of them. The only explanation can be that that government had in some way wounded them, in some way forfeited their confidence—either this, or that the people of the South had some inherent defect of cowardice or irresolution:—either Jefferson Davis unworthy, or the whole population of the South in fault and disgrace. A severe alternative, of which the reader may take the supposition he pleases.

When Mr. Davis, after the disasters of Gettysburg and Vicksburg, found his appeals for volunteers unavailing, and when he must have been sensible of his loss of the popular confidence, we find him at once taking a new breadth of despotism in his government—a measure, indeed, calculated to produce a certain re-animation of the war, and this for a certain period, but having no depth of public spirit in it, and although postponing the catastrophe, yet making it more certain and disastrous at the last. We refer to the enlargement of the conscription law. First, on the 15th of July, 1863, came a proclamation of the President extending the limits of the conscription, which in the former year had been of persons between the ages of eighteen and thirty-five, to include all up to the age of forty-five; then an act of Congress extending the term of the conscript age to fifty-five years; added to this a law repealing all substitutions in the military service, and actually compelling the seventy or eighty thousand persons who had furnished substitutes to take up arms themselves, and that without returning them the money they had paid or releasing the substitutes they had employed—an example of the very effrontery of fraud and despotism; and lastly, at the close of the year, a law to clinch the whole matter, declaring every man between eighteen and fifty-five years of age to belong to the army, subject at once to the articles of war, military discipline and military penalties, and requiring him to report within a certain time, or be liable to death as a deserter. The whole people of the South were made soldiers under martial law. The country was converted into a vast camp, and the government of Jefferson Davis into one of the most thorough military despotisms of the age.

But the levy *en masse* was not all. The twin measure of conscription, that which completed the despotic character of the government at Richmond, was impressment. They were logical correspondents; they made as a whole a government in which the lives of the citizens and all the production and labor of the country, were put under military control. It was the maximum of the demands of a despotism.

After the disasters of 1863, complaints of the want of food arose simultaneously with those of the deficiency of men; and it was evident to the intelligent that the same decay of public spirit that denied the claims of military service, also withheld the meaner contributions of food and supply for the army. Both necessities grew out of the same unwilling spirit in the Confederacy. There was really no scarcity of food to the absurd extent represented by Mr. Davis when he declared that it was "*but the one* danger to be regarded with apprehension"—as if in an extensive and fruitful land like the South, there could be danger of the starvation of a whole population! What necessities did really exist were mostly artificial, or of the government's own creation. There was plenty of food in the South; but it was badly distributed by a Commissary who was unwise and rapacious; who had no idea of equalizing the supplies of the country, or conciliating the generosity of the people. Again, the apparent deficiency was greatly due to the wretched currency of the Confederacy; and that by a law certain and irresistible in its effects. As a currency depreciates, a rise in prices takes place; it affords for the time a temporary accommodation to the producer. But it is remarkable that this rise does not keep equal pace on the inverse scale of comparisons with the decline of the currency; that it cannot do so, owing to the constant contest between buyer and seller, which delays and embarrasses the adjustment; and that the consequence is, that when a currency depreciates there is a general disposition to withhold from market and to hoard supplies which would otherwise be converted into money. These results were excessively realized in the Confederacy, where the currency was rapidly verging to worthlessness, and where hoarders and engrossers were found in every department of industry and in every class of society.

In the early months of the war, when General Beauregard was preparing to fight the battle of Manassas, he had written a letter to a farmer in Orange county, representing that the army was in need of sixty wagon-loads of corn and provisions, and engaging to pay for the same and the expense of hauling, as soon as the funds could be obtained from Richmond. The letter was read the following Sunday to all the churches in Orange county. The response was that the next day the sixty wagons, loaded with corn, were sent to General Beauregard, free of charge, and with the message that he should also keep the wagons and teams for the use of his army. Such was the patriotic generosity of a single county in Virginia; it was indicative of public spirit in the Confederacy. How great a change must have befallen that spirit, when, two years later, we find the same class of producers who then hastened with donations for the army, avaricious and chaffering traders in the life-blood of their own country, refusing to sell their grain to the government, perhaps haggling about the price of pork per pound, when their sons and brothers in the army were living on a quarter of a pound of meat a day, and sometimes had none at all.

Truly the patriotism of the Confederacy had wofully declined—had fallen by a whole heaven—in view of a government compelled to recruit supplies for its army in a war for its existence on the alternative of begging to buy them or of taking them with a ruthless hand. The army was badly fed; it was worse clothed. It was said:—"Day by day the clothes made for the soldiers exhibit less wool and more cotton." Thousands of these poor fellows were clothed in the Federal uniforms which had been captured. Thousands were destitute of shoes; and it was reported that nearly half of Longstreet's corps were barefoot, when the snows laid on the ground at the close of the year 1863. Meanwhile the railway system of the Confederacy was giving out; even if supplies were found it was difficult to transport them; and thus distress from every point stared the people of the South, while the enemy continued to invade their towns and States, to offer liberty to their slaves, to enrol them in his armies, and to defy their retaliation.

Great and bitter as were the wants of the government for supplies, nothing could have been worse than the law into which it wildly and madly plunged for a remedy. The law of impressment was excessive; it alarmed the sentiment of the whole country; it destroyed the last vestiges of civil rights in the Confederacy. To show to what extent the government of Mr. Davis contemplated its powers, it may be mentioned that his dull creature, Northrop, the Commissary-General had proposed to him to seize plantations throughout the South, and to work them on government account;* and

* "The plan is for the Government to take possession of the plan-

that the President had, only after hesitation, declined this high-handed scheme to adopt the more uniform, but scarcely less cruel law of impressments. This law authorized the government to seize or impress all the produce necessary for the army. It provided that a board of commissioners should be appointed in each State who should determine, every sixty days, the prices which the government should pay for each article of produce impressed within the State. A central board of commissioners was also appointed for all the States. The act authorized the agents of the government to seize all the produce of the farmer, except so much as was necessary to sustain himself and family.

Denunciations of the law arose on all sides. It was inseparable from abuses. The newspapers complained of the rude and rapacious action of "the press-gangs." The meaner citizens resorted to all possible methods to save their property from impressment; many of them were driven to sell clandestinely or openly their stores to non-producers out of the army, who were willing and anxious to pay fifty or a hundred per cent. more than the government paid. On the other hand the few who were really patriotic and disposed to contribute to the war, who still maintained a romantic enthusiasm in the contest, had their feelings hurt; they were touched in their pride and sense of justice that the govern-

---

tations, or such portions of them as the owners do not intend to seed with grain, etc., and to employ negroes belonging thereto in raising such agricultural products as may be deemed necessary. Officers and soldiers who have been rendered by wounds or disease unfit for further service in the field could be employed as superintendents and overseers * * * Let the emergency be urged upon the President, while there is yet time to save ourselves."—*Letter of Northrop to Secretary of War*, April 25, 1863.

ment should treat them with rudeness and suspicion. Yet another and more important class of citizens resented the law in a more serious light—as an act of unexampled despotism. There were men even in the Confederate Congress who were bold enough to declare that impressment and other acts of misrule and oppression in the administration of Mr. Davis had extracted all virtue from the cause, and that the war simply remained as a choice of despots, one at Washington and one at Richmond. "I have heard it frequently stated," said Senator Toombs, of Georgia, "and it has been maintained in some of the newspapers in Richmond, that we should not sacrifice liberty to independence; but I tell you, my countrymen, the two are inseparable. If we lose our liberty, we shall also lose our independence; and when our Congress determined to support our armies by impressment, gathering supplies wherever they found them most convenient, and forcing them from those from whom their agents might choose to take them, in violation of the fundamental principles of our Constitution, which requires all burdens to be uniform and just, and paying for them such prices as they chose, they made a fatal blunder, which cannot be persisted in without endangering our cause, and probably working ruin to our government. The moment they departed from the plain rule laid down in the Constitution—that impressment of private property should only be made in cases where absolute necessity required them—they laid the foundation for discontent among the people; they discouraged labor, and incorporated a principle which is not only in violation of the Constitution, but fatal to the rights of property. The Constitution cannot be dispensed with in time of war any more than in time of peace. If it is overthrown we are already conquered."

CHAPTER XXI.

The Scarcity of Food in the South in Connection with the Subsistence of Prisoners—Secret History of the Administration of the Confederate Prisons—No Provision for Feeding Prisoners—A Brutal Incident at the Libby—Anecdote of a Yankee Boatswain—Commissary Northrop Recommends that the Prisoners be Chucked into the James River—Laws of the Confederacy concerning Prisoners—Exceeding Humanity of Quartermaster-General Lawton—Northrop defeats it—His *Coup d'Etat* on a Drove of Beeves—Northrop Responsible for the Maltreatment of Prisoners—Sorrowful Story of Wirz—"The Wrong Man" Hung—Measure of Mr. Davis's Responsibility for the Sufferings of the Prisoners—His Extraordinary Affection for Northrop—Mr. Foote on the "Pepper Doctor"—Senator Orr has a Flea put in his Ear—The Subject of Discipline in the Confederate Prisons—An Argument to Relieve Mr. Davis from the Charge of Deliberate Cruelty—The Authentic Version of the Libby "Gunpowder Plot"—The Spy's Story—Richmond Sleeping on the Crust of a Volcano—Why the Prisoners were Distributed to Salisbury and Andersonville.

IN connection with the scarcity of food and necessary supplies in the South occurs a subject of interest which we may conveniently examine here. We refer to that large volume of complaint against Mr. Davis for the maltreatment of Northern prisoners, especially in the article of subsistence. We have already, on the subject of the Confederate commissariat, made some suggestions which throw light on this matter; but we find no more proper place in our work than the present to sum a brief account of the administration of the Confederate prisons. We propose thus to go over rapidly the history of the subsistence of Federal prisoners in the South—a subject so serious and interesting as to have founded extensive ex aminations both at Washington and Richmond, but the secret history of which is scarcely yet known.

It is remarkable that in the early periods of the war there was no system whatever, no organized provision for subsisting the prisoners who soon commenced to accumulate on the hands of the government. There was an officer, of the rank of lieutenant, who had charge of the unfortunate creatures, who subsisted them by irregular purchases in the Richmond markets, and who was left to determine, as of his own discretion, the measure and article of food. He was removed for a singular freak some weeks after the battle of Manassas. Having had a drunken quarrel with the quartermaster as to who should bury the dead of the prison, he had left two corpses in front of the office of the latter, in a wagon halted in one of the most public streets near the Capitol, and, unhitching the horses in sight of a horrified crowd, had abandoned the "dead Yankees" to take their chances of burial as the authorities, other than himself, might determine. It was a day's scandal in Richmond, and the brutal officer was removed. But for forty-eight hours nearly two thousand prisoners were without a mouthful of food, until a subordinate of the prison, moved by their cries or alarmed by their mutiny, found some barrels of corn-meal in the stores of the prison, and fed it to them in buckets of mush.

It was through this humane diligence that Captain Warner, a generous and efficient man, became afterwards charged with the subsistence of the prisoners. The Captain often told in Richmond, with great emotion, his experience with the prisoners, mutinous and savage for want of food; for surely there is no fiercer devil in the human composition, none that dares more than hunger. He was walking in the prisoners' galleries of the Libby, explaining that a difficulty had occurred in their supplies of food, but that they should have illimitable stores on the morrow, when an immense Yankee boatswain clutched him by the collar, and dragged him into a circle of angry faces, desperate from hunger. "You are a good commissary," said Jack, "and I am a good prisoner; I am the best prisoner you ever saw in the world; but, d——n me, if I had not rather face one hundred of Jeff. Davis's cannon than be starved like a dog." "I felt rather *unhappy* for a few moments," said Captain Warner, "but I promised the fellow, who shook me, heavy as I was, as if I was no more than a baby in his hands, that if he would let me go, he should have some grub in half an hour. I found nothing in the store-house of the prison but three barrels of meal. I made it into hot mush, filled some buckets with it, and had it passed in to the prisoners. But you may bet I didn't go inside. I called to Jack through the grate that I had got him the healthiest supper I could, and not to let the men burn their mouths."

The next day Captain Warner represented to General Winder, the principal officer in charge of the prisoners, that there was no subsistence for them, and that they were in the actual pangs of hunger. He was directed at once to make a requisition on Colonel Northrop, the cross-grained and eccentric Commissary-General—an officer whose idea of importance was to have a fit of insolence whenever he was approached, and who was either gruff or hysterical in his official intercourse.

"I know nothing of Yankee prisoners," he said; "throw them all into the James river!"

"At least," said Captain Warner, "tell me how I am to keep my accounts for the prisoners' subsistence."

"Sir," said Northrop, slightly inclining his eyes to the anxious inquirer, "I have not the will or the time to speak with you. Chuck the scoundrels into the river!"

Here was a quandary. There was no law to charge the Commissary-General with the subsistence of prisoners; he insisted that it belonged to the quartermaster's department;

the latter denied it, and, in a dead-lock of quibbles the prisoners might be left to starve. The ingenuity of a lawyer was required to solve the dispute. Captain Warner had been appointed Commissary of Prisons and yet Northrop refused to acknowledge his authority or to fill his requisitions, and was completely obscure and impracticable on a question of humanity. Happily a convenient law or military regulation was hunted up, to the effect that a bonded commissary might be assigned to perform certain duties of quartermaster at his post. Under this law Captain Warner might draw his supplies from the Quartermaster-General and might be independent of the odious Northrop. Another obscure statute was discovered; it was an act of the early Congress at Montgomery; it consisted only of three or four lines, but it was very important. It provided with rare humanity that the prisoners of war should have the same rations as Confederate soldiers in the field.

Under the arrangement indicated by these laws the prisoners were comfortably, and even generously, subsisted for many months. The arrangement was perfected not long after the battle of Manassas. Food was then abundant in Richmond, and the best beef sold for only eight cents a pound. When supplies became scarce; when the foolish law authorizing impressments and assigning "government prices," drove nearly every producer from the market, it became a matter of extreme difficulty to feed the prisoners and to divide what could be obtained between their necessities and those of the Confederate troops in the field. The Commissary of Prisons, acting independently of Northrop, employed travelling agents to purchase supplies at the best prices, and never allowed his solicitude for the unhappy men in his charge to be impaired by demands in other departments of the government.

As evidence of this solicitude it may be mentioned that in the winter of 1863, a memorable season of scarcity, it was proposed to buy supplies for the prisoners in some of the upper counties of Virginia, where Confederate money was refused, and that to effect the humane undertaking, General Lawton, then Quartermaster-General, was willing to draw a requisition for fifty thousand dollars in gold.

But these purchases were defeated by an unforeseen interference. Commissary Northrop had opposed all purchases of supplies outside of his department; he complained that Captain Warner paid larger prices than the government maximum; he insisted that as the first care was to provide for the troops in the field, he should have the first option of all marketable supplies; and at last he assumed to "impress" the subsistence puchased for the prisoners and to divert it to his own department. A fierce war was waged between him and Warner; rival committees of investigation were raised in Congress; and the supplies of the Libby became a bone of contention. On one occasion Warner's agents had brought down from Augusta county a drove of one hundred and seventy-five beeves, and Northrop had performed a *coup d'etat* by impressing them on the skirts of Richmond. Not to be entirely outdone, Captain Warner, in the winter of 1863, loaded sixty-three cars in North Carolina with sweet potatoes, brought them to the Libby, pounded them and then sifted them through the wire-nets he tore from the windows, and composed a curious bread made of equal measures of mash of potatoes, flour and corn-meal. "It was the best bread I ever ate," says Captain Warner. But even this invention was spoiled by Northrop. He had determined to take control of all the subsistence of the Confederacy, and to interdict all special purchases for the consumption of prisoners. The first result was a regulation requiring the Commissary of Prisons to purchase from the Commissary-General; and ultimately, in the spring of 1864, a law was passed virtually abolishing the former office and transferring the subsistence of prisoners to the tender mercies of the man who had wished the thousands of them in Richmond at the bottom of James river.

From this time whatever there was of distress for food among the prisoners is to be properly and distinctly charged to one man in the Confederacy—Northrop. It is a pity that this was not known when poor Wirz, the miserable scapegoat of Confederate maladministration, was sent to the gallows; and we may understand the remorseful remark of the Judge-Advocate of the court that condemned him, when better acquainted with the system under which the Southern prisons were managed—he is reported to have declared that "he had hung the wrong man!"

A few words of this tragic episode, this fearful misadventure of Northern vengeance, may properly be introduced here. Captain Wirz died an innocent man. His history was one of the most harmless we have ever known. In 1861 he had come to Richmond, a private in a company from Louisiana, called the Madison Infantry. He was detailed as a sentinel at the Libby; there his fidelity and intelligence were noticed, and he was promoted to a clerkship in the prison. From this capacity he was sometimes called to undertake slight executive duties about the prison, and for this obtained a commission. He acquired such reputation for his diligence and energy that when Secretary Mallory wished in 1863 a trusty agent to convey some ordnance to the coast of Louisiana, Wirz was indicated to him as the man of all others for a service so difficult. When he had got the cannon by almost superhuman efforts to the Mississippi river, General Pemberton seized it, and Wirz returned disgusted to Richmond, and half resolved to quit the service, from which he had once before obtained a furlough to recruit his health in Europe. At this time General Winder was establishing the prison at Andersonville; he had sent his son down, a youth, commissioned as lieutenant to take charge of it; but it was suggested that an officer of higher rank and more experience should go. Captain Wirz was urgently solicited to undertake the mission, and as warmly refused it. At last he consented to go, but on the express promise of General Winder that he was only to make a brief stay to relieve an embarrassment about the youth and inexperience of his son, and that he would be recalled in a few weeks. Winder never relieved him, and the unhappy man was left there to fall a victim to a fate he had never provoked or never suspected!

For whatever there was of maltreatment of Northern prisoners, the responsibility of Mr. Davis is to be measured as that of any other part of his administration. The President, himself, had an easy and humane temper, unless in fits of enraged vanity. No one ever accused him of cruelty; but if he employed such cruel and incompetent agents as Northrop, continuing to employ him after repeated exposures of his unworthiness, it is but fair that he should suffer something of responsibility for the abuses we have described. The law of agency is as certain in politics as in any other affair of life. The President of the Southern Confederacy, although defended from the bulk of those atrocious Northern inventions concerning cruelty to prisoners, is yet to be blamed, not lightly, for continuing in his employment such agents as Winder and Northrop, each a favorite creature, the last extravagantly so, and both of them repeatedly brought to his attention as incompetent and scandalous officers.

His affection for Northrop was grotesque, inexplicable, insane, "The pepper doctor from South Carolina" was as great a curiosity at the head of the Confederate Commissariat as Memminger, the eccentric, with tall beaver and black bag, mumbling his soliloquies on the street, was at the head of the Confederate Treasury. Mr. Davis could plead no ignorance of the idiosyncrasies or insanities of Northrop. They were laughed at or derided, by nearly every person in the Confederacy; or they were sternly accused in Congress. He was thus spoken of in this body:—"A certain Commissary-General who is a curse to our country has been invested with authority to control the matter of subsistence. This man has placed our government in the attitude charged by the enemy, and has attempted to starve the prisoners in our hands." Mr. Foote, of Tennessee, added the following graphic touch: "This Commissary-General, who I am told was a sort of pepper-doctor down in Charleston, and I must say looking as like a vegetarian as his practice would indicate, has actually made an elaborate report to the Secretary of War, showing, that for the subsistence of a human Yankee carcass, a vegetable diet is the most proper that can be adopted!"

One other instance of remonstrance by Congress against Northrop deserves to be related. Senator Orr, of South Carolina, backed by several Congressmen, attempted to procure his removal, moved by the outcry from the army and the country against an officer especially hateful and ignorant, who was ridiculed for his grotesque incompetency, who had been lampooned as a vegetarian, and who had been accused as almost insane. "Gentlemen," replied Mr. Davis, "you do not know Mr. Northrop as I do. I assure you he is a great military genius, and if he had not preferred his present position, I would have given him the command of one of the armies in the field." And so both Federal prisoners and Lee's army were left to starve on the theoretic genius of the pepper-doctor; and Congress, abashed and impotent, was again forced to surrender to the supreme pleasure of Mr. Davis, and to accept one of his worst creatures, one most fatal and shameful to the Confederacy.

While we are treating the subject of the administration of the Confederate prisons, we may not omit the subject of their discipline; although it is significantly to be noticed that but few complaints of the enemy were lodged on this account, and that they mostly related to the article of food and supplies, in which principally it was alleged that the Federal prisoners were sufferers. The distress for food was the main complaint. The remark is very significant; for it appears that the Federal prisoners were punished or pinched only in a respect in which the whole army and people of the South were, alike, sufferers; and the thought obviously occurs that if Jefferson Davis had really a disposition of cruelty towards these unfortunates, he might have gratified it through means much more direct and effective than that of dealing out to them insufficient rations; that a harsh and murderous discipline would have been much more to such purpose than stinted allowances of food. The Federal prisoners suffered only in that respect in which the whole South suffered. The fact is powerfully significant in relieving Mr. Davis of the charge of cruelty to prisoners; although even in this respect we are not disposed to acquit him of obstinate carelessness in the supervision of his agents and subordinates, and of that responsibility which ensues from an act of omission or attaches to a case of neglect.

If there had really been a disposition in the head of the Confederate government to maltreat prisoners, we repeat the means were much more easy and obvious in a harsh discipline than in insufficient doles of subsistence. But the fact is that the discipline of the Confederate prisons, was mild and lax to a fault. The incontestable proof of this easy and imperfect discipline is the vast number of prisoners who escaped to the North. There were insufficient guards of Southern prisons their inmates had such great breadth of license that they were almost constantly in a condition of mutiny and revolt; and if there were occasional acts of restraint and terrorism on the part of the Confederate authorities, it was because the prisoners had become insolent from the very excess of freedom allowed them; were ill-contained by their guards and were constantly encouraged to efforts at escape and to attempts of revolt by the lax and insufficient discipline which the means of the South afforded to govern and secure them.

Much has been told, gloomily and melodramatically, of a mine of gunpowder under the Libby prison, dug there on the event of the Dahlgren raiders, and designed to blow the prisoners to destruction, should any attempt for their rescue be made. The story has been told with great dramatic effect; but the truth of it is very simple, and illustrates the disposition to construct horrors about Southern prisons. It was told to the prisoners that such a mine was under their feet to deter them from a revolt, which was then plainly threatened; but, indeed, the Confederacy had no such quantity of gunpowder to spare for a puerile scare-crow. The story quieted the prisoners, and probably averted a scene of horror that was being prepared for Richmond, and that was known to not more than three men—these officers connected with the Libby prison

It has been confessed since the war that the keeper of this prison, aware of his insufficient force to guard it and prevent escapes, dreading almost each night, while Richmond slept secure, that a determined revolt of the prisoners might over whelm the few hundred men who guarded it, hit upon the plan of employing among them a spy, introduced in the character of a Federal captive, who regularly gave information of the various plots of the prisoners to which he gained confidence. At the time the raid of Dahlgren was afoot, the spy reported that the prisoners had been made aware of this movement outside to assist their escape, and had prepared at a signal to batter out the walls which confined them, and to unite in a foray through the streets of Richmond, including the murder of Jefferson Davis and the indiscriminate pillage of the citizens. A fearful plot was exposed. Beams had been detached from the rafters of the prison, to be used as battering rams. There were then men enough in the prisons of Richmond to constitute an army. In the Libby prison alone there were eleven hundred inmates; in Crew and Pemberton's Factory, across the street, there were twenty-five hundred; and including the men confined on Belle Isle, there were not less than fifteen thousand prisoners in and around Richmond, guarded by a few hundred men, and who might any moment, by a bold and concerted movement have obtained their liberty (even without the assistance of such raids as Dahlgren's), and have collected in the Confederate capital an enraged and impetuous army, that would have made their way with blood and fire through every street. The extent of the peril was never popularly known in Richmond. It slept each night on the crust of a volcano. It is almost incredible now, that when Lee's army was away, the safety of Richmond should have been watched by two local battalions, and so when fifteen thousand prisoners had only between them and their liberty and revenge, a thin wall, or a few cannon planted on the boundary of their range. The true romance of the Dahlgren raid was not the night-fight on the turnpike and in the forest, but the secret story of Libby Prison; the meditation of fifteen thousand men, to make their way as furies into the streets of Richmond, and to give a whole city to fire and sword. The story was hushed up; the "gunpowder plot" that had been used to affright the conspirators, was treated only as a vague rumor in the newspapers; but it is remarkable that after this date, Mr. Davis was busy to distribute the prisoners through the South, sending them to distant places, as Salisbury and Andersonville; relieving Richmond of an incubus of terror of which it had happily been unconscious, and where only the happy ignorance of all the Confederate Government did and proposed had secured it from alarm.

CHAPTER XXII.

Brilliant Military Effects of Conscription and Impressment—The Richmond Government, the Harshest Despotism of the Age—New Hopes of the War—The South not Deficient in Resources—Pictures of Plenty—The Shadow of Jefferson Davis on the Prospect—The Renewed Confidence of the South in the War Explained—The Position of the Northern Democratic Party in 1864—A Great Advantage which the South had in the War—What a Richmond Journal Said of the Situation—Why the South Failed in the War—False Theory of Deficient Resources—Moral Desertion of the Confederate Cause—Proof of it in the Behavior of Southern Men since the War—The Southern Character Corrupted by the Misrule and Misuse of President Davis—Peculiarities of the Campaign of 1864—Its Fierce Battles—The True Situation Around Richmond—A Ten Minutes' Battle—Lee Better Situated at Richmond than in the Wilderness—A Maxim of Napoleon—No Alarm in Richmond—Manners in the Filthy and Accursed City—Mr Davis's Household—His Want of Moral Influence in Richmond—Exclamation of a Joyous Editor—The Confidence of the Country Healthier than that of the Capitol—A Southern Lady's Pictures of Country-Life—Prospect of Peace on the Horizon—A Picture of the Arena of the War.

THE measures of conscription and impressment, which completed at Richmond one of the harshest despotisms of the age, yet developed a brilliant and imposing array of Confederate force for the great campaign of 1864, which both sides had determined should be decisive of the war. All the resources of the South were carried to the front and displayed there. The war had now reached every man and every family in the Confederacy; it had extorted a tribute from every household; it had taxed every sinew of the country, which now turned upon the enemy a concentrated and formidable aspect, a strained and desperate expression that might well have made him anxious for what was plainly the last issue and the dominant campaign of the contest.

The hopes of the South flared up again at the beginning of the campaign of 1864. There was a brilliant return of confidence. The question of food had passed away with the short crops of 1863, and Mr. Davis had said, with reason:—"The facts demonstrate that, with judicious legislation, we shall be enabled to meet all the exigencies of the war from our abundant resources." Indeed, as we have elsewhere indicated, and making allowance for the partial failure of a single year's crop of grain, the resources of the South, both in men and subsistence to prosecute the war were ample; and as we may hereafter see, they were not insufficient, not exhausted, when the South chose to lay down its arms in surrender, and more than six millions of people declared themselves defeated, professing that they were so from the wear of their resources, not from any great catastrophe of their arms. The difficulty was—and had been, ever since the second year of the war—the unwillingness of the people to support the misgovernment of Mr. Davis, not their physical inability to prosecute the war, and to supply men and material for a contest, which, if prolonged, could not have been otherwise than successful.

If there be any who doubt that the difficulty of men and supplies was in the decline of the spirit of the South, and who are disposed to insist that it was in the decay of resources, we have only to ask them to estimate the real, abundant, physical power of the Confederacy in the last year of the war, the events of which we are proposing to relate. It was then accounted that the conscription would bring more than four hundred thousand men into the field. Subsistence, instead of being scarce, was superabundant, no matter how illy the government of Mr. Davis bestowed it. A writer who followed the invading armies of the North, in the campaign of 1864, thus describes some of the aspects of the route: "Wherever the Federal soldier has penetrated, he has found granaries filled with corn until they overflow; gardens in which grow all the luxuries of the season; pastures and hills not deserted by flocks and herds; yards frequented by fowls, and dove-cotes not abandoned by the innocent inmates. The cavalry horses, in the season, waded through clover knee-deep, and the growing wheat brushed their sides as they passed."

In addition to this plenty of the quick and fruitful land of the South, manufactures of necessary articles of the war had become prosperous. There was no longer any scarcity of iron, implements, and machinery. Establishments for the manufacture of cannon, small arms, powder, shot, shell, wagons, ambulances, and all the materials of war, were more than supplied the demand. The limited commerce through the blockade had, by a wise law, been made tributary to the government, and for every pound of cotton exported, the owner had to sign a bond, conditioned that at least one half the value be invested in goods and merchandise on account of the government, and brought into the Confederacy within sixty days. It was thus that the material resources of the South abounded in season for the campaign of 1864. Nothing was wanting to quicken them but confidence in the administration of Mr. Davis.

There was confidence enough in the naked prospect of the war, as stripped of the shadow which Jefferson Davis, alone, threw upon it. It was not only that accumulation of material resources we have noticed which was the ground of the renewed hope of the South as it entered on the last year of the war. There was another and greater reason for it. The North, in conducting the war, had constantly the disadvantage of a divided public sentiment; and there was a near prospect in the approaching Presidential election that this occasion of a great popular dissent might be turned to the account of the South, and increase the encouragement which it had already greatly derived from the political controversies of the enemy. In fact, it is to be admitted that the division of public opinion in the North, had already thrown a great weight on the balance of the war in favor of the South. It was an advantage of the latter that has not been justly estimated in the comparisons which Southern men have been fond to make between the resources of the contestants. It reduces them to something like equality, when we consider that the political division in the North must have detracted from its power to make war in proportion to the numbers that it carried off from the support of the government; that the comparison is to be justly made as between the resources which were *available* on each side, not those merely apparent on a statistical parallel of population and wealth, as described in the census. There were, as yet, comparatively no political parties in the South. In the North they divided it nearly by halves, and that on the immediate question of the prosecution of hostilities; and the approach of a Presidential election threatened yet further to disturb that public sentiment which was essential to carry on and sustain the war. We may safely conclude that it was at no great physical disadvantage that the South, with all her strength brought to the surface by conscription and impressment, with all her resources employed in the war, re-entered the contest in the year 1864, and commenced the campaign on the torn, yet unpenetrated, borders of Virginia and Georgia.

A Richmond journal, in January, 1864, thus described the situation:—"The South not only is not conquered; but, *if she choses*, she never can be. In a population of five millions, there is one in five capable of making resistance; capable of exerting effective effort, in some form, in opposing an aggressive power. If true to herself, the South is capable of successfully resisting a million of men. Can a people thus possessing an army of at least four hundred thousand brave men be conquered by any foreign power unless they chose to be? The North boasts twenty millions people. One in twenty of this number is more than it has yet succeeded in placing upon its muster rolls. The plain deduction from this statement of the case, is, that if the South has suffered reverses in the contest to the extent of bringing her cause into any sort of peril, it has been either from want of valor in the people, or of capacity in the government. It is for the public to determine where the blame lies; our own opinion is well-known. The whole male population, between the ages of eighteen and forty-five, with a few necessary exceptions, have been placed at the disposal of the government; and our impressment laws have exposed to it the whole available substance of the country, which they have seized with a strong and used with a lavish hand. If our cause has been brought into peril, it need not remain so for one moment, if those who are charged with responsibility but perform their duty with wisdom, with honesty, and with ability."

There has been an explanation of the South's failure in the war, very consoling to the pride of its people and much over-asserted in its newspapers:—that it was the victim of physical necessities, and that it succumbed only to these; that it lost its cause from a deficiency of men and materials. This excuse, is, of course, pleasant to the vanity of the South; it founds the tender and romantic theory of a great and spirited nation overcome by accidents, yet preserving its honor to the

23

last, and asserting a certain *eclat* in misfortune. But the theory is false, illogical and not without a mean stripe of hypocrisy in it. The eyes of the world cannot deny that since the surrender of the South there have been found population and subsistence enough in it to support a defensive war for many years—sufficient to furnish many such wars as those which Paraguay and Crete have maintained in circumstances vastly more unequal and adverse than those in which the Confederates contended for their independence. We cannot afford at the expense of history to gratify the vanity of the South, or even to console its mortification on defeat. If the plain truth is to be told, the South lost the contest, because of the moral desertion by her people of the cause they had espoused; not from their physical prostration or actual destitution of means to continue the war.

Unhappily as proofs of the moral delinquency in which the South surrendered, we have its behavior since the war. A great nation, who had lost a contest for its independence only through the accident of a power superior in material, would necessarily retain and cherish some of the resentments of the contest. But when we see almost the whole people of the South professing that they have retained absolutely nothing of the animosity of the war; when we find their newspapers actually representing as a merit that the Southern people feel precisely as *if there had been no war*, that they are ready to treat Northern men as their friends and brothers, that they have brought back their minds as blank pieces of paper to be inscribed with new lessons of love and duty to the Washington Government, we must be convinced that the South surrendered in the war as a moral delinquent, a conscious culprit, and not as a brave nation giving way to a physical power, and yet retaining its honor in history.

How are such displays of indifference in the South concerning the past war consistent with the honorable regard of its own heroes in it, or even the tender memory of its dead? But of these displays we design no remark here, except to apply them to the question whether the South surrendered from a mere physical distress, or from a moral infirmity. Where a people contending for their liberty have been overmatched by force and yet retain the spirit of their cause as a moral sentiment—which they have a right to do—they may submit and not cow, they may forgive without forgetting. The other alternative is of a people not bravely worn out in war, but surrendering from a broken spirit, a decayed courage. Their conduct following the contest easily shows in what condition they left it. How can we account but that the South surrendered from an infirm spirit rather than from physical misfortune, when we find her people now professing to wash their hands of the war, to have forgotten all its passions, to treat allusions to it with indifference, and receiving as the highest teachings of their politicians, that they should behave, speak and converse, as if no war had ever happened!

But our criticism of the causes of the surrender of the South must not outrun the course of our narrative. We have only referred to it here, and naturally, in view of the amount of physical resources it displayed at the beginning of the last campaign of the war and of the just hopes which might have been inspired by that campaign, had the South retained to its close any thing of the former animation of the war. And that it did not retain such we refer constantly and inevitably to the maladministration of Mr. Davis. Even if the South surrendered at the last in a prostrate and depraved spirit, and in view of the resources which we have enumerated as collected in the last year of the war, we do not mention it as a disgrace of her people, but rather in unwilling mournful reflection upon a government that by persistent misconduct and trifling had brought the spirit of the country to such a dishonorable pass. The best and bravest people may be demoralized by a bad government. The people of the South, whatever faults they had, were, as we have repeated in these pages, a courageous and virtuous people sustaining a noble cause; they had illustrated a martial virtue unexcelled in modern times; they had proved that the age of chivalry was not extinct; and if at the last we shall find them quitting the contest in evident disgust, and preferring the single pang of surrender to the useless and prolonged torture of the government of Jefferson Davis, it was not so much that their character had been changed by misfortune as that it had been corrupted by misrule and misuse. In all that there was of the decay of the resolution and devotion of the South, the black hand and the weak spirit of Mr. Davis are visible. Who can intelligently doubt that with a better direction and inspiration than this man afforded, that without his chilling influence and mistakes, the strength which the South developed in the campaign of 1864, would have carried it to victory through the disturbance and hesitation of the North, especially in view of the fact which we shall hereafter see, that victory, despite all of Mr. Davis's former misgovernment hung in the balance until a single supreme stroke of his folly cut the cords and cast to the ground all that the South had thrown in the last scale of the war!

There was something remarkable of the campaign of 1864 in Virginia. It was the desperate, persistent, almost breathless fury of its battles, as if both contestants were aware that they were struggling in the death-lock, and that their feet were on the brink of the fate of the war. Grant came to his work with a nerve and directness which had been found in no other Northern General. He did not tumble back, as Burnside had done from the hills of Fredericksburg, or lose his head as Hooker had done at Chancellorsville. He was evidently resolved to do more than fight one battle and then withdraw, after the fashion of former years. Now, he had the whole North at his back. He was furnished with an authority over the entire military force of his nation, never before possessed by any commander, unless that commander was an absolute sovereign in the field. On the other hand, Lee had made up his mind to fight with quick, decisive strokes, as if he knew the value of time in view of the enemy's accumulation of resources. There was none of the usual margin of strategems and delays. Neither side declined the contest until it had been fought to the doors of Richmond. When Grant, in the early days of May, first crossed the Rapidan, Lee did not hesitate a moment, but sprung upon his flank in the Wilderness with the leap of a tiger. Thence the way to Richmond was blazed by battles, and posted with monuments of carnage—a route of blood, a broad, red, macerating stripe across the wide hills where the mountains of Virginia descend to the plains.

The summer campaign ended with Grant within sight of Richmond. The true situation was, that he had reached a point, after the loss of nearly a hundred thousand lives, where, if he had moved by water, he might have arrived without the loss of a man; where, on delivering a battle for Richmond (in attempting to cross the Chickahominy), he was defeated in the space of *ten minutes* by the army he had hoped to drive into the capital; and where he sustained such a defeat as to deter him thereafter from direct attack, and to throw him back upon the resources of a slow and dastardly strategy. So far the situation was yet favorable for Richmond. A public meeting was called in New York to render the "thanks of the nation" to Grant for his victories on paper, the mere accomplishment of certain distances on the map; but the same day gold was quoted in Wall street at 285—about its maximum in the war—and the city of Richmond was quietly, without the ostentation of public assemblies, paying a hearty gratitude to Lee, for the assurance he yet gave it of safety, and was reposing on an undiminished confidence in his arms.

On a just military calculation it was plain that Lee was better situated before Richmond than in the Wilderness or at Spottsylvania Court-house. His movement towards the capital was rendered necessary by the configuration of the soil and the lines of the rivers he had to defend; the latter having their sources remote from the city, and emptying their waters in the neighboring York. He had gained manifest advantages by each change of his lines. When he was on the Rapidan his stores and reinforcements had to be brought up from Richmond; now they were nearer and more available. Grant had passed over a certain geographical space, without gaining any ground in a military sense. Had he passed down the lower Rappahannock, he might have come to the Piping Tree, within eleven miles of Richmond, without an engagement with General Lee, or he might have come up the Peninsula, perhaps to Fair Oaks, without firing a shot or losing a man. If he adopted the more circuitous course to invite battle, deliberately counting on "depletion," he could scarcely have calculated that even with his army of one hundred and fifty thousand men, the odds would have been overwhelming, when the issue came to be that of an open field against a fortified place. Napoleon declared as an axiom of war, that "fifty thousand National Guards, with three thousand gunners, will defend a fortified capital against an army of three hundred thousand men." Almost to the last days of the Confederacy, the army of Lee was nearly equal in numbers to, and greater in actual efficiency than those whom Napoleon assumed could hold their position against twice the force which at any time assailed Richmond. There was no good reason, except that fatal one, sufficient to explain every catastrophe—demoralization—why General Lee should not have held Richmond and Petersburg against any number which the enemy, within the limits of his physical resources, could bring against them.

The government of Mr. Davis was not yet alarmed. It had no reason to be alarmed except for the chances of its own mistakes. Nobody in Richmond was alarmed—not even so much as when McClellan, in 1862, had displayed his standards on the banks of the Chickahominy. There was the same recklessness of vice in this city that it had displayed so early in the war, and that had pointed it out as the centre of all the crime and iniquity in the South. There were the same "faro banks," on Main and other streets, with numbers painted in large gilt figures over the door, and illuminated at night; the same flashily dressed young men with villainous faces, who hung about the street corners during the day, and were gamblers, garroters and plugs at night; the same able-bodied, red-faced and brawny individuals who mixed bad liquors in the bar-rooms, and who held exemptions from military duty as consumptive invalids, or for some reason had been recommended by the Surgeon-General to keep in cheerful company and take gentle exercise; the same men who frequented the innumerable bar-rooms, paying five dollars for a drink of the bad liquors, and who, mistaken for men of fortune, happened to be out-door patients of hospitals, with a daily allowance for stimulants, or government clerks on salaries, the monthly amounts of which, would not pay for a single night's carousal. The society of Richmond was given over to unabashed vice and revelry, to continue thus until the partial doom of Sodom should overtake it. The filthy and accursed city was indeed a commentary on the administration of Mr. Davis; for that he should have made of his capital such a place indicates his own unworthiness, and, no matter what local or particular excuses are made, men will think how weak and bad must have been the government, immediately around which the moral atmosphere was so impure. It has often been boasted of Richmond, that it never lost its confidence during the war; but we must confess that much of this confidence was a vile recklessness that lived in the twenty-four hours, not all the serious and manly faith which calculates the morrow, and reposes on its superiority to fortune. To the last vice kept open doors in Richmond. For the present it had taken out a new lease of its abodes, as it supposed itself secured by the immediate presence of Lee's army, and confidently expected for Grant, the sequel of McClellan.

Mr. Davis, himself, was not an immoral man. However, in midsummer of 1864, there were curious stories about the President's household, and the money that was squandered by the luxurious tastes of his wife, and her excessive love of display. In secret session of Congress, there were complaints that the President did not live as democratically as he might, or should; and one member was bold enough to mention the incident that a large sum had been diverted from the Treasury to cover the expense of transporting, in box cars, all the way from Mississippi, the splendid horses which Mrs. Davis displayed on Main street, while the whole

South was groaning in poverty. A joint resolution was whirled through Congress with extraordinary alacrity, giving additional compensation and emolument to Mr. Davis, under the name of "lights and fuel for the Presidential mansion," and forage in the Presidential stables for four horses during the war. But notwithstanding the supplies of money, of which his wife gave evidence in various ostentation, there was but little social bounty in the President's household. He gave but few entertainments, and even his occasional "receptions" were neglected by the best people in Richmond. There were no instances of elegant hospitality, no examples of those refinements which a President is supposed to give to the manners and society of his capital. Thus, although Mr. Davis was much above most of the vices in Richmond, it is yet remarkable what little correction he administered to them, and what a listless observer he was of the social corruption that besieged the very doors of his mansion. The worst that can be said of him in this connection is, that he gave none of those examples of decorous social life which the President of a republic is supposed to impart, at least, within the limits of his capital, where he is as much the censor of manners as he is the ruler of public affairs.

When Grant's army approached Richmond, Mr. Davis was in better health and in better spirits than he had yet been during the war. He had recovered from his neuralgia; he was healthy and frivolous. We have described the inner life of Richmond about this time as indicative of the little impression Grant's approach made upon it—although, as we have slightly and incidentally seen, it is interesting in other respects. The sounds of hostile cannon fell unheeded on the ears of revellers. Not for a day did Mr. Davis change the unpopular routine of his household, abate the luxury of his table, or his allowance of Havana cigars, or neglect, weather permitting, his easy evening ride on his shabby grey horse, while his more pretentious wife gathered on the wheels of her equipage the dust through which Lee's barefoot soldiers might have trudged an hour before. In this indifference in Richmond, there is much that is unpleasant, much that is the subject of detraction; but we have exhibited it in its most excessive phases to show how little affected Mr. Davis and the population around him were by Grant's array in front of them, and to suggest that while part of this indifference was only bad and reckless, yet another part must have proceeded from a common popular confidence in the war, when a whole community is found involved in so great a neglect of danger.

"If," exclaimed a joyous Richmond editor, "those highly excited official circles of Washington, and delighted newspaper readers of New York and Boston, could but see the tranquil serenity of these embowered streets at this day; how peacefully our people go about their daily business; how quietly they buy and sell, or even marry and are given in marriage;" but the same writer fatally added, finishing his period of exclamation, unconscious of the significance: "*as in the day when Noah entered the ark!*"

Among the people of the country as compared with those in the capital the confidence in the war was much healthier. Through the South, beyond Richmond, the dirty patch of the Confederacy, there was an increased alacrity to contribute to the war, more willingness to bear its burdens in the prospect of a speedy peace, and some hope of improvement in the administration of Mr. Davis. The people had recovered much of their former animation; they again showed examples of readiness, of fortitude, and of noble sacrifices; it appeared that they had taken new resolution, and had determined to strain every nerve in what they supposed to be the last stadium of the war. In every period of the contest there was a remarkable contrast between the licentiousness of the capital of the Confederacy and the hardy and virtuous simplicy of the country people. It was never illustrated more strongly than in the times of which we write. The South generally was aroused to a new and sustained effort for independence, and the evidences of this resolution were to be found in the simplicity and industry of almost every household at a distance from Richmond.

A Southern lady has thus graphically described the interior of these rustic and virtuous homes:—"We were carried back to the times of our grandmothers. Our women were actively interested in discovering the coloring properties of roots, barks, and berries, and experimenting with alum, copperas, soda, and other alkalies and mineral mordants in dyeing cotton and wool for domestic manufacture. On approaching a country house rather late, the ear would be greeted, not with the sound of the piano or the Spanish guitar, but with the hum of the spinning-wheel brought out from the hiding-place to which it had been driven before the triumph of mechanical skill, and the "bang-bang" of the old-fashioned and long-disused loom. The whereabouts of the mistress of the mansion might be inferred from the place whence the sound proceeded; for she was probably herself engaged in, or superintending the work of a servant in the weaving or spinning-room. It was beautiful to watch the snowy cotton and wool drawn out from the fleecy roll into long threads, and wound up so dexterously on the spindle. It was delightful to watch the magic shuttle shoot to and fro under the threads of the warp, and to hear the strange music of the almost obsolete loom, and to see the stout fabric grow under ingenious hands. With commendable pride we beheld the Southern gentleman clad in the comfortable homespun suit, and our ladies wearing domestic dresses that challenged comparison with the plaids and merinos of commercial manufacture."

From the pictures we have given of the South, both of its capital and country in the summer months of 1864, the reader will conclude how much more cheerful and assured had become the prospect of the war, and how improved was the spirit of the Confederacy in view of it. In every direction the armies of the North had been brought to a dead halt; hope had sprung again in the heart of the Confederacy; the sources of political weakness in the North were being multiplied; a prospect of peace was on the horizon, its rumors in the air. The strained nerve of the South, its beating heart, its sinews thrown to the surface, told of the last lock of the contest, that final match of strength and courage in which it already held the adversary in its arms and appeared about to trip his uncertain foothold.

CHAPTER XXIII.

The Situation at Atlanta, Georgia, more Favorable than that at Richmond—Johnston's Retreat, the Masterpiece of His Military Life—Its Incidents, and its Triumph over Sherman—The Military Condition of the South one of Brilliant Promise—The Confederacy had now to Accomplish only "Negative" Results—Mr. Davis's Private Correspondents in the Chicago Convention—Secrets of "the Presidential Bureau of Correspondence"—A Remarkable Article in the New York *Tribune*—Compositions and Designs of the Peace Party in the North—Bold Declaration of the New York *World*—The Northern Democratic Party Looking to Richmond rather than to Washington—How Much Depended on the Prudence of Mr. Davis—How His Course should have been Shaped in such a Crisis—General Johnston Busy at Atlanta—An Opportunity to Operate in Sherman's Rear—A Conversation of General Johnston and Senator Wigfall—An Urgent Application to President Davis, to Transfer Forrest's Cavalry to Sherman's Rear—Important and Critical Nature of this Enterprise—Senator Hill Undertakes a Mission to the President—He "Goes Back" upon Johnston—A Special Messenger Sent to Richmond—Anecdote of Mrs. Davis and a Washerwoman—Order Removing Johnston from Command, the Death-Warrant of the Confederacy—Secret History of this Order—The Fruit of an Intrigue in Richmond—The Part Played by General Bragg—Underhanded Correspondence of Mr. Davis with General Hood—The Latter Described by General Sherman and a Richmond Wit—Demoralizing and Terrible Consequences of the Removal of Johnston—"The Beginning of the End"—Reflection on the Narrow Chances which make History—Bitter Remarks of a Richmond Journalist.

We have described the situation at Richmond. Its correspondent on the other side of the Alleghanies—the situation at Atlanta, Georgia—was even more favorable. General Johnston held Atlanta more securely than Lee did Richmond. We have already said something of the military character of the former. His opportunities of distinguishing himself had not been so great and prolonged as those of Lee; but, however various might be the popular criticism of him, or however cold and envious might be the regards of Mr. Davis, it could not be said of him that he ever lost an army, or any considerable body of troops, or incurred any disaster, or even disadvantage that obscured the prospects of the Confederacy for a moment.

General Johnston was now executing the masterpiece of his military life. He had fought down to Atlanta with far more success and brilliancy than Lee had fought down to Richmond, with more incidents of advantage, and to greatly better effect. His retrograde from Dalton to Atlanta has been described as a future study in military schools, and as exact as a figure in geometry—his plan of campaign being the avoidance of pitched battles and the substitution of flank movements, interspersed with actions between detachments and sometimes rising to a general engagement. He had performed the wonder of conducting an army in retreat through nearly one hundred and fifty miles of intricate country, absolutely without any loss in material or prisoners; he had brought along every thing, every gun, every wagon, every camp-kettle; he had inflicted a loss upon the enemy of forty-five thousand men, more than four times his own; and in pursuance of his plan of reducing the numerical superiority of Sherman's army so as "to cope with it on equal ground by the time the Chattahoochee was passed," he had now that army south of the stream where its defeat would be inevitably its destruction, and where, on the other hand, the Confederates would have a place of refuge in Atlanta which their commander, writing officially to Richmond had described as "too strong to be assaulted and too extensive to be invested." Never was any situation of the war so advantageous for the Confederates, and so critical and tremulous for the enemy, unable, as he was, to go further, brought to a place which he dared not to assault, and which he was unable to invest and suspended one hundred and forty miles in a hostile country by a single line of communication. The fears of the giddy enemy were excessive, almost to demoralization; the assurances of Johnston were as perfect as human foresight could make them. We repeat that his position in Atlanta was more secure than that of Lee in Richmond. Judging prospective by past events, it was impossible to doubt that he would have held Sherman as well as Lee held Grant. He could at least have done this; and it was probable he would have done more, for if he had succeeded in destroying Sherman's line of land communication, which was obviously easier to reach than that of Grant over water, he might have forced his enemy to a retreat, in which surrender or annihilation would be the choice.

No wonder that the heart of the Confederacy was elated, and that the tiptoe of expectation was the attitude of the most intelligent. The campaign of 1864 found the two best men in real command and in the two principal positions—Lee in Virginia, Johnston in Georgia. The military condition of the country was, as we have seen, in various respects never so prosperous as it was at midsummer; for these two great commanders had so done their work that it was then morally certain that the last supreme effort of the enemy was going to fail; and failing it was impossible to doubt that the year would be the last of the war, and would terminate in the proclaimed independence of the Confederacy.

The question of peace already trembled on the balance in the North, and the number of rumors concerning it show how busily employed was the public mind with the prospect of an early termination of the war, and how eager it was to anticipate it. So equally had parties come to be divided in the North, when the Chicago Convention nominated McClellan for President, that the entire Democratic party was bold enough to declare, in the most deliberate manner, that the war was a "failure." Scarcely any Northern man of any political persuasion, outside of fanaticism, doubted that if Johnston defeated Sherman, or that if he even held his own—in short, that if the South accomplished mere *negative* results, in holding Richmond and Atlanta—the peace party which was at this time the whole Democratic party, would come into power, turn the war into a Convention of States, and decide there the claims of the South, which, it was a foregone conclusion, and a logical necessity, could not be less than independence. Mr. Davis could not fail to perceive the significance of the Chicago Convention, and was certainly intelligent enough to understand the condition of parties in the North. He had private correspondents in that Convention. Indeed it is well known that during the entire war, Mr. Davis maintained secret communications with many distinguished Northern politicians, generally those of the Democratic party. The letters and documents he received from them were so numerous that they were kept in a special, private archive, entitled the Presidential Bureau of Correspondence. These confidences were kept from Congress, and even from his Cabinet; few persons in Richmond ever knew of the existence of such a bureau; no curiosity was ever admitted to its papers; and so anxious was Mr. Davis to conceal them that it is a curious fact that, some days before the surrender of Richmond, he had them conveyed to a secret place, where they are yet supposed to be safely deposited. In this "underground" correspondence Mr. Davis had been well informed of the Chicago Convention; that "it meant peace for the North and independence for the South," as a distinguished gentleman of New England wrote him, and that all there was of doubt of the success of the Chicago nominees depended on the success of his own administration at Richmond, and that the Democratic party of the North was held in the hollow of his hand.

But as to the real desire for peace in the North, which had now divided it nearly by halves, Mr. Davis did not need to look to evidences in his Presidential Bureau; he might have learned it in the newspapers and common publications of the day. It was deeply significant that the question of peace was no longer discussed in the North in wary whispers, and under the shadow of the danger of an accusation; it was no longer the discovery of eavesdroppers and the pursuit of spies—not even the subject of a clamor for "disloyalty." It had become a topic of bold, open argument; it was on the unfaltering and multiplied tongues of the press; it was spoken of without disguise, and without abatement. Nor was it any longer the stinted thought of any particular political party. Some of the best men of the Republican party raised their voices for peace; they joined the Democrats, as if in a sentiment of a general nature, but where they must have known, as well as they, the logical consequence of this sentiment in the independence of the South, as the one condition of peace, and where to fall back from such conclusion, or to attempt to flank it by circumlocution, could only have been an affectation to cheat the public, or to console their own consciences. It was not without some surprise that the people of the South read in such a paper as the New York *Tribune*:—"We feel certain that two-thirds of the American people on either side of the dividing line anxiously, absorbingly, desire peace; and are ready to make all needful sacrifices to secure it. Then why shall it be long withheld. Let us know, as soon as may be, the most that the rebel chiefs will do to secure peace; let us know what is the 'ultimatum' on our side." Almost in the same breath of the New York Press, the *World* gave a practical expression to a purpose which Mr. Greeley had been content to leave in the vagueness of a sentimental appeal. It furnished the true exposition of the Chicago Convention. It said: "The new President, to be nominated at Chicago, and elected in November, must be a man ready and willing to meet any and every overture for peace, a man who shall represent truly the dignity and power of the nation, and who will not be unwilling even to tender an armistice, and suggest a National Convention of all the States."

Such signs of public sentiment in the North could not have been lost on Mr. Davis. He must have known how near the Confederacy was to peace and independence, the consummation of its hopes. He must have understood what his New England correspondent advised: that the Democratic party of the North had for the time turned its attention from what was taking place at Washington, to fix it upon the administration at Richmond, and that upon its wisdom now singly depended the condition of parties in the North, and the ultimate question of peace. The Democratic party asked Jefferson Davis rather than its own leaders to sustain it. Richmond and Atlanta were its arguments, and it looked to Mr. Davis to preserve their force. It only asked that the Confederacy should for a few months hold its own, and that Mr. Davis should not interrupt or imperil the existing state of affairs by any act of imprudence. Scarcely ever did a single man control issues so vast and critical. It was a condition which required the utmost delicacy, the utmost prudence; a condition in which rather the *status quo* was to be maintained than new experiments to be hazarded—much less changes to be made originating in caprice. Mr. Davis stood near the boundary of peace; he had only to fold his arms, only to wait on Lee and Johnston. But unhappily he was one of those men whom the consciousness of power makes pragmatical, who are never satisfied to accept events without the appearance of controlling them, and who, from vanity rather than impatience, had much rather risk taking fortune by assault, than to wait for it in unconspicuous circumstances, and in wise obscurity.

Meanwhile, General Johnston, never looking aside to any political complications in the war, was giving a characteristically single and severe attention to his purely military work. He was steadily devoting himself to the defences of Atlanta; heavy rifled cannon were brought up from Mobile and planted on its ramparts; a large number of negroes were employed on its earthworks; and the militia of Georgia were being assembled to garrison Atlanta, which Sherman now dared not to approach, and could not approach, without risking an attack of Johnston's whole army on his most exposed flank.

One other movement now only remained to complete the discomfiture of the enemy. It was plain and inviting; and it seemed indeed as if all events had been marshalled in favor of Johnston. The defeat by Forrest's cavalry in northern Mississippi of an expedition of the enemy under Sturgis designed to protect and operate in Sherman's rear, left that rear uncovered, and presented the spectacle of an enemy a hundred and forty miles in the interior of Georgia, holding a single line of communication which might be easily destroyed by cavalry. General Johnston at once dispatched to Richmond a request that Forrest's cavalry might be transferred from Mississippi, where it was then roving as an independent command, representing that if it got on Sherman's line, it could destroy it beyond the possibility of further use. He did not doubt that the government would at once see an opportunity so plain and splendid; he was in the highest spirits from all his prospects of advantage in the campaign; he supposed that what he had done was appreciated at Richmond, and that what he proposed would now be ordered with alacrity. To his infinite surprise and alarm, he received an order from Richmond denying his request and prohibiting him from any command of Forrest's cavalry to move it to the rear of Sherman.

At this time Senator Wigfall happened to be in Georgia. General Johnston, surprised at the singular treatment he had received from President Davis, knowing nothing of what was taking place in Richmond to discredit him, invited Mr. Wigfall to visit his camp, and in an earnest conversation entreated that Senator to hasten back to the capital, and to use all possible influence to prevail upon Mr. Davis to transfer Forrest to Georgia. He explained the great importance of such a movement. He disclaimed any desire to repair Mr. Davis's confidence in himself or to conciliate him personally; he was careless of injustice to himself; he was only deeply hurt that any opportunity for the good of the country should be neglected through a personal dislike of him by the President, a dislike which he considered himself unfortunate to have incurred, and to which he would not be made a party in any recrimination or protest further than the interests of the public service to which he was attached demanded. He spoke with his usual magnanimity, and in noble and touching terms. Mr. Wigfall grimly replied that the President had as little love for himself as for Johnston. He explained that his intermediation would only injure the cause for which he was invoked to act, and he therefore declined the mission.

Mr. Wigfall was on bad terms with B. H. Hill, Senator

from Georgia; but he knew him to be an obsequious politician and, to some extent, a favorite of Mr. Davis, well-qualified to influence the President by his adroit servility, and to exercise an influence over him denied to wiser and purer counsellors. In the inspiration of his conversation with Johnston, the Senator from Texas was willing to lay aside his private feelings, and to use a medium to which he was personally averse to accomplish a public benefit. He suggested B. H. Hill for the mission to Richmond. The suggestion was adopted; Mr. Hill was called into council with Johnston and some of his corps commanders; the clear-headed General submitted to him all his plans, assured him of the safety of Atlanta, pointed out the opportunity of operating on Sherman's rear; and at the close of the conference. the Senator expressed himself as fully satisfied with all that Johnston proposed and requested. He left with the promise warmly expressed that he would go at once to Richmond and use all the influence he had or could assemble to persuade the President to sustain General Johnston, and especially to give him command of Forrest's cavalry for the critical operation he designed.

The promise was never kept. The confidence with General Johnston was not only violated but betrayed. Senator Hill went to Richmond; but the gossip was that he "went back" upon Johnston, and joined his enemies and detractors who he found had secured the ear of Mr. Davis. The fact may be that Senator Hill was at first sincere in what he had undertaken in behalf of an injured General, but that coming to Richmond, he found the President so impatient of any thing said in favor of Johnston, and so well-disposed towards those who brought him any tale to the discredit of this commander, that, weak and servile as he was, a man always more anxious to court favor for himself than for others, he was easily led away from his first intentions and by another step of descent in sincerity was involved in the intrigue which he found busy in Richmond to depose Johnston, and to make a pretext on which Mr. Davis might gratify the malice he had nursed against this great and good commander. Whatever the explanation, it is certain that Senator Hill, a short time after reaching Richmond, was active in the intrigue referred to; that he circulated stories to alarm the more foolish of the public for the safety of Atlanta; that he was in frequent conversation with General Bragg, whom the President had, previous to this occasion, sent as a well-disguised spy into Johnston's camp; and that he was in correspondence with one of the corps commanders of the Army of Tennessee whom Mr. Davis had already designated as one of his favorites.

General Johnston was ignorant of this intrigue. He anxiously awaited at Atlanta, the result of Hill's mission, the signal for action; and while day after day he suffered disappointment, he yet busied himself adding to the defences of Atlanta, assured that even at the worst he might expect from Mr. Davis's temper, he could yet defy and wear out the enemy, although enviously denied and robbed of the opportunity of finishing his work with a conspicuous victory. Hearing nothing from Hill, he was yet resolved to leave no means unemployed to operate on the mind of the President. He sent a special messenger to Richmond, furnished with full and detailed dispatches, which were to be submitted to the President at the earliest possible moment. For two weeks this messenger unsuccessfully sought an audience of Mr. Davis. Trifles, especially in weak governments, sometimes govern great events. An anecdote obtained circulation in

Richmond that the President could not see Johnston's messenger, because he was over-busy with an affair of Mrs. Davis, she having quarelled with a laundress in one of the hospitals who had formerly been discharged from her service as a waiting-woman; that there was a deficiency of *eleven dollars* in the monthly hospital account of the laundress, and that Mrs. Davis was moving President, Cabinet, and all sources of authority to have the woman punished, giving the first but little time to attend to the cares of State, until he had appeased the clamor in his household. It was a story, perhaps, told for amusement, and designed as a caricature of those anecdotes which serve as popular illustrations of famous persons, which would be excessively absurd if they were not obviously characteristic, and which, if not true, yet deserve in a measure to be true.

On the 17th day of July, General Johnston was standing on the fortification of Atlanta, conversing with his chief engineer. A dispatch was handed to him; there were no marks of importance upon it; he read it without a change of countenance. *It was an order removing him from the command of the army;* brief, decisive; he should "immediately turn over the command of the army and department of Tennessee to General Hood."

It was a day never to be forgotten, for it contained the doom of the South. On the slight piece of paper that Johnston read silently, looking over the great army that he had hoped to lead to victory, that had been his pride, and joy, glory, and that, standing upon the ramparts, he now saw, for the last time, stretched before him, there was written not only his removal, not only this of cruel and sneering brevity to himself, but the sentence that murdered tens of thousands of brave soldiers, the message of greatest joy and encouragement to the enemy, the death-warrant of the Southern Confederacy.

Why did Mr. Davis remove General Johnston? The pretence put before the public was, that this commander had not expressed sufficient confidence of his ability to hold Atlanta; while the fact was that Johnston, properly resenting the pragmatism of the President, and annoyed by the fire of cross questions from the War Department, at Richmond, had simply been cold and reluctant in his replies, instead of being fulsome, as a weak General might have been, in such circumstances; and when at last removed, he made the neat and cutting reply to the Secretary of War:—"Confident language by a military commander is not usually regarded as evidence of incompetency." He did right not to commit himself to an inquisition by which there is reason to believe Mr. Davis designed to entrap him. The latter could have really had no doubt as to Johnston's determination and spirit to hold Atlanta, for the evidence of these was his daily employment in strengthening its defences; and the fact was that his family was remaining in the town at the time he was removed. Not a single charge of disaster incurred, or opportunity omitted, could be brought against this wise and ready commander. It is especially remarkable that while the retrograde of Lee from the Rapidan to Richmond had had the effect of adding to his reputation, and had been adorned with the thanks of Mr. Davis and his Congress, the correspondent movement of Johnston, in Georgia, attended, as we have seen, with more success, and ending in better advantages, should have excited the ire of the President, and should have been used to raise a clamor as against a shameful and disastrous defeat.*

---

* The following is from a private letter of General Johnston, not intended for publication, but due to history :—"After his experience in the Wilderness, General Lee adopted as thorough a defensive as mine, and added by it to his great fame. The only other difference

The true history of Johnston's removal is yet to be written. It is already discovered, as far as evidence can make it plain, that an intrigue to remove him was commenced in Richmond, at the time he first moved from Dalton, at the very commencement of the campaign, and that Mr. Davis only awaited a convenient opportunity and an available pretext to put his sinister design in execution. The fact was that the appointment of Johnston to the Army of Tennessee had been wrung from Mr. Davis by a public sentiment which had compelled him to make a show of obedience to it; and he was resolved to find the earliest pretence to get rid of an appointment which he had made so unwillingly, which had offended his vanity, and which, as the triumph of a rival in the affections of the people—one innocently so—rankled in his heart. He had been compelled to remove his favorite General Bragg—the commander who had, on the 1st of January, 1863, dispatched from the field of Murfreesboro, "God has given us a happy New Year," and who, at the close of this year, had been driven through the length of Tennessee, had been forced from the mountain-barrier of Georgia, and yet clung to the command of an army which not only distrusted, but despised him. Bragg was displaced for Johnston. But the former was consoled by the sinecure but sonorous appointment of "military adviser," at Richmond, a sort of ornamental generalissimo which made the *Examiner* exclaim:—"We are driving the red battle car and not a gilded coach, with room enough

---

between our operations, was due to General Grant's bull-headedness and Sherman's extreme caution, which carried the armies in Virginia to Petersburg in less than half the time in which Sherman reached Atlanta. From our relative losses, I might have expected to be very soon stronger than Sherman. His army beaten on the east of the Chattahoochee, might have been destroyed."

on the foot-board for uniformed *chasseurs* with marshals' batons. Cut behind. We are driving artillery into the fight."

But Bragg was used not altogether for ornament. He was a great and useful part of the intrigue against Johnston. He was employed by the President to visit Johnston in the lines around Atlanta; he was cordially received by this commander; and he gave no intimation that his visit was of an official nature. He observed that some of the public workshops had been removed, and that there were no large supplies deposited in the town—circumstances no more significant than sending the wagons of an army to the rear on a day of battle; and he hurried back to Mr. Davis to furnish him a pretence on which he might act as he desired, in the report that Atlanta was about to be evacuated! Another party to the intrigue, and who was in communication with Bragg and the President, was General Hood himself, who, there is reason to believe, had been designated as the successor of Johnston while his army was yet in motion from Dalton. We have heretofore referred to a bad practice of Mr. Davis in holding underhanded secret correspondence with subordinate commanders in the field, so as to diminish the authority of the General in command, and to hold the latter under a disreputable surveillance. He had done so with Pemberton. And we must suppose that he had done so with Hood. For how else is it possible to explain the evidence that the latter had written a private letter, since divulged in some circles, while on the retreat from Dalton, that he expected soon to be raised to the chief command of the army; that he, generally so ready for a fight, had so stoutly resisted General Johnston's first proposition to give battle on the Etowah river, and was apparently so well pleased with the continuation of his retreat to Atlanta; and that when at last the removal of Johnston and his own appointment reached there, and when the whole army was struck with wonder or convulsed with indignation, he alone, of fifty thousand men, received it without surprise; and that in his readiness to take command, he neglected even the compliments, if we may not say civilities, which custom required to the retiring General.

The news of General Johnston's removal fell upon the ears of his army like a clap of thunder from clear skies. When Sherman heard of it, he was radiant and jocose; and one of his staff-officers tells of his making a motion with the thumb of one hand around the forefinger of the other, as if already wrapping around it the weak and maimed commander who had displaced his old and tried antagonist. The man whom the folly of Mr. Davis had raised to the command of a great army, not less numerous than that with which General Lee had fought the campaign of the Rapidan, was described by one of the wits of Richmond as having "a lion's heart and a wooden head." Courage was cheap in the army of Tennessee; and in the constitution and temper of Confederate troops, the wise General was much to be preferred to the pugnacious one. General Johnston had obtained the admiration and affection of his troops; but what is more, as the foundation of all discipline and efficiency in armies, their steady confidence. His removal chilled and blasted the spirit of the army, which for months he had cultivated and trained; it sowed in a single day the South broadcast with the seeds of distrust; it produced fruits such as inconsequence, folly, and subserviency, never produced before. If Mr. Davis could have heard the rumors which filled the camps of the Army of Tennessee when it was known that their trusted and beloved commander was to be taken from them; if he could have been sensible of the expressions of anger and discontent which traversed the country as fast as the telegraph carried the news of this last ill-tempered and ill-timed freak of the Executive; if he could have observed the rejoicings in Washington, and the dismay of every Northern friend of the Confederacy, at this unexpected and inconsequent folly, he might possibly have realized the terrible extent of the disaster he had done by a single stroke of his pen. In one day, in one capricious moment, he had struck down the prospect which, in the midsummer of 1864, had held the South in expectation of an early peace. He had signed an order, unconsciously we may believe, but recklessly we must declare, for the general and final ruin of his country. It was "the beginning of the end," the first of the train of events that led distinctly to the final catastrophe, the explosion of the Confederacy.

In history we are often grieved and tantalized at the narrow chances on which are determined the most important events. We say to ourselves, if such and such things had not been so, if there had been another adjustment of mere circumstances, a great disaster might have been averted, or a good cause might have been saved. It is a common emotion in those who study the order of events. But, in the case referred to, of the one act of Mr. Davis that visibly and immediately turned the balance ot the war, there is added to such displeasure of the reader as comes from an unexpected alteration of history, a feeling of irritation; since such alteration was not the effect of an accident, but of a voluntary, deliberate act, which should have foreseen its consequences, and which, too, originated in the worst motives of the human heart, conceived in malice, matured by fraud, and executed by stealth.

"We must," said a Richmond journalist, "think of these things, for these are the causes which produce the effects. It is manifestly absurd to put up and pull down a commander in the field according to the crude views or peevish fancies of a functionary in Richmond. Such conduct of a government would paralyze the greatest military genius, ruin the oldest army, and render success in war absolutely impossible. Now is it not hard, is it not cruelly hard, that the struggle of eight millions, who sacrifice their lives, sacrifice their money, who groan in the excess of exertion, who wrench every muscle till the blood starts with the sweat—should come to naught—should end in the ruin of us all—in order that the predilections and antipathies, the pitiful personal feelings of a single man may be indulged?"

CHAPTER XXIV.

Mr. Davis's Idea of a "Fighting General"—Hood's Battles and Mistakes—Fall of Atlanta—A Powerful Appeal to Mr. Davis to Restore Johnston to Command—Anecdote of Mr. Davis and His Physician—Demoralization of all the Confederate Armies—One Hundred Thousand Deserters—Effect of the Disasters on Mr. Davis—He Attempts to Re-animate the People by Braggart Speeches—A Remarkable Speech at Augusta—The Error and Weakness of the Policy of Inflation of Public Confidence—The Temper of the South Misunderstood by Mr. Davis—Partial Sincerity of his Expressions of Confidence in the War—His Over-Sanguine Temperament—Some Instances of It—Mr. Davis Constantly Blind to the True Condition of Affairs—Extraordinary Self-Delusion—Extravagance of Hope, as an Infirmity of Character—A Shrewd Suspicion of one Motive the President had to Remove Johnston—His Weak Ambition to Conduct a Military Campaign—How his Vanity Betrayed him at Macon—His Visits to the Armies Ominous—The Country Surprised by Hood's Eccentric Movement towards Tennessee—Mr. Davis's Prophecy of Sherman's Retreat—Fatal Error of the Davis-Hood Campaign—It is Arranged at one End, without ever Looking to the other End—General Johnston Foresees Sherman's March to the Sea—Interesting Extract from a Private Letter of the Former—A Baptist Clergyman's Evangely in Richmond—Mr. Davis on "Vital Points" of the Confederacy—An Error in his Calculation—Decline of the War Spirit in the South—General Hardee at Savannah—His Grim Telegram to Bragg—Fall of Savannah—March of Sherman towards Richmond—Apparition of the Army of Tennessee in the Pine Woods of North Carolina.

General Hood had been appointed by President Davis as a "fighting General," and he at once proceeded to make good the recommendation. In one week he fought three vain, ineffectual battles, attempting to break the enemy's lines. They were the most brilliant, reckless, massive and headlong charges of the war. It appeared as if he emulated Grant in reducing the art of war to competitive slaughter, although it should have been plain to him that the resources of the South afforded no margin for fanciful battles. It was a fatal imitation. General Johnston had left the Army of Tennessee with a heavy heart for his country, for he knew what was expected of his successor, and he knew that the expectation involved destruction, both to that army and to the Confederacy.

Hood retired his reduced army into Atlanta, only to make another mistake. General Johnston had earnestly sought the transfer of Forrest's cavalry to operate in Sherman's rear, knowing how necessary it was to keep the little cavalry that properly belonged to his army, to watch the movements of the enemy and to entangle his flanks. Hood sent off his entire cavalry towards Chattanooga; Sherman, with his flanks now easily protected, moved to the South, repulsed an attempt to dislodge him, broke the Macon road, severed Atlanta entirely from its supplies—and "the Gate City" fell, Hood retreating from it under the cover of an ill-starred night.

It was a disaster of fearful import to the South, but only such as had been expected by intelligent persons who foresaw the consequences of Johnston's removal. It was the occasion however of a new appeal to Mr. Davis; and for some time a brave endeavor was made to repair as far as possible the disaster, and to avert the demoralization which was now swiftly pervading the Confederacy. All in Georgia was not yet lost; there yet remained between Atlanta and Macon the army of Hood which had secured its retreat, shattered and demoralized it is true, but which might yet respond to the inspiration of the return of its old commander, and thus be enabled to check the further advance of the flushed and insolent enemy. It was not too late to restore Johnston to command; it was the natural and obvious remedy; and it was supposed that, after a lesson so plain and severe as Mr. Davis had derived from his removal, he would be more accessible to the popular appeal and argument, and might relent in his personal enmity toward the unjustly treated commander. He had removed Johnston for the ostensible reason that he had not been perfectly confident of holding Atlanta. Why should he not remove Hood for the solid and greater reason that he had lost it?

An urgent and imposing appeal for the restoration of Johnston was prepared. Nearly all the newspapers joined in it. Members of Congress visited the President as petitioners; every influence around him was, as far as possible, employed to change his purposes concerning Johnston, and to shake his obstinacy; and even the intercessions of many of those who were recognized favorites of Mr. Davis were secured to reinforce the appeal. He was inexorable. On one occasion his family physician ventured to tell him that the public expectation was that he would relent, and that Johnston would be restored to command. "Doctor," replied Mr. Davis, "do you believe in homœopathy—*similia similibus curantur*—like cures like? Anyhow, I am not disposed to practise it in my government. I will not attempt to cure disasters of the country by imposing upon it the very man in whom these disasters originated, and whom I hold to be the author of the greatest misfortunes of the Confederacy. The people may be sure that I shall not give them another dose of Johnston."

Nothing being done by any change in the administration at Richmond, or any new disposition of the commander in the field to break the fall of Atlanta, the worst consequences of this event were rapidly realized. The most deplorable effect was the demoralization, which was not confined to the army yet commanded by Hood, but which quickly spread through all the camps of the Confederacy, and involved the whole people. Two or three months after the great disaster, it was estimated that the desertions from the Confederate armies for the yet unfinished year had reached one hundred thousand men! The narrowed limits of the war, the threatened loss of the vast agricultural interest in Georgia, the depletion of the armies, were subjects of painful contemplation, where but a short time before had reigned the prospect of an early peace. The discouragement of the people was expressed in sneers, lamentations, and misgivings of the future.

Mr. Davis was not moved by the popular discontent and alarm to give up any of his personal prejudices. But he could not be wholly insensible to these appeals; he saw that he had committed a great mistake and produced a great disaster, and he proposed in his characteristic way to cover up the latter by boastful speeches and messages—by putting a fine complexion on the affairs of the country, when they were verging to the worst. He had tried this weak remedy more than once in the history of the war, experimenting upon the popular sentiment by braggadocio. He now proposed to visit the camps of Hood, in Georgia, to harangue the people by the way, and to try what his ingenuity of words might accomplish to cure the popular despondency. Some of these speeches are curiosities in the way of swollen and braggart rhetoric.

At Augusta, Georgia, he said: "Those who see no hope "now, who have lost confidence, are to me like those of "whose distorted vision it is said, they behold spots upon the "sun. Such are the croakers who seem to forget the "battles that have been won, and the men who have fought; "who forget that in the magnitude of those battles and the "heroism of those men, this struggle exceeds all that his-"tory records. We commenced the fight without an army, "without a navy, without arsenals, without mechanics, with-"out money, and without credit. Four years we have "stemmed the tide of invasion, and *to-day are stronger than* "*when the war began;* better able now than ever to repulse "the Vandal who is seeking our overthrow. Once we im- "ported the commonest articles of daily use, and brought in "from beyond our borders even bread and meat. Now the "State of Georgia alone produces food enough not only for "her own people, and the army within it, but feeds, too, the "army of Virginia.* Once we had no arms, and could receive "no soldier but those who came to us armed. Now we have "arms for all, and are begging men to bear them. This city "of Augusta alone produces more powder than the army can "burn. All things are fair, and this Confederacy is not yet "'played out,' as those declare who spread their own des- "pondency over the whole body politic."

Of the absurd exaltation of such speeches a part must have necessarily been insincere. There is something to be accounted to braggadocio—to the bad calculation of raising the spirits of a fatigued and despondent people, by false pictures of hope and delusive promises of success.

As the author has had other occasion to observe of Mr. Davis, "his flippant prophecies of speedy success were doubtless intended to animate the South. But in this respect it was the thought of a small mind, a shallow trick; and it had the fault, too, of being calculated without reference to a peculiar temper of the Southern people in the war. That temper was one of impatience, almost of mutiny, under peculiar hardships; and thoughtful men remarked it more than once in the exhibitions of the war. It grew out of the very elements of Southern society. Here was a people of singularly high spirit, who had enjoyed a previous prosperity perhaps greater than that of any other community of equal numbers on earth, who had lived, although perhaps some-

---

* A curious commentary on the necessity of the Impressment Law.

times without cultivation, yet always in ease, and who had their due share of republican indisposition to submit to severe exercises of authority. A people so sensitive should have been lightly taxed with disappointments, and the policy of amusing them with promises was essentially a delicate and dangerous one. It would have been the task of a true statesman to have moderated their expectations, and to have educated then to just conceptions of the trials of the war. Instead of such prudent cultivations of strength, Mr. Davis always went to the opposite extreme of inflaming the army and people with promises, and while foolishly congratulating himself on the momentary excitements that flared out under such appeals, he did not perceive that the heart of the country was being steadily consumed by this policy, and that with each false appeal to public confidence he lessened his hold upon it."

But the singular remark is to be added of such speeches as we have reported the President making at Augusta, that it was not entirely insincere, and that while some of it may be ascribed to braggadocio, some of it must be put down to his self-delusion. He undoubtedly believed much of what he said. There is nothing more remarkable of this extraordinary man than an over-sanguine temperament, partaking largely of conceit, which kept him to the last blind to the true condition of affairs, and even presented him increased in confidence, self-complacent as his power continued to decline, lively and hopeful when all around him had been committed to despair. The man who could be so insolently confident as towards the close of the year 1864, when the disasters we have referred to had been largely increased, to reply to a suggestion of European recognition, that the Confederacy was past the necessity for it, and to decline the attempt to secure such countenance and aid from the French Emperor, as not needed to secure the success of the South; and who, when Sherman had marched through Georgia, and South Carolina and North Carolina, almost to the borders of Virginia, prophesied that he would be speedily destroyed, and that peace and independence were only a few months distant, might well be accounted as suffering from self-delusion, and not altogether insincere, in speaking so hopefully of the condition of the South to an audience in Georgia, when that State had not yet been lost to the Confederacy, and when the enemy that had entered it had not yet passed beyond Atlanta.

We are forced to the reflection on this extravagance of hope in the character of Mr. Davis, the singular fatuity that kept him constantly insensible of the real condition about him, that whatever happiness it may have bestowed upon the individual, it is an infirmity of weak minds, and never more out of place and more deplorable than in the serious government of men. The common observation of life teaches us that such a disposition is characteristic of weak and disappointed men. It is the source of constant failure, for it excludes the judgment. It is only he who can measure events that can control them; the just conception must precede the effective execution; and it may be announced almost in the form of an axiom—at least, in the style of a correct antithesis—that he who cannot, in some measure, govern events, has, in no measure, the right to govern men.

But to return to the progress of Mr. Davis's journey in Georgia. He lost no time, beyond that required in making speeches, in hastening to Hood's lines. It had been already suspected, by a few persons in Richmond, that a part of the motive which the President had in removing Johnston, was to exhibit some of his own military ideas, and impress his own views on the campaign in Georgia; knowing well that Hood would permit such interference, and would consent, as long as he had the nominal rank which he coveted, to be used as his instrument, whereas Johnston would certainly have resented it. It was an opportunity for Mr. Davis, which the deference of Hood gave, to display himself in the field, and to gratify the ambition which he had long indulged of the personal conduct or direction of a campaign. Before he reached Hood's line, he announced so plainly, in a speech, in Macon, his purpose to produce some great military phenomenon, that he not only moved the expectations of those who heard him, but excited the suspicion of the enemy; so greatly betraying himself by the imprudence of his vanity, that General Grant has since written of this speech, that it "disclosed the plans of the Confederates, *thus enabling General Sherman to fully meet them.*"

The visit of the President to any of the armies of the Confederacy had always been ominous. Thereafter, the country had generally heard of obvious campaigns discomfitted or overruled, and the substitution of some far-fetched and empirical plan of operations, such as might well proceed from the vanity of a man who had mistaken his vocation. Mr. Davis, as we have elsewhere noticed, imagined, after the fashion of vain men, that his forte laid in what he was really weakest. He was excessively fanciful in military matters, and to the last, he continued to believe that he was a master of the art of war. He thought to illustrate genius, while he was only proving the affectation of it, in fondness for novelties, in moving out of the beaten track of campaigns, and in surprising the public by sudden and violent eccentricities.

Surprise he accomplished enough; for the country soon

beheld, with feelings akin to amazement, Hood's army turned northward and marching in the direction of Tennessee! The first night Mr. Davis reached Hood's lines, he said, as if he had not already advertised sufficiently to the enemy as well as to the South his plan of operations—speaking to Cheatham's command:—"Be of good cheer, for, in a short while your faces will be turned homeward, and your feet pressing Tennessee soil." The novelty of the movement, and the indiscreet admissions of the President, in his various addresses, were such that for a long time the wondering people in Richmond would believe neither. The newspapers there had daily contests as to the whereabouts of Hood; and it was suggested that the speeches of the President were forgeries or extravagances of the telegraph, or that they had been made in an unnatural excitement. At Macon, he had alluded with something of vexation to the depletion in General Hood's ranks, caused by "absenteeism," and promised if the deserters would return to duty, that General Sherman should incur "the fate that befell the army of the French Empire in its retreat from Moscow. Our cavalry," he said, "and our people will harass and destroy his army as the Cossacks did that of Napoleon; and the Yankee General, like he, will escape only with a body-guard."

The foundation of these boasts, the military conceit that gave rise to them, and which was the indisputable product if Mr. Davis's brain, and, indeed, ostentatiously advertised by him, was the movement of Hood's army to the rear of Atlanta, on the calculation that, destroying the railroad between the Chattahoochee and Chattanooga, and crossing the Tennessee river, burning the bridge behind it, it might isolate Atlanta from Chattanooga, and the latter from Nashville, and thus cut off Sherman from his primary and second ary bases. Yet this was but one end of the campaign. Mr. Davis appeared to have absolutely never looked at the other end; to have never questioned what Sherman would do; to have taken for granted that he would have followed Hood with unequal pace and in the dismay of retreat he had described; and to have never had his mind crossed by the thought that Sherman might march through the rich and inviting country, which the withdrawal of Hood's army had left undefended, to the sea. It was a campaign characteristic of the partial and unilateral mind of Mr. Davis. What insanity must have inspired a movement that thus uncovered a vital and most resourceful part of the Confederacy, and yet assumed that the enemy would not take advantage of it! Mr. Davis must have known that there was nothing between Sherman and Augusta, or Savannah, but about two thousand of Wheeler's ill-mounted and ill-disciplined cavalry; that there was nothing to be expected of the Georgia militia, since Governor Brown, whose action in the war had already become sinister, had withdrawn them from Hood, and retired them to their homes, as soon as Atlanta had fallen; that General Beauregard had no troops to spare from Charleston; that Savannah was almost without a garrison; and that that part of Georgia, which was the granary of the South, laid at Sherman's mercy, the fair, warm fields inviting him, while Hood's army, at the beginning of winter, marched northward to the cold mountain ridges, and with an uncertain destination. He prepared a trap, blabbed of its ingenuity, exposed it to the enemy, and then supposed that he would walk directly into it, without once considering the chances of his going in another direction!

General Johnston was remaining as a private citizen in Macon. His ready and even mind knew what was coming.

In a private letter to a friend in Richmond, he wrote: "I could not tell the public what I would have done if left in command. I do not hesitate to tell you, though, that if I had been left in command of that army, it is very unlikely that Atlanta would have been abandoned. At all events, ten or twelve thousand soldiers, whose lives have been thrown away, would have been saved. Nor would I have left Sherman, with a force about equal to my own, in the heart of Georgia, to make such an excursion as our army is now engaged in. If Sherman understands his game, he can now cut off General Lee's supplies, which pass through this place, and break up all our establishments for the repair of arms and preparation of ammunition; and this without risk, without the chance of being compelled to fight—a necessity which he can avoid by marching to Charleston, Savannah, Pensacola, or Mobile. At this season the country can furnish his army an abundance of food and forage. Sherman, in his extreme caution, may not venture upon such a course. Should he do so, he will win."

Sherman did understand his game. He marched through an undefended country to the sea, impeded only by the plunder of his soldiers; he closed the year with the capture of Savannah, a "Christmas gift" to his government; he became the terror of the South, the messenger of doom; his fierce, lurid warfare spreading fear and dismay through the country, failing to disturb the equanimity, the confidence, the self-complacent routine of but one man in the Confederacy—he, Jefferson Davis!

"God had put a hook in Sherman's nose, and was leading him to destruction," said Doctor Burroughs, a puddy, little Baptist clergyman of Richmond, who affected intimacy with the President, and who would have said or done anything to jump with his humor. The President was satisfied with the revelation. He had said in November, 1864, when Congress met in Richmond: "The Confederacy has no vital points. If Richmond, and Wilmington, and Charleston, and Savannah; and Mobile were all captured, the Confederacy would remain as defiant as ever." This might be true in a certain sense; but the declaration implied, as its first condition, that the spirit of the people, despite of temporary disasters, was to remain erect and unbroken. Could it be said that that spirit was thus firm, when it had become the chief care of those who remained out of the army, to dodge the conscription, when "details" were purchased at tens of thousands of dollars, and when it was commonly said in Richmond, that it was "easier for a camel to go through the eye of a needle than for a rich man to enter Camp Lee"—the rendezvous for conscripts; when delegations were being plotted in all parts of the South for peace missions to Washington; when the desertions from Lee's army, that of best *morale* in the Confederacy, were reported to average fifty a day; when North Carolina swarmed with deserters, so numerous, and desperate in their resistance, that whole regiments had to be sent to re. claim them; when gold was quoted at 1 for 60 in Richmond; when Mr. Davis had already (in his message to Congress in November) suggested the arming of the slaves, as if Negro soldiers might do what white citizens, with their vastly superior interests in the contest, were no longer forward in accomplishing; when all thoughtful persons walked with bent heads; when there was nothing of social cheer in the Confederacy, only the bad and reckless revelry which expresses the levity of despair; when the newspapers were filled with complaints of Mr. Davis; when the *Examiner* printed its famous "*Eheu Jam Satis*" article, and when those journals which had hitherto defended the President had now nothing to offer, but falsehood's last refuge—silence?

But Mr. Davis remained blind and insolent; his eyes filletted, his ears sealed, his imagination drunken. If the public had really known something of the history then secretly transpiring of Sherman's march through Georgia they would have been aghast at the folly of the President, or they might possibly have been amused at the grotesqueness of some of his affectations of confidence. General Hardee had been appointed to take command in Georgia. He represented to the government the exact condition of affairs, and the necessity of sending him troops, both for the defence of his department, and as an eventual protection to General Lee. The estimate was that Sherman had forty-five thousand muskets, and Hardee was willing to take the field against him with twenty thousand. Not a soldier or a gun was sent him, and he was left to his unassisted resources.* He set about securing the service of the militia and reserves of Georgia and South Carolina, and took measures for placing all important points in his department in such condition of defence as his means would allow. He went to Macon, Georgia, where there were valuable public shops, soon after Sherman began his march southward.

---

* Every soldier and gun not absolutely indispensable to hold the coast line, had been sent to Lee or Johnston long ago. The troops left in Hardee's department, mostly heavy artillerists, were distributed in forts and defences along one hundred and fifty miles of coast, and were at every point confronted by the land or naval forces of the enemy. The weakening of any one point would have been followed by an attack upon it, probably a successful one, by an enemy constantly on the alert, and whose naval resources gave him great advantages for concentration. The loss of one point in a system of coast defences more or less dependent, involved the eventual loss of the whole system.

There he could do no more than collect a force of Georgia reserves, under command of Howell Cobb, and the reserve artillery of the Army of Tennessee, which had been sent back to that point by Hood, prepared to defend the place. Sherman passed by without attacking Macon, and Hardee then proceeded to Savannah, which was now evidently Sherman's destination.

At Savannah, General Hardee received from the "military adviser" of the President, the redoubtable Bragg, a telegram advising him to take the field against Sherman! He replied with bitter humor that his whole available force at Savannah then consisted of one hundred and eighty Georgia militia, and he suggested most respectfully that Mr. Davis could scarcely desire him to assume the offensive against Sherman's army with that force!

Events moved rapidly beyond the limits of our narrative assigned to this chapter. It is not our design to attend the march of Sherman from Savannah to Charleston, to Branchville, through North Carolina, towards Richmond. It is only to notice the improvidence and folly of Mr. Davis. which, as we have seen laid bare all the length and breadth of the Confederacy outside of a small circle around Richmond and a slip of territory in Virginia, and which at the last gathered from all quarters of the South, outside the Richmond lines, not more than fourteen thousand men on the front of Sherman, advanced near Raleigh. What had become of that splendid army from which Johnston had parted at Atlanta, and which was to achieve the wonders conceived by Mr. Davis, to illustrate his military genius, and to revive the memories of Napoleon? When in the forests of North Carolina it made its reappearance, only *four thousand* men answered to the roll-call of the Army of Tennessee; men worn and haggard from the hard service of winter, their faded gray jackets stained with the mud of six States in which they had fought or marched within the past three months, and not more than a corporal's guard gathered around some of the regimental colors that had waved defiantly at Atlanta, but since then had never been carried to a single victory!

CHAPTER XXV.

Inflamed Aspect of the War on the Side of the North—The Causes which Produced it—How the Cruel and Inhuman Spirit of the North had Increased—The Warfare of Sherman—His Contract with his Soldiers for Plunder—His Army Re-created by the Davis-Hood Campaign—The Track of his March through the Carolinas—General Hampton's Reflections on the Burning of Columbia—Sheridan Competes with Sherman in Atrocities—Devastation of the Valley of Virginia—Approved by Public Sentiment in the North—The Last Period of the War that of Revengeful Punishment of the South—General Grant Involved in the Savage Warfare—A New Theory of the Enemy's Raids—Their Extraordinary Moral Effect on the South—Change of Warfare on the Confederate side, Correspondent to the Increased Atrocities of the Enemy—Mr. Davis Refuses any Plan of Open and Manly Retaliation—How he Treated his Friends, and how his Enemies—A Curious Sort of Obstinacy—Reminiscences of General Lee in Pennsylvania—General Early's Feat of Incendiarism—Secret Expeditions to Fire Northern Cities, etc.—A Mean and Paltry Substitute for Legitimate Retaliation—Curious Method of Taking Revenge upon the North—Mr. Davis's Responsibility for Firing Northern Cities and Robbing Northern Banks—Revelations of the St. Albans Raiders and the Chesapeake "Pirates"—One of Morgan's Men to Fire Chicago—To what Extent these Bad Enterprises were Countenanced by Mr. Davis—Secrets of the Confederate Passport Office—Revelations of a Member of Congress—Mr. Davis and "Confidence Men"—A Peep at his Ante-Room—Romantic Story of an Italian Adventurer in Richmond—The *Carbonari* and the Assassination of Abraham Lincoln—Mr. Davis Innocent of any Conspiracy against the Life of Lincoln—A Playful Allusion to the Abduction of the Northern President—What Mr. Davis Thought of his Rival at Washington.

ABOUT the time of Sherman's march through the South, the war on the enemy's side assumed an aspect so new, and so exaggerated, and so decided, that we cannot pass it without notice. The fall of Atlanta, the encouragement it bestowed on all the armies of the North, the consequent defeat and diminution of the Democratic party, the re-election of Lincoln, made the enemy so confident of success, that there was no longer any occasion to bridle the real passions of the war, or to practice any show of moderation. It was remarked throughout the war that the North became insolent and ferocious as it gained successes. Now, since it had passed, as it supposed, the crisis of the war, and was assured of speedy and complete victory, the mask of humanity, already thin enough, was thrown off, and the formerly pent up hate of the North had full sway. It appeared as if a calculation had been made of using the little time left of the war in making excessive reprisals of vengeance for what the North had suffered in nearly four years of bloody contest, and while the memories of its own losses were yet fresh and exasperated. It was as if, expecting an early termination of hostilities, the enemy had resolved to expend all he could of rage on the antagonist who had so long baffled, punished, and scorned him, while such acts of ferocity might obtain some appearance of justification in a state of war, and before the South might come under the shelter of a declaration of peace.

In earlier periods of the war the North had practised outrages, and had shown a savage disposition, which the South then imagined could not be exceeded, and which it supposed was the limit of its sufferings. But now the atrocities of Sherman, of Hunter, of Sheridan, went far past all former experiences of the war, and a dense, disfiguring chapter of horrors was to precede the illuminated "*Finis*," the decked scroll of peace. When Butler governed in New Orleans, he had banished people from that city, but only such as were "registered enemies," those being called so who refused to forswear their allegiance to the Confederacy; about the period of Pope's irruption into Virginia, the Northern Congress had passed a law, popularly known in the South as "the plunder act," but which authorized the taking only of such private property of "rebels," as might be available for military use; at various times of the war, citizens had been imprisoned and executed, and in some instances as felons, but even these capital outrages had been done under some affected forms of law, and with some show of trial. Now, Sherman did not hesitate to exile from their homes whole and indiscriminate populations, men, women, and children, as when, in his characteristic slang, he "wiped out" Atlanta; now, all private property, of every species and in every place, dwelling-houses, furniture in the chambers of the sick, jewelry on the persons of ladies, were given over to the marauder or the incendiary, and every soldier in Sherman's army was a licensed plunderer; now, peaceful citizens were dragged to unwholesome prisons, were driven as cattle in the rear of the invading army, or were shot down at the doors of their houses, for no other offence than that of attempting to defend their property.

The immediate occasion of license which Sherman gave to his army is interesting, as it has been suggested by General Johnston. The latter commander has explained that one of his calculations in resting at Atlanta, and there taxing the time of the enemy, was that he expected a considerable part of Sherman's army to be discharged, as the time for which the troops enlisted expired. This army had been formed in 1861 for three years; the terms of most of the regiments had been served out, and a very large number refused to re-enlist. But the capture of Atlanta came in time to relieve the Federal General from the unwillingness of his soldiers to continue the campaign; and what inducements were offered to secure their re-enlistment may be inferred from the license which they indulged in the long marches of the months that followed. It was a matter of contract. The Federal soldiers were induced to believe that they had done enough for glory, that they had now only to fight for booty; and when the modern Vandal marched from Atlanta his sword pointed to the private wealth of three States as the argument for re-enlistment.

The wretched Davis-Hood device which had uncovered these States, had re-created Sherman's army, and, besides giving it opportunity, had supplied it with animation to make the most of it.

The narrative of Sherman's march through the Carolinas will be read over the world as a graphic and fearfully picturesque illustration of the barbarities of war, when the apocrypha or more doubtful stories of Goth and Vandal are forgotten. Wide-spreading columns of smoke rose wherever went that army of destruction. These fearful evidences of its march stood constantly in the sky, signals by which the marauders who had wandered miles away to plunder were guided back to the main army. Pillagers, incendiaries, "bummers." black and white thieves, recruited on the march and conveniently called "emigrants," were put under the charge of men who had escaped from the Confederate prisons, on the calculation that such officers would be most cruel and ferocious, and that they might have an opportunity to avenge the memories of Andersonville and Salisbury. These predatory and murderous bands spared nothing. On the black, slow length of an army choked with emigrant trains, laden with plunder, picturesque with a barbaric caravansary, there were carried devastation, ruin and horror. The smoke of a hundred conflagrations arose to the sunlit sky, and at night a gleam brighter and more lurid than that on the horizon of evening, shot from every verge. The land was desolated and scorched, dwelling-houses were robbed and then wantonly fired, the shrines of religion were violated, women were insulted, and in many a household there was an agony more bitter than death. Looking over the smoking ruins of the once beautiful city of Columbia, his own cherished home involved in the destruction, General Wade Hampton wrote to the conqueror, who had just threatened him because some Federal pillagers had been killed by men defending their property:—"You are particular in defining and claiming 'war rights.' May I ask if you enumerate among them the right to fire upon a defenceless city without notice; to burn that city to the ground after it had been surrendered by the authorities, who claimed, though in vain, that protection which is always accorded in civilized warfare to non-combatants; to fire the dwelling-houses of citizens, after robbing them, and to perpetrate even darker crimes than these—crimes too black to be mentioned?"

The outrages of Sherman were not only sustained but encouraged by a public sentiment in the North; and the contagion of his example was soon illustrated in all the Federal armies. In the Valley of Virginia—where Jackson had planted crimson, glorious memories, and where Early had just made a counterpart of Hood's wretched campaign, and had left behind him a monument of shame—Sheridan vied with Sherman in the work of destruction, and appeared to envy him for the popularity of the ruffian and the incendiary. "I have destroyed," he wrote gleefully, "over two thousand barns filled with wheat, hay and farming implements, and over seventy mills filled with wheat and flour." The bright, tempered sword was laid aside for the indiscriminating, relentless, merciless torch. A spectator in Sheridan's army touched by scenes he was compelled to witness has thus written of them:—"The wailing of women and children mingling with the crackling of flames, has sounded from scores of dwellings. I have seen mothers weeping over the loss of that which was necessary to their children's lives, setting aside their own, their last cow, their last bit of flour pilfered by stragglers, the last morsel that they had in the world to eat or drink. Young girls with flushed cheeks, and pale with tearful or tearless eye, have pleaded with or cursed the men whom the necessities of war (!) have forced to burn the buildings reared by their fathers, and turn them into paupers in a day, The completeness of the desolation is awful."*

Yet what one Northern man looked upon with a sickened heart was a pleasing picture to millions in the North, who regarded it as a sign of their power or a token of their triumph, who had their vanity pleased or their hate gratified by it. The extent of this disposition to punish the South, conceived at a time when victory should have made the enemy generous—the breadth and depth of that vindictive sentiment, which acquired such sudden growth after the fall of Atlanta, and when all danger of the war to the North was supposed to have passed, appears almost incredible; and, yet examined, it is perfectly undeniable. A passion appears to have seized the whole people of the North to crowd the last

---

* A committee, consisting of thirty-six citizens and the same number of magistrates, appointed by the county court of Rockingham for the purpose of making an estimate of the losses of that county by the execution of General Sheridan's orders, made an investigation and reported as follows :—

Dwelling-houses burned, 30 ; barns burned, 450 ; mills burned, 31 ; fencing destroyed (miles) 100 ; bushels of wheat destroyed, 100,000 ; bushels of corn destroyed, 50,000 ; tons of hay destroyed, 6,233 ; cattle carried off, 1750 ; horses carried off, 1750 ; sheep carried off, 4,200 ; hogs carried off, 3,350 ; factories burned, 3 ; furnace destroyed, 1. In addition to which there was an immense amount of farming utensils of every description destroyed, many of them of great value, such as McCormick's reapers, and threshing machines ; also household and kitchen furniture, money, bonds, plates, etc., etc., the whole loss being estimated at the enormous sum of $25,000,000.

period of the war with vindictive measures, and to disfigure it with scenes of savage warfare. The South was to be made "sick of war" as Sheridan suggested, and nearly the whole North applauded the sentiment. As significant evidence of the growth of this passion for vengeful hostilities, the increase of savage disposition in the war, we find General Grant—a commander who had never before fought women and children, and who had hitherto been considered by the South as conducting a legitimate contest of arms—involved by it, actually giving those orders, which Sheridan executed as his lieutenant, but for which the latter has hitherto been willing to reap all the infamy, and esteem it glory. Such outrages could not have been ordered by the highest General in the Federal armies; could not have been countenanced by the newspaper press; could not have failed to awaken a response of pity or indignation, save some desultory expressions of sentimentalism or some appeals of party in Democratic journals, unless there had been a large popular sentiment to sustain such conversion of the war to the methods and codes of the barbarian.

While the aspect of vengeful war was thus put on by the main armies of the North, another means was employed which not only served to harass the South, but is remarkable for the effect it had upon the imagination of its people, and the advantage thus contributed to the enemy. We refer to those numerous raids by which the South was cut up—those expeditions of cavalry which traversed every part of the country, and appeared in places where a Federal soldier had never before been seen. The Southern newspapers were in the habit of consoling themselves that these raids accomplished but little of material injury, such only as could be soon repaired, and they were often foolishly inclined to ridicule and caricature them as profitless adventures. But it was a great mistake. These frequent and far penetrating raids of the enemy, even when they inflicted but the most trifling injuries on the physical resources and material of the South, did as much to determine the war in favor of the North as many considerable battles. It was the alarm they created, the effect they had on the imagination of the people of the South, the sense of insecurity which they spread through the length and breadth of the country, the bringing home to every household the fear of an armed enemy, the apparition of "the Yankee," which more than the defeats of main armies in the field made the South "sick of war," and disposed to abandon it. These raids of the enemy, multiplied in the last period of the war we are now considering, operated largely to the demoralization of the South, and were doubtless organized for that purpose, rather than for the amount of material injury they might inflict. A feeling of insecurity entered every household in the Confederacy. There was not a square mile outside the lines of Richmond where the enemy's cavalry might not put in an unexpected appearance; and thus those who had hitherto lived remote from the war had now its terrors brought to their doors. For one act of outrage committed by these raiders, a hundred persons suffered in alarm. It was impossible to say what point they might not next visit, or who might not be their next victims. The imagination of almost the whole people of the Confederacy was strained and their spirits worn by a constant anxiety; and thus, while the main Federal armies spread death and devastation as far as they could reach, the enterprise of raiders carried to remote parts of the country the fear if not the actual experience of war—almost an equal agent of demoralization.

To the various outrages of the enemy what of response had President Davis to make? To the new and inflamed aspect of the war assumed by the North we shall see as a feeble correspondent some change in the warfare of the South. But it was a change of the most paltry pattern, and of the most curious character.

Mr. Davis had constantly refused any open retaliation upon the enemy, from motives which, in a preceding chapter we have discussed. He was not willing to risk being tried as a felon in a Federal court of justice, in the event of the "rebellion" being subdued. He wrote in his messages with a most violent mania of Yankees; he multiplied threats of retaliation; but his record on this subject, as we have seen, was that of swaggering menace, followed by prompt abasement. He was fierce and alarming enough in his words, but when it came to acts it appeared that his passion had given way, and that he had recovered the sweet and Christian temper of forgiveness. His stern self-will, his *hauteur*, his obstinacy were for his own people; he could be very firm and very bitter, when he differed from a Southern officer, or when his own rightful counsellors approached him with respectful advice or remonstrance; he could defy the indignation of his own people in maintaining a minion or a measure; while all that he had of graceful gentleness appeared to be reserved for the foe, and it is remarkable that he was never so politic and yielding as when the public enemy commanded him to come down from his high ground, to belie his pronunciamentos and to take back his threats.

When Northern pictorials exhibited in Richmond were almost weekly filled with carefully executed wood cuts of gibbets and "rebels" dangling from them, not a single victim of retaliation had ever been claimed by the gallows.

When the enemy destroyed the products of labor, devastated vast tracts of country, and drove out the inhabitants whom they did not destroy, Lee's army in Pennsylvania made levies on the inhabitants less severe than those which the Confederate government made daily on its own citizens. The policy of the Confederate invading armies had been the rigid protection of the enemy's private property. The orders of General Lee in Pennsylvania had been, that "all persons complying with requisitions for supplies shall be paid the market price for the articles furnished;" and where Confederate money was refused, they were to be satisfied with "a receipt specifying the kind and quantity of the property received or taken and the market price," which as a certificate of indebtedness, might, after the close of the war be recovered in gold or silver! Even but a little while before Sherman began his grand raid, General Early had an opportunity to devastate the country immediately about Washington, and yet had come back, looking mean for having burned a single house, and pleading as an absurd extenuation, a snobbish excuse, that this single act had been reluctantly done in retaliation for General Hunter's destruction of Governor John Letcher's house—as if no one else in Virginia or in the South had lost home or property by the enemy's act, and might not as well as the retired Governor whom Early avenged, have invoked the law of retaliation.

But tame as was the government of Mr. Davis, on the subject of retaliation, and subdued as were the people of the South in their sentiment of retributive justice, the vast increase of the enemy's outrages, at the time of Sherman's march, and towards the close of the last year of the war, could not fail to effect some response. But it was a most singular response. Mr. Davis yet persisted in abstaining from open and regular retaliation. But while he was thus silent, there were whispers in Richmond of strange and secret expeditions which were to burn Northern cities, to fire transports, to abduct hostages, and to give to the North, in a mysterious way, some taste of the horrors of war, to accomplish some degree of revenge for what the South was suffering. Nor were these whispers always low and covert. There were suggestions in the newspapers that the North might not have all of plunder and incendiarism, that houses in New York and Chicago might pay for those burned in Georgia, that the South was not as helpless in the way of revenge as her enemies supposed, that the trodden worm might turn and sting. The author recollects a remarkable article in that journal of Richmond, known peculiarily as the organ of Mr. Davis, and to which rumor assigned Mr. Benjamin, Secretary of State, as a regular contributor—the *Sentinel*—warning the North that but a few secret hands might suffice to commit her finest cities to the flames, and to inflict an injury as great as that which Sherman's army had done to Atlanta. It was a new mode of warfare thus suggested; it was, of course, not large enough to affect, to any considerable degree, the fate of the contest; it was not useful, and scarcely considered as such; it was *revengeful.*

We are sensible that a great effort has been made to relieve Mr. Davis of responsibility for the various predatory and incendiary enterprises toward the North, partial and unworthy correspondents as these were, for the atrocities of Sherman and Sheridan. These atrocities were bad enough; but there were obvious open modes of retaliation, such as were allowed by the honorable laws of war; and it was, indeed, shameful, if Mr. Davis, not having the nerve to take these methods of manly and courageous retribution, not daring to doom to death a single prisoner captured from Sherman's pillagers, and taken in the act of murder and felony, should yet have attempted to take revenge in a *secret*, cowardly and indiscriminate way, by promoting or countenancing conspiracies, to burn houses and rob banks in the North, to fire upon transports, taking the risk of involving innocent persons, and to destroy, under cover of night, the shelters of women and children. Yet on this painful subject we must write the truth of history. To those who contend that these bad enterprises was the work of lawless and abandoned adventurers, and that the Confederate Government had no part in them, we are forced to remark the significance of the fact that such a phase of the war, on the side of the South, had never before taken place, as it might have done, had it proceeded only from a bad element in the population; and that the number of these enterprises, their cotemporary relation, and the distinct period they occupied—being a series of acts rather than desultory performances—are evidences of a purpose and organization which, under the circumstances, only some official direction and authority in the South could have accomplished.

Under the severe passport system of the Confederacy, scarcely a man could leave its limits without it being known to the authorities—and certainly not when he went through ports of the Confederacy, or through the lines of its armies. Passports were given in the utmost stinginess. Especially could not any officer or soldier of the Confederate armies leave the country unless he obtained a passport from the War Department at Richmond, and then the business which took him from the regular military service had to be stated most explicitly. Yet the St. Albans raiders were found to be, mostly, commissioned officers in the Confederate army.

Yet the party that, in the autumn or winter of 1864, made the "piratical" seizures in Chesapeake Bay, was of Confederate soldiers, who had been furnished with passports from the War Department, and who had gone on their expedition directly through General Lee's lines. And yet again the emissary to burn Chicago—an officer of Morgan's command—had gone through the port of Wilmington, and had exhibited there a passport signed by Secretary Seddon, besides possessing a general letter of introduction from the President himself.

The whole truth of these vengeful episodes of the war, in relation to the responsibility of Mr. Davis, is that while he carefully abstained from furnishing any direct authority for them, he gave a secret countenance to them, under the system of passports in the War Department, and afforded their emissaries and agents facilities of departure from the Confederacy. The *modus operandi* has been privately described by a distinguished Congressman. The expeditions of oakum and turpentine were not very close secrets in Richmond. Not a few members of Congress were in favor of almost any measure of revenge upon the North, even to the burning of hotels and steamboats. In some cases they applied to Mr. Davis to authorize such an illegitimate warfare, informing him of the expeditions that were plotted; they were waived away or treated with noncommittal speeches. But "my experience was," said the member referred to, "that, although the commissions or details were not given, I never had any trouble in getting passports from the War Department, and in getting 'the boys' through the lines."

It was a paltry and detestable warfare; on the part of Mr. Davis, a subterfuge, and, with respect to the whole Southern people, the evidence of a descent from the true spirit of the war to a mean spitefulness, a disposition to wanton acts of revenge when they had come to despair of success. It was a profound pity that Mr. Davis could not conceive—at least not execute—the just idea of a bold and open retaliation. The proper subjects of such retaliation were before him in the miscreants of Sherman's and Sheridan's armies; many of these were in his power as prisoners; and to go behind them, and substitute in a secret way, as victims of his revenge, peaceful people in the North, was an unmanly device and a cruel absurdity.

To the men who came to him with schemes of vengeance upon the enemy, Mr. Davis was frequently accessible without the intermediation of Congressmen or powerful friends. He had such a weak credulity that every adventurer, with an extraordinary and insane invention, found it not difficult to obtain his ear. Men who professed to have found out some new form of liquid fire, patentees of extraordinary torpedoes that would destroy whole fleets, the Mississippi inventor of a flying machine to freight ordnance and to fire down upon the enemy at the height of half a mile, were mingled in the President's ante-room with men who proposed immense financial schemes, after the fashion of extracting sunbeams from cucumbers, and geniuses of diplomacy who were anxious to spend their time in the grand Hotel du Louvre and to test its famous vintages, whereof each glass would cost about three pounds of cotton. There never was a lack of "confidence-men" about Mr. Davis, and among them those who proposed to dispatch the war by such means as we have described, and who even suggested viler works of destruction.

With respect to the credulity that entertained such wild and reckless propositions, an incident happened in Richmond that would be incredible but for the evidences which the author has from one of the parties to it. This incident—or romance we may call it—has never before been published, and there are persons who, having thought it effectually suppressed and concealed, will be surprised to find at this day a minute account of it.

About the close of the year 1864 a stranger appeared in Richmond, of elegant dress and manners, speaking both English and Italian, and whose dark and peculiar features supported the statement that he was a native of Italy. He made himself exceedingly agreeable to the company at the Exchange Hotel, although practicing something of the reserve of the nobleman; and he was observed with not a little curiosity, until gossip settled on the discovery that he had been seen to visit the State Department, and that, therefore, considering, too, his *distingue* appearence, he must be charged with a "mission" of importance. Dining one day at the hotel, he took advantage of a casual remark to draw into conversation Mr. Boteler, a member of Congress from Virginia, a gentleman who was supposed to have a great taste for learning. The latter had noticed the sound escaping from a gas jet over the table. The conversation turned upon the possibility of producing musical notes from such a source; chemistry, acoustics and other branches of science were discussed, greatly to Mr. Boteler's relish; and at last the Italian gracefully insisted that the Congressman should accompany him to his room to witness some scientific experiments in which he was then engaged. The experiments were shown; Mr. Boteler saw at once that their adjustments were those of a scientific man, and for hours he roamed with his strange acquaintance over the fields of science, literature, and art, wondering at his varied accomplishments and fascinated by the charm of his manners. As

Mr. Boteler rose to depart, the stranger said with the air of communicating an important confidence:—"I have some thing to say to you. The pleasure I have experienced in your company, and the position I know you occupy in your government, encourage me to make a communication that will interest you. I have a mission to Richmond, and I have already partially discharged it, and am now only waiting on your government for a sum of money that is necessary. I belong to the society of *Carbonari!* It sympathizes with the Southern Confederacy; and it is the only power in Europe that can compel its recognition, for Napoleon III. is secretly a member of the society, and dares not disobey its mandates. More than this"—and his brow darkened—"I hold in my hand the life of Abraham Lincoln; the victim whom the *Carbonari* designate cannot elude them."

What impression this important and terrible disclosure made upon Mr. Boteler is not known; but he has never denied that he believed what the man told him. He even went to the extent of appointing a day to accompany the strange *diplomat* to the State Department, and actually engaged to add his influence to the impressions which the latter already reported he had made upon Secretary Benjamin, but to what extent of aiding the mission he did not mention. The day came; Mr. Boteler attended at the hotel. The Italian was not to be found; he had left the hotel hurriedly that morning. Suspicions were aroused at the State Department. Pursuit was ordered on all the roads leading out from Richmond, and fortunately the man, disguised as a peddler, was overtaken and arrested a few miles from the city. He resisted the officers stoutly and with great insolence; for some time the search to which he was subjected revealed nothing contraband or suspicious; he was about to be dismissed with apologies, when one of the officers examining his boots discovered that the heels might be screwed off, and found snugly ensconced therein several sheets of tissue paper inscribed with plans of all the fortifications of Richmond, and with a correspondence giving all the details of its defences! The man was carried back to Richmond as a spy. But he was never tried, never punished, and we do not know what became of him—the government being unwilling to give publicity to the incident, and anxious to hush up an affair, in which its credulity had been so ridiculously practiced upon by an adventurer, who, at best, was nothing more than a *charlatan*.

The singular story suggests here a remark which we should make in justice to Mr. Davis—and that is with reference to the allusion it contains to the assassination of Mr. Lincoln. There have been those who have believed—few believe it now—that the strange warfare which the South proposed to conduct by secret agents and emissaries in the North, and in which we have seen Mr. Davis might have borne an indirect share, might possibly have extended to a conspiracy against the life of the Northern President. It is an absurd and foul imagination, without a particle of evidence to support it, and with every probability pointing to the contrary. Irregular and nefarious as we must consider the warfare that we have just described, as designed for an indiscriminate revenge upon the people of the North, rather than for the legitimate ends of the war, or in the true and manly spirit of retaliation, Mr. Davis never could have carried it to the point of cold-blooded assassination, and that as against a President whose death could not possibly benefit the South, and who, at the time, was more tolerable to it than the man who would succeed him. Briefly, Mr. Davis was equally incapable of the crime and of the folly of such an act. As to the safety of Mr. Lincoln, the author, living in Richmond during the war, and having access to most of its political conversation, never heard a threatening breath, but on one occasion, and that a playful allusion in the War Department, to capturing him and using him as a hostage to compel an exchange of prisoners. Possibly that allusion might have grown to a serious plan of abduction; but even to this there is not the slightest evidence that Mr. Davis was a party. He bore Mr. Lincoln no ill-will, and it is remarkable that he never designated him personally in his bitter criticisms on the conduct of his government, or reflected the popular disposition in the South to caricature and abuse him. On the contrary, he had a certain personal esteem for his rival at Washington. He regarded him as an honest, weak man, who had been used beyond his real disposition by the adroitness and malignity of party;* he certainly had neither motive nor desire to injure him in his person, much less to kill him, and to inflame the North by a crime which civilization has

* Since the war, Mr. Davis is thus reported in a conversation in his prison at Fortress Monroe, referring to the assassination of the Northern President:—"Of Mr. Lincoln he spoke, not in affected terms of regard or admiration, but paying a simple and sincere tribute to his goodness of character, honesty of purpose, and Christian desire to be faithful to his duties according to such light as was given him. Also to his official purity and freedom from avarice. The Southern press labored, in the early part of the war, to render Mr. Lincoln abhorred and contemptible; but such efforts were against his judgment, and met such opposition as his multiplied cares and labors would permit. From no ruler the United States could have, might terms so generous have been expected by the South. Mr. Lincoln was kind of heart, naturally longing for the glory and repose of a second term to be spent in peace."

stamped as the extreme of infamy. Surely the President of the Southern Confederacy has enough of deserved censure to bear, without throwing upon him the suspicion of a foul crime, in which there is not a particle of evidence or a grain of consistency.

CHAPTER XXVI.

A New Breadth and Volume of Opposition to President Davis—Approach to an Internal Revolution in the Confederacy—A *Coup d'Etat* Threatened in Richmond—Animation of the Confederate Congress—Appeals to It by the Richmond *Examiner* and Charleston *Mercury*—Senator Wigfall on President Davis—A Revolutionary Opportunity Lost by Congress—Movement to Make General Lee Military Dictator—He Resists it—In what Sense he Accepted the Office of Commander-in-Chief—His Private Understanding with Mr. Davis—The Secret and Curious History of a Military Dictatorship in the Confederacy—A Remarkable Correspondence of General Lee with the President—Some Peculiarities of the Character of Lee—His Quiet and Negative Disposition—General Lee Excessively and Servilely Admired in the South—Defects in his Character—A Great Man nevertheless—Why he Refused to be Used by the Opposition against Mr. Davis—How he Secured the Favor of the President—Their Personal Relations—Mr. Davis Affects not to be Sensible of the Revolutionary Design against his Administration—A Remarkable and Dishonorable Evasion by the President—His Correspondenee with the Legislature of Virginia—His Secret Resentment of the Revolutionary Demands Made upon Him—Anecdote of Mrs. Davis—A Defiant Speech in the Executive Mansion—Scandalous Quarrel between the President and Congress—A Lame Conclusion of a Revolution.

THE disasters which ensued in the close of the year 1864, created a popular sentiment towards Mr. Davis, that needed, to rise to the force and dignity of a great revolution, but one, yet an indispensable condition—spirited leadership. They were the occasion of a breadth and volume of opposition to his administration that would have overwhelmed it, could it only have improved its organization, and secure the leader whom popular preference had designated. How near the Confederacy came to an internal revolution, while it yet waged war, though feebly, against the public enemy; how narrowly Mr. Davis missed the chance of dethronement; and how critically short of success fell an effort to re-animate the flagging war in the South by the repudiation of Mr. Davis, have been but little known to the world. It is the period of the war of profoundest interest, although so unconspicuous or unknown in the common history of the contest. Behind the panorama of battles, a great struggle of moral forces was going on, imperfectly seen by the world, only scantily related in the newspapers, mistaken in the North as nothing more than a passing political effervescence in the South, one of its scandalous party quarrels, an episodial excitement, but which was really a movement of historical moment, and constitutes, perhaps, the most interesting passage in the stormy and unequal annals of the Southern Confederacy.

Heretofore, in treating of the dulness and servility of the Confederate Congress, we have referred to a brief and exceptional animation in it, towards the end of the war. It came from an opposition to President Davis, in which Congress was led by a few men of power, incited by the press, and aroused and alarmed by the evidently declining fortunes of the Confederacy. If it had had the intellectual capacity and the nerve, or if certain conditions had been supplied, its disposition would have carried it to the extent of a *coup d'etat* against Mr. Davis. It was astonishing how, in the last periods of the war, it threw off its servile habit to the President. It became as men often do who have long lived in mean and interested compliance, and then break away from it, sudden and violent in its resentment. In this disposition it was spurred by the newspapers. The Richmond *Examiner* wrote: "It will be for Congress to repair as it best can the mischief done the public service by a weak and impracticable Executive; to look at the reduction of our forces in the field; the decay of military discipline; the demoralization of our armies, and the jeopardy to which our cause has been put by a long course of trifling conduct, childish pride of opinion, unworthy obstinacy, official obtuseness, conceit, defiance of public opinion, imperoiusness, and despotic affectation on the part of those intrusted with the execution of the war."

In less passionate phrase, but with not less determined purpose, the Charleston *Mercury* said: "Congress must assume its duties under the Constitution as an independent element of power. It must abandon the idea that it is only a secret power for registering the will of the President. It must be the people standing forth in the light of day, clothed with the whole legislative power of the Government, and with their agent, the President, instrumental for their deliverance. . . . But if President Davis is to be treated as 'our Moses,' we really do not see the use of Congress. If the people, through their representatives in Congress, are to exercise no power but at the bidding of the Executive, Congress is a nonentity. It is worse, it is the tool of the Executive by which the Constitution is practically overthrown, and a military dictatorship established in its stead; characterized by a base assumption of power on the part of the Executive, and a baser betrayal of trust on the part of Congress."

But the opposition that thus sprang up in the later years of the war between the Confederate Congress and the President, although stimulated by public opinion, and carried to the point of personal exasperation, was singularly without results. Some of this opposition in Congress was merely petulant. Mr. Foote represented it in the Lower House with voluble speeches, but without weight of character to impress even his shallow audience. In the Senate, General Wigfall, who had returned from the army to the political arena, was more formidable. Perhaps the greatest orator of the South, he spoke with powerful effect, in language that could mount from the most even and classical flow of words to the most rugged and eccentric force, and sometimes penetrating his audience with the electrical passion that would blaze in his seamed and fierce face. The Richmond papers feared to report his bitter and vindictive speeches. Only the *Examiner* dared to tell of the fires in which he roasted that "amalgam of malice and mediocrity," as he described the august person of Mr. Davis. But after all, these were fruitless censures and declamations, and, as we shall see, no positive measure of importance ever grew out of them, beyond a formal relinquishment of the control of military affairs to General Lee, which he practically never accepted.

The fact is—and it is a fact that has never had its just proportion of mention in the current histories of the war—there was in the last year of hostilities a serious and determined thought in the minds of the Southern people to get up a counter-revolution in the Confederacy, or, at least, to overthrow the military authority of Mr. Davis; and that the Congress, while weakly assuming to respond to this design, really belittled and abandoned it and reduced it to nothing more than a wordy and indecent controversy with the President. It never represented the depth of the public sentiment in the Confederacy on this subject. It fell utterly below the occasion, and, at last degraded an opportunity that might have produced the most important historical results and possibly have saved the Confederacy, to a low competition in recriminating and fruitless words.

Every revolution, to be effective, must have distinctness of purpose, a plain and well-defined object in view, and, secondly, a leader capable of representing its design and of conveying its inspiration. It was on the second condition that the revolution, aimed at the maladministration of Mr. Davis, failed. The condition of the country in which was presented the necessity for such a movement, was obvious, and there was no variety of opinion, among those who were aggrieved, as to the remedy. It was thus clearly indicated in a Richmond journal: "A remedy for all discontent has suggested itself to the mind of every man who thinks, and has been advised by a thousand mouths in the same breath. It is the creation of a new officer—a Commander-in-chief—who shall exercise supreme control over the armies and military affairs of the Confederacy; and the appointment of General Lee to be that officer. Such an act, if made in good faith, and solidly guarded against counteracting influences, would restore public confidence, and give the country heart for a new effort equal to that which it has hitherto made. It would do more to bring down the price of gold and restore faith in the currency, than any law that the Secretary can devise, however wise in principle, and however ingenious in detail. The people would be satisfied that their means are not thrown away; that the best use of their blood and property would be made that could be made. The adoption of such a measure would be the new birth of the Southern Confederacy. But it must be a real, substantial measure, guarantied by the representatives of the nation; not a sham—not a duplex—general order, creating another Beauregard or Johnston "Department under the control of the President." And it must be adopted in time—that is to say, now."

As the train of disasters had progressed, all eyes had been turned upon General Lee as the remaining hope of the Confederacy. There was an anxiety to put on his broad shoulders the burden of the public cares, and to trust him for a safe deliverance. General Lee could not have been insensible to this trust and confidence of the people. His modesty could not have barred the knowledge of it; it was in the thoughts and speeches of all men; it was before his eye in every newspaper he read; it was the daily conversation of the people; it reached his ear in every tone of expression. His judgment, approved by so many events, his constancy under heavy trials, his lordly equanimity in the face of misfortune, his economy and readiness of resources were the only signals of hope and deliverance in what was now the darkest and most painful time of the war.

Briefly, there was but one influence in the Confederacy that could have fully carried out the revolutionary purpose of the people; that, Lee;—and he, unfortunately, and to a most curious extent, was found impracticable. He could not be brought to accept the position of Commander-in-chief of all the forces of the Confederacy. It is true he apparently accepted this appointment. It was thus announced by him to the public:

"In obedience to General Order, No. 3, from the Adjutant and Inspector-General's office, February 6, 1865, I assume command of the military forces of the Confederate States. Deeply impressed with the difficulties and responsibility of the position, and humbly invoking the guidance of Almighty God, I rely for success upon the courage and fortitude of the army, sustained by the patriotism and firmness of the people, confident that their united efforts, under the blessing of Heaven, will secure peace and independence."

But General Lee did not accept the position in the sense and to the extent that Congress had intended. He insisted upon believing that the President was still "constitutionally" Commander-in-chief; and while accepting the position to which Congress and the country had called him, in terms so as to satisfy public sentiment, and end a controversy in which he was unpleasantly involved, he did it with a private reservation to respect the views of the President, quite equivalent to the former written conditions that had been attached to the position. This explanation is necessary to understand a part of Confederate history which has been generally confused; and proofs of it we shall soon see in the sequel, where the unfortunate judgment of the President was still visible, and took its accustomed precedence in the conduct of military affairs.

The history of the movement to place General Lee in command of all the Confederate armies, is as yet unwritten, and contains some facts as characteristic of the man as they are generally interesting. The movement, as conceived by the people, had, as we have seen, really the breadth and incisiveness of a revolutionary design; it was not less than to divide Mr. Davis's administration and to appropriate to another his powers as commander-in-chief. Such an idea had vaguely floated in the public mind almost from the beginning of the war; it was precipitated by the dissatisfaction which Mr. Davis particularly gave in his administration of the military affairs of the Confederacy; but even, apart from this, it may be said that a serious reflection occurred to thoughtful minds during the past civil struggle, and on both sides of it, whether the office of President, as combining that of commander-in-chief, was not really too large and incongruous, and whether, in case of actual war, the latter authority should not be separated, or the powers of the President, as the leader and director of armies be held only as a convenient fiction of constitutional law, not designed to be practically, much less pretentiously and pragmatically, executed. But we have no space here for an excursion on the speculation, interesting as it is, and suggestive, somewhat, of an anomaly; inasmuch as we believe the time has not yet come for the American people to elect their Presidents for the qualifications of military leaders.

Whether or not this qualification had been considered in the case of Mr. Davis, when he had been selected by a Senatorial caucus, in Washington, as head of the Southern Confederacy—and on this question we have seen the curious evidence that the first programme of the conspirators had Mr. Hunter, of Virginia, for President, and Mr. Davis as commander-in-chief, the latter being thus assigned in view of his military experience in Mexico—it is certain that he regarded his military office as no fiction, that he insisted upon practically executing it, and that he displayed it even in the smallest details, and to a point of insufferable pragmatism.

It has been popularly reported that General Lee discouraged the movement to invest him with the military authority of the Confederacy, because of scruples that it violated the letter of the Constitution. But such scruples, if they were entertained, were paltry and illogical; for, we repeat, the movement was essentially one of revolutionary design, it was to be estimated as such, and the only question was whether General Lee would consent to assume the part assigned him on the supreme plea of the safety of the republic. He could not but be fully sensible of this plea, for no one knew better than he the military deficiencies of Mr. Davis, and his infirmities as Commander-in-chief. To be sure, with his natural restraint of speech, he had never breathed a word of distrust of Mr. Davis; but on this subject we need not the evidence of confessions. General Lee could not help knowing the incompetency of the President in military matters; it had been brought home to him; and he had had recent and singular experiences of it, since the summer campaign of 1864 had forced him back to Richmond. Since that time the President had been in opposition to him to an extent little known to the public. The people of Richmond would have trembled had they known that after General Lee drew in his defences around the capital, and when Grant shifted his operations south of the James river, he wrote a private letter of warning to Mr. Davis, telling him that he even then had but little hopes of holding the city, and that the loss of his communications, with the numerous cavalry of the enemy operating upon them appeared to be only a question of time; but what would have been the feelings of this people, thus startled and distressed, to have known the additional fact that Mr. Davis, so far from being properly impressed by this letter, despised its warning, and even resented it, in way of reply, by urging Lee to send troops from the small and critical force that scarcely covered the approaches to the capital to aid in defence of Charleston! Yet such are the facts, strange and astounding as they may be. More than this, the President had embarrassed the plans of General Lee from the moment the latter had come directly under his eye in Richmond; he had starved the army, by sustaining Commissary Northrop, in the face of universal opposition to this singular creature; he had almost destroyed its discipline by repeated pardons of deserters; and when General Longstreet, Lee's most important lieutenant, had ventured to write as a commentary on one of these writs of pardon that four hundred men out of a brigade of twelve or fifteen hundred were at that time confined in the guard-house for desertion, thus indicating the condition of the discipline of the army, Mr. Davis had returned the paper with the imperial endorsement that "the act of the Executive was not the subject of comment by an officer in the field!"

Understanding then the condition in which the position of Commander-in-chief was urged upon General Lee, the question forcibly occurs why he should have so strenuously declined this solicitation of public confidence. The scruple that to accept it would contravene the letter of the Constitution is, as we have seen, scarcely tenable; and his opinion could not have been undecided of the necessity of a radical change in the military affairs of the Confederacy. General Lee declining the position of Commander-in-chief, and actively discouraging the only hopeful turn which popular confidence had taken in the extremity of affairs, yet refused to give, to the public, at least, any explanation of his course. It must be found and estimated in the character of the man. We think we discover it in certain peculiarities of his character:—an anxiety to avoid the accumulation of responsibilities, yet coupled with a strict sense of the duty that has been accepted; an indisposition, not ungenerous, but severely resolved to do nothing more than is nominated in the bond of public service. It was as if he had said to those who proffered him the high trust of military dictator:—"Gentlemen, I accepted the position of the Army of Northern Virginia; I shall do my best by that army, I shall fight it to the best advantage; it employs all my solicitude, its safety and success are my studies, night and day; but I am not willing to go outside of that army to assume new responsibilities; its limits confine, alike, my duty and my ambition."

The future philosophic historian will probably make an elaborate, difficult judgment of this choice of General Lee. We shall not attempt here to anticipate that judgment; but we indicate the subject as one for profound criticism. It was the moral effect that was mostly sought in the appointment urged upon him. The Confederacy had to be saved in extreme and desperate circumstances; and General Lee was the only man within its limits who could have commanded public confidence to the extent of reanimating the declining cause, and effecting another lease of the war. He did not do it. It is remarkable of him—and we scarcely know whether in a good sense, for, however excellent may be a degree of reticence, a cold and barren silence is not admirable—that never, at any time of the war, and not even in the company of the most intimate friends on whom he might have bestowed his confidence without imprudence, did he ever express the least opinion as to the chances of the war.* Curiosity was

* It is quite certain from all the evidences in the case, and especially from his private letters bewailing the secession of his State, that General Lee's heart was not in the war. He accepted it as a necessity, doing what it required exactly, and even punctiliously, yet coldly. Since the war he testified faithfully to the Reconstruction Committee that he had never anything to do with the affairs and fortunes of the Confederate cause outside the limits of his army. He proposed nothing of a general nature in the war, with the single exception of arming the slaves ; and this departure from his usual negativeness, the writer has had ingeniously explained to him, to the effect that General Lee had a strong though secret affection for Emancipation, and imagined an opportunity of accomplishing that by a convenient circuit, together with whatever might be the particular benefits of the measure in recruiting his army.

His lack of animosity in the war—as we find him protesting it to the Reconstruction Committee, since the surrender of the Confederacy —is illustrated by a number of anecdotes. In another historical work by this author, are the following:—"In all his official intercourse and private conversation, he never breathed a vindictive sentiment towards the enemy who so severely taxed his resources and ingenuity, and put against him so many advantages in superior means and numbers. He had none of that *Yankee-phobia* common in the Southern army ; he spoke of the Northern people without malevolence, and in a style that deprecated their political delusions rather than denounced their crimes ; and he generally referred to the enemy in quiet and indifferent words, quite in contrast to the epithets and anathemas which were popularly showered on 'the Yankees.' On one occasion, a spectator describes him riding up to the Rockbridge Artillery, which was fiercely engaging the enemy, and greeting his

kept on the stretch, but with little avail, to learn his views of the probable fate of the struggle. A Virginia newspaper

---

son Robert, who, as a private soldier, was bravely working one of the guns. 'How d'ye do, father?' was all that Robert had to say as he continued his duty at his gun; and General Lee replied quietly: 'That's right, my son; drive *those people* back.' At another time, in sight of the enemy on the Rapidan, General Lee was standing near his lines, conversing with two of his officers, one of whom was known to be not only a hard fighter and a hard swearer, but a cordial hater of the Yankees. After a silence of some moments, the latter officer, looking at the Yankees with a dark scowl on his face, exclaimed, most emphatically, 'I wish they were all dead.' General Lee, with the grace and manner peculiar to himself, replied, 'How can you say so, General! Now I wish they were all at home, attending to their own business, and leaving us to do the same.' He then moved off, when the first speaker, waiting until he was out of earshot, turned to his companion, and in the most earnest tone said, 'I would not say so before General Lee, but I wish they were all dead *and in hell!*' When this 'amendment' to the wish was afterwards repeated to General Lee, in spite of his goodness and customary reproof of profanity, he could not refrain from laughing heartily at the speech, which was so characterictic of one of his favorite officers."

To the last day of the Confederacy, General Lee appears to have preserved his singular indisposition to incur responsibility. In a recent reminiscence of Appomattox Court-house, General Grant is reported to have said: "Lee remarked that he hoped I would offer as magnanimous terms to the other Confederate armies as his had received. I told him he should, if he wished to serve his friends, go to the other armies in person, and prevail upon them to surrender. He said *he would wish to see Mr. Davis first!*"

To his retirement since the war, General Lee has carried that vacancy of opinion, so remarkable in him. He is said to be in the habit of refusing to converse of the war—a refusal which, we must say, has much more the appearance of an absurd prudery, an old-maidish estimate of proprieties, than that of a wise and delicate reserve. The late war was a great historical event; it not only supports conversation, but is a natural topic of the intelligence of our times.

said, shortly after the battle of the Wilderness, when the public mind was in a momentary conflict of hopes and fears, that there were men in the South, who would bestow half their fortunes for three words from General Lee, giving his opinion of the military situation. "What does he think about?" said the journalist referred to. "None of us can read the thoughts of that impenetrable bosom. It is appropriate that the hero of this story should not be garrulous; the sadness of the time renders it fitting that the helmsman should guide the ship with few words spoken. * * * * When he first came to Richmond, they said he had no manners; he attended to his business, and spoke little. They sent him to Western Virginia—a small theatre, when Beauregard was at Manassas, and Johnston was at Winchester; he went, and made no comment. The campaign failed—they called him Turveydrop—he did not attempt to excuse himself. Soon we find him in a blaze of glory, the hero of the battles around Richmond. He is still silent. He marches to Manassas, and achieves another great victory. Not a word escapes him. He

---

Why should General Lee shun intelligent references to the war? Indeed, as a great actor in it, he owes, as a duty, both to history and to present public opinion, to give whatever information he can of it; and, at least, he might be glad to illuminate some of its passages in cheerful conversation among his friends. But it is said that he will tolerate no conversation on the subject. When visitors call on him, he makes it a precedent condition that they shall make no allusion to the war; and whenever the subject is approached, he turns the conversation to the weather, the crops, or some other commonplace. A gentleman, hunting some historical materials, recently applied to him for aid, or, at least, for the benefit of some directions; and he replied that he had not a scrap of writing about the war, not even a memorandum book to preserve the dates of his battles, and that he could absolutely furnish nothing from his recollections!

takes Winchester, is foiled at Sharpsburg for the want of men —defeats Burnside at Fredericksburg—Hooker at Chancellorsville—but he breaks not his silence. He has the terrible trial of Gettysburg—he only remarked, 'It was my fault' —and then, in the present year (1864), he has conducted this greatest of all his campaigns. Silent still. When will he speak? Has he nothing to say? What does he think of our affairs? Should he speak, how the country would hang upon every word that fell from him!"

We have recited, in another part of this work, many of the virtues of General Lee, and much that was admirable; and yet there are faults in this military idol of the South, which neither the partiality of friends, nor the glare of cotemporary eulogium, can entirely conceal or compensate. His most notable defect was that he never had or conveyed any inspiration in the war. He had gone into it with but little personal animation, as a matter of severe and unwelcome duty, and he never attempted any animation of his troops greater than his own. He was mechanical in the war; he never inflamed his troops; he had not that passion, that faculty of inspiration which is at once the most brilliant and valuable quality of the military commander. Nothing could be more characteristic of his quiet conception of the war, than when asked by a committee of the Federal Congress if the soldiers of the Confederacy were not less acrimonious after the surrender, than were the people generally of the South, he replied:—"My troops looked upon the war as a necessary evil, and went through it." It was a low sentiment for an army; and General Lee in his testimony evidently made the mistake of transferring his own passionless character to his soldiers. A great army must have an inspiration beyond the mere conviction of performing a painful duty; it must have resentment, passion, ambition, those emotions which stir men to die at the call of their leader; and, however admirable General Lee may have been, in his own person, from his *quasi* asceticism in the war, it is certain that in this respect he was defective as a commander.

The discriminating reader will perceive that we are not writing an encomium of General Lee; we are attempting a just account of the man, and we must maintain both the debtor and creditor sides in Fame's great ledger. We suppose there are some silly and coarse people in the world, who resent any shadow in the portraiture of the heroes they accept as depreciation; who can bear nothing but the raw and garish colors of the dauber of praise; but we are persuaded that the true harmony of all human character, and its truthfulness require that mixture of light and shade which Nature displays even in the most perfect creations. The writer is an admirer of General Lee, but not a servile one. He perceives at least one serious shadow in his character, that marked and somewhat marred his career. It was a negativeness that bordered on a weak neutrality, which perhaps originated rather in a moral casuistry than in constitutional timidity. It was the lack of self-assertion rather through a morbid conscience, than a weakness of will or intellect; an indisposition of the man to go beyond a technical or professional line of duty, or to do any works of supererogation. Anyhow, we can but consider it a fault of character. It is true that General Lee may, to some extent, have been admirable in illustrating a type of greatness without that vigorous, aggressive selfishness, that has usually imprinted history with remarkable successes, and which, according to a certain theory of human greatness, is a necessary element of it; but it is not admirable when this lack of selfishness becomes a weak amiability, the lack of individualism, of force, degenerating to a degree of negativeness and indifference. We have no idea of disputing the greatness of General Lee, and we mention an infirmity only to deplore it by the side of so many virtues. If his sense of duty was morbid and paltry in some regards, yet the quality of mind from which these excesses sprung was a noble one; and, taken with the even development of his faculties and the purity of his character, constituted that pleasing, Washington-like type of greatness, which partakes both of the moral and intellectual, and fairly distributes the practical virtues of life. No candid person will doubt the fair and honorable place which General Lee holds in the history of the war; although he may be permitted to doubt whether, with something of the egotism of genius, he might not have made it more brilliant with respect to his own fame, and more useful in serving the true interests of his country.

The man whom the South most loved, and would have most honored, refused the duties which they would have imposed upon him, as supreme military ruler of the Confederacy. In the sense in which the office of Commander-in-chief was urged upon him, he would have absorbed nearly all the powers of Mr. Davis, the government of the Confederacy being almost purely military, and all its concerns capable of being rated as military affairs. But in the sense in which he accepted the nominal title, he took nothing from Mr. Davis's powers, still deferring to his authority, and using the discretion which the popular choice conferred upon him only in the tone of suggestion to the President, whom he still considered his superior.

The kindly relations between himself and Mr. Davis were not for a moment disturbed, although the partizans of the two were in the most violent collision. General Lee had from his natural habit of self-negation and deferential etiquette, the happy faculty of managing the President to a degree which others dared not attempt; and although he might not have been always guilty of calculating the vanity of the latter, the deference and respect he showed, bred out of his natural disposition, were very soothing and grateful to Mr. Davis, and secured the greatest amount of Executive favor for the modest and uncomplaining commander. But whatever the motives that governed President Davis in his attachment to Lee, it was a fortunate instance of well-bestowed confidence. The Confederacy had reason to congratulate itself that, for once, the obstinacy of the President was set out in the direction of what was right—that Robert E. Lee was a single exception to that caprice, which had removed Johnston, which had persecuted Beauregard, and which had once driven Stonewall Jackson to the point of sending in his resignation to the War Department;* which had made such appointments

* It has been stated in an unscrupulous panegyric of Mr. Davis, as additional evidence of his just perceptions of military worth, that he steadily sustained Jackson as well as Lee. The statement has generally been accepted as true, in ignorance of the curious fact of a quarrel which Mr. Davis—or at least the War Department—had with this famous commander, and in consequence of which he sent in his resignation from the army as early as January, 1862. It was an instance of one of the characteristic dissensions of the President; he wishing to put General Loring over Jackson in the campaign of the Valley of Virginia (as he did "granny" Holmes over Price in the Trans-Mississippi), or, at least, refusing to subject the former to the authority that Jackson claimed to direct his forces. The letter of resignation was actually sent to Richmond. Jackson proposed to submit to "the will of God," as he humbly interpreted what others considered the human injustice of Mr. Davis. Governor Letcher, hearing of such a letter, took the bold liberty of withdrawing and suppressing it; wrote to Jackson to consider the claims which the *State*

as Lovell, Bragg, Pemberton, Hood, Holmes; and which only needed, to cap the climax of grotesque selections to command Confederate armies, that Northrop, Mr. Davis's last discovery of military genius in the guise of the civilian, should be sent to the field along with Henry A. Wise, the supreme absurdity of the war, a shallow-brained and large-mouthed charlatan—in peace, the elder edition of George Francis Train, Colorado Jewett, and other notoriety hunters—in war, a scare-crow made up of buckskin leggings, flint-lock pistols, and profanity.

But although there was no personal controversy between Mr. Davis and General Lee, the latter continuing undisturbed in the confidence and favor of the Executive, as commanding the army of Virginia, and the former being yet supreme military ruler of the whole Confederacy, it is interesting to observe what was the conduct of the President towards the last effort of popular opposition to his administration, which was practically to depose him. There was no quarrel with Lee, but there was a deadly one with the party that attempted to use him, and to put him in the attitude of the superior of the President in military affairs. Yet the conduct of Mr. Davis was very singular, and is not easily understood, unless we regard him as attempting the most violent affectation. In his public commentary on what could not have been less than an attempt to degrade him, he exhibited no temper whatever; he even made a show of alacrity to have Lee appointed com-

of Virginia had upon him, and which were involved in his relations with the Confederacy and Mr. Davis, however unpleasant they might be; and, at last, prevailed upon him to withdraw his resignation, and to retain "the sword which might have been dropped in an obscure quarrel, and was yet to carve out the most brilliant name of the war."

mander-in-chief; but all the time affecting not to understand the object which the popular mind had in this appointment—the real design of Congress. He might have been unwilling to expose to the world the breadth and depth of the disaffection of the Confederacy towards himself, the prospect of an intestine conflict in the midst of war; or he might have been unwilling to show to Congress how deeply he was wounded by its vote of want of confidence, and to give to his enemies the pleasure of seeing him suffer from shame or resentment. Whatever the motive, the President took the movement against his authority with affected ease, and sought to evade its significance by professing not to understand it, and putting upon it a construction of which it was logically and essentially incapable. It was an attempt at evasion, the most remarkable of all his sinister diversions on popular sentiment.

The Legislature of Virginia passed a resolution declaring that "the appointment of General Robert E. Lee to the command of all the armies of the Confederate States would promote their efficiency, and operate powerfully to reanimate the spirits of the armies, as well as of the people of the several States, and to inspire increased confidence in the final success of our cause." President Davis replied that he had desired to surrender all military affairs to General Lee, but that the latter persisted in his refusal to accept a trust of such magnitude. He said: "The opinion expressed by the General Assembly in regard to General R. E. Lee, has my full concurrence. Virginia cannot have a higher regard for him, or greater confidence in his character and ability, than is entertained by me. When General Lee took command of the Army of Northern Virginia, he was in command of all the armies of the Confederate States by my order of assignment. He continued in this general command, as well as in the immediate command of the Army of Northern Virginia, as long as I would resist his opinion that it was necessary for him to be relieved from one of these two duties. Ready as he has ever shown himself to be to perform any service that I desired him to render to his country, he left it for me to choose between his withdrawal from the command of the army in the field, and relieving him of the general command of all the armies of the Confederate States. It was only when satisfied of this necessity that I came to the conclusion to relieve him from the general command, believing that the safety of the capital and the success of our cause depended, in a great measure, on then retaining him in the command in the field of the Army of Northern Virginia. On several subsequent occasions, the desire on my part to enlarge the sphere of General Lee's usefulness, has led to renewed consideration of the subject, and he has always expressed his inability to assume command of other armies than those now confided to him, unless relieved of the immediate command in the field of that now opposed to General Grant."

We are almost forced to a sense of pity that so disingenuous a statement, and one of such duplicity as that contained in the correspondence indicated above, should have originated from the President of the Southern Confederacy. The position which General Lee held in 1862, described above as "command of all the armies of the Confederate States," had attached to it the condition "*with the advice and direction of the President*;" and General Lee, having that circumscribed authority, was nothing more than part of "Mr. Davis's military family," his advisor or confessor; while the present demand was that he should have independent, supreme control of the armies, and supercede the military authority of the President. Mr. Davis must have known the extent of this demand, must have known that there was nothing conditioned of his "advice and direction" in the appointment now sought for Lee; must have known that the public sentiment was not to be satisfied with the repetition of the folly of this duplex command, as in 1862—the wretched and worn farce of the *alter ego* in his military administration. He must have known the extent of the revolutionary design upon his authority; any one who understood the force of words could see it; any one who looked at the popular excitement could not help perceiving that the question was of the substance of the government, and any one whose vanity was so easily alarmed as that of Mr. Davis, could not have remained insensible of a conspiracy so great against his authority. It was an affectation of ignorance and of indifference, that, of itself, would have been pitiful enough, without the addition to it of studied misrepresentation—of what we are painfully compelled to designate a positive act of falsehood.

But while Mr. Davis practised an appearance of carelessness, in public, with regard to the popular discontent that threatened him so seriously, and while he found General Lee accommodating him with personal assurances of undiminished deference to his authority, he nursed, in private, a fierce and unrelenting resentment. He felt, although unwilling from shame or from policy to acknowledge it in public, that the Virginia Legislature and the Confederate Congress had done him an unpardonable indignity in asking him to give up the greater portion of the authority which the early choice of the people had conferred upon him, and which he undoubtedly held under the letter of the guaranties of the Constitution. It was a deep and rankling wound. In his private conversation, and in his household, there were said to be unrestrained expressions of rage and defiance. On one occasion, Mr. Henry, a Senator from Tennessee, who had formerly been the ablest and most eloquent advocate of the President in the higher branch of Congress, was paying a social visit to the Executive mansion, when Mrs. Davis said abruptly, "So you, too, Mr. Henry, have turned against my husband!" "Madam," replied the Senator, "I voted that General Lee should be appointed commander-in-chief; not because I had ceased my confidence in or respect for your husband, but the people required it; their confidence, it appears, has not been so constant as mine; and you should know that in matters of government, for a ruler not to have the people's confidence is almost as bad as to deserve the deprivation. At least, Mr. Davis may console himself with the consciousness that he has not deserved the condemnation which the people wills." "I think," replied the lady, warmly, "I am the person to advise Mr. Davis; and if I were he, I would die or be hung before I would submit to the humiliation that Congress intended him."

With Mr. Davis so much inflamed, in fact, by the action of Congress, and with that body, on the other hand, smarting under the sense of defeat which it has sustained from the impracticableness of General Lee, there was but little prospect of any serious and effective legislation for the remaining days of the Confederacy. An open war was declared between them soon after the *fiasco* of Lee. The work of making laws and the public cares were subordinated to an angry, personal controversy; messages and resolutions of censure were bandied between the President and Congress, while legislation stood at a dead-lock. It appeared they could agree upon nothing, and that every incident of intercourse was a new exasperation. It was a scandalous quarrel. Congress sat in secret session, but its doors were imperfectly closed, and the walls could not contain the screaming rhetorics from which

Mr. Davis suffered. The contest continued until public indignation became fatigued with both parties, and until the popular excitement, which had so recently aimed at the dignity of a revolution, was turned to disgust or indifference.

CHAPTER XXVII.

Resignation of Mr. Seddon from President Davis's Cabinet—Ugly Developments in the War Department—How Mr. Seddon's Resignation was Forced by a Delegation of Congress—Mr. Davis's Angry Defiance—Daring Response of Congress—Condition of the Confederate Treasury—Empirical Remedies in Congress—A Frightful Tax Law—The Infirm Temper of Congress—Heroic Appeals of the Press—The South yet far from Material Exhaustion—Remarkable Statement of General Lee respecting the Resources of the Confederacy—Application of it to Theory of the Failure of the War—A Proposition to Arm the Slaves, a Desperate Remedy—Reluctant Recommendation of it by Mr. Davis—Summary of Arguments for and against it—Public Opinion Decided by a Letter from General Lee—A Gross Fallacy Contained in this Measure—Remarkable Concession of the Confederate Government to the Anti-Slavery Party of the North—Jefferson Davis, as an Abolitionist—Reflections on the Little Regret Shown by the South for the Loss of Slavery—The Law of Negro Enlistments as Finally Passed—A Farcical Conclusion—A Negro Parade in Capitol Square—Congress Expiring in a Recrimination with President Davis.

THE wordy warfare of the last days of the Confederate Congress produced, as we have already indicated, nothing but public demoralization. In the midst of the greatest distresses and abuses, it was able to effect no considerable measure of re-organization, to execute no practical scheme of relief. Nothing was done, beyond some partial and imperfect laws that accomplished but little good, to strengthen the army, to improve the condition of the treasury, or to revive the confidence of the people. We have remarked in the preceding chapter, that, in the midst of necessities so great, Congress did not produce a single measure of importance, and we have shown how it was defeated in its controversy with the President. A slight exception to this observation may be named in the forced resignation of Mr. James Seddon, Secretary of War; but as the design to reform Mr. Davis's Cabinet was arrested there, and as Mr. Seddon resigned from a large share of personal motive, and without consulting the President, the event had neither great effect nor significance.

But it was the occasion of a manifestation of temper on the part of Mr. Davis that was not without interest. Mr. Seddon was one of the President's "pets;" he had succeeded Mr. Benjamin in the office of Secretary of War; an utterly heartless politician, a conspirator by nature, of little ability but with great disposition for intrigue, a man always in the condition of servility to some other, and one not above the suspicion of administering his office for private gain, he had become in his office as odious to the public as he had proved useful to Mr. Davis. Mr. Foote had brought out by a committee of investigation in Congress a curious incident in his administration—a small circumstance, but one so neatly proved and so sharply defined that it gave a fatal wound to his reputation. It appeared in unquestioned evidence that while Mr. Seddon had been impressing the grain of the Virginia farmers at nominal prices, he had sold his own crop of wheat to the government at forty dollars a bushel, then the equivalent of two dollars in gold; and that the price thus established thereafter for this staple, and which he had raised for his own selfish profit, had had the effect of suddenly depreciating the whole currency of the Confederacy. In a failing and sensitive currency subject to alarms it is surprising what vast and sudden effects may be produced by apparently the slightest causes. In the summer of 1864, the paper money of the Confederacy had shown some symptoms of revival, and was then received and paid at the rate of twenty for one. But when it was known that a member of Mr. Davis's Cabinet who was supposed to know the true state of affairs had doubled the price of wheat, the twenty dollar scale was discarded every where, and in a single day, as it were, without any military disaster, without any other event than that in the wheat market, the currency of the Confederacy fell from twenty for one to forty for one; in effect cheating Mr. Seddon out of his profits, but inspiring a popular distrust of the money, from which it never recovered.

In January, 1865, the Virginia delegation in Congress addressed to the President an earnest petition for a change in his Cabinet, expressing their want of confidence in the capacity and services of its members. They represented that the public spirit was depressed, that the apprehensions for the public safety were increased by the belief that the public misfortunes were at least partially the result of mismanagement, and that one of the most important measures to be adopted was a reconstruction of the Cabinet. Mr. Seddon, being a Virginian, and recognizing the censure as coming from Virginians, and therefore as peculiarly applicable to himself, and conscious of the excessive unpopularity he had incurred in the administration of his office, determined to resign, and thus appease the public indignation against himself.

Mr. Davis was unaware of this determination of his Secretary until his letter of resignation was sent in to be accepted. He declined to accept it, and earnestly besought Mr. Seddon to continue in office, as his resignation would be interpreted as a triumph of Congress and would found other insolent demands on the Executive. Mr. Seddon insisted on resigning; he had no hope of repairing his reputation, and it is not improbable that he wished to withdraw from the catastrophe he saw approaching, and to retreat to the seclusion of his country home. But Mr. Davis was determined that the event should not bear any significance of concession on his part, either to the demands of Congress or the clamor of the people. He went out of his way; he made a violent occasion in a correspondence published in the newspapers to declare that Mr. Seddon's resignation would in no manner change the policy or course of his administration. In words not to be mistaken he thus threw down his defiance to Congress and the country, and practically proclaimed that he held his government above public sentiment and inaccessible to its appeals.

To this defiance Congress replied with a spirit which, if translated into action, would have been admirable enough. It declared, through an address of the Virginia delegation, replying to the President's ill-tempered publication: "That the friendly advice of a delegation, or the more authentic counsel of Congress, should be repelled in such a manner, with such claims, and at such a time, is a circumstance which we deplore for the sake of the country, and, let us add, for the sake of the President. It will not provoke us to a resentful controversy; it cannot abate our devotion to the public cause; it does not alter our principles of action. But since, by the publication of this correspondence, members of the Cabinet have (probably with their consent) been placed before the tribunal of public opinion, at issue with the Virginia delegation upon the question whether they should have remained or been retained in office, notwithstanding the condition of our country and all the indications of public sentiment, this delegation do not recoil from that issue."

In the midst of other distresses, the condition of the Confederate Treasury had fallen to a point from which it was next to impossibility to recover it. The extent of the public grief and alarm on this subject may be judged from the measures which were proposed to meet the crisis. There were still vast stores of cotton and tobacco in the South, and it was proposed in Congress, to lay a special and heavy export duty on them as long as there was a chance of working them to market through the blockade. There were members who favored yet more exacting measures, who thought that in the altered condition and circumstances of the government, it should take the cotton and tobacco, as it already did the wheat, corn, meat and other products of the country. The latter had been taken at rates far below their market value—why should the cotton and tobacco be spared; and if the government did not take them the enemy would, and the accumulation of these staples at different points were already standing invitations to the rapacity of the Federal armies. Another measure of financial relief was debated. It was proposed to call upon the States to give up to the Confederate government the benefit of their separate State credits; but this application had been made more than a year before to the extent of having the States endorse the Confederate debt, had been rejected by most of them and favorably answered by a few, and it was scarcely to be supposed that they were better prepared now to signify thus their confidence in the issue of the war, and to pin their credit on Mr. Memminger's notes. The result was that neither scheme of finance referred to was perfected by Congress; that on this subject, as on others, it squandered public expectation in wandering and fruitless debate. There were other schemes to be counted by the dozen, and not necessary to be repeated here. They were merely evidences of the uncertainty of Congress. Nothing was actually done to relieve the Treasury. Indeed it was not until March, 1865, that Congress agreed upon a measure of taxation; and the monstrous provisions of this—such as a tax of twenty-five per cent. on all profits of business which exceeded twenty-five per cent. of the capital invested in it, and a tax of twenty-five per cent., payable in kind, on all the gold and silver in the Confederacy—could never have been carried into execution if the enemy had not intervened to end, alike, all the troubles and all the aspirations of the Southern Confederacy in the early days of April, 1865. On the subject of Confederate finance, there was to the end of the war a vast expenditure of ingenuity; but it is remarkable that in the last session of Congress, not a single measure was produced on this subject beyond a tax bill. The empiricisms displayed in this Congress; the violence of reforms suggested, but never carried out; the increased volume of debate, yet the scantiness of results; a condition in which legislation was no longer matured through leaders, but lost in the differences of the views of individuals, and in which all party organization was gone but that which was held together by the sympathy of opposition to Mr. Davis, suggested that weak and wandering condition of mind which precedes settled despair, that vague uneasiness in which men, expecting great misfortunes, lose their readiness and self-possession, and cannot bear to have either their hopes or their fears defined.

While the affairs of the Confederacy thus visibly declined, and while the neglects and distresses of its government were thus unrepaired or unrelieved, it is to be remarked that the press of the South never ceased its appeals to the public. It was the one element in the contest that, to the last, never lost its integrity or fervor. The ability, the genius, the dexterity which the newspaper press illustrated in educating and inspiring the South in its great contest of arms, especially when viewed in contrast with the intellectual barrenness it has shown in later years, constitutes really a historical feature of the war. The Richmond press had a power and brilliancy that were remarked over the world; and it might scarcely be recognized in the servile and insipid papers now issued from the diminished capital of Virginia. During the war it boasted, among its contributors, such names as John M. Daniel, John Mitchell, Robert W. Hughes, Patrick Henry Aylett and Judah P. Benjamin. The pens of such men were busy to the last, in the attempt to animate the South and to improve its confidence in the war.

Within three months of the fall of Richmond, one of its journals printed the picture which has been so repeatedly upheld in these pages—sufficiency of all the material resources of the South to continue the war, provided only the spirit of the people could be revived, so as to use them. It said:—"Several persons have employed themselves lately in preparing statistical tables of the wealth, food, and fighting men, remaining in the Confederacy, subject to the command of the government. They prove conclusively that the amount of all these things is still very great—enormous—sufficient to support far greater efforts than the Confederacy has yet made. To question the accuracy of their facts is far from our purpose; indeed their truth has been so long and so well known to all who have examined the subject, that the proof and tabular exposition seem to them quite superfluous, and even uninteresting. Material exhaustion is not yet felt by the mass of the nation; not felt in the slightest or most distant degree. It will never be felt. But the nation may soon suffer from moral exhaustion. The country will never be unable, if willing, to supply the wants of its government, but it may easily become unwilling; and then no pressure of legislation will be of much value. Pressure will obtain only those few drops which trickle from the squeezed orange, and soon get nothing at all. These Southern States are lands of Goshen.—A hot summer and a fertile soil will always produce a superabundance of bread and meat. They contain five millions of the best fighting people in the world, and can always supply three hundred thousand arms-bearing men in the prime of life. The extent of their territory is so great, that its real occupation by the armed forces of two or three such nations as that we are fighting is inconceivable. The enemy is perfectly aware of the fact, and does not base his hope of subjugation on the practical application of main strength, but upon the submission of the will, and consequent inability, to contend to the last extremity, which he expects to see at some time spread over the land. That is, in fact, the only contingency on which the subjugation of the South is possible. The Southern States are in no danger so long as the spirit of the people is what it has hitherto been. But let us not be blind to the truth, that there is such a thing possible as a decay of national confidence and a death of national spirit. There is such a thing as *heart-break* for nations as for individuals. There are such things as hopelessness and despair, lethargy and apathy. A conviction that all that it will do must come to naught, all sacrifices it can make be rendered vain by an irremediable cause,—a conviction resting on rational grounds, both of reflection and experiment, will produce this state of feeling in any nation, however heroic and however obstinate."

Neither was the picture, nor the reflections subscribed to it overdrawn. On the 11th of February 1865, General Lee wrote deliberately and conscientiously in one of his general orders:—"*Our resources, fitly and vigorously employed, are ample.*" With what consistency, in the face of this supreme and unquestionable testimony—the testimony of a man who never made an extravagant statement, and whose word no one in the South had ever disputed—could it be said that the Confederacy surrendered, not more than sixty days later, from actual physical inability to carry on the war! The fact is that those who hunt excuses for the loss of the Southern Confederacy in merely external circumstances, and neglect the maladministration of Mr. Davis and its consequences in their estimate, are generally persons who seek to cover up by a gross and impudent fallacy their own implication in the follies of the President of whom they were partizans, and to conceal their own share of responsibility in the work of destruction.

In the list of reforms and rumors debated in the last session of Congress, and bandied between that body and the President, one more remains to be noticed—a measure after the fashion of the legislation we have already, vast in conception, but an utter failure in execution. It was a measure of profound interest; and although a dwarfed birth was the consequence of the excessive labor of debate, the whole subject is so vitally connected with moral questions in the war, that we cannot pass it with the slight notice it has heretofore obtained from those who are inclined to measure the spaces of history by the external event produced, rather than by the principle involved.

We refer to the proposition to arm the Negro slaves in the South, and to enlist them in the Confederate service. Such an idea had, as early as the autumn of 1864, found some expression in the newspapers, the uniform theory being that the Negro soldier should be emancipated at the end of the war, and that this prospect would hold out an appropriate reward for his services, and stimulate them to the highest degree of efficiency. But the discussion was general, speculative, and several months elapsed after the first allusions we have described, and before the arming of the slaves was considered as a probable measure, and had become a subject of practical argument. The public mind had to be brought up by degrees to the calm contemplation of a reform so radical; had to be delicately managed to support so great a surprise, and to put itself on familiar terms with so thorough a change of its traditions and old associations.

Mr. Davis slowly and reluctantly progressed to the open advocacy of the employment of the slaves as soldiers. In his official message of the 7th of November, 1864, he thought that no necessity had yet arisen for resort to such a measure; but he added: "Should the alternative ever be presented of subjugation, or of the employment of the slave as a soldier, there seems no reason to doubt what should then be our decision." As events progressed, and under influences hereafter to be indicated, Mr. Davis was forced from this equivocal position and was found recommending to Congress the enlistment of the Negro in all the breadth of this measure; and, at last, when in March, 1865, an imperfect bill was passed to obtain Negro recruits, he wrote, with but little consistency in view of his earlier message, although justly enough with reference to the delay: "Much benefit is anticipated from this measure, though far less than would have resulted from its adoption *at an earlier date,* so as to afford time for their organization and instruction during the winter months."

Meanwhile the question of employing Negro soldiers had been debated from a variety of stand-points, with great excitement, and upon a singularly nice balance of arguments, affirmative and negative. In favor of the measure it was urged that the Negro could be effectively used as a soldier, that the experiment had already been determined in the Northern armies, where two hundred thousand Negroes had already been put under arms and had proved serviceable soldiers; that the military experience of all nations had shown that a severe discipline was capable of making soldiers from almost any human material; and that the South could use the Negro to better advantage as a soldier than the North could; that it could offer superior inducements to his good service by making him a freeman in his own home, instead of turning him adrift at the end of the war in a strange and inhospitable country, and that it could furnish him officers who could better understand his nature, and better develope his good qualities than could his military taskmaster in the North. These views were not a little plausible, and they founded some pleasant calculations. It was estimated by Secretary Benjamin that there were six hundred and eighty thousand black men in the South of the same ages as the whites then doing military service. Again, if there was any doubt of their efficiency at the front, and until they were educated to bear the fire of the enemy there, they might be employed in other parts of the military field—they might be put in the trenches; and General Ewell, who commanded the immediate defences of Richmond had declared that with a Negro force thus employed on the interior lines of the capital, fifteen thousand white soldiers might be liberated from a disagreeable duty and be used by Lee on the enemy's front. As to emancipation as a reward of the Negro's services, it was said that Slavery was already in an expiring condition in the South on account of the shock given to it by the invasions and raids of the enemy, and the uncertainty of this property represented in the low prices it brought, the price of an average slave such as would have commanded before the war twelve or fifteen hundred dollars being now scarcely more than fifty dollars estimated in gold; and it was argued with great ingenuity and not without force, that, by a measure of emancipation the South might make a virtue of necessity, remove a cause of estrangement, however unjust, between it and the Christian world, and possibly neutralize that large party in the North, whose sympathy and interest in the war were mainly employed with the Negro, and would cease on his liberation.

These arguments were not without weight. Yet the reply to them was scarcely less in volume and power. It was said that the measure would be virtually to stake success in the war on the capacity and fidelity of Negro troops of which the South had no assurance; that they would desert at every opportunity; that the white soldiers of the South would never bear association with them, and that their introduction into the army would be the signal of disaffection and mutiny; that the proposed liberation of slaves becoming soldiers was to give up the most important of the objects of the war, and to abandon every ground assumed at its commencement: that it would be a fatal confession of weakness to the enemy, and that it would be a resort to a low and dishonorable alliance far more shameful that that of which the North had been guilty in recruiting its armies. The cry of "Abolitionism" was used with most effect. It was declared that the South was about to inflict upon itself the very evil to avoid which it had professed to the world that it had separated from the North, and that thus while lowering the dignity of its cause it would also divest it of its justification, and expose it to history as a useless and wanton controversy.

The tremulous balance of the Southern mind on the subject of Negro enlistments—the almost equal match of arguments, for and against—was determined by a single event, by the influence which one man in the Confederacy threw into the scale. It illustrates, indeed, the wonderful power which General Lee had to command the opinions and confidence of the people of the South, and suggests what must have been his vast superiority to Mr. Davis in this respect, that when, on the subject referred to, departing from his usual reticence or his indifference to the general affairs of the Confedracy—probably for a peculiar reason, as we have elsewhere intimated—he recommended, in a plain, open letter, the arming of the slaves, from that moment the measure should have obtained a decided, almost overwhelming popular majority in its favor, and been urged on Congress by the almost unanimous voice of the country. Before the declaration of Lee, the measure had been in such suspense that it was difficult to say on which side lay the majority of public opinion. Now Congress could have no doubt of the popularity of the measure; the recommendation of General Lee had reinforced its advocates, and had reconciled nearly the whole country to to it; and the only thing to fear was that the large slave-holding interest in Congress would prove too strong for both Lee and the people.

In a letter to Mr. Barksdale, a member of the House of Representatives, from Mississippi, and a confidential friend of Mr. Davis, General Lee declared that no time was to be lost in securing the military service of the slaves. He said:—"The enemy will certainly use them against us if he can get possession of them; and as his present numerical superiority will enable him to penetrate many parts of the country, I cannot see the wisdom of the policy of holding them to await his arrival, when we may, by timely action and judicious management, use them to arrest his progress." He advanced the opinion from his military experience, that the Negroes, under proper conditions, would make efficient soldiers, remarking that they furnished a more promising material than many armies of which we read in history, that owed their efficiency to discipline alone. On the subject of emancipation, and the stimulants to be supplied to obtain recruits, he wrote:—"I think those who are employed should be freed. It would be neither just nor wise, in my opinion, to require them to serve as slaves. The best course to pursue, it seems to me, would be to call for such as are willing to come with the consent of their owners. An impressment or draft would not be likely to bring out the best class, and the use of coercion would make the measure distasteful to them and to their owners. I have no doubt that if Congress would authorize their reception into service, and empower the President to call upon individuals or States for such as they are willing to contribute, with the condition of emancipation to all enrolled, a sufficient number would be forthcoming to enable us to try the experiment. If it proved successful, most of the objections to the measure would disappear, and if individuals still remained unwilling to send their negroes to the army, the force of public opinion in the States would soon bring about such legislation as would remove all obstacles."

It is a matter of greatest surprise that there should have occurred, neither to General Lee nor to President Davis, while occupied with the various arguments we have related on either side of the question of Negro enlistments, the great and important fallacy so obviously contained in such a measure. This fallacy was overlooked, and yet is not too much to say that it constitutes a page for the most important reflections on any part of the war. It is true enough that the object of the war was not the tenure of property in slaves, as claimed only by a narrow, insolent and selfish aristocracy of slave-holders, and to the extent of a remark of the Charleston *Mercury*, that "if the slaves were armed, South Carolina could no longer have any interest in prosecuting the war." But although Negro enlistments and consequent emancipation could not be construed—as we have seen the attempt made—to be an abandonment of the object of the war, which surely had higher objects than to protect a certain species of personal property, yet it is profoundly remarkable that this measure, in the shape prepared by President Davis and General Lee, contained a full justification of the Anti-Slavery party in the North, and to that extent, at least, surrendered the contest.

It cut under the traditions and theories of three generations in the South. The one essential, exclusive argument, outside of all technical reasonings, which supported Negro slavery in the South, was that that condition accommodated the fact of the natural inferiority of the Negro, that he obtained his best development, his maximum of civilization and happiness in the condition of a slave. Beyond this argument, all that has been written or spoken of "the Slavery Question," may be taken for technical defences—as, for instance, the guarranty of the Constitution; for if the slave-holder was *morally* a criminal, he was no better than any other criminal, who might boast or congratulate himself that the law did not reach his case, that the statute was defective—or as excesses or palliatives; for if the slave was well treated, contented, etc., this could not compensate for his loss of liberty any more than in the case of any other prisoner, if the fact was that he was captured from the condition to which nature had assigned him. Briefly, the *justification* of slavery in the South was the inferiority of the Negro; it being inferred from this that nature designed him to live in subordination to the white man, and that he was better placed as a slave for his own happiness than if thrust into a violent equality with a superior race. Yet we find Mr. Davis and his counsellors, in their scheme to use the Negro as a soldier side by side with the white man, thrusting him into an unnatural equality, and, in the promises of emancipation, virtually proclaiming that his former condition as a slave was an unhappy and injurious one, and holding out to him his freedom as a better state, something most desirable, a reward, a blessing, calculated to make him risk his life for it. It was a fatal inconsistency. By a few strokes of the pen the Confederate government had subscribed to the main tenet of the Abolition party in the North and all its consequences, standing exposed and stultified before the world. We repeat that the only ground on which the South could justify Slavery, was that it kept the Negro in his proper situation, in the condition that was best for him, where he reached his highest moral, intellectual and physical development, and could enjoy the full sum of his natural happiness; in short, that while living with the white man, in the relation of slave, he was in a state superior and better for him than that of freedom. Yet this important theory was destroyed by the Confederate government when it proposed that the Negro's freedom should be given to him as a reward for services to his country; and the very assumption of his capacity and fidelity in this service was the best argument that could be presented to show the injustice and oppression, and crime of slavery. If the Negro was fit to be a soldier, he was not fit to be a slave. If his freedom was to be offered as a reward, then it was a *desideratum*, a boon—it was a better state—a natural good of which the laws of the South had deprived him. Now this was the whole theory of the Abolitionists; and the world found it subscribed to, in circumstances which might be thought to compel sincerity—in what might be easily construed as an honest confession in a season of affliction and misfortune—by no less a person than Jefferson Davis.

The concession which was thus made to the Abolition party of the North by the Confederate Government on the subject of Slavery probably had an effect of which the mind of the South was unconscious, to reconcile it to the final loss of its peculiar institution that was soon to ensue in the conclusion of the war. It explains to some degree the easy assent which the South gave to the extinction of Slavery at the last, and indicates the progress which had been made in lessening its attachment to an institution which it had once esteemed essential to every interest it had on the face of the earth, and which had been placed as the corner-stone in the structure of the Southern Confederacy. There is no more just and profound surprise to the thoughtful historian than the little regret which the people of the South have manifested for the loss of Slavery, as compared with other consequences of the failure of the Confederate cause—and that too after the long and impassioned defence of this institution against the Abolitionists of the North; and the suggestion forcibly occurs how much of this defence must have been conventional and constrained, due simply to the resentment of Northern interference in this system of labor, rather than giving proofs of real attachment to it. Any how the little sorrow that the South has bestowed upon the death of Slavery, compared with other losses of the war, proves conclusively enough that it was an inferior object of the contest—surely not the chief cause and end of the war, as Northern writers have been forward to misrepresent.

But we return from these speculations to notice the practical result from them in the action of Congress. The result was, as we have intimated, to the last degree paltry and imperfect. For three months Congress labored in debate and had convulsive intercourse with the President; and the birth was a bill passed not until the 7th of March 1865—not much more than three weeks before the fall of Richmond—that brought the whole matter to an impotent and ridiculous conclusion. The law, as finally enacted was merely to authorize the President to receive into the military service such able-bodied slaves as might be patriotically tendered by their masters, to be employed in whatever capacity he might direct; no change to be made in the relation of owners of slaves, at least so far as it appeared in the bill. The fruits of this emasculated measure were two companies of blacks organized from some Negro vagabonds in Richmond, which were allowed to give balls at the Libby Prison and were exhibited in fine, fresh uniforms on Capitol Square, as decoys to obtain sable recruits. But the mass of their colored brethren looked on the parade with unenvious eyes, and little boys exhibited the early prejudices of race by pelting the fine uniforms with mud. The paltriness of the law referred to, was a stock of ridicule and the occasion of a new contempt for Congress. It was seriously interesting only as showing that vague desperation in the Confederacy which caught at straws; an indication of the want of nerve in it to make a practical and distinct effort for safety; and a specimen of those absurdly small laws of Congress, measured with reference to the necessities for which its legislation was invoked.

All hopes of reviving the war by any action of Congress had faded out and disappeared. The day of its final dissolution was near at hand; and yet there was nothing but trifles and quarrels to the end. It is, indeed, remarkable of the Confederate Congress, which had lived so dishonorably, giving so much of imbecile and disgraceful record to the Southern story of the war, that it should have fitly expired in a weak and disreputable recrimination with President Davis.

Its last official act was to raise a committee in the Senate to report upon a message in which Mr. Davis had reproved it for designing to abandon the affairs of the Confederacy, and to leave important interests unprovided for, as the enemy approached and pressed upon the capital. He wrote: "The capital of the Confederate States is now threatened, and it is in greater danger than it has heretofore been during the war." Congress replied that it had finished its legislation, that it proposed to adjourn, and that whatever culpability there might be for any improvidence of the Government, it did not lie at the doors of the legislative department. It adjourned on the 18th of March, 1865, unwilling to witness the end which it saw approaching, and repeating the cowardice of its flight in 1862, refused to take any official lot in the final catastrophe. Thus meanly expired a legislative body, remarkable in the annals of the world for its weakness and ignorance, whose record was a constant degradation of the Confederate name, and whose composition and nature will afford to the future historian an especial study among the contradictions and curiosities of the late war.

CHAPTER XXVIII.

An Unexpected Test of the Spirit of the South—The Fortress Monroe Peace Commission—Mr. Blair's Visit to Richmond—Review of Peace Movements in the Confederacy—Critical Analysis of the Peace Party in the South—Three Elements or Classes in it—Mr. Davis Ultimately Joins the Third Class of Peace Men—Governor Vance's Exposition of this Class—Correspondence between him and President Davis—The Idea in this Correspondence Renewed, a Year thereafter—The Fortress Monroe Commission, the Result—Secret Design of Mr. Davis to Kill off the Peace Movement—How this Design was Served by the Official Report of the Commissioners—A Day of Speech-Making in Richmond—Speeches of Mr. Hunter and Mr. Benjamin—Unexpected Appearance of Mr. Davis in Metropolitan Hall—The Most Eloquent Speech of his Life—It was never Reported—Summary of it—A Brief Excitement in the South Followed by a Failure of Resolution—The Character of the Southern People Impaired—Fatal Defect of Mr. Davis as a Ruler in his Ignorance of the People—His Power to Inspire the People Gone—A Curious Reason for the Failure to Re-animate the South after the Fortress Monroe Commission—Doubts Thrown on the Truth of the Report of the Commissioners—Singular and Remarkable Delusion of the South as to the Consequences of Submission—Extent of the False Trust in the Enemy's Generosity—"Subjugation" Treated as a Scare-Crow—Hopes of Saving Something from the Abolition of Slavery—A Singular Conversation of President Lincoln—An Amiable Episode of the Fortress Monroe Commission—Impressive Warnings in Richmond Against a "Deceptive Reconstruction"—To what Degree the South was Conquered by Anticipations of the Generosity of the North—A Justification of the War on Retrospect—Examples of the Credulity of the South—How it has Lingered Since the War.

In the month of February, 1865, an event came from an unexpected quarter, and apparently of the enemy's own motion, which, for a time, afforded some prospect of re-animating the South in the war, and arming it with a new resolution to continue it, even despite the disaffection and distrust which had been produced by its own government. This event was the memorable Fortress Monroe Commission; the declaration there of the harsh and arrogant ultimatum of the North; the rebuff of the Southern Commissioners; and what was apparently the authentic statement of the consequences of the surrender of the South, which were thought by some persons, calculated to raise the efforts of the Confederacy, regarding it, as they did, in that condition and spirit where the insolent demands of an enemy are more likely to give increase of resentment and resolution than to compel assent and produce the indifference of despair. But this test of the true condition of the Southern mind—the question whether the point to which its hopes had sunk, was that where an increased menace would sink it still further, or that where it would cause it to rebound—was yet to be determined; and the decision was eagerly looked for by parties standing on each side of the question, and each looking at it from his own stand-point of speculation.

In the preceding month of January, Mr. Francis P. Blair had visited Richmond, coming from Washington; and although he disclaimed any official character, his earnest application to Mr. Davis for a letter that would signify his willingness to send or receive commissioners authorized to treat of peace, disclosed a distinct purpose in which he must have been serving the views of the Federal Government. The letter was given. But it was in Mr. Davis's usual equivocal and circumlocutory way when approaching the powers at Washington; it being addressed to Mr. Blair himself, and containing such a specimen of diplomatic certainty and perspicuity, as that he was willing to "renew the effort to enter into forms by which the public interests are to be subserved." The result of the irregular and tentative mission of Mr. Blair, was that President Lincoln and his Secretary of State, Mr. Seward, were met near Fortress Monroe by three commissioners appointed by Mr. Davis (Vice-President Stephens, Senator Hunter, and Judge Campbell); that a conference of some hours took place; and—what is most remarkable—that although this conference resulted in not a single article of agreement, it ended with mutual satisfaction —the South promising itself that a *sine qua non* so harsh as that which was submitted would give fresh inspiration to its war, and the North (or the dominant party there) congratulating itself that the Washington Government might be trusted to abate none of the objects of the war, to show no weak mercy to "rebels," who might be regarded as already driven to the attitude of supplication, but to exact all demands it had ever made upon an enemy now sure to be conquered.

But before proceeding to the minutes of this conference, we must go back over a considerable space in the chronological order of the war. The true internal history of the Fortress Monroe Commission commences more than a year later than the time it actually met on board a steamer moored near the shores of Virginia. From the time the military fortunes of the Confederacy commenced to decline, and in exact inverse proportion to this decline, there had grown up a peace party in the South proposing in reality terms of submission, but scarcely venturing in public to do more than insist that the Richmond Government should open negotiations with the enemy on the pretence, which it knew to be false but which served its purpose of deceiving the people, that terms much short of subjugation could be obtained. We are thus describing the majority of the peace party in the South. But that party was really composed of three elements; and it is from failure to observe the distinctions of opinion in it, the want of a correct analysis, that it has suffered from a confused and sometimes unjust commentary from most of the writers who have assumed to criticise it. First, there was the old Union party proper, the "submissionists," who formed the early bulk of what came to be generally designated as the peace party of the South. Secondly, there was a large number of persons acting with them to the point of asking that an effort should be made at negotiations, under the delusion, which their more designing associates busily practiced upon them, that terms might be obtained from the enemy short of the sacrifice of the independence of the South. What was the hypocritical pretence of the "submissionists" was the sincere belief of those we may call the "optimists." This second element in the "peace movement" thus named for convenience, became, as we shall hereafter see, considerably enlarged and powerful towards the end of the war under the operation of peculiar influences. But there was a third party or class in this movement, yet more remarkable and of the most curious construction—which so far from coinciding with the "submissionists" was really the party of extreme Southern views, representing the most determined spirit of resistance to the North, yet joining persistently in the demand for peace negotiations, on the calculation that the result of them in what they imagined would be the rejection of all propositions other than the abject submission and ruin of the South, would inflame the war, and strengthen the resolution of the Confederacy to continue it.

To this third party belonged Governor Vance of North Carolina; and to it was finally won over President Davis, but not without difficulty, and not until near the close of the war. A correspondence between these men, more than a year before the date of the Fortress Monroe Commission, furnishes the proper logical commencement of the peace movement, so far as Mr. Davis was involved in it, and should be studied as a preface to the negotiations that preceded but a few weeks the close of the war. The letter of Governor Vance was brief and pithy, as follows:—

STATE OF NORTH CAROLINA, EXECUTIVE DEPARTMENT.
RALEIGH, December 30, 1863.

His Excellency President Davis: MY DEAR SIR:—After a careful consideration of all the sources of discontent in North Carolina, I have concluded that it will be impossible to remove it except by making some effort at negotiation with the enemy. The recent action of the Federal House of Representatives, though meaning very little, has greatly excited the public hope that the Northern mind is looking toward peace. I am promised by all men who advocate this course, that, if fair terms are rejected, it will tend greatly to strengthen and intensify the war feeling, and will rally all classes to a more cordial support of the Government. And, although our position is well-known, as demanding only to be let alone, yet it seems to me that for the sake of humanity, without having any weak or improper motives attributed to us, we might, with propriety, constantly tender negotiations. In doing so, we would keep conspicuously before the world a disclaimer of the responsibility for the great slaughter of our race, and convince the humblest of our citizens—who sometimes forget the actual situation—that the Government is tender of their lives and happiness, and would not prolong their sufferings unnecessarily one moment. Though statesmen might regard this as useless, the people will not, and I think our cause will be strengthened thereby. I have not suggested the method of these negotiations, or their terms. The effort to obtain peace is the principal matter. Allow me to beg your earnest consideration of this suggestion.

Very respectfully yours,
Z. B. VANCE.

On the 8th of January, 1864, President Davis wrote a long letter in reply, only some passages of which it is necessary to consider here. He wrote:—"We have made three distinct efforts to communicate with the authorities at Washington, and have been invariably unsuccessful. Commissioners were sent before hostilities were begun, and the Washington Government refused to receive them or hear what they had to say. A second time I sent a military officer with a communication addressed by myself to President Lincoln. The letter was received by General Scott, who did not permit the officer to see Mr. Lincoln, but promised that an answer would be sent. No answer has ever been received. The third time, a few months ago, a gentleman was sent, whose position, character, and reputation were such as to insure his reception, if the enemy were not determined to receive no proposals whatever from the government. Vice-President Stephens made a patriotic tender of his services, in the hope of being able to promote the cause of humanity; and although little belief was entertained of his success, I cheerfully yielded to his suggestion, that the experiment should be tried. The enemy refused to let him pass through their lines, or to hold any conference with them. He was stopped before he reached Fortress Monroe, on his way to Washington. To attempt again (in the face of these repeated rejections of all conference with us) to send commissioners or agents to propose peace, is to invite insult and contumely, and to subject ourselves to indignity, without the slightest chance of being listened to. . . .

"I cannot recall, at this time, one instance in which I have failed to announce that our only desire was peace, and the only terms which formed a *sine qua non* were precisely those that you suggested, namely, 'a demand only to be let alone.' But suppose it were practicable to obtain a conference through commissioners with the Government of President Lincoln, is it at this moment that we are to consider it desirable, or even at all admissible? Have we not just been apprized by that despot that we can only expect his gracious pardon by emancipating all our slaves, swearing allegiance and obedience to him and his proclamation, and becoming, in point of fact, the slaves of our own Negroes."

It appears from this correspondence, that Mr. Davis was then unwilling to essay negotiations with Washington; and from a close inspection of his letter, we cannot see that he fully apprehended Governor Vance's proposition. He rather manifested the idea to take the peace movement in its direct, literal and, perhaps, honest sense, as coming from that second class we have named in the composition of the peace party of the South—men who sincerely believed that the war might be mitigated or some of the consequences of surrender saved, if an opportunity could be secured to communicate and negotiate with the enemy. Mr. Davis appears to have been sufficiently disabused of such confidence in the generosity of the enemy, and greatly anxious to expel it from the popular mind of the South. He never contracted that confidence again; for although we have the story of Messrs. Clay and Thompson attempting to communicate with President Lincoln from Niagara Falls in the mid-summer of 1864, it is now well known that that so called "peace commission" was rather an experiment on the Democratic party of the North, then about to engage in a Presidential campaign, than the expression of a real desire to get to Washington and obtain the ear of Abraham Lincoln. After the correspondence with Governor Vance, Mr. Davis does not really appear in the operations of the peace party until more than a year, fraught with great fortunes, had elapsed—the date of the Fortress Monroe commission; and then only as representing that third element of the party we have described.

As the falling fortunes of the war pressed upon him, and as the clamors of the people assailed him, he appeared to the public to have retracted his opposition to the peace movement, and to have altered the views which he had expressed in the letter from which we have quoted. But the real fact was, that, without giving up anything of his opinions of the unyielding disposition of the enemy, he had taken the sudden resolution of trying Governor Vance's plan of consenting to an effort at negotiation with the enemy, which would appease the malcontents, and, if successful, as he had reason to expect, would intensify and strengthen the war feeling in the South. Thus, while in the minds of some leading persons in the Confederacy, the interview of the Southern commissioners with President Lincoln and Mr. Seward was a sincere experiment on the sentiment and temper of the Northern Government, Mr. Davis had, in fact, consented to it with the especial view of obtaining an ultimatum from the enemy so harsh as to exasperate the people of the South, and to put before them a plain alternative, which he calculated would be a continuation of the war, or an unconditional submission too absolute to be entertained. The secret thought in Richmond of the Fortress Monroe commission was thus, strangely enough, to kill off the "peace conferences" rather than to improve the growing tendency to negotiation. In some respects Mr. Davis calculated aright; but the scheme of re-animation utterly failed for peculiar reasons, which remain to be examined.

Of what took place at Fortress Monroe the following account was given under the official imprint of the Confederate Government, and published to the people of the South as a sufficient history of the negotiation:—

"*To the Senate and House of Representatives*
of the Confederate States of America:

"Having recently received a written notification, which satisfied me that the President of the United States was disposed to confer, informally with unofficial agents that might be sent by me, with a view to the restoration of peace, I requested Hon. Alexander H.

Stephens, Hon. R. M. T. Hunter, and Hon. John A. Campbell, to proceed through our lines, to hold a conference with Mr. Lincoln, or such persons as he might depute to represent him.

"I herewith submit, for the information of Congress, the report of the eminent citizens above named, showing that the enemy refuse to enter into negotiations with the Confederate States, or any one of them separately, or to give our people any other terms or guarantees than those which a conqueror may grant, or permit us to have peace on any other basis than our unconditional submission to their rule, coupled with the acceptance of their recent legislation, including an amendment to the Constitution for the emancipation of Negro slaves, and with the right, on the part of the Federal Congress, to legislate on the subject of the relations between the white and black population of each State.

"Such is, as I understand, the effect of the amendment to the Constitution, which has been adopted by the Congress of the United States.

"JEFFERSON DAVIS.

"EXECUTIVE OFFICE, Feb. 5, 1865."

RICHMOND, February 6th.

To the President of the Confederate States:

SIR—Under your letter of appointment of commissioners, of the 8th, we proceeded to seek an informal conference with Abraham Lincoln, President of the United States, upon the subject mentioned in the letter. A conference was granted, and took place on the 30th, on board the steamer anchored in Hampton Roads, where we met President Lincoln and Hon. Mr. Seward, Secretary of State of the United States. It continued for several hours, and was both full and explicit. We learned from them that the message of President Lincoln to the Congress of the United States, in December last, explains clearly his sentiments as to the terms, conditions, and mode of proceeding by which peace can be secured to the people; and we were not informed that they would be modified or altered to obtain that end. We understood from him that no terms or proposals of any treaty or agreements looking to an ultimate settlement would be entertained or made by him with the authorities of the Confederate States, because that would be recognition of their existence as a separate power, which, under no circumstances, would be done; and for like reasons, that no such terms would be entertained by him from the States separately; that no extended truce or armistice, as at present advised, would be granted or allowed, without the satisfaction or assurance in advance, of the complete restoration of the authority of the constitution and laws of the United States over all places within the States of the Confederacy; that whatever consequence may follow from the re-establishments of that authority, it must be accepted; but all individuals subject to the pains and penalties under the laws of the United States, might rely upon a very liberal use of the power confided to him to remit those pains and penalties if peace be restored. During the conference, the proposed amendments to the Constitution of the United States, adopted by Congress on the 31st, were brought to our notice.

These amendments provide that neither slavery nor involuntary servitude, except for crime, should exist within the United States or any place within its jurisdiction, and Congress should have power to enforce the amendments by appropriate legislation.

Of all the correspondence that preceded the conference herein mentioned, and leading to the same, you have heretofore been informed.

Very respectfully, your obedient servants,

A. H. STEPHENS,
R. M. T. HUNTER,
J. A. CAMPBELL.

According to this report, the commission had accomplished what Mr. Davis had desired in his scheme to revive or to increase in the South the animosity of the war. In substance it was the distinct, enlarged and insolent demand of Mr. Lincoln and his government, that the South should submit unconditionally to the rule of the Union and conform to the advanced position of that government on the subject of Slavery, which included an amendment to the Constitution abolishing this domestic institution of the South, a bill establishing a Freedmen's Bureau, and much other incidental legislation, stipulated as "laws of the United States," looking to a new construction of relations between the Negroes and the white men of the South, and to consequences even beyond a full concession to the original party of Abolition in the North. This was the version which the commissioners evidently desired should be made of their report by the popular mind of the South; to which, indeed, it was more addressed than to Mr. Davis. The report was carefully prepared, and every word of it appears to have been skilfully adjusted. It was designed to exclude all hopes of further negotiation for peace, and to summon the South to new and desperate resolution. It was a very scant document, and made the impression that those who represented the Federal government were singularly harsh and formal. There was nothing to break the force with which Mr. Davis had designed that it should strike the imagination of the South, and excite alike its resentment and its resolution.

As if in evidence of the design we have imputed to the government of Mr. Davis, the return of the commissioners was at once made the signal of numerous addresses to the people, in which the President himself, and such of the members of his Cabinet as had any faculty for oratory, took the stand of the speaker, and in their speeches, joined in the attempt to rally the spirit of the people with precisely the same argument—that almost any increase of trial and suffering in the war was preferable to submission to the insolent demands of the enemy. It was an attempt to infuse into the war a new element of desperate passion, as the reply of spirited men to the arrogance of a hated foe. The people of the South were to be taught to believe that the result of the conference at Fortress Monroe proved that every avenue to an honorable peace was closed, but what might be hewn out by the sword, and that they were fighting not only for the original prize of the war—independence—but for safety from the worst consequences in case the enemy should obtain their submission. Such a conclusion, it was argued, should nerve the arms of those who had hitherto been steadfast in the fight, and, on the other hand, rescue those who had been enfeebled by the imagination of reconciliation and generosity on the part of the enemy, and secure their adhesion to the prosecution of the war.

A day was taken for public speaking in Richmond, and calls were published in the newspapers for the people to hold mass-meetings, and renew their testimony of devotion to the Confederacy. In the African church, in the theatre, and in a large hall in the capitol, speakers' stands were erected and occupied the same day; business was suspended; and a long procession, in which walked some of the cabinet officers of Mr. Davis, designated as orators of the day, passed through the streets. The African church—which the white politicians of Richmond had for years been in the habit of appropriating for public meetings, as if there was no invasion of sanctity of so lowly a house of God as that where Negroes worshipped—was packed with an excited audience; its foul air rent with shouts and huzzas, and its crazed floor shaken under applause. The speaking continued until near sunset, and was resumed at night. The newspapers devoted almost their whole space to reports of the day, and described it as a triumph, a resurrection, a regeneration of the war no longer to be doubted. It was curious to observe how the different orators served the purpose which had brought them together. Mr. Hunter, one of the commissioners, addressed the multitude, and gave them to understand that Mr Lincoln had turned from the propositions of peace with cold insolence—

an insolence which he described as monstrous, since the Federal President "might have offered something to a people with two hundred thousand soldiers, and such soldiers under arms." The frightful apparition of subjugation was next introduced. "I will not attempt," said Mr. Hunter, "to draw a picture of subjugation. It would require a pencil dipped in blood to paint its gloom." Mr. Benjamin, Secretary of State, followed with yet more artful appeals to the multitude. He affected to witness the animation which he designed to produce, and spoke of it with exciting praises. "How great the difference in one short week! It seems an age, so magical has been the change! Hope beams in every countenance. We now know in our hearts that this people must conquer its freedom or die!" It is remarkable that the Confederate Congress, a few days later, adopted the same adroit style of taking for granted a change of popular sentiment. In an address to the people, it declared: "Thanks be to God, who controls and overrules the counsels of men, the haughty insolence of our enemies which they hoped would intimidate and break the spirit of our people is producing the very contrary effect."

To the volume of rhetorical appeal, President Davis himself added the most remarkable speech of his life. Two or three days before the meeting at the African church, and not more than six hours after the return of the commissioners, he had ascended the speaker's stand in the most unexpected way. It was the last public speech of the President of the Southern Confederacy, but, in all its circumstances, the most splendid and dramatic oration he had ever made. He appeared before the public without any announcement whatever. A meeting had been called at Metropolitan Hall, on Franklin street, by Governor Smith, to adopt resolutions on the part of the State of Virginia, responsive to what had taken place at Fortress Monroe; and there was a general surprise of the audience when the thin figure of Mr. Davis, in a worn suit of gray, stalked into the hall, and ascended the speaker's stand.

We have heretofore spoken of the power of Mr. Davis as an orator. On this occasion the author sat near him, and he does not recollect ever to have been so much moved by the power of words spoken for the same space of time. It appeared that the animation of a great occasion had for once raised all there was best in Mr. Davis; and to look upon the shifting lights on the feeble, stricken face, and to hear the beautiful and choice words that dropped so easily from his lips, inspired a strange pity, a strange doubt, that this "old man eloquent" was the weak and unfit President whom a large majority of his people had been recently occupied in despising and abusing. For more than an hour he held the audience by an appeal of surpassing eloquence. The speech was extempore, for he was frequently interrupted, and always spoke appropriately and at length to the subject suggested by the exclamations of the audience. There were no reporters present to preserve a speech which should have been historical; and, indeed, there was but one man connected with the Richmond press who fully understood the art of the short-hand writer. Mr. Davis frequently paused in his delivery; his broken health admonished him that he was attempting too much; but frequent cries of "go on" impelled him to speak at a length which he had not at first proposed. When he first appeared, erect at the speaker's stand, holding with his glittering eye the assembled crowd, there were tremendous cheers, and a smile of strange sweetness came to his lips as if the welcome assured him that decried as he was by the newspapers, and pursued by the clamor of politicians, he had still a place in the hearts of his countrymen. He spoke with an even, tuneful flow of words; the choicest language appeared to come from his lips without an effort; spare of gestures, his dilated form and a voice the lowest notes of which were distinctly audible, and which anon rose as a sound of a trumpet, were yet sufficient to convey the strongest emotions, and to lift the hearts of his hearers to the level of his grand discourse. The sentiment of his speech was that of imperious unconquerable defiance to the enemy; their insolent officials at Fortress Monroe little knew that they "talked *to their masters*," and that it would be their turn to ask for peace "before the summer solstice was reckoned;" and then changing the subject, he surveyed the whole field of the war, enumerated new hopes, and, at last, speaking of the private soldiers of the Confederacy, he commemorated their heroism and devotion, drew a picture of their sufferings, and in withering tones cursed the speculators who had traded and profited in their distress, and said the day might soon come when their ill-gotten gold would be divided in the camps of the country's defenders! He closed with a remarkable illustration drawn from history. He referred to the judgment which the world had passed upon Kossuth who had been so weak as to abandon the cause of Hungary with an army of *thirty thousand* men in the field. He spoke of the disgrace of surrender, if the Confederates should abandon their cause with an army on their side and actually in the field more numerous than those which had made the most brilliant pages in European history; an army more numerous than that with which Napoleon achieved his reputation; an army standing among its homesteads; an army in which each individual man was superior in every martial quality to each individual man in the ranks of the invader, and reared with ideas of independence, and in the habits of command!

The effect of these rhetorical stimulants could scarcely have been less than some temporary excitement. Hearing the huzzas in Richmond and reading the congratulations in the newspapers, the President and many around him were cheated into the belief that the people of the South had taken heart again, and that the war was about to be dated from a new era of popular enthusiasm. But the delusion was soon to be dispelled. There was no depth in the popular feeling thus excited; it was a spasmodic revival, or short fever of the public mind, ending in the most sickly and shameful response to what was undoubtedly, in all its circumstances, one of the most powerful appeals ever calculated to stir the heart and nerve the resolution of a people fighting for liberty. The sources of popular enthusiasm were dried up in the South, and it was past that period when any thing could be expected from it, beyond a temporary excitement for the most unparalleled insult, or a brief resentment of the most arrogant menace. The test to which we have referred in the opening of this chapter, as of the point to which the hope and spirit of the South had descended had been determined, and had proved to be such as where the bravado of an enemy, instead of raising men to new and passionate exertion, sinks them to the abject and timid counsels of submission. The condition of the South, following the brief excitement of appeals such as we have described, was, among the best of its people, a dull, helpless expectation, a blank despondency, and, among the worst of them, an increased alacrity to pursue the phantom of negotiation, and finally, as of course, to submit to the enemy.

Mr. Davis had calculated too much on the integrity of the Southern character. He had not yet realized—and to the last moment of the existence of the Southern Confederacy he never did realize—that that character had been impaired by what had been the terrible experiences of the war; and he persisted in believing that the troops which yet defended Richmond were soldiers of the same spirit as those who had won the battle of Manassas. He trusted too much in what he believed to be the unchangeable courage, the irreversible resolution, the untameable manhood of the Southern soldier A month after the African church revival, and when back sliders were numerous, he wrote in reproof of Congress, then meditating an adjournment, that he yet "reposed entire trust in the courage and constancy of the people." It was on the violent hypothesis of that constancy that he was insensible, to the last, of the condition of the country, and made most of those ludicrous miscalculations and grotesque prophecies which amused the North, and which divided the South on the question whether it should resent them as trifling with its intelligence, or pity and despise them as displaying, unconsciously, the real weakness of his judgment. A single, but a great misassumption explains much of that curious over-confidence of the President, which we have seen in other parts of this narrative, and have discussed on various grounds of speculation, and as proceeding from a mixture of causes. He was blind to the true condition of the South, partly because of the false media through which he viewed it. He looked at it through armies, which he yet supposed to be of men similar to those who had successfully fought the enemy five to one, and who, having won such victories once, might do it again. The mere list of Confederate victories was too often used as an argument, and an enumeration of names without any logical order in them—an instance of mere exclamations, *ad captandum vulgus*, drowning the voice of reason—was often thought sufficient to silence those who were inclined to debate seriously the prospects of the war, or who ventured to express misgivings of the future.

The people of the South were never understood by their President; and this first condition of a wise and powerful government—insight into the character of the people—was never performed. The principle of a wise democracy but repeats the apothegm of Machiavelli, that a nation is wiser and more constant than its leading men. A truth announced from sources so various, and inscribed alike by the wisdom and the experience of all ages, was conspicuously illustrated in the Southern Confederacy. President Davis never understood the people he was appointed to govern; and whatever there was of weakness and inconstancy in them—and there were certainly such exhibitions—were exceeded by his own weakness and inconstancy; and it is remarkable that he could never see them, either as exaggerated reflections of himself, or as effects of his own ignorance in government. If the people of the South are somewhat to be blamed for the want of proper spirit in the war, which they at last exhibited, Mr. Davis is much more to be blamed for having been in a great part the cause of such popular delinquency, and for not having performed the first duty of a wise governor—that of acquainting himself with the character of the people, and thus cultivating their virtues that they might over-balance their vices.

The Southern people had their virtues and their vices—their good and their bad traits of character, as any other people. All that there was among the first, of lively and peculiar courage as in contempt of danger, quickness of imagination, extravagant sensitiveness to indignity, a passion for romance, had been misdirected and abused in the war; and all that there was among the last, of variableness of temper, as in a tendency to despond easily, impatience of expectation, a disposition to brave peril rather than to wait on fortune, an insobriety of hopes and fears were brought out and cultivated by the ignorant and uncertain administration of Mr. Davis. The best qualities of his people he failed to develop, and their faults he unconsciously enlarged to his and their ruin. No wonder that they commenced to dissociate themselves from a government, which from ignorance of their character alone, could never have been in sympathy with them; to support its existence, without upholding its authority, to acquiesce, instead of applauding. Mr. Davis still held in his hands the reins of authority; but his power to inspire the people was gone, diminishing from the moment he became—instead of the orator, who had so easily inspired them by his speeches at the commencement of the war—the ruler who, by a long course of mistakes and abuses, was to impair their character and to forfeit their confidence. Now his words had to be taken along with his acts. The oration he made at Metropolitan Hall, designed to excite anew the spirit of the war, which his actions for nearly four years had depressed, was beautiful, admirable words as caught by the ears of his auditors; but when submitted to the reflections of their minds they were but dead types, the unavailing pretences of a man upon whom the public had already passed an irreversible judgment. Little did he know when animated in that oration, he accepted the mere temporary glow of an audience for a tribute and confirmation from the people, how powerless he had become to make a permanent impression on either the mind or heart of the South. Little did he feel when thus speaking, he prophesied the independence of the Confederacy "before the summer solstice," and pointed with disdain to the enemy he doomed, how near his own feet were to the brink of destructiou. Alas! the military events for the next few weeks were to nullify all that eloquence could accomplish, were to terminate the existence of the Southern Confederacy, and were to consign to a dim and voiceless prison him who, once, by his words had commanded the affairs and ruled the affections of six millions of people!

But there remains yet another reason to account for the failure to re-animate the South after the Fortress Monroe Commission—a reason that makes a historical discovery of such importance, and so connected with the times in which we live—with, indeed, the whole future of the South—that we must earnestly invoke for it the attention of the reader. In another part of this chapter, analyzing the peace party in the Confederacy, we have already referred to the rapid and wonderful growth of an opinion in the South, that, at the last, generous terms might be expected from the enemy; and although we have seen that this opinion was apparently so discouraged by the Fortress Monroe Commission—its discouragement being the very design of that commission, on the part of the President—yet we are bound to notice that, after the first effects of the representations of Mr. Davis and his commissioners, the people of the South came generally to believe that the report of the Commissioners was a false or garbled statement, that the enemy was not really so harsh and inaccessible as he was represented to be; and that the real disposition of the North was for a generous reconciliation, and a "reconstruction" of the Union, in which the South would lose nothing but Slavery, and probably not that without some measure of compensation. The extent of this delusion, and the singular fact of its rapid growth under the very means taken to suppress it, is a subject of great historical importance. It explains how a mistaken faith in Northern generosity, added to the distrust of Mr. Davis's administration in continuation of the war, gave the last blow to the Confederate cause, and broke down the war in the South; it accounts, in a great degree, for the sudden and abrupt termination of the contest, when the South was so far from the physical necessity of surrender; and it furnishes reflections, the most obvious and interesting, upon the present situation of parties at Washington.

In a political review written since the war, by the author, (and from which he had drawn some of the facts stated here concerning the Fortress Monroe Commission) the false hope of the South in the moderation of the enemy, which precipitated the cause of the Confederacy and expedited its surrender, has been explained fully. With some slight changes in the context and expression it may supply some passages here, consistent with what we have written, and aiding the idea we desire to convey:—

"In the last stage of the war, and contributing to its termination, there was a marked decline of hostility to the Yankee in the sense of dread of the consequences of submission. The wonder is that expectations of the enemy's generosity should have been indulged to such an extent, when the outrages of Sherman were fresh, and when the enemy was really in his fiercest and most destructive moods, and the atrocity of his arms at its height. The explanation is very peculiar, and one must have closely studied public sentiment in the South to understand its curious condition on this particular subject toward the end of the war. It was an effect produced entirely by politicians who had had frequent opportunities in various conferences, regular or irregular, with Northern men to inform and mitigate public opinion as to the real designs of the enemy. The idea was spread, sometimes insidiously, that although the North was violent in the war, its excesses in this might be forgiven, as proceeding not so much from cruelty as from a false notion of military necessity, and that its political design was really of the most moderate and indifferent description, meaning only the re-establishment of the Union, and the restoration of the *status quo* in every other particular. The reports brought back from the conferences referred to, were generally those of the most polite and pleasant personal intercourse, of hearty fellowship and kind entertainment on the enemy's part. Many of the politicians who had enjoyed such interviews, or who had Northern correspondence, had heard, in a confused way, of the most liberal propositions, and were ready to assure their weary countrymen of almost any terms of peace, on the single condition of laying down their arms, and trusting themselves to the generosity of the North.

Under these representations, generally made privately and insidiously, and never venturing in the columns of the press, where the death's head of "Subjugation" was constantly displayed, the idea grew in the Southern mind that the Yankee was not such a terrible monster after all, that the newspapers had been practicing scare-crows on the people, and that the government had only for its own selfish purposes exaggerated the demands of the enemy, and painted the terrors of submission. The extent of this delusion in the last days of the Confederacy, can scarcely be conceived by one not admitted to those under-currents of opinion which make the secret history of governments in great wars. It was a whispered thought, an adroit suggestion, rather than a declared idea making its appearance in the press, or circulated in open debate. While the newspapers displayed the horrors of submission, and John Mitchell wrote, in serial articles, the parallel between Ireland and the conquered South, and President Davis continued the stereotype of "death preferable to defeat," the idea went secretly and steadily abroad, in the South that the Yankee was not as black as he was painted, and that surrender was not the chief of evils.

Of this delusion toward the end of the war (so inconsistent with the public tone of the South and especially with the defiance of Mr. Davis) the author ventures to make this curious remark: that many men in the South were even led to doubt of the loss of Slavery in the final adjustment with the enemy, and on this particular account, were induced to relinquish the contest. This supposition may appear very extravagant at this day; but it should be remembered that at the time referred to, the South had very imperfect communications with the North, that she was a prey to rumors, and that politicians were busy with the story of the generous temper of the enemy. People were told in whispered conversations that it was not impossible that, at some time after the surrender of their arms, Slavery might be recovered from the yielding disposition of the North; a second supposition was yet more probable, to the effect that they might expect pecuniary compensation, if they promptly and gracefully accepted emancipation, and rumors were already flying in the air that President Lincoln had intimated such a proposition to Alexander H. Stephens, in the conference at Fortress Monroe.

Mr. Stephens has since confessed (if we are to believe a Georgia newspaper), that in that conference, Mr. Lincoln said to him:—

"Your people might, after all, get four hundred thousand dollars for the slaves, and you would be surprised if I should call the names of some of those who favor such a proposition." But this important disclosure has been so severely suppressed since the death of Mr. Lincoln, as an injury to his memory in Northern estimation, that the public, even to this day, is scarcely aware of it, or is unprepared to credit it. Certainly, it would have been more direct for Mr. Stephens to have made this disclosure in his public report of the conference, instead of submitting the bald statement he did, and locking in his breast so important a secret.

Unfortunately for the object of Mr. Davis, there leaked out some other private versions of the conference which showed the official report to be partial and sinister, and suggested a friendly and generous disposition of President Lincoln quite at variance with the spirit in which he was officially represented to have replied to the Commissioners.

In private accounts of the conference, Mr. Seward was especially represented as kindly, and very much disposed to enter into a general amicable conversation with the Confederate Commissioners. He asked Mr. Hunter, with amiable solicitude, of many of those they had mutually known in former days, in Washington, and inquired particularly of the health of Mr. Davis. There were no marks of harshness in the conference, and no attendance of ceremonies and forms. At parting, Mr. Seward shook Mr. Hunter by the hand very warmly, and said, with effusion:—"God bless you, Hunter!"

The author recollects to have made some reference to this and other incidents of personal amiability in this famous conference, and to have designed publishing it in the Richmond *Examiner;* but Mr. Daniel ruled it out sharply, and for a special reason. He always forbade the publication of any of the amenities of the war; he thought they were likely to mislead as to the true character and conduct of the enemy, and to soften the resolution of the South."

But, without reference to the conference at Fortress Monroe, or to the disputes concerning what took place there, there can be no doubt of the general fact that the South surrendered before it was actually compelled to do so by the arms of the North, and from a false and ill-considered trust in the moderation of the latter. The explanation of the almost abrupt conclusion of the war, stated in its broadest terms was the expectation of a mild, and even magnanimous treatment of the enemy—the mollification of dread of the Yankee—coupled with an entire want of confidence in the Davis Administration; the consequence of which was that the people of the South were demoralized, and their virtue and resolution corrupted. There are thus stated three causes of the failure of the Confederacy—and all of them outside the hypothesis of physical inability to carry on the war. Of the existence of that we are now treating there can be no doubt. The popular mind of the South, all official protestations to the contrary, expected a generous treatment after the war, and had lost its faith in the conventional terrors of subjugation, so long maintained in the newspapers and in the public demonstrations of the Richmond Government. The people who had been variously called "rebels" and "brethren" in the North, believed that one term was for war, the other for peace, and that on the declaration of the latter, they would take their equal and accustomed places in the Union. In vain, Mr. Davis sought to combat this idea, and, in the light of his interpretations of the Fortress Monroe Commission, to argue the people into the belief that subjugation or war was the only alternative before them. There were many who answered that these were only interpretations, effected, too, by some fraud or ingenuity in the language of the conference, and made by a man who was likely to take a partial view of the matter, and interested, perhaps, to present a dishonest one. In vain, advisers more competent and persuasive than Mr. Davis, warned the Southern people of the treachery of the North, and reminded them of former lessons of its deception and cruelty. In vain, the press exhorted them, "better go down fighting, better be subjugated and conquered than live to recollect that we brought our ruin upon our heads by a *deceptive reconstruction!*" They were prophetic words. The South never awoke from its delusion, until it had become the victim of "deceptive reconstruction;" until there were fastened upon it the chains of political tyranny it now wears; and until those terrors of subjugation, to which it had sealed its ears in the last periods of the war, as silly or distorted imaginations, were realized almost literally in the acts of the Congress at Washington.

When the war was first declared for the independence of the South, there were those who doubted whether there had up to that time been sufficient of actual experience of the hardship and oppression of the North to support a popular justification of rebellion, and to furnish moral animation enough to sustain it. The doubt was a reasonable one. However right a revolution may be on abstract principles, or for protection in the future, the experience of the world shows that in such contests the spirit and resources of a people are never fully developed, and that to arouse them, there must be some actual, present experience of the rod of the oppressor. A whole people will justify a rebellion when they fight for relief from some oppression, present and visible; but only the more thoughtful of them will appreciate a war for the integrity of an abstract principle or for some good, distant in the future. It has been singularly reserved for the South to obtain *after* the war the actual experience of oppression and of that sort of despotism which, if it had existed at the commencement of hostilities would have amply sustained them in popular estimation, and supplied much greater animation to their arms. Now such justification of the war is obtained in regarding the present condition of the South, in which all that was ever feared of the oppression of the North is fully realized. It is a justification retrospective, but none the less true or effective on that account.

Yet we are forced to reflect on the credulity that had to wait the present actual realization of the outrages of Northern despotism, to understand the usefulness and justice of the past war, and that refused to see the consequences of surren der until they were brought home to their doors. The delu sive faith in the generosity of the North that hastened the surrender of the South before her arms had been conquered, and betrayed her to a treacherous enemy—the weak belief that the latter meditated no practical tyranny over those who were invited to return to the blessings of free government—prove how persistent has been the South in her credulity, respecting all designs of the North, and how yielding to all the professions of the latter. This disposition is no new thing; it is part of the history of the South, cotemporary with three generations, and not yet expired. She showed it, when she refused, long before the war, to accept the lesson that the transfer of political power to the North would be used to oppress her; she showed it when she hesitated to believe, on the incoming of the government of Abraham Lincoln, that it had any actual designs upon Slavery, and was, for some time, inclined to doubt whether the war was not undertaken on a false alarm or an over-remote speculation; she showed it, when she regarded the terrors of subjugation as imaginary, and insisted upon believing, against the counsels of her greatest and wisest men, that the victorious North would be liberal and just, and that she would be taken back into the Union, without hindrance or delay; and—wonderful to say—to this very day, she shows it in still trusting to the moderation of a party hostile to her, in yet looking for a time when a sentiment of returning justice in the North will undo the tangled skein of "reconstruction," and restore to her something of the faith in which she surrendered. That surrender, we repeat, was made not so much under the compulsion of military necessities, as from the persuasions of a false political hypothesis. It was the fruit of the credulity of the South;—and it is credulity for her yet to believe that she will not be required to eat the fruit of her own choosing to its inmost core of bitterness.

CHAPTER XXIX.

A Cruel Rumor in Richmond—Description of General Lee's Lines—The Fatal Battle of the 2d of April—Sabbath Scenes in Richmond—A Telegram Delivered in St. Paul's Church—No Authentic Announcement concerning the Evacuation of Richmond—A Scene on a Hotel Balcony—Sudden and Wild Excitement in the City—Scenes of a Panic—Where is the President?—Mr. Davis Concealed—His Mean and Obscure Exit from the City—General Breckinridge at the War Department—A Curious Scene in the Third Story of the Capitol—Disgraceful Conduct of the Citizens of Richmond—A Mission of Mayor Mayo—How Richmond was Fired—Responsibility of President Davis for the Conflagration—Congregation of Horrors—Picturesque *Entrée* of the Federal Army—The Burnt District—A Thronged Theatre Unnaturally Illuminated—Terrible Quiet of the Night after the Fire—The War Virtually Ended—President Davis Insensible of the Importance of the Loss of Richmond—His Confidence Grotesque—An Issue Between Him and a Richmond Editor—The Picture of a Southern Confederacy Reduced to Jefferson Davis in Flight.

WE have heretofore referred to the peculiar distress produced in the South by the multitude of rumors, mostly proceeding from the secret habits and recluse disposition of the government of Mr. Davis. About the last of the important and certainly the most cruel of the false rumors of Richmond, was one circulated there but two days before the final battles in front of Petersburg. These were dark days; the public gloomy and despondent; worn and dejected faces in the streets of Richmond. No one outside the circle of Mr. Davis's confidences knew what strength Lee had, or what was the "situation." Into this mist of ignorance and despondency darted a ray of light. An early morning train from Petersburg sped to the capital with the news that General Lee had made a night attack on the enemy, and in the summary phrase of the report (not official, but averred to be the forerunner of such) had "crushed his whole line." The news was generally believed in Richmond; and although the government must have obtained its contradiction in a few moments by the telegraph, of which it had exclusive possession, it, with as little feeling as of judgment, allowed the pleasant delusion to linger in the excited minds of the people. Such was the credit the report obtained that it was told at the bedside of John M. Daniel, chief editor of the *Examiner*, as a comfort to the dying man, then almost in his last agonies, and too feeble to do more than nod his satisfaction. Next day, John Mitchell regretted, in the *Examiner*, that its editor, who had labored so much for the Southern Confederacy had died almost at the moment that its arms had gained a great victory, and when it had probably crossed the fitful boundary of its fortunes, and passed into the grand illumination of final success. Alas for human hopes, and false comforts for the dead and dying!—a few days later, and Richmond was crowned with an illumination—but it was of the flames of fire that signaled the approach of the enemy, and waved over the grave of the Southern Confederacy.

No one in or about Richmond—not even General Lee himself, surveying his slight army, and comparing it with the hosts of Grant before him—could have imagined how near was the end; nor did Grant himself conceive it until the hour he ordered the fatal attack. As long as the enemy could be kept from the west of Richmond, the seige of the city might be indefinitely prolonged; his line already extended thirty miles, but on the west it ended on the bank of Hatcher's Run, and had failed, after repeated attempts, to reach the South-Side railroad, which connected with the Danville railroad and maintained all that was left of the communications of Richmond. An unexpected reinforcement of cavalry (Sheridan's corps) enabled Grant to make a strong movement to develope his left; but before that operation was finished, it became a mere episode, for as it weakened Lee's lines in front of Petersbúrg, the enemy conceived suddenly the grand design of giving the lesser movement to the winds, and breaking through directly upon his prize, which was no longer the railroad, but Richmond itself. In the morning of the 2d of April, General Lee saw his line broken at three points, at each of which a whole Federal corps had attacked, and all day long the enemy was closing on the works immediately enveloping Petersburg. But the work, decisive of the war, was done in two hours. At eleven o'clock in the morning, General Lee wrote a dispatch to President Davis at Richmond, advising him that the army could not hold its position, and that preparations should be made to evacuate the capital that night! He might have added in the dispatch what he remarked to one of his staff-officers, as with embittered, but lofty face, he saw his army breaking up in the broad sunshine:—"It has happened as I told them in Richmond: the line has been stretched until it has broke."

No sound of the battle—not an echo, not a breath—had yet reached the doomed city. It was a lovely Sabbath day, and Richmond basked in its beauty and enjoyed more than usual remission from the cares of the week. There were no sounds as of the vexed thoroughfare; the long streets laid open, not a vehicle upon them; the murmur of the river gave tones only to soothe the ear, and the silent pulses of the sunshine beat slowly in the misty warm air that laid on the landscape. It was a day of careless thoughts. The usual Sunday crowd lounged near the post-office, exchanging rumors of the war, or the latest depraved gossip of Richmond society. Hundreds wended their way to the churches, while not a few of "their country's hope" trod the paths beaten as sheep-walks to the back-entrances of the whiskey-shops on Main street, and sought consolation in the shades of "the Chickahominy," "the Rebel," and "the Wilderness." Ladies dressed in old finery, in which the fashions of many years were mingled, were satisfied to make a display at St. Paul's about equal to the holiday wardrobes in better days of the Negroes at the African Church. At the former church worshipped Mr. Davis. He now sat stiff and alone in "the President's pew"—where no one outside his family had ever dared to intrude since Mrs. Davis had ordered the sexton to remove two ladies who had ventured there, and who, on turning their faces to the admonition to leave delivered before the whole congregation, had proved, to the dismay and well-deserved mortification of the President's wife, to be the daughters of General Lee. Mr. Davis was an earnest worshipper. But a Sunday before this memorable one, he, General Lee and Secretary Trenholm had gone together to the communion-table, and many eyes in the congregation had been moistened to see these three men, on whom depended so many of human hopes, kneeling side by side to partake of the most precious and comforting sacrament of the church. Now a very different scene was to be witnessed.

In the midst of the services, a man walked noisily into the church, and handed the President a slip of paper. Mr. Davis read the paper, rose, and walked out of the church without agitation, but his face and manner evidently constrained; an uneasy whisper ran through the crowd of worshippers, and many hastened into the street. The congregation was soon dismissed. The rumor had already gained the street that Richmond was to be evacuated; it was confirmed to a few who penetrated the closed doors of the War Department, or made persistent inquiries at the telegraph office; but, although the government had no motive now to suppress the sad truth, but, on the contrary, was in duty bound to inform the people and to prepare them for the exigency, it is remarkable that there was no authentic announcement of the intended evacuation, no published order on the subject, no official notification of any sort; and that news in which every man's household was involved, was left to wander all day as a vague rumor in the streets, only to be confirmed by the actual, visible fact of the authorities leaving the city. In these singular circumstances, many persons for many hours of this memorable day doubted the truth of what they heard only in the streets; many clung to undefined hopes; many remained in blank dismay, unable to conceive suddenly the magnitude of their misfortune, and having no details by which to determine or guide their action. Thus for a considerable part of the afternoon, Richmond remained without visible excitement; for hours there were on the streets no active preparations to evacuate; a whole population was kept unnecessarily in suspense, blank, hesitating, knowing not what to believe or how to act;—but it was the calm before the storm.

A little past noon some regiments of Longstreet's command, on the north of James river, were seen marching through the city, on their way to reinforce General Lee in the battle he was then supposed to be making to save or recover his lines before Petersburg. The soldiers moved with a slouching step; and, once, on their disordered march, it is said groans were called for Jefferson Davis. Formerly, when Confederate soldiers had passed through Richmond, there had been music, cheers, crowds of shouting spectators, throngs of ladies standing on the balconies of the principal hotels on Main street, to wave their adieux, perchance, to scatter flowers on them, at least to bestow upon them sweet and inspiring countenances. Now, as they passed through the thoroughfare, only a few spectators looked on sadly or cynically; no note of music cheered the sullen procession of men, marching sadly and wearily to Death; a few blank faces appeared at the windows; and on the balcony of the American Hotel, only two or three ladies stood. It was melancholy to see one of them limply wave a single handkerchief in a hesitating way, and then stop, pale and wounded, as not a single soldier cheered or recognized the compliment.

As the day wore on, it was noticed that wagons were driven to the doors of the Departments, and to the public storehouses—many of them branded as government wagons, many nondescripts—and all moving off towards the Danville depot. The accumulation of stores there, and of ticketed boxes, left no doubt that the city was to be evacuated. Signs of hurry increased; wagons, no longer driven in order, tore through the streets; men seemed suddenly possessed with a mania to run to their houses, to snatch from them some hasty baggage, and to rush to the nearest exit from the city. In less than an hour from the first appearance of the wagon trains on the streets, the whole population of Richmond was involved in a panic.

What scenes ensued it is impossible to describe. What a change fell upon this city, palled its wanton and hitherto unabashed revelry, and spread terror through its wicked streets, like a thunderbolt from the unclouded expanse of heaven, can only be imagined, as the comparison indicates, in the light of some sudden wrath visited from the skies. For four years Richmond had lived in the easy riot of the war. Now it appeared as if the day of judgment had been called upon it. Now there was hurrying to and fro. Now the panic-stricken city broke up as if riven by lightning, into black, torn crowds of maddened men, conscience-stricken fugitives, sobered revelers, blanched woman and children, fleeing wildly through the streets, over the bridges of the river, through every avenue of escape from the terrible day of judgment—the chariots of fire and wrath that were next day to enter the doomed city. It was a scene never to be forgotten in the memories of Richmond. The night was hoarse with the roar of the great flight.

But where, in this dramatic and tumultuous scene, was President Davis? When he had received news of Lee's defeat he had slunk from his pew in St. Paul's church, and while the fountains of his government were being broken up, and the great final catastrophe had mounted the stage, the principal actor was wanting; he, the President, the leader, the historical hero, had never shown his face, had never spoken a word, was satisfied to prepare secretly a sumptous private baggage, and to fly from Richmond—a low, unnoticed fugitive—under cover of the night. In such scenes a great leader is naturally sought for by the love and solicitude of his people; there are words of noble farewell to his countrymen; there are touching souvenirs of parting with his officers. But there were none of these in Mr. Davis's case, and, indeed, no stronger proof could have been given of the popular contempt and neglect into which he had fallen than his mean and obscure exit from Richmond. He did not show himself to the public, as a great leader might be expected to do in such a supreme calamity; he attempted no inspiration, comfort or advice; hid in his house, busy only with his private preparations, inquired of by no one, without any mark of public solicitude for him, without the least notice from popular sympathy or anxiety, the unhappy, degraded President of the Southern Confederacy, never showed his face in the last catastrophe of his capital, until he stole on the cars that was to bear him to a place of safety, and fled from the doomed city, unmarked among the meanest of its fugitives. He left no word of tender or noble farewell for Richmond, and the last souvenir of his power was an order to burn the city that for four years had given him shelter, countenance and hospitality.

He left behind him every circumstance to dismay the people. The Congress had meanly adjourned some days before; the President was not visible; not a single member of the Cabinet could be found but General Breckinridge (the successor of Mr. Seddon in the War Department), who remained steadily in his office until nightfall, giving the last orders that were necessary for the destruction or distribution of the archives, and answering the inquiries of the few citizens who were allowed access to him. The reporter of the associated press who was aware that eight o'clock had been designated by General Lee as the hour for evacuation, unless meantime he succeeded in re-establishing his lines, in which event he would telegraph again, attended the room of General Breckinridge at that hour, and was admitted. He came out with a blank face. "There is no hope," said General Breckinridge, and he walked quietly from the room and from the building to the house where the President was then concealed, making private preparations for his flight. There was no last council or conference. All that there was of deliberative assembly—all that remained of the once proud and loquacious government of Jefferson Davis—was to appoint the rendezvous and time for flight, the Cabinet members being instructed to meet the President at the Danville depot, a little before midnight.

The Capitol appeared deserted, but as night fell, it was noticed that the main door was ajar. Hid away in an obscure room in the third story, the City Council was anxiously debating what ceremonies were necessary for the surrender of the city, since the President was supposed to have already fled, or to be concealed for the present in Manchester, and the duty of surrendering the capital was thus devolved upon its municipal authorities. It was a cowardly debate removed from the observation of the citizens. One of the councilmen was ostentatiously dressed in a Confederate uniform. So extreme was the concern for the safety of the city, such the anxiety for its readiest humiliation, that it was arranged that a notification of surrender should be given before the next day broke, and three hours past midnight, the Mayor, despite his eighty years of age, was started in a dilapidated vehicle on the mission of surrendering Richmond before the enemy could get in sight of it. It was the first of a train of disgraceful humiliations. The city that showed such hot and indecent haste to surrender; that next day presented the spectacle of some of its leading citizens rushing bareheaded to Federal officers in the street, asking for the delicious consolation of taking the oath of allegiance (one of them—a former financial agent of the Confederacy—obtaining the reply, "When we are ready to administer the oath of allegiance we'll send for you, you d—d scoundrel;") that in two days after the enemy's occupation was publishing a "Union" newspaper from the office of the *Whig*, with the boast that "the old flag" had been concealed in its garret during the whole war; and that within a week after the surrender showed the statistic of seventeen thousand three hundred and sixty-seven food tickets calling for eighty-six thousand five hundred and fifty-five rations, as the measure of its population willing to live on the bounty of "the hated Yankee"—is yet that self-styled "heroic city" of Richmond, which professes to have lived within a peculiar enclosure of glory during the war, which has insolently claimed comparison in history with such places as Saragossa and Londonderry, and which yet cherishes its blunt and withered laurels as capital of the Southern Confederacy.

Before the Mayor could mount on his mission to the enemy, a new and surpassing terror fell upon the city. It had been fired in various quarters, and there were already gleams of conflagration on the dark horizon. While the heaving and tumultuous city was even at this hour of the night filled with pillagers and marauders—convicts from the penitentary, who had escaped, their guards having fled, and lawless soldiers who were no longer under any control, the main command of General Ewell having already tramped across the bridges over the river—the wakeful and anxious eyes of thousands of terrified citizens looking from their windows beheld this new apparition of horror rising from the black wastes of the night. Word came that the Shockoe Warehouse was fired; then, again, that three other large warehouses containing tobacco had been given to the flames. It was too late; the hand of the government was recognized in it.

The conflagration had proceeded from a strange negligence of President Davis. It was a standing order in the Confederacy, that cotton and tobacco should be burned on the approach of the enemy; and some weeks before, in a general discussion, in the newspapers, as to what might possibly take place in Richmond, it was suggested that the little there was of these staples, in the city, should be removed, and impounded in the Fai˙ Grounds outside the city, where they might be conveniently and cleanly destroyed in case of necessity. The suggestion was never heeded by Mr. Davis. The cotton and tobacco remained stored in large and scattered warehouses in the most thickly built parts of the city. In the trepidation of his flight, and in the excessive concern for his own safety, Mr. Davis appears to have left the order for burning the cotton and tobacco unchanged; at least the supposition of neglect is most charitable, for it is hardly to be supposed that he would have deliberately imperilled the homes of sixty thousand people, to destroy and to deprive the enemy of some insignificant stores of the total value of which it has been computed that it would not furnish one day's rations for the whole of Grant's army!

Richmond in flames was a fitting souvenir of its departed President—a characteristic concluding example of the mismanagement and thoughtlessness of the government whose record for four years had been that of brilliant wrecks. It was well for the sensibilities of Mr. Davis that he did not witness the last supreme ruin and distress his folly caused, and which history has placed at his doors as an inextinguishable signal of shame and crime. The flames that devoured his capital were seen by him only in faint reflections on the sky; the sheets of fire and smoke that flapped in the mid air were not over his own head; the keen cries of distress, though given to the racing winds, could not overtake his rapid flight. For the present he was safe and amused; and while Richmond burned, he was setting up a childish caricature of a new government in the obscure town of Danville.

The morning of the 3d of April was ushered in with a congregation of horrors. The first grey streaks of the dawn were broken by the explosions of the iron-clads in the James river, blown up by orders of Admiral Semmes. The air was rent as by the report of a hundred cannon. Men rushed through the streets crying out that Richmond was bombarded; but even the voices of alarm could scarcely be lifted above the roaring, the hissing and the crackling of the flames as they leaped from house to house, and licked the faces of the swaying crowds. By ten o'clock—when several thousands of the enemy had already marched into the city—the scene had become fearfully sublime. It was a scene in which the horrors of a great conflagration struggled for the fore-part of the picture, while the Grand Army, brilliant with steel and banners, breaking into the circle of fire with passionate cheers, and the crash of triumphant martial music, dazzled the spectator and confounded his imagination. The flames had already spread over the chief business portion of the city; brands were flying toward the Capitol; and it seemed at one time, as if the whole of Richmond would be destroyed—that the whole wicked city would rush skyward in a pyramid of fire. A change in the wind, however, drove back the fire from the high plateau above Franklin street, where, if the flames had once lodged, they would soon have traversed the length and breadth of the city. But the business portion of the city, south of this street, and bounded east and west by Fifteenth and Eighth streets, was doomed from the time the torch was applied to the Shockoe Warehouse, where the flames rising to the height of six stories, and radiating front and rear, were soon beyond control. The Government could not have selected a better point from which to scatter the destroying element, and to secure a complete conflagration of the most valuable part of Richmond.

All that was terrible in sounds was added to all that was terrible in sights While glittering regiments carried their straight lines of steel through the smoke; while smoke-masked robbers fought for their plunder; while the lower streets appeared as a great pit of fire, the crater of destruction; while alarmed citizens, who had left their property a ruin or a spoil, found a brief refuge on the sward of the Capitol Square, whose emerald green was already strewn with brands—the seeds of fire that the merciless winds had sown to the very doors of the Capitol; while the lengthening arms of the conflagration appeared to almost reach around those who had fled to the picturesque hill for a breath of fresh air, sounds as terrible, and more various than those of battle, assailed the ear, and smote the already over-taxed imagination. There were shells at the Confederate Arsenal exposed to the fire, from the rapid progress of which they could no longer be rescued, and for hours the explosions of them tore the air and shook the houses in their vicinity. Crowds of Negroes roamed through the streets, their wild, coarse voices raised in hymns of jubilation, thanking God for their freedom; and a few steps farther might be heard the blasphemous shouts of those who fought with the red-handed fire for their prey.

Above all these scenes of terror hung a great vail of smoke. It rose solemnly to the sky, and through it the trimmed disc of the sun, "no bigger than the moon," shone dull and ghastly. It was a combination to which description fails to do justice, and in which it is impossible to distress the mind with all of its details. There were crowds, mad with cowardice, swaying under excitement, trampling on each other; there were lurid figures of pillagers in the smoke and flame; there were keen cries of distress that cleft the volume of military music; and thus, on this thronged theatre, unnaturally illuminated, and in an auditorium of almost unearthly sounds, expired much of the pride, the luxury, the licentiousness and the cruelty of Richmond.

32

When night descended, a death-like quiet fell upon what remained of the city. It represented a feeling of reaction; and far beyond the sleepless forms of those who mechanically laid down in the shadows of the ruins of Richmond to think of the events of a day never to be forgotten, there were millions in all parts of the country to whom the same night brought a sense of remission from a great excitement. The tens of thousands who had sung the doxology in New York, and whose voices of praise to God had risen in the open air, while the smoke of Richmond's torment ascended the sky, laid down at the close of the day with hearts as overstrained as those which kept vigil in the punished and despairing capital of the Confederacy. For each the decisive event of the war had happened, although in the opposite senses of hope and fear; but the excesses of despair and joy are alike, in reducing the mind to a momentary blankness, to the cessation of an active interest. A war which had been waged for four years had practically, virtually ended in a day, and the country was sunk into meditation—awaking after the night of the 3d of April, to show but little interest in the chronological order that alone remained to gather up the details, to distribute the characters, and to conclude the story.

Only one notable man in the South seemed thoroughly insensible of the meaning of that day. Intoxicated with rage and disappointment, foolishly disposed to resent as an incident of misfortune what was really the finishing blow of fate, furious at what he thought the incredulity of those who listened in pitiful silence to his new schemes of triumph, Jefferson Davis was proceeding to continue the war with behavior so extravagant and grotesque as to excite the ridicule of his enemies, to move the pity of his friends, and to rob himself even of that last consolation of a failing cause

—the dignity of a calm and intelligent submission. It is the great man who can make the distinction between the challenge of misfortune and the sentence of fate, and who knows how to conform his conduct to the one or the other. Mr. Davis could not see it. He had not the nature to accept gracefully the irreparable. He could not understand the effects of the fall of Richmond. But a short while before the catastrophe, and as if in calculation of it, he had stated that if Richmond fell, the war would still go on; and he had added to some of his friends in intimate conversation on the subject, that he even ventured to hope that after such an event, the war would proceed with increased spirit on the part of the South. It is memorable that the press published the following reply to the inflation of the President:—"The evacuation of Richmond would be the loss of all respect and authority towards the Confederate Government, the disintegration of the army, and the abandonment of the scheme of an independent Southern Confederation. Each contestant in the war has made Richmond the central object of all its plans and all its exertions. It has become the symbol of the Confederacy. Its loss would be material ruin to the cause, and, in a moral point of view, absolutely destructive, crushing the heart and extinguishing the last hope of the country. Our armies would lose the incentive inspired by a great and worthy object of defence. Our military policy would be totally at sea; we should be without a hope or an object; without civil or military organization; without a treasury or a commissariat; without the means of keeping alive a wholesome and active public sentiment; without any of the appliances for supporting a cause depending upon popular faith and enthusiasm; without the emblems or the semblance of nationality." A few days were to determine whether Mr. Davis or his critic was right; which view was to supervene on the loss of the Confederate capital. It proved a sequel in which we shall presently follow Mr. Davis—a view even more sorrowful and humiliating than that which the Richmond journalist had predicted; for what remained of the picture of the Southern Confederacy, after the catastrophe of Richmond is, as we shall see, mainly the single figure of the President in flight, and, at last, his surrender with not one defender from all the vast armies of the South, standing between him and the enemy.

CHAPTER XXX.

Some Further Reflections on the Character of President Davis—A Historical Comparison—Secret History of his Flight from Richmond—A Vessel Awaiting Him on the Coast of Florida—Concealment of Important Records of the Confederacy—Trepidation of Mr. Davis's Departure from Richmond—What Became of the Gold in the Treasury—The President's Proclamation at Danville—A Singular Conversation—Fatuity and Blindness of Mr. Davis—Continuation of his Flight to Greensboro', North Carolina—Infamous and Insulting Conduct of the People there—The President Housed, for nearly a Week, in a Box Car—A Lady to the Rescue—Memorable Interview of President Davis and Generals Johnston and Beauregard—A Bitter Speech from Johnston—The President Dictates an Important Letter—Meditations of his Journey through North Carolina—He Conceives a New Prospect—"Hoping Against Hope"—A Dramatic and Painful Scene at Abbeville, South Carolina—The Last Council of the Southern Confederacy—"*All is Lost*"—Disbandment of the Confederate Troops at Abbeville—Mr. Davis's Misconduct on Receiving the News of the Assassination of Abraham Lincoln—The Presidential Party at Washington, Georgia—Mr. Davis Disguised as an Emigrant—His Capture—Wicked and Absurd Story of his being Disguised in a Woman's Dress—A Bloody Defiance—Mrs. Davis in the Scene—The President's Parley with His Captors—A Sorrowful Cavalcade to Macon, Georgia.

In another part of our work we have suggested a comparison between President Davis and a character whom the historian Gibbon has vividly portrayed, and whom Bulwer, from the standpoint of elegant fiction, has adorned, making a brilliant, romantic figure quite unlike the severe description in history—Rienzi, the last of the Roman Tribunes. The comparison, as it will suggest itself to the reader, is remarkably fine and forcible. The two men are examples of that mixed character, always fated to various and opposite criticism, alike liable to the extremes of censure and of praise, where the virtues and the vices flourish on an uncertain boundary, and are often intertwined; where great weaknesses are coupled with admirable accomplishments, and where the defects of practical judgment are found in union with the finest scholarly culture, rendering the attainments of the latter rather curious than useful. The two tribunes were alike in their ambition, alike in their historical mission, alike in abusing the most extraordinary gifts of fortune. They had the same quality of ambition, at once intensified and degraded by much of personal vanity; they made the same mistake of strong, selfish aspirations for public spirit; they had the same affection for the gauds of authority, proceeding not so much from the love of elegant luxury as from that of the symbol and adornment of power; they had the same connubial entanglements, alike governed by their wives, and divided between the endearments of the private chamber and the cares of State. And yet they were great orators and scholars; they represented the best culture of their times; and they were pure men, though, in the sense of being such, not so much from the hardihood of virtue as from the refinements of taste. They failed, alike, from the same ignorance of government, the same ill distribution of obstinacies and weaknesses, haughty refusals in one instance, and mean compliances in another, the same repulse of counsellors, the same paltry intrigues of the closet and the boudoir, the same contempt of fortune, presuming upon its favors as natural rights or irrevocable gifts. They experienced the same extremes of public opinion—popular adultation at the commencement of their career and damning neglect at its close; and they, alike, lost the affections of their people, by using with arrogance the powers they had bestowed, playing the tyrant rather from the vanity of power, rather through conceited and thankless use of it than from any natural cruelty, or through exercises of anger or revenge.

The comparison is most striking, towards the end of the careers of the two tribunes. The feebleness of the surrender of Rome brings to mind the forty cavalrymen, that, first, in the morning of the 3d of April, rode into Richmond without hindrance, and planted their guidons on the Capitol; and the apathy of the citizens who looked with contempt on their former idol, Rienzi, the friend of Petrarch, the great orator, the elegant favorite of the forum, suggests at least the indifference with which Jefferson Davis was dismissed from the stage of his country's extreme distress and calamity.

"The Roman hero," says Gibbon, "was fast declining from the meridian of fame and power; and the people who had gazed with astonishment on the ascending meteor, began to mark the irregularity of its course, and the vicissitudes of light and obscurity. More eloquent than judicious, more enterprising than resolute, the faculties of Rienzi were not balanced by cool and commanding reason: he magnified in a ten-fold proportion the objects of hope and fear; and prudence which could not have erected, did not presume to fortify his throne. In the blaze of prosperity, his virtues were insensibly tinctured with the adjacent vices; justice with cruelty, liberality with profusion, and the desire of fame with puerile and ostentatious vanity * * * In the pride of victory, he forfeited what yet remained of his civil virtues, without acquiring the fame of military prowess. A free and vigorous opposition was formed in the city; and when the tribune proposed in the public council to impose a new tax, and to regulate the government of Perugia, thirty-nine members voted against his measures; repelled the infamous charge of treachery and corruption; and urged him to prove, by their forcible exclusion, that if the populace adhered to his cause, it was already disclaimed by the most respectable citizens * * * At the head of one hundred and fifty soldiers, the count of Minorbino introduced himself into Rome; barricaded the quarter of the Colonna; and found the enterprise as easy as it had seemed impossible. From the first alarm, the bell of the Capitol incessantly tolled; but, instead of repairing to the well-known sound, the people were silent and inactive; and the pusillanimous Rienzi, deploring their ingratitude with sighs and tears, abdicated the government and palace of the republic."

Rienzi, at another time, attempted to escape from his capital in the disguise of a baker. Jefferson Davis's effort at escape was perhaps not less mean in its last resources. But Rienzi did what the chief of the Southern Confederacy did not do; and at the last he was unwilling to leave his capital, without at least the dignity of an adieu, without some words addressed to the people, without something of invocation not to be omitted in any extremity of despair, or to be forgotten in any haste of personal alarm.

We have seen that Jefferson Davis fled from Richmond, without a word of public explanation, with none of that benediction or encouragement which a great leader is expected to impart to his people in such a catastrophe. He escaped with the ignominy of an obscure, mean fugitive, if not positively in the character of a deserter. Some explanation has been offered of his singular neglect on this occasion of those whom, in his day of power, he was accustomed, after the affectation of a fond and paternal ruler, to call "his people," in the statement that the government at Richmond had no expectation of Lee's disaster, and was thus painfully hurried in its evacuation of the capital.

The statement is untrue, and the excuse is unavailing. The writer well knows, what has not heretofore been imparted to public curiosity, that Jefferson Davis had, many weeks before Lee's catastrophe, made the most careful and exacting preparations for his escape. The matter had been fully consulted with his Cabinet, in profound secresy; and it had been agreed that, to secure the escape of the President and his principal officers, the *Shenandoah* should be ordered to cruise off the coast of Florida, to take the distinguished fugitives on board, who had selected the coast for their exit from the Confederacy, and their extrication from its falling fortunes. These orders had been sent to the Confederate cruiser many days before Lee's lines were broken. It was calculated that, in the last resource of the surrender of Lee's army, and of the neutralization of other organized forces of the Confederacy, the President's party might make an easy and deliberate escape in the way agreed upon, as the communications with the Florida coast were then scarcely doubtful, and once on the *Shenandoah*, a fast sailer, the most valuable remnant of the Confederate navy, they might soon obtain an asylum on a foreign shore. Other preparations were made for the flight; all the papers of the government were revised, and marked for destruction, abandonment, or preservation, according to their contents;* and even Mr. Davis's private baggage was

---

* By the way, it is remarkable that so little has been obtained, by the capture or discovery of documents, of the secret history of the Confederacy. True, there have been collected at Washington some documentary relics, under the title of "Rebel Archives;" and the pretentious construction of a Bureau to take care of them, and certain foolish provisions against the access to them of public curiosity, have given the idea of some value and mystery attached to them. But they are historically worthless, scarcely anything more than the official platitudes, dry and barren amplifications of stories which have been told a hundred times in the newspapers. There was captured in Richmond only the refuse of the Confederate archives. It is a curious and romantic fact, not generally known, that the bulk of the valuable papers of the Confederate Government, including the

put in order for transportation. Of course, the public knew nothing of these preparations, and it did not even suspect

---

correspondence of Jefferson Davis, exists to-day in concealment; that many days before the fall of Richmond there was a careful selection of important papers, especially those in the office of the President, and letters which involved confidences in the North and in Europe, and that these were secretly conveyed out of Richmond, and deposited in a place where they remain concealed to this time, and will probably not be unearthed in this generation. Where is this repository of the secrets of the Confederate Government the author is not prepared to say. Indeed, he has never been able to obtain other than very general information of the present place of these papers, and even as to the limits of the locality he was bound by obligations of private confidence, which it is impossible to violate.

The author can only assure the reader of three facts: that they still exist; that there are living persons who know of their concealment; and that they contain important evidences of the secret history of Mr. Davis's Government. He has repeatedly sought access to them out of historical curiosity, but he has been invariably met with the explanation that, while this indulgence might be allowed him, for such legitimate purpose, it would be unsafe, for private reasons, and the information if published might be diverted to serious consequences to persons of importance yet living, and within the jurisdiction of the government. It has been impossible to surmount this objection, and there is no doubt that many of these papers do really involve discoveries of some curious negotiations in the war, the parties to which might astound the public. During the war it was well known, in some circles of confidence in Richmond—as we have observed in the text of another part of this work—that Mr. Davis entertained a large secret correspondence in the North; that he had sources of comfort, information, and advice there; and indeed it would have been strange, considering the volume of disaffection in the North—a remarkable peculiarity of the late war—if it had not found some expression in secret negotiations, or some sort of surreptitious communication with the Confederate authorities. Of the extent of such correspondence the popular imagination has

them. We have already referred to a bitter suspicion in Richmond, that whatever the misfortune of the Southern Confederacy, Mr. Davis would be certain to provide for his personal safety, above that of all others; and indeed, we have been forced to suggest that, for this mean reason, the President had invariably blanched at any retaliation upon the enemy involving the penalty of death. But many people resented this thought or suspicion; they persisted in believing that President Davis would stand with the army when the

---

probably fallen short. As an instance of the volume of "disloyalty" and venality in the North, the writer may mention the case of a single secret document which he was once permitted to see in Richmond, wherein certain parties offered to assist the Confederacy, by supplying its Western armies for a whole year from the granaries and magazines of the North. Such important letters and other secret papers were kept in what was called "the *Presidential* Archives." These archives—a part of the documentary history of the government of Mr. Davis, of which we have had occasion to speak in connection with its political intrigues in the summer of 1864—we repeat, still exist, were preserved from the wreck and fire of Richmond, and at this moment are under the seal of a personal confidence with Mr. Davis; while the Federal authorities congratulating themselves that they seized the archives of the Southern Confederacy, had only captured its waste paper.

However imperfect the revelations that have yet been made of the inner or secret government of Mr. Davis, yet the world may know, and it is at least some historical satisfaction, that the most valuable papers of the Southern Confederacy, including the correspondence of the President, reported to have been held with important parties in the North and in Europe, and which might yet involve the personal safety of some of them, and possibly found prosecutions, did not perish in the catastrophe of Richmond; that they are yet preserved in a manner and place to defy discovery, and secure against loss or mutilation—dedicated, perhaps, to the curiosity of a distant generation.

Confederate flag was lowered, and accept a common lot with them and the people; and they called to mind his heroic words, spoken to the troops in Virginia in 1861, at the beginning of the war: "When the last line of bayonets is levelled I will be with you."

In the last chapter, we left Mr. Davis hurrying from St. Paul's church. He walked unattended to his house. After having safely bestowed his important papers, and by this measure consulted to some degree his personal safety, it might be supposed that Mr. Davis would be prepared to leave Richmond with some appearance of self-possession and dignity. But after all the provisions for his flight, the signal for it was so sudden and dramatic—announced to him in the shape of Lee's dread telegram—as to have some effect of surprise at least, breaking down his equanimity, and reducing him to that condition of fluster and tremulousness with which the weak man receives the news of misfortune, no matter how long he has vaguely expected it, and practised against the moment of its announcement.

He nervously prepared at his house his private baggage, and he never ventured in the streets until, under cover of the night, he got, unobserved, on the train that was to convey him from Richmond. He did not forget the gold in the Treasury; that, amounting to less than forty thousand dollars, it had been proposed some days before, in Congress, to distribute as largesses to the discontented soldiers; but Mr. Davis had insisted upon reserving it for exigencies, and it was now secured in his baggage. He did forget his sword. That, a costly present from some of his admirers in England, had been sent to the Richmond Armory for some repairs; it was abandoned to the fire there. The last seen of this relic of the Southern Confederacy was a twisted and gnarled stem of steel, on private exhibition in a lager-beer saloon in Richmond, garnished with a certificate that it was what remained of Jeff. Davis's sword, and that the curiosity might be purchased for two hundred dollars.

Mr. Davis was accompanied at the first stage of his flight by some of his personal staff, and three members of his Cabinet: General Breckinridge, Secretary of War, Mr. Benjamin, Secretary of State, and Mr. Reagan, Postmaster-General. His wife was in North Carolina. The party journeyed without accident or adventure to Danville, sitting mostly in moody silence, as the train shrieked through the night that a few miles further was being torn by explosions, through whose fitful chasms of light Lee's army marched as into impenetrable darkness. Arrived at Danville, Mr. Davis issued a proclamation; out of place there, inaccessible to the army, and which would have been much more fitly made before he had abandoned the post of danger in Richmond.

This proclamation merits the curiosity, and, in some sense, the sympathy of the reader:—

DANVILLE, VA., April 5, 1865.

The General-in-Chief found it necessary to make such movements of his troops as to uncover the capital. It would be unwise to conceal the moral and material injury to our cause resulting from the occupation of our capital by the enemy. It is equally unwise and unworthy of us to allow our own energies to falter, and our efforts to become relaxed under reverses, however calamitous they may be. For many months the largest and finest army of the Confederacy, under a leader whose presence inspires equal confidence in the troops and the people, has been greatly trammelled by the necessity of keeping constant watch over the approaches to the capital, and has thus been forced to forego more than one opportunity for promising enterprise. It is for us, my countrymen, to show by our bearing under reverses, how wretched has been the self-deception of those who have believed us less able to endure misfortune with fortitude than to encounter dangers with courage.

We have now entered upon a new phase of the struggle. Relieved from the necessity of guarding particular points, our army will be free to move from point to point, to strike the enemy in detail far from his base. Let us but will it, and we are free.

Animated by that confidence in your spirit and fortitude which never yet failed me, I announce to you, fellow-countrymen, that it is my purpose to maintain your cause with my whole heart and soul; that I will never consent to abandon to the enemy one foot of the soil of any of the States of the Confederacy. That Virginia—noble State—whose ancient renown has been eclipsed by her still more glorious recent history; whose bosom has been bared to receive the main shock of this war; whose sons and daughters have exhibited heroism so sublime as to render her illustrious in all time to come—that Virginia, with the help of the people, and by the blessing of Providence, *shall be held and defended*, and no peace ever be made with the infamous invaders of her territory.

If, by the stress of numbers, we should ever be compelled to a temporary withdrawal from her limits, or those of any other border State, we will return until the baffled and exhausted enemy shall abandon in despair his endless and impossible task of making slaves of a people resolved to be free.

Let us, then, not despond, my countrymen, but, relying on God, meet the foe with fresh defiance, and with unconquered and unconquerable hearts.

JEFFERSON DAVIS.

The proclamation was a characteristic effusion of the sanguine disposition of the President. While walking the streets of Danville, he was met by two gentlemen who had occupied offices in one of the Departments of Richmond, and who now, with visible anxiety, but with great respect, asked him if he had yet received any news from Lee's army. "No," replied Mr. Davis; "but, gentlemen, no news is good news under the circumstances, and General Lee probably knows what to do with the enemy, without consulting me." And, with a smile, he added, "Make the most of your holiday, gentlemen, for we'll soon have you at work again." What miracle could he thus have expected from Lee? What transformations of public opinion, that the authority and civil routine of the government were thus easily to be resumed? It was the evidence of a fatuity, the example of a blindness, proof against that enlightenment which is supposed to be afforded when misfortune wreaks its worst and last—the illumination of the past which the kindness of nature grants before the moment of death—the period of *eclaircissement* at the close of the life drama, when the entanglements of the plot are loosened, and nothing remains but the expiring hero and the final catastrophe.

Even when the news of the surrender of Lee's army got to Danville (which it did on the 10th of April), Mr. Davis was not yet ready to abandon hope. But it was noticeable that the exaltation of spirits he had obtained after having passed, as he conceived, the boundary of danger, and got on the side of supposed personal safety, did not long survive. With courage again impaired by the nervous haste and trepidation of flight, and with hopes diminished, but not extinguished, the President and his party, on the news of Lee's surrender, turned their faces to the South. They travelled by railroad to Greensboro', North Carolina, and here the President paused to obtain an interview with Generals Johnston and Beauregard. Something of assurance might be obtained from them; they might appeal to their soldiers not to lay down their arms, as Lee's troops had done; and if once could be effected only the semblance of continuing the war, the example of such a resolution, or, perhaps, a victory, no matter how small or obscure the field, would rally the confidence of the people in its vicinity, and spread gradually through the country. Such were the weak speculations of the President. Sorrowfully, General Breckinridge, undertook a journey on horseback to General Johnston's camp, to acquaint him with the President's desire for an interview; moved by the earnest entreaties of Mr. Davis, pitying the fallen chief, to whom he had been so near in office, but well knowing that his mission was vain, and sharing none of the fluttering hopes of Mr. Davis, or of the vivid delusions which tormented the last days of his official life.

At Greensboro' occurred an episode on which every candid reader of the history of the war, no matter what his standpoint, must put a condemnation, and which no Southern man can remember, without affixing it with a stigma of shame. There is nothing which tests character more truly than the fall into misfortune of a friend or of an enemy. Surely a mean nature is never more despicable than in its maltreatment of misfortune, and its cowardly refuge, on such occasions, in old resentments, or in selfish calculations. There were many in the South who dissented from the government of Mr. Davis, who were hostile to his administration, who gave him no confidence and bore him no affection, as a ruler; yet even among these, the truly noble and the sincere could have respected the misfortunes of the President, when they found him a distressed fugitive. They would have obeyed the promptings of but an ordinary human generosity, to have visited him at the stages of his distressed and weary flight, to tender some hospitality, or to offer an honorable condolence. But even such manifestations of humanity did a North Carolina town, containing several thousand souls, refuse to show to the man who, but a few weeks before, had been their supreme magistrate and chief, who was yet such under the unexpired forms of the Confederacy, and who now came among them a broken, aged fugitive, making a feeble flight from the enemy, and encumbered with a helpless family. For nearly a week, while remaining at Greensboro', *the President and his family lived in a box-car on the railroad, having no other shelter!* When he arrived, not a house in Greensboro' was open to him. Not the slightest hospitality was offered; and if any thing could be added to the shame of this cruel neglect and insult of the unhappy President, it was the cowardly excuse made by the citizens, that they were unwilling to alleviate his distress, or, indeed, to offer him shelter, because they feared that the enemy, on some future visit to this humane and honorable town, might resent it. But for the honor of humanity, there occurred one exception to the shameful exhibition of a North Carolina community; and it—as the reader may anticipate—came from a *woman,* a lady well qualified by her social position and worth to rebuke conduct of such infamy and cowardice. It was not until some days after his arrival that Mrs. C. S. L'Hommedieu, a lady residing in Greensboro', and well-known in society as the daughter of Dr. Tooley, of Natchez, Mississippi, learned that the President was in town, ignominiously housed in a box-car, and shunned by the citizens, except those who visited him from brutal curiosity; and this true and brave lady at once addressed him a note, begging him to make her house his home, and to honor her by commanding any thing in it The President had to decline the invitation, as he was then making preparations to depart; but he was deeply affected; in no circumstances—to his credit be it said—was he ever unmindful of what was due from the fine and generous breeding of the gentleman, and, although hurried in his departure from Greensboro', he did not omit to address to the lady a beautiful letter of thanks, anxious to commemorate, and unable otherwise to reward her goodness and generosity.

The resumption of Mr. Davis's flight toward the South was in consequence of what had taken place in his interview with Generals Johnston and Beauregard. It was an interview of inevitable embarrassment and pain. The two Generals were those who had experienced most of the prejudice and injustice of the President; he had always felt aversion for them; and it would have been an almost impossible excess of Christian magnamity if they had not returned something of resentment and coldness to the man who, they believed, had arrogantly domineered over them, and more than once sought their ruin. We have seen how unceremoniously and cruelly Johnston had been hustled off the stage at Atlanta. True, he had now been restored to command; but under circumstances which made it no concession to the public, and no favor to him, for he was restored only to the conduct of a campaign that was already lost, and put in command of a broken and disorganized force that Sherman had already driven through two States. When some time before public sentiment was demanding his return to service, he wrote bitterly that he was quite sure that if the authorities at Richmond restored him to command, they were resolved not to act toward him in good faith and with proper support, but to put him in circumstances where defeat was inevitable, and thus confirm to the populace the military judgment of the President. He had no reason to thank Mr. Davis for his present command in the forests of North Carolina, where the President had now come to him to ask little less than a miracle at his hands. As for General Beauregard, his painful relations with Mr. Davis had been public gossip ever since the battle of Manassas. There had been, too, a recent unpleasantness, fresh in the minds of both, on account of General Beauregard having evacuated Charleston against the orders of the President; although what idea the latter could have had, within the limits of sanity, in attempting to hold this city after Sherman's army had flanked it, is difficult to imagine.

These three men were now to meet, to consult of the condition of the country; and the occasion invoked that they should rise above personal feelings in the circumstances of a great public sorrow and anxiety. There was obtained for the interview a mean room on the second floor of a house owned by a Confederate officer. Mr. Davis sat cold, dignified, evidently braced for an unpleasant task. He spoke in a musing, absent way; and it was remarked that, while speaking, he never looked toward either commander, his eyes being amused by a strip of paper which he was twisting in his hands. His heart must have beat with a great anxiety, for he must have known how much depended on these Generals countenancing his plans of continuing the war; and yet he spoke as one who had merely resolved to state his case, and who cared not to influence the decision one way or the other. It was as if he had said openly to his Generals, "if you decide to continue the war, to keep your armies in the field, well and good; but understand, it is no obligation conferred upon me, I shall regard it as no concession to me." And yet his heart secretly hung on their replies, and beneath his cold exterior the practised eye might have seen the deep underplay of the nerve, the flutter of suppressed emotion.

The President spoke at great length. General Johnston sat at as great a distance from him as the room allowed. He was evidently impatient; he knew what was coming; he had anticipated all that the President said before he had come into the room, and he listened as one oppressed with the fulness and readiness of reply. Yet, when the President stopped speaking, he remained profoundly silent. "General Johnston," Mr. Davis said, "we should like now to hear your views." It was a reply that came with a bluntness and defiance that brought a sudden color to the cheeks of the President. "Sir," blurted out General Johnston, "my views are that our people are tired of the war, feel themselves whipped and will not fight!" In these few words he had said all that was necessary; and he spoke them suddenly, without preface. But he continued to speak in short, decisive jerky sentences, as if in haste to deliver his mind. He suggested that the enemy's military power and resources were now greater than they had ever been. What could the President hope to oppose to them in the present demoralized condition of the South? "My men," he said, "are daily deserting in large numbers, and are taking my artillery teams to aid their escape to their homes. Since Lee's defeat they regard the war as at an end. If I march out of North Carolina, her people will all leave my ranks. It will be the same as I proceed south through South Carolina and Georgia, and I shall expect to retain no man beyond the by-road or cow-path that leads to his house. My small force is melting away like snow before the sun, and I am hopeless of recruiting it. We may, perhaps, obtain terms which we ought to accept."

A silence ensued. It was broken by the President, saying, in a low, even tone: "What do you say, General Beauregard?" "I concur in all General Johnston has said," he replied.

There was another pause in the conversation, when presently General Johnston, as if regretting the cruel plainness of his remarks and thinking he had wounded enough the unhappy President, who was still twisting abstractedly the piece of paper in his hands, proceeded to suggest, at some length, the hope of getting favorable terms from the enemy. He thought it would be legitimate, and according with military usage for him to open a correspondence with General Sherman, to see how far the Generals in the field might go in arranging terms of peace. Mr. Davis could not but be sensible of the wisdom of this suggestion, although he listened coldly to it, and it was very little of consolation for the destruction of such towering and grotesque hopes as he had brought into the interview. General Breckinridge, who had been present at the whole of the interview, now ventured to advise that General Johnston should at once, and on the spot, address a letter to Sherman to prepare an interview. "No," replied General Johnston—probably anxious to show a mark of deference to the President, out of pity for the mortification already inflicted upon him—"let the President dictate the letter." The letter, proposing a suspension of hostilities, was dictated by the President. And thus Mr. Davis himself, virtually subscribed the token of submission of the Confederate army, second in importance and numbers to that of Lee; yet unwilling to go further in the sequel, and to write gracefully his entire submission to the inevitable.

On the 16th of April, the President, his staff and cabinet left Greensboro'. It was a slow travel in ambulances and on horseback, and the dejection of the party was visible enough. Mr. Davis was the first to rally from it. When he and his companions had left Richmond, it was in the belief of the majority that Lee could avoid surrender but a few days longer, and with the intention, as we have already said, of making their way to the Florida coast and embarking there for a foreign land. The President had clung, at Danville, to the hope that Lee might effect a retreat to south-western Virginia, and he had remained there long enough to see that hope disappointed. Again, when he had sought General Johnston's demoralized and inconsiderable army, it had been from a feeble diversion of hope that it might not yield to the example of Lee's surrender, and that, under the inspiration of the presence and the direct command of the President, it might be induced to keep the field. That expectation had been brought to a painful end; and it appeared as if the

President would be recommitted now to the original design of fleeing the Confederacy, and would now make an earnest effort at escape. But his mind was disordered and undecided; and it was distressing to see how he hesitated between assured safety in flight from the country and the possible hope that the cause of the Confederacy might not be beyond redemption. Anyhow, there were no signs yet that he was pursued by the enemy; and he had appeared to consider himself sure of ultimately making good his escape, after he had once got out of sight of Richmond. He had shown great trepidation in getting out of the capital, but in the leisure of a journey, unmolested by pursuit and entertained by the fresh air and pleasing sights of spring, he had time to recover, to some extent, his self-possession, and to cast about for something to be saved from the wreck of his hopes.

In the meditations of his journey through North Carolina the fugitive President, although anxious for his personal safety, appears to have conceived the alternative of venturing to the south-west, within reach of the forces of Taylor and Forrest, in the hope of reviving the fortunes of the Confederacy within a limited territory. He suggested the alternative to General Breckinridge, as they travelled together, after the news of Johnston's surrender, but received only an evasive reply; the latter not sharing his hopes, but unwilling to mortify them by a candid declaration of opinion. Mr. Davis was remarkable for a sanguine temperament, but it was that which we observe in weak characters, "hoping against hope," fickle, flaring, extravagant, rather than that practical energy which renews itself on disaster and conquers fortune. The vision he had conjured up of a limited Confederacy around the mouths of the Mississippi might have looked plausible upon paper, but it was fatally defective in omitting the moral condition of the South. The unhappy President had not yet perceived that he had lost the faculty of encouraging others, that the Southern people were in despair, and that, wherever he might go, he would find their countenances averted, their hopes abandoned, and their thoughts already committed to submission. But he was to realize very shortly how morally deserted and practically helpless he was. His first discovery of it was at Abbeville, South Carolina, where occurred one of the most pathetic scenes in history, over which the tenderness and charity of some of the actors have been disposed to draw the curtain, committing its sorrows to secresy.

Mr. Davis reached Abbeville on the 1st of May. So far he had been accompanied by the fragments of five brigades, amounting in number to less than one thousand men, and reorganized into two battalions, at the front and in rear of the long train which signalled his flight and foolishly obstructed his effort at escape. There were already painful evidences of the demoralization of the escort, and the story told almost at every mile, by stragglers from Johnston's command, was not calculated to inspire them. At Abbeville Mr. Davis resolved upon a council of war. It was composed of the five brigade commanders, and General Braxton Bragg (for the year past the "military adviser" of the President) was admitted to this last scene of the deliberations of the lost cause.

In the council Mr. Davis spoke with more than his accustomed facility and earnestness, inspired by hope, but without volubility or extravagance. He made a statement of surpassing plausibility. The South, he declared, was suffering from a panic; it yet had resources to continue the war; it was for those who remained with arms in their hands to give an example to reanimate others; such an act of devotion, besides being the most sublime thing in history, might yet save the country, and erect again its declining resolution.

"It is but necessary," he said, "that the brave men yet with me should renew their determination to continue the war; they will be a nucleus for rapid reinforcements, and will raise the signal of reanimation for the whole country." No one of the council answered him at length; the replies of the commanders were almost sunk to whispers; the scene was becoming painful; and it was at last agreed that each in his turn should announce his decision. Each answered slowly, reluctantly, in the negative; the only words added were that though they considered the war hopeless, they would not disband their men until they had guarded the President to a place of safety.

"No," exclaimed Mr. Davis, passionately. "I will listen now to no proposition for my safety. I appeal to you for the cause of the country." Again he urged the commanders to accept his views.

"We were silent," says General Basil Duke, one of the council, "for we could not agree with him, and we respected him too much to reply."

Mr. Davis yet stood erect, raised his hands to his head, as if in pain, and suddenly exclaimed, "*all hope is gone!*" added haughtily, "I see that the friends of the South are prepared to consent to her degradation;" and then sweeping the company with a proud and despairing glance, he attempted to pass from the room.

But the blow was too much for his feeble organization. His face was white with anger and disappointment, and the mist of unshed tears was in his eyes—tears which pride struggled to keep back. The sentiment that all was lost went through his heart like the slow and measured thrust of a sword; as the wound sunk into it, it left him speechless; loose and tottering, he would have fallen to the floor, had not General Breckinridge ended the scene by leading him faltering from the room. In a dead and oppressive silence the deserted leader, the fallen chief, secured a decent retreat for agonies which tears only could relieve.

It was the last council of the Confederacy. The hateful selfishness which originates in the attempt of each individual to extricate himself from a common misfortune soon broke out, no longer restrained by the presence of the President. The soldiers were discharged; but they clamored that they had no money to take them home. What of the Treasury gold that remained was divided among them. So fearful were they of marauders that many buried their coin in the woods, and in unfrequented places. With the disbandment of the troops Mr. Benjamin suggested a separation of the Cabinet officers from the President, making an excuse that so large a party would advertise their flight, and increase the chances of capture. Mr. Davis was left to make his way to Georgia, Postmaster-general Reagan continuing to journey with him, and General Breckinridge only to a point where he thought it convenient to leave for Florida. There were also in the party two or three of his staff officers, and a few straggling soldiers, who still kept up some show of an escort. Mrs. Davis had already preceded her husband to Georgia, and he now travelled slowly, and almost desolately, on horseback, having arranged that she should await him in the town of Washington.

From this place, the now hunted President was soon driven again on his journey by news of the occupation of Augusta. He had also received news of the assassination of President Lincoln, and that event, he declared, confirmed his resolution not to leave the country. He inferred from the newspapers that he was accused as an accomplice in the crime, and he remarked to one of his staff officers that he "would prefer death to the dishonor of leaving the country under such an imputation." But with such a sentiment, it will occur to the reader that it would have been noble and decorous for Mr. Davis to have surrendered himself at the nearest Federal post, and to have demanded a trial. It would have placed him in a grand and winning attitude, one becoming a great man, one honorable to himself and the South, and redeeming him more than anything else in the eyes of the world. But unfortunately, he accepted the base alternative of continuing his flight, and that too with the artifice of a mean disguise.

On continuing his journey, accompanied by his wife, whom he had overtaken at Washington, it was determined that the President and his friends should thereafter travel as an *emigrant party*. Mr. Reagan was still in his company. General Breckinridge had left outside the town of Washington, taking with him forty-five Kentucky soldiers—a straggling remnant of Morgan's old brigade. Ten mounted men had offered to escort Mrs. Davis, and although they had accepted their paroles, justly considered that they might protect a distressed lady from marauders. All tokens of the President's importance, in dress and air, were laid aside; a covered wagon, pack-mule and cooking utensils were provided at Washington; and it was designed that Mr. Davis, his wife, and his wife's sister should pass as a simple country family emigrating from Georgia, and having fallen in with straggling soldiers for their protection. Mr. Davis's dignity was laid aside without much difficulty. Carlisle says: "A king in the midst of his body-guard, with all his trumpets, war-horses and gilt standard-bearers, will look great, though he be little; but only some Roman Carus can give audience to satrap ambassadors while seated on the ground, with a woolen cap, and supping on boiled peas, like a common soldier." Mr. Davis, in the dress of a country farmer, had none of these traces of imperialism which cling to those "born to the purple." His features, just and handsome, without being remarkable, were those which might command by assumed airs, or might be practiced to particular expressions, but scarcely those which could assert superiority without an effort and at a glance. He incurred but little chance of detection in the dress he had assumed of an honest, well-to-do emigrant.

But the last device of the distinguished fugitive, the only one in which he had shown any ingenuity, and had confessed his real anxiety for escape, was in vain, and he was captured three day's journey from Washington. He had scarcely expected to fall in with any enemy north of the Chattahoochie river, the boundary of "the department of the Southwest," and there he had designed to part with his wife, and to commit her to her journey to the *Shenandoah*. He was overtaken by a small body of Federal cavalry, originally sent out to post a skirmish line through that part of Georgia, reaching to Augusta, but now diverted to his pursuit.

The wicked and absurd story that Mr. Davis was captured disguised in female attire is scarcely now credited. He was aroused in the early grey of the morning by a faithful negro servant (the same who has since attended his broken fortunes), who had been awakened by the sound of firing in the woods. The President had not laid off his clothes, and, in a moment, he had issued from the tent where he had been sleeping. The woods were filled with mounted troops, ill-defined in the mist of the breaking morning, and, noticing that they were deploying, as if to surround the camp, he quickly imagined their character and design, and returned within the tent, either to alarm Mrs. Davis or there to submit decently to capture. She besought him to escape, and, urging him to an opening in the tent, threw over his shoulders a shawl which he had been accustomed to wear. His horse, a fleet and spirited one, was tied to a tree at some distance. He was within a few steps of the animal that might have borne him out of danger, when a Federal soldier halted him, and demanded to know if he was armed.

In relating the encounter afterwards, in his prison at Fortress Monroe, Mr. Davis reported himself as saying, "If I were armed you would not be living to ask the question." If he did say so, it was a sorry bravado—and, as none of his captors appear to have recollected such words of defiance, we are permitted to hope that Mr. Davis's memory is at fault, and that he submitted to his fate really with more dignity than he claims for himself. While he was parleying with the soldier, Colonel Pritchard, commanding the body of cavalry, rode up, and, addressing him by name, demanded his surrender. Not one of his escort or companions came to his aid. He submitted, walked back to the tent, and, in the presence of his wife, asked Colonel Pritchard that she might continue her journey. The reply of the Colonel was that his orders were to arrest all the party. Mr. Davis rejoined, with sarcasm: "Then, sir, what has been said is true, your government *does* make war upon women!" These were the only words of displeasure or of bitterness in the dialogue of the capture. The unhappy prisoner, after these words, was coldly silent. Asking no questions of his fate, not intruded upon by any curiosity of his captors, conversing only with the faithful and devoted wife from whom he was not yet divided, and whose whispers of affectionate solicitude by his side were all to lighten the journey, he rode moodily in the cavalcade back to Macon, where first he was to learn the extent of his misery, and to commence the dread career of the penalties he had accumulated by four long and bitter years of war.

CHAPTER XXXI.

Mistake of the Federal Government in the Imprisonment of Mr. Davis—An Intrigue of Secretary Stanton—How Mr. Davis Repaired his Reputation in Prison—Celebration of his Release in Richmond—A Transport of Affection for him in the South—Ingenious Explanation of the Sensitiveness of the Southern People concerning Criticisms of Mr. Davis—This Disposition Unreasonable, and really. Injurious to the Whole South—Mr. Davis in Canada—A Commercial Errand to England—The Ex-President of the Southern Confederacy as a Commission-Merchant—The Proposition of an Infamous and Hideous Traffic in Historical Notoriety—Reflections on the Employments of Confederate Leaders since the War—An Important Distinction—Honorable Example of General Lee—The Prosecution of Mr. Davis Dismissed—An Order of *Nolle Prosequi*—The Great Significance of this Event—Imperfect Commentaries of the Dull and Barren Press of the South—The Discharge of Mr. Davis, the Greatest Triumph the South could have Obtained after the War—The Event Important in Three Aspects—Exit of Mr. Davis from the Political Stage.

But little remains to be told of a life, in which the blank of imprisonment has been closely followed by the obscurity of neglect.

It has been well said that if the Federal authorities, cap turing Jefferson Davis, had turned him loose, or had wisely refrained from treating him with invidious or exceptional rigor, he would have remained to-day the most unpopular man in the South. He would have been subject not only to those censures and derisions of his countrymen which assailed him in the last periods of his administration, but to the natural increase and exasperation of them from the failure of the war, and in the bitter daily experience of evils, of which he would have stood, in the estimation of his people, the chief author, the embodied, living cause, constantly displayed before their eyes. Such an effect would have been logical; and the Government at Washington would have been wise if it had thus left Mr. Davis to the natural operations of the sentiment of his own countrymen, the results of which would have been not only to appropriately punish him, but to aid the reaction, so much desired, in the South in favor of the restoration of the Federal authority.

Indeed, it is known that the Federal government was first impressed with this view; that Mr. Davis was not pursued through the Carolinas, and that there was every disposition to wink at his escape, until Mr. Stanton, Secretary of War, procured his capture on an accusation which he probably invented merely to furnish an immediate occasion for pursuit. The true explanation of the infamous and absurd charge against Mr. Davis of complicity in the assassination of President Lincoln is that it was a fictitious process got up by Mr. Stanton, to defeat ingeniously the first intentions of the government towards the distinguished fugitive; and that, for the gratification of his malice, the North had imposed upon it, for four years, the embarrassment of an impracticable prisoner, and fell into the irretrievable mistake of making him a martyr rather than an example. Mr. Davis was pursued as a murderer, not as a traitor; but when once the gates of Fortress Monroe closed upon him, the Federal Government found itself embarrassed by divided public opinions in the North, urging the most various dispositions of the prisoner, and it finally discovered that, so far as the people of the South were concerned, instead of "making treason odious" to them in the person of Jefferson Davis, it was making itself superlatively odious in the character of his jailor and persecutor.

The imprisonment of Mr. Davis was the best thing that could have happened for his fame. What he suffered, lying as a prisoner in a casemate of Fortress Monroe for two years, and for the first few weeks degraded by fetters, and especially the manner of his suffering, not only disarmed much of the old resentment of his countrymen, but displayed him in an attitude so touching, and in conduct so becoming and noble, that, when released on bail in the month of May, 1867, he found himself welcomed by nearly every heart in the South, and hailed with a pride and tenderness that his countrymen had not before shown him, even in the best of his former estate.

Old enmities were forgotten, old offences were forgiven, and not an injurious memory of the past war was allowed to disturb the tribute which the whole South seemed now anxious to pay to the martyr of "the lost cause." He came back to Richmond as one who, by his sufferings, had conquered the resentment of his people; he found himself holding a brilliant levee at the Spotswood Hotel, which some of the newspapers maliciously compared with the mean assemblies which President Lincoln and General Grant had drawn in the same city; men thronged the hotel, asking to see "*our* President;" and, at last, such were the demonstrations of popular affection, that the judicious friends of the pleased recipient had to compel him to desist from encouraging them, for fear that they might attract jealous attention at Washington, and have the effect of returning him to the pain and obscurity of his prison.

This transport of public opinion in the South concerning its ex-President, is easily explained. Mr. Davis had certainly borne imprisonment with a dignity scarcely to be expected from him. The actual extent of his sufferings, the patience with which he bore them, his brave abstention from the common complaints and revilings of the prison, at once entreated for him the pity of his countrymen, and commanded their admiration. Again, the North committed the mistake of making him an exception to the general rule of its treatment of the leading men of the Confederacy; from this point it was easy for his countrymen to imagine him as a vicarious sufferer, bearing punishment for the sins of the whole South; yet further, this habitual view easily passed into the romantic regard of him as an impersonation of the cause of the Southern Confederacy; and it is remarkable that, in this regard, the argument or the invocation is most frequently made that any severe criticism of Mr. Davis from Southern sources is to be deprecated and resented.

This is probably the whole ingenious explanation of the recent transport of affection of the Southern people for Mr. Davis, and its extreme sensitiveness to any commentary on the errors of his administration. It contains an illogical argument—one naturally heard most from the women of the South and persons of weak mind; and it makes an appeal mixed with the transitory passions and interests of the day, and utterly unworthy to touch the severe conscience of the historian. His duties to Jefferson Davis are the same as to any other actor in history; and paltry, indeed, is the idea that he should withhold any truth for fear of wounding the sensibilities with which a living generation of men would conceal the chief actor among them. And sensibilities, too, utterly mistaken as we account them; for we hold that Mr. Davis, so far from being the impersonation of what was good and reverential in the lost cause of the South, represented only its follies and the reasons of its failure; and if we have striven to make clear any particular point in this work, it is that that cause is best to be vindicated, and the merit and honor of the South maintained therein, on the hypothesis of the unworthiness of the man who presumed to conduct it, and who sacrificed and betrayed in it the true courage and virtue of his countrymen!

On his enlargement on bail, Mr. Davis, after a brief stay in Richmond, and an unpleasant visit to New York, retired to Canada. Thence, in the summer of 1868, he proceeded to England, in pursuance of an offer of a commission house in Liverpool to take him in as a partner, and thus afford him a handsome pecuniary profit or bonus. The terms of this singular proposition, as reported in the newspapers, were that Mr. Davis was to become a member of the house referred to without the contribution of any capital, and that he should continue to reside in America, if he preferred to do so, representing the interests of the firm at New Orleans. On arriving in England, Mr. Davis did not find the house of that character as to induce the advertisement of his name in connection with it; and, partly through the persuasions of friends who recognized the offer attempted to be imposed upon his credulity or his avarice, as a disreputable advertising "dodge,"—a scheme of trading through the name of the ex-President of the Southern Confederacy,—the matter was dropped, but not until it had obtained for Mr. Davis considerable scandal. Since then he has been residing, alternately, in England and in France, living quietly but comfortably; his descent into obscurity being rather faster than most of revolutionary refugees, who have generally continued to be objects of curiosity after having ceased to excite any other interest.

But although Mr. Davis declined the peculiar adventure in commercial life just referred to, it is greatly to be regretted that he ever entertained it; that he ever came near to a descent so unexampled from that historical heroism and dignity which he was expected to support in the sight of Europe and the world. His commercial errand to England was, indeed, a mortifying episode; and for some time it was feared by his countrymen that the unfortunate ex-President of the South, at the end of his public career, might fall to exhibiting the dregs of his character, in a way to shame them as well as to disgrace himself. The people of the South have always prided themselves upon their nice and delicate observances of honor, and, in this respect, Mr. Davis had been their master of ceremonies, their pattern of deportment, the very prince of punctilios. It would have been excessively awkward if he had turned out to be an excellent accountant of pelf, doing precisely at Liverpool what the South has so often reviled as "the Yankee trick" of utilizing public and social advantages, turning such to the mean account of dollars and cents. The world would have accused him of selling out his historical fame, and turning the Southern Confederacy into a tradesman's advertisement! He had not money enough to buy an interest in a large commission-house; he had no skill or experience in commercial affairs; there must have been some consideration for a place so lucrative as that temptingly offered to him; and in the range of human speculation, it could have been none other than that Mr. Davis had formerly been President of the Southern Confederacy; and that there was a certain available commercial notoriety in that bulk of blood and tears of a despairing people that the American member would contribute to the firm!

We admit something for the exigencies of misfortune. A bankrupt cannot be select in his choice of occupation. But certainly it would have exceeded all that could be allowed in this respect, that the former ruler of a noble and cultivated community should descend to a commission merchant, with his capital in trade a historical name, and his profits accruing out of the eight millions of people who had served him in a disastrous cause. There is something inexpressibly low and offensive in the idea. History demands, even in the extremity of misfortune, a certain dignity from those who have shared in its lofty scenes. If Mr. Davis has been compelled to choose a hard and honorable poverty, it is far better than that he should have accepted this gilded shame in the streets of Liverpool. There are many ways to fortune; but Mr. Davis could scarcely find one so easy and degraded as that of spelling his name in golden letters, and selling out his historical fame as commercial capital. It is this barter which would have been offensive to honorable instincts—not the grade of employment, as long as it was honest. There are those who will say that it is both decent and noble for any unfortunate man to win his livelihood from a sacrifice of his pride; that labor is honorable, and that the day is past when even the insolent aristocracy, in which Mr. Davis was bred, may deride the vulgarity of trade. We shall not dispute on these points. Labor *is* honorable; it has been decorated by modern opinion. But the true and precise complaints of those who deprecated the descent of Mr. Davis to the counting-room, was that the former chief of the Southern Confederacy, as partner of the Liverpool commission house, would have meanly *avoided* labor by a commercial sinecure, the place of a distinguished loafer, in which he might live on the reputation of the past. It would be said, and apparently not without justice, that he had sold his name and that of his people purely as an advertisement, to avoid the real and honorable exigencies of labor. What is historical dignity, what the glory of heroes, what all the noble proprieties of a nation's misfortune, when the chief of eight millions of people might hang out a tradesman's signboard over all of it, and make of the grand catastrophe a first-rate commercial advertisement!

The case of Mr. Davis thus employed and that of other leading men of the Southern Confederacy, working in obscure occupations for a livelihood, are essentially different, in the fact of the latter being really engaged in labor, and being really capable of the services which they undertake to render, and which they actually perform. If General Johnston manages a railroad, or if General Lee supervises a college, they are capable of doing the duties required of them ; there is a real service, a real consideration for which they are paid. But if General Lee is offered a large sum of money to have his name appear in some money-making enterprise, where his services would be nominal, and only the benefit of his name was sought—and it is notorious that he has been thus tempted by joint-stock concerns, insurance companies, etc., in all parts of the United States—he would wrong his conscience, and shame his great reputation in history to accept it. The distinction is interesting and valuable. If we have asked the reader's attention at some length on the subject, it is not to pursue an old and trite speculation about the rights and honor of labor, etc., or, yet, to indulge in an essay, however interesting, on the decline and fall of historical characters, but to indicate a question of great practical importance in the present condition of Southern society, where so many persons are thrown back upon resources of livelihood much below their former aspirations and habits, and where some safe rule is required to determine the question of dignity in these descents of fortune. We believe that such a rule is suggested in the distinction we have made between Jefferson Davis seeking a sinecure partnership in a commercial firm, and other Confederate leaders engaged in occupations much below their former positions, yet rendering in them actual and capable services. There can be no general guide as to how the dignity of a past career may be maintained in poverty, beyond the plain consideration that a man, fallen from his former estate, may with honor betake himself to those resources of livelihood which are most becoming and most decorous within the limits of his remaining faculties and opportunities. Surely it is to be hoped that within those of Mr. Davis, however slender may be his remnants of pecuniary fortune, some resource for his age may be secured—if even in the open charity of his countrymen—more honorable than that of advertising member of a foreign trade-firm.

After nearly four years of hesitation—after a most injurious exhibition of doubtfulness and weakness—the North has managed to rid itself of the awkward prisoner whom the stupidity or blind rage of Mr. Stanton imposed upon it. At the term of the United States Circuit Court, held in Richmond, December, 1868, a *nolle prosequi* was entered in the case of Mr. Davis, as on an indictment for treason, and the prosecution on that charge, at least, was thus dismissed. This conclusion had been foreseen, or it had been strongly imagined; yet it was the occasion of much rejoicing in the South, and of not a little disembarrassment and relief on the part of the North. The newspapers of the South teemed with congratulations of Mr. Davis; but they have generally stopped there in the apprehension of the event, and have been singularly deficient in their commentaries on it.

Indeed, it is very surprising that the vast importance of this event, as affecting the *morale* of the past war, and as involving the whole political history of the country, should have escaped the apprehension of the press of the South; and especially, too, when it is apparently so much concerned to discover whatever there is of hope and encouragement for this section, and affects so much the tone of optimism in public affairs. The most important triumph that the South could have possibly achieved since the war, the most significant event that has happened since its close, the most interesting revelation that has lately been given to the world from behind the scenes of our political history, has been overlooked by a dull and barren press. The mere congratulations affecting the person of Mr. Davis, with which the newspapers have generally stopped short in their commentaries on the abandonment of his prosecution, are utterly inconsiderable, compared with the true significance of this event, and the extent of the triumph of the whole South on it.

There can be no doubt that the North would have been glad to exact of Mr. Davis the furthest penalties of the law, if it could have made out a case for the prosecution; that it was immensely anxious to convict him. There were thousands in the North who even clamored for his blood, and many who would have been glad to doom him to the cell of the felon. This, to be sure, was a mistake; for, as we have already suggested, it is the kind and degree of punishment that determines whether the victim shall be an example or a martyr, and that the true economy of punishments is their moderation. But for the thousands who thus demanded the severity of the laws upon Mr. Davis, there were millions who desired his conviction in another and indispensable sense—that of "making treason odious," that of obtaining a moral vindication of the North in the past war, and securing the future in its interest. The extent of the anxiety of the North to procure such a vindication—all, indeed, that was wanting to crown the great victory of its arms, and to complete its satisfaction—has never been fully confessed. It has scrupled at nothing. Its whole government in the South is based on the idea of justifying the war; and its system of test-oaths in that section was probably designed, as well as for other reasons, to obtain a factitious declaration of public opinion there, in favor of the legitimacy of its past contest of arms.

The full sense then of the abandonment of the indictment of Mr. Davis for treason, is the confession of the North, that it despaired of obtaining such a justification of the war on its side as would have been implied in his conviction; and, in even proportion to this confession, the claim of the South that the balance of justification was on its side, that it held the vantage ground on whatever questions of law the war involved. Here is a vast admission, and it is as unequivocal as it is important. The trial of Jefferson Davis was the trial of the North. It was to determine whether a man could be punished as a traitor for acting on an opinion which had divided three generations of Americans, and even the founders themselves of the Federal Constitution; whether the party and sectional dogma on which the North had waged war, could be affirmed on the legal decision of a constitutional question. Such a trial the North has declined. It has shrunk from the august arbitration on which it once proposed to enter in sight of the world to "make treason odious;" it has feared to risk the question whether it had really any superiority over the South in any respect but that of number of its arms; it has decided not to attempt, even at its own judicial bar, the justification of its cause—the determination whether the war was the invocation of a violated Constitution, or the temptation of sectional hate and ambition; and it leaves to the South whatever implications may arise from the facts of its rival having withdrawn his challenge and abandoned the contest.

The release of Mr. Davis has become one of the most important events of his life—not so much so with reference to his own fortunes, as in its application to the whole political history of the country. It is interesting in three aspects. It suggests a vindication of the cause of the Southern Confederacy —such a vindication as is to be desired next to success; it supplies some reflections upon the permanence and vitality of the old schools of American politics; and it has the surprising and most remarkable effect of exhibiting a tendency of the American mind to the conservatism of the past, in the midst of the public passions of the day—of disclosing an under current in the mad career to Consolidation that is apparently, but not really and entirely sweeping every thing before it. Perhaps the South may think herself too ready to despair of her record in the war and of restoration to something of her ancient rights, since she has seen the chief of her so-called "rebellion," a defiant and feared litigant in a Federal court of justice, and walking forth released, even from accusation.— Such is the significance of the last public attitude of Jefferson Davis—such the unexpected loftiness and interest of his exit from the stage of American politics.

THE END.

www.ingramcontent.com/pod-product-compliance
Lightning Source LLC
LaVergne TN
LVHW021258110826
845150LV00003B/424

9781425560638